The Gallup Poll

Public Opinion 1981

GEORGE H. GALLUP, founder and chairman of
The Gallup Poll, received a Ph.D. in psychology from
the University of Iowa in 1928. From his undergraduate
days he has had three prime interests: survey research,
public opinion, and politics.
Dr. Gallup is the author of many articles on public
opinion and advertising research and he has published
the following books: *The Pulse of Democracy* (1940);
A Guide Book to Public Opinion Polls (1944); *The Gallup
Political Almanac* (1952); *Secrets of Long Life* (1960);
The Miracle Ahead (1964); *The Sophisticated Poll
Watcher's Guide* (Rev. 1976); *The Gallup Poll,
1935–1971* (1972); *The Gallup Poll: Public Opinion, 1972–1977* (1978);
1978 (1979); *1979* (1980); *1980* (1981); *1981* (1982).

Other Gallup Poll Publications Available from Scholarly Resources

The Gallup Poll: Public Opinion, 1980
ISBN 0-8420-2181-7 (1981)

The Gallup Poll: Public Opinion, 1979
ISBN 0-8420-2170-1 (1980)

The Gallup Poll: Public Opinion, 1978
ISBN 0-8420-2159-0 (1979)

The Gallup Poll: Public Opinion, 1972–1977
2 volumes ISBN 0-8420-2129-9 (1978)

The International Gallup Polls: Public Opinion, 1979
ISBN 0-8420-2180-9 (1981)

The International Gallup Polls: Public Opinion, 1978
ISBN 0-8420-2162-0 (1980)

The Gallup Poll

Public Opinion 1981

Dr. George H. Gallup
Founder and Chairman

 Scholarly Resources Inc.
Wilmington, Delaware

ACKNOWLEDGMENTS

The preparation of this volume has involved the entire staff of the Gallup Poll and their contributions are gratefully acknowledged. I particularly wish to thank James Shriver, III, managing editor of the Gallup Poll, and Professor Fred L. Israel of the City College of New York, who has been the principal coordinator of this volume and of the eight volumes that preceded it.

G.H.G.

Scholarly Resources Inc.
104 Greenhill Avenue
Wilmington, DE 19805

Library of Congress Catalog Card Number: 79-56557
International Standard Serial Number: 0195-962X
International Standard Book Number: 0-8420-2200-7

CONTENTS

PREFACE

[This introductory essay by Dr. George Gallup is excerpted from a section entitled "How Polls Operate" from his book *The Sophisticated Poll Watcher's Guide.*]

THE CROSS-SECTION

The most puzzling aspect of modern polls to the layman is the cross-section or sample. How, for example, is it possible to interview 1,000 or 2,000 persons out of a present electorate of about 150 million and be sure that the relatively few selected will reflect accurately the attitudes, interests, and behavior of the entire population of voting age?

Unless the poll watcher understands the nature of sampling and the steps that must be taken to assure its representativeness, the whole operation of scientific polling is likely to have little meaning, and even less significance, to him.

With the goal in mind of making the process understandable, and at the risk of being too elementary, I have decided to start with some simple facts about the nature of sampling—a procedure, I might add, that is as old as man himself.

When a housewife wants to test the quality of the soup she is making, she tastes only a teaspoonful or two. She knows that if the soup is thoroughly stirred. one teaspoonful is enough to tell her whether she has the right mixture of ingredients.

In somewhat the same manner, a bacteriologist tests the quality of water in a reservoir by taking a few samples, maybe not more than a few drops from a half-dozen different points. He knows that pollutants of a chemical or bacteriological nature will disperse widely and evenly throughout a body of water. He can be certain that his tiny sample will accurately reflect the presence of harmful bacteria or other pollutants in the whole body of water.

Perhaps a more dramatic example is to be found in the blood tests given routinely in clinics and hospitals. The medical technician requires only a few drops of blood to discover abnormal conditions. He does not have to draw a quart of blood to be sure that his sample is representative.

These examples, of course, deal with the physical world. People are not as much alike as drops of water, or of blood. If they were, then the world of individuals could be sampled by selecting only a half-dozen persons anywhere. People are widely different because their experiences are widely different.

Interestingly, this in itself comes about largely through a sampling process. Every human being gathers his views about people and about life by his own sampling. And, it should be added, he almost invariably ends with a distorted picture because his experience is unique. For example, he draws conclusions about "California" by looking out of his car or airplane window, by observing the people he meets at the airport or on the streets, and by his treatment in restaurants, hotels, and other places. This individual has no hesitancy in telling his friends back home what California is really like—although his views, obviously, are based upon very limited sampling.

The Black man, living his life in the ghetto, working under conditions that are often unpleasant and for wages that are likely to be less than those of the white man who lives in the suburban community, arrives at his own views about racial equality. His sample, likewise, is unrepresentative even though it may be typical of fellow Blacks living under the same conditions. By the same token, well-to-do whites living in the suburbs with the advantages of a college education and travel have equally distorted views of equality. These distortions come about because their sampling, likewise, is based upon atypical experiences.

Although every individual on the face of the earth is completely unique, in the mass he does conform to certain patterns of behavior. No one has expressed this better than A. Conan Doyle, author of the Sherlock Holmes series. He has one of his characters make this observation:

> While the individual man is an insoluble puzzle, in the aggregate he becomes a mathematical certainty. You can never foretell what any one man will do, but you can say with precision what an average number will be up to. Individuals vary, but averages remain constant.

Whenever the range of differences is great—either in nature or man—the sampling process must be conducted with great care to make certain that all major variations or departures from the norm are embraced.

Since some differences that exist may be unknown to the researcher, his best procedure to be sure of representativeness is to select samples from the population by a chance or random process. Only if he follows this procedure can he be reasonably certain that he has covered all major variations that exist.

This principle can be illustrated in the following manner. Suppose that a government agency, such as the Bureau of the Census, maintained an up-to-date alphabetical list of the names of all persons living in the United States eighteen years of age and older. Such a file, at the present time, would include approximately 148 million names.

Now suppose that a survey organization wished to draw a representative sample of this entire group, a sample, say of 10,000 persons. Such a representative sample could be selected by dividing 150,000,000 by 10,000—which produces a figure of 15,000. If the researcher goes systematically through the entire file and records the name of every 15,000th listed, he can be sure that his sample is representative.

The researcher will find that this chance selection, in the manner described, has produced almost the right percentage of Catholics and Protestants, the proper proportion of persons in each age and educational level. The distribution of persons by occupation, sex, race, and income should be broadly representative and consistent with the best available census data. It is important, however, to emphasize the words "broadly representative." The sample—even of 10,000— most likely would not include a single person belonging to the Fox Indian tribe or a single resident of Magnolia, Arkansas. It might not include a single citizen of Afghanistan heritage or a single Zoroastrian.

For the purposes served by polls, a sample normally needs to be only broadly representative. A study could be designed to discover the attitudes of American Indians, in which case the Fox Indians should be properly represented. And a specially designed study of Arkansas would likely embrace interviews with residents of Magnolia.

But for all practical purposes, individuals making up these groups constitute such a small part of the whole population of the United States that their inclusion, or exclusion, makes virtually no difference in reaching conclusions about the total population or even of important segments of the population.

Unfortunately, there is no master file in the United States of persons over the age of eighteen that is available to the researcher. Moreover, even a few weeks after the decennial census such a file would be out of date. Some citizens would have died, some would have moved, and still others would have reached the age of eighteen.

Unlike some European countries, no attempt is made in the United States to keep voter registration lists complete and up to date. Because of this failure to maintain accurate lists of citizens and of registered voters, survey organizations are forced to devise their own systems to select samples that are representative of the population to be surveyed.

Any number of sampling systems can be invented so long as one all-important goal is kept in mind. Whatever the system, the end result of its use must be to give every individual an equal opportunity of being selected. Actually, not every individual will have an equal chance, since some persons will be hospitalized, some in mental or penal institutions, and some in the armed forces in foreign lands. But while these individuals help make up the total United States citizenry, most are disenfranchised by the voting laws of the various states or find difficulty in implementing their opinions at election time. Typically, therefore, they are not included in survey cross-sections.

The Gallup Poll has designed its sample by choosing at random not individuals as described previously, but small districts such as census tracts, census enumeration districts, and townships. A random selection of these small geographical areas provides a good starting point for building a national sample.

The United States population is first arranged by states in geographical order and then within the individual states by districts, also in geographical order. A sampling interval number is determined by dividing the total population of the nation by the number of interviewing locations deemed adequate for a general purpose sample of the population eighteen years of age and older. In the case of the Gallup Poll sample, the number of locations, so selected, is approximately 300.

At the time of this writing, the population of the United States eighteen years and older is approximately 150,000,000. Dividing 150,000,000 by 300 yields a sampling interval of 500,000. A random starting number is then chosen between 1 and 500,000 in order to select the first location. The remaining 299 locations are determined by the simple process of adding 500,000 successively until all 300 locations are chosen throughout the nation.

A geographical sampling unit having been designated, the process of selection is continued by choosing at random a given number of individuals within each unit. Suppose that the sampling unit is a census tract in Scranton, Pennsylvania. Using block statistics, published by the Census Bureau for cities of this size, a block, or a group of blocks, within the tract is chosen by a random method analogous to the procedure used to select the location.

Within a block or groups of blocks so selected, the interviewer is given a random starting point. Proceeding from this point, the interviewer meets his assignment by taking every successive occupied dwelling. Or, as an alternative procedure, he can be instructed to take every third or every fifth or every tenth dwelling unit and to conduct interviews in these designated homes.

In this systematic selection plan, the choice of the dwelling is taken out of the hands of the interviewer. As a reminder to the reader, it should be pointed out that the area or district has been selected by a random procedure; next, the dwelling within the district has been chosen at random. All that now remains is to select, at random, the individual to be interviewed within the household.

This can be done in several ways. A list can be compiled by the interviewer of all persons of voting age residing within each home. From such a household list, he can then select individuals to be interviewed by a random method. Ingenious methods are employed to accomplish this end. One survey organization in Europe, for example, instructs the interviewer to talk to the person in the household whose birthday falls on the nearest date.

Now the process is complete. The district has been selected at random; the dwelling unit within the district has been selected at random; and the individual within the dwelling unit has been selected at random. The end result is that every individual in the nation of voting age has had an equal chance of being selected.

This is the theory. In actual practice, problems arise, particularly in respect to the last stage of the process. The dwelling unit chosen may be vacant, the individual selected within a household may not be at home when the interviewer calls. Of course, the interviewer can return the next day; in fact, he or she can make a half-dozen call backs without finding the person. Each call back adds that much to the cost of the survey and adds, likewise, to the time required to complete the study.

Even with a dozen call backs, some individuals are never found and are never interviewed. They may be in the hospital, visiting relatives, on vacation, on a business trip, not at home except at very late hours, too old or too ill to be interviewed—and a few may even refuse to be interviewed.

Since no nationwide survey has ever reached every person designated by any random selection procedure, special measures must be employed to deal with this situation. In the early 1950s, the Gallup Poll introduced a system called Time-Place interviewing. After an intensive study of the time of day when different members of a household are at home, an interviewing plan was devised that enabled interviewers to reach the highest proportion of persons at the time of their first call.

Since most persons are employed outside the home, interviewing normally must be done in the late afternoon and evening hours, and on weekends. These are the times when men, and especially younger men, are likely to be at home and therefore available to be interviewed.

In various nations, survey organizations are working out new ways to meet this problem of the individual selected for the sample who is not at home. These new procedures may meet more perfectly the ideal requirements of random sampling.

Many ardent advocates of the procedure described as "quota sampling" are still to be found. This, it should be pointed out, was the system generally employed by the leading survey organizations in the pre-1948 era.

The quota system is simplicity itself. If the state of New York has 10% of the total population of the United States, then 10% of all interviews must come from this state. In the case of a national sample of 10,000, this would mean 1,000 interviews.

Going one step further, since New York City contains roughly 40% of the population of the state, then 40% of the 1,000 interviews must be allocated to New York City, or 400. And since Brooklyn has roughly a third of the total population of New York City, a third of the 400 interviews, or 133, must be made in this borough. In similar fashion, all of the 1,000 interviews made in the state of New York can be distributed among the various cities, towns, and rural areas. Other states are dealt with in similar fashion.

Making still further use of census data, the interviews to be made in each city, town, or rural areas can be assigned on an occupational basis: so many white-collar workers, so many blue-collar workers, so many farmers, so many business and professional people, so many retired persons, and so many on the welfare rolls. The allocation can also be made on the basis of rents paid. The interviewer, for example, may be given a "quota" of calls to be made in residential areas with the highest rental values, in areas with medium priced rentals, and in low rental areas.

Typically, in the quota sampling system, the survey organization predetermines the number of men and women and the age, the income, the occupation, and the race of the individuals assigned to each interviewer.

In setting such quotas, however, important factors may be overlooked. In 1960, for example, a quota sample that failed to assign the right proportion of Catholic voters would have miscalculated John Kennedy's political strength. An individual's religious beliefs, obviously, cannot be ascertained by his appearance or by the place where he dwells; this applies to other factors as well.

Not only do theoretical considerations fault the quota system but so do the problems that face the interviewer. When the selection of individuals is left to him, he tends to seek out the easiest-to-interview respondents. He is prone to avoid the worst slum areas, and consequently he turns up with interviews that are likely to be skewed on the high income and educational side. Typically, a quick look at the results of quota sampling will reveal too many persons with a college education, too many persons with average and above average incomes, and in political polls, too many Republicans. Therefore, one of the many advantages of the random procedure is that the selection of respondents is taken out of the hands of the interviewer. In the random method, the interviewer is told exactly where to go and when to go.

Another consideration with cross-sections is keeping them up to date. Although America's population is highly mobile, fortunately for polltakers the basic structure of society changes little. Perhaps the greatest change in America in recent years has been the rising level of education. In 1935, when the Gallup Poll first published poll results, only 7.2% of the adult population had attended college for one year or more. Today that figure is 27%.

How does a research organization know that the sample it has designed meets proper standards? Normally, examination of the socioeconomic data gathered by the interviewer at the end of each interview provides the answer. As the completed interview forms are returned from the field to the Princeton office of the Gallup Poll, the facts from each are punched into IBM cards. In addition to the questions that have dealt with issues and other matters of interest, the interviewer has asked each person to state his occupation, age, how far he went in school, his religious preference, whether he owns or rents his dwelling, and many other questions of a factual nature.

Since the Census Bureau Current Population Surveys provide data on each one of these factors, even a hasty examination will tell whether the cross-section is fairly accurate—that is, whether the important factors line up properly with the known facts, specifically:
   —the educational level of those interviewed
   —the age level
   —the income level
   —the proportion of males to females
   —the distribution by occupations

—the proportion of whites to nonwhites
—the geographical distribution of cases
—the city-size distribution.

Typically, when the educational level is correct (that is, when the sample has included the right proportion of those who have attended college, high school, grade school, or no school), when the geographical distribution is right and all areas of the nation have been covered in the correct proportion, when the right proportion of those in each income level has been reached, and the right percentages of whites and nonwhites and of men and women are included—then usually other factors tend to fall in line. These include such factors as religious preference, political party preference, and most other factors that bear upon voting behavior, buying behavior, tastes, interests, and the like.

After checking all of the above "controls," it would be unusual to find that every group making up the total population is represented in the sample in the exact percentage that it should be. Some groups may be slightly larger or smaller than they should be. The nonwhite population eighteen years and older, which makes up 11% of the total population, may be found to be less, or more, than this percentage of the returned interviews. Those who have attended high school in the obtained interviews may number 58%, when actually the true figure should be 54%.

Ways have been developed to correct situations such as these that arise out of the over-representation or under-representation of given groups. The sample can be balanced, that is, corrected so that each group is included in the proportion it represents in the total population. When this procedure is followed, the assumption is made that persons within each group who are interviewed are representative of the group in question. But there are obvious limitations to this. If only a few persons are found in a given category, then the danger is always present that they may not be typical or representative of the people who make up this particular group or cell.

On the whole, experience has shown that this process of weighting by the computer actually does produce more accurate samples. Normally, results are changed by only negligible amounts—seldom by more than 1 or 2 percentage points.

A persistent misconception about polling procedures is that a new sample must be designed for measuring each major issue. Actually, Gallup Poll cross-sections are always based upon samples of the entire voting age population. Every citizen has a right to voice his opinion on every issue and to have it recorded. For this reason, all surveys of public opinion seek to reach a representative cross-section of the entire population of voting age.

Some people ask if we go back to the same persons with different polls. The answer, in the case of the Gallup Poll, is "no"; the same person is not interviewed again. Some survey research is based upon fixed cross-sections or "panels." The same persons are reinterviewed from time to time to measure shifts in opinion.

There are certain advantages to this system—it is possible to determine to what extent overall changes cloak individual changes. But a practical disadvantage is that the size of the sample remains fixed. Unless the panel is very large, reliable information cannot be produced for smaller subgroups. In the case of the Gallup Poll, the same question can be placed on any number of surveys and the total sample expanded accordingly, since the same persons are not reinterviewed.

Panels have other limitations. One has to do with determining the level of knowledge. Having asked a citizen what he knows about a certain issue in the first interview, he may very well take the trouble to read about it when he sees an article later in his newspaper or magazine. There is, moreover, a widespread feeling among researchers that the repeated interviewing of the same person tends to make him a "pro" and to render him atypical for this reason. But the evidence is not clear-cut on this point. The greatest weakness, perhaps, is that panels tend to fall apart; persons change their place of residence and cannot be found for a second or subsequent measurement; some refuse to participate more than once and must be replaced by substitutes.

THE SIZE OF SAMPLES

When the subject of public-opinion polls comes up, many people are quick to say that they do not know of anyone who has ever been polled.

The likelihood of any single individual, eighteen years of age or older, being polled in a sample of 1,500 persons is about one chance in 90,000. With samples of this size, and with the frequency that surveys are scheduled by the Gallup Poll, the chance that any single individual will be interviewed—even during a period of two decades—is less than one in 200.

An early experience of mine illustrates dramatically the relative unimportance of numbers in achieving accuracy in polls and the vital importance of reaching a true cross-section of the population sampled.

In the decade preceding the 1936 presidential election, the *Literary Digest* conducted straw polls during elections, with a fair measure of success. The *Literary Digest*'s polling procedure consisted of mailing out millions of postcard ballots to persons whose names were found in telephone directories or on lists of automobile owners.

The system worked so long as voters in average and above-average income groups were as likely to vote Democratic as Republican; and conversely, those in the lower income brackets—the have-nots—were as likely to vote for either party's candidate for the presidency.

With the advent of the New Deal, however, the American electorate became sharply stratified, with many persons in the above average income groups who had been Democrats shifting to the Republican banner, and those below average to the Democratic.

Obviously, a polling system that reached telephone subscribers and automobile owners—the perquisites of the better-off in this era—was certain to overestimate Republican strength in the 1936 election. And that is precisely what did happen. The *Literary Digest*'s final preelection poll showed Landon winning by 57% and Franklin D. Roosevelt losing with 43% of the two-party popular vote.

Landon did not win, as everyone knows. In fact, Roosevelt won by a whopping majority—62.5% to Landon's 37.5%. The error, more than 19 percentage points, was one of the greatest in polling history.

The outcome of the election spelled disaster for the *Literary Digest*'s method of polling, and was a boon to the new type of scientific sampling that was introduced for the first time in that presidential election by my organization, Elmo Roper's, and Archibald Crossley's.

The *Literary Digest* had mailed out 10,000,000 postcard ballots—enough to reach approximately one family in every three at that point in history. A total of 2,376,523 persons took the trouble to mark their postcard ballots and return them.

Experiments with new sampling techniques had been undertaken by my organization as early as 1933. By 1935 the evidence was clear-cut that an important change had come about in the party orientation of voters—that the process of polarization had shifted higher income voters to the right, lower income voters to the left.

When the presidential campaign opened in 1936, it was apparent that the *Literary Digest*'s polling method would produce an inaccurate figure. Tests indicated that a large majority of individuals who were telephone subscribers preferred Landon to FDR, while only 18% of those persons on relief rolls favored Landon.

To warn the public of the likely failure of the *Literary Digest,* I prepared a special newspaper article that was widely printed on July 12, 1936—at the beginning of the campaign. The article stated that the *Literary Digest* would be wrong in its predictions and that it would probably show Landon winning with 56% of the popular vote to 44% for Roosevelt. The reasons why the poll would go wrong were spelled out in detail.

Outraged, the *Literary Digest* editor wrote: "Never before has anyone foretold what our poll was going to show even before it started . . . Our fine statistical friend (George Gallup) should be advised that the Digest would carry on with those old fashioned methods that have produced correct forecasts exactly one hundred percent of the time."

When the election had taken place, our early assessment of what the *Literary Digest* poll would find proved to be almost a perfect prediction of the *Digest*'s final results—actually within 1 percentage point. While this may seem to have been a foolhardy stunt, actually there was little risk. A sample of only 3,000 postcard ballots had been mailed by my office to the same lists of persons who received the

Literary Digest ballot. Because of the workings of the laws of probability, that 3,000 sample should have provided virtually the same result as the *Literary Digest*'s 2,376,523 which, in fact, it did.

Through its own polling, based upon modern sampling procedures, the Gallup Poll, in the 1936 election, reported that the only sure states for Landon were Maine, Vermont, and New Hampshire. The final results showed Roosevelt with 56% of the popular vote to 44% for Landon. The error was 6.8 percentage points, the largest ever made by the Gallup Poll. But because it was on the "right" side, the public gave us full credit, actually more than we deserved.

The *Literary Digest* is not the only poll that has found itself to be on the "wrong" side. All polls, at one time or another, find themselves in this awkward position, including the Gallup Poll in the election of 1948. Ironically, the error in 1936—a deviation of 6.8 percentage points from the true figure—was greater than the error in 1948—5.4 percentage points. But the public's reaction was vastly different.

The failure of polls to have the winning candidate ahead in final results is seldom due to the failure of the poll to include enough persons in its sample. Other factors are likely to prove to be far more important, as will be pointed out later.

Examination of probability tables quickly reveals why polling organizations can use relatively small samples. But first the reader should be reminded that sampling human beings can never produce findings that are *absolutely* accurate except by mere chance, or luck. The aim of the researcher is to come as close as possible to absolute accuracy.

Since money and time are always important considerations in survey operations, the goal is to arrive at sample sizes that will produce results within acceptable margins of error. Fortunately, reasonably accurate findings can be obtained with surprisingly small samples.

Again, it is essential to distinguish between theory and practice. Probability tables are based upon mathematical theory. In actual survey work, these tables provide an important guide, but they can't be applied too literally.

With this qualification in mind, the size of samples to be used in national surveys can now be described. Suppose, for example, that a sample comprises only 600 individuals. What is the theoretical margin of error? If the sample is a perfectly drawn random sample, then the chances are 95 in 100 that the results of a poll of 600 in which those interviewed divide 60% in favor, 40% opposed (or the reverse) will be within 4 percentage points of the true figure; that is, the division in the population is somewhere between 56% and 64% in favor. The odds are even that the error will be less than 2 percentage points—between 58% and 62% in favor, 42% to 38% opposed.

What this means, in the example cited above, is that the odds are 19 to 1 that in repeated samplings the figure for the issue would vary in the case of those favoring the issue from 56% to 64%; the percentage of those opposed would vary between 44% and 36% in repeated samples. So, on the basis of a national sample of only 600 cases, one could say that the odds are great that the addition of many cases—

even millions of cases—would not likely change the majority side to the minority side.

Now, if this sample is doubled in size—from 600 to 1,200—the error factor using the 95 in 100 criterion or confidence level is decreased from 4 percentage points to 2.8 percentage points; if it is doubled again—from 1,200 to 2,400—there is a further decrease—from 2.8 to 2.0, always assuming a mathematically random sample.

Even if a poll were to embrace a total of 2,000,000 individuals, there would still be a chance of error, although tiny. Most survey organizations try to operate within an error range of 4 percentage points at the 95 in 100 confidence level. Accuracy greater than this is not demanded on most issues, nor in most elections, except, of course, those that are extremely close.

Obviously, in many fields an error factor as large as 4 percentage points would be completely unacceptable. In fact, in measuring the rate of unemployment, the government and the press place significance on a change as small as 0.1%. At present, unemployment figures are based upon nationwide samples carried out by the U.S. Bureau of Labor Statistics in the same general manner as polls are conducted. The government bases its findings on samples of some 50,000 persons. But samples even of this size are not sufficient to warrant placing confidence in a change as small as 0.1%. And yet such a change is often headlined on the front pages as indicating a real and significant change in the employment status of the nation.

Even if one were totally unfamiliar with the laws of probability, empirical evidence would suffice to demonstrate that the amassing of thousands of cases does not change results except to a minor extent.

An experiment conducted early in the Gallup Poll's history will illustrate this point. At the time—in the middle 1930s—the National Recovery Act (N.R.A.) was a hotly debated issue. Survey results were tabulated as the ballots from all areas of the United States were returned. The figures below are those actually obtained as each lot of new ballots was tabulated.

NUMBER OF RETURNED BALLOTS	PERCENT VOTING IN FAVOR OF THE N.R.A.
First 500	54.9%
First 1,000	53.9
First 5,000	55.4
First 10,000	55.4
First 30,000	55.5

From these results it can be seen that if only 500 ballots had been received, the figure would have differed little from the final result. In fact the greatest difference found in the whole series is only 1.6 percentage points from the final result.

This example represents a typical experience of researchers in this field. But one precaution needs to be observed. The returns must come from a representative sample of the population being surveyed; otherwise they could be as misleading as trying to project the results of a national election from the vote registered late in the afternoon of election day in a New Hampshire village.

The theoretical error, as noted earlier, can be used only as a guide. The expected errors in most surveys are usually somewhat larger. In actual survey practice, some sample design elements tend to reduce the range of error, as stratification does; some tend to increase the range of error as, for example, clustering. But these are technical matters to be dealt with in textbooks on statistics.

Survey organizations should, on the basis of their intimate knowledge of their sampling procedures and the analysis of their data, draw up their own tables of suggested tolerances to enable laymen to interpret their survey findings intelligently.

The normal sampling unit of the Gallup Poll consists of 1,500 individuals of voting age, that is, eighteen years and over. A sample of this size gives reasonable assurance that the margin of error for results representing the entire country will be less than 3 percentage points based on the factor of size alone.

The margin for sampling error is obviously greater for subgroups. For example, the views of individuals who have attended college are frequently reported. Since about one-fourth of all persons over eighteen years have attended college, the margin of error must be computed on the basis of one-fourth the total sample of 1,500, or 375. Instead of a margin of error of 3 percentage points, the error factor increases to 6 or 7 percentage points in the typical cluster sample.

In dealing with some issues, interest focuses on the views of subgroups such as Blacks, labor union members, Catholics, or young voters—all representing rather small segments of the total population. Significant findings for these subgroups are possible only by building up the size of the total sample.

This can be done in the case of the Gallup Poll by including the same question or questions in successive surveys. Since different, but comparable, persons are interviewed in each study, subgroup samples can be enlarged accordingly. Thus, in a single survey approximately 165 Blacks and other nonwhites would be interviewed in a sample of 1,500, since they constitute 11% of the total voting-age population. On three successive surveys a total of 495 would be reached—enough to provide a reasonably stable base to indicate their views on important political and social issues.

Since much interest before and after elections is directed toward the way different groups in the population vote, it has been the practice of the Gallup Poll to increase the size of its samples during the final month before election day to be in a position to report the political preferences of the many groups that make up the total population—information that cannot be obtained by analyzing the actual election returns. Election results, for example, do not reveal how women voted as opposed to men, how the different age groups voted, how different religious groups voted, how different income levels voted. Many other facts about the public's voting habits can be obtained only through the survey method.

During the heat of election campaigns, critics have asserted on occasion that the Gallup Poll increases its sample size solely to make more certain of being "right." Examination of trend figures effectively answers this criticism. The results reported on the basis of the standard sampling unit have not varied, on the average, more than 1 or 2 percentage points from the first enlarged sample in all of the national elections of the last two decades, and this, of course, is within the margin of error expected.

Persons unfamiliar with the laws of probability invariably assume that the size of the sample must bear a fixed relationship to the size of the "universe" sampled. For example, such individuals are likely to assume that if a polling organization is sampling opinions of the whole United States, a far larger sample is necessary than if the same kind of survey is to be conducted in a single state, or in a single city. Or, to put this in another way, the assumption is that since the population of the United States is roughly ten times that of New York State, then the sample of the United States should be ten times as large.

The laws of probability, however, do not work in this fashion. Whenever the population to be surveyed is many times the size of the sample (which it typically is), the size of samples must be almost the same. If one were conducting a poll in Baton Rouge, Louisiana, on a mayoralty race, the size of the sample should be virtually the same as for the whole United States. The same principle applies to a state.

Two examples, drawn from everyday life, may help to explain this rather mystifying fact. Suppose that a hotel cook has two kinds of soup on the stove—one in a very large pot, another in a small pot. After thoroughly stirring the soup in both pots, the cook need not take a greater number of spoonsful from the large pot or fewer spoonsful from the small pot to taste the quality of the soup, since the quality should be the same.

The second example, taken from the statistician's world, may shed further light on this phenomenon. Assume that 100,000 black and white balls are placed in a large cask. The white balls number 70,000; the black balls, 30,000. Into another cask, a much smaller one, are placed 1,000 balls, divided in exactly the same proportion: 700 white balls, 300 black balls.

Now the balls in each cask are thoroughly mixed and a person, blindfolded, is asked to draw out of each cask exactly 100 balls. The likelihood of drawing 70 white balls and 30 black balls is virtually the same, despite the fact that one cask contains 100 times as many balls as the other.

If this principle were understood then hours of Senate floor time could have been saved in recent years. Senator Albert Gore, of Tennessee, a few years ago, had this to say about the Gallup Poll's sampling unit of 1,500—as reported in the *Congressional Record*:

As a layman I would question that a straw poll of less than 1 per cent of the people could under any reasonable circumstance be regarded as a fair and meaningful cross-section. This would be something more than 500 times as large a sample as Dr. Gallup takes.

In the same discussion on the Senate floor, Senator Russell Long of Lousiana added these remarks:

I believe one reason why the poll information could not be an accurate reflection of what the people are thinking is depicted in this example. Suppose we should try to find how many persons should be polled in a city the size of New Orleans in order to determine how an election should go. In a city that size, about 600,000 people, a number of 1,000 would be an appropriate number to sample to see how the election was likely to go. . . . In my home town of Baton Rouge, Lousiana, I might very well sample perhaps 300 or 400 people and come up with a fairly accurate guess as to how the city or the parish would go, especially if a scientific principle were used. But if I were to sample only a single person or two or three in that entire city, the chances are slim that I would come up with an accurate guess.

If the reader has followed the explanation of the workings of the laws of probability, and of earlier statements about the size of samples, he will be aware of two errors in the senator's reasoning. Since both cities, New Orleans and Baton Rouge, have populations many times the size of the sample he suggested, both require samples of the same size. The second is his assumption that any good researcher would possibly attempt to draw conclusions about either city on the basis of "a single person or two."

The size of the "universe" to be sampled is typically very great in the case of most surveys; in fact, it is usually many times the size of the samples to be obtained. A different principle applies when the "universe" is small. The size of a sample needed to assess opinions of the residents of a community of 1,000 voters is obviously different from that required for a city that is much larger. A sample of 1,000 in such a town would not be a sample; it would be a complete canvass.

DEVELOPING POLL QUESTIONS

Nothing is so difficult, nor so important, as the selection and wording of poll questions. In fact, most of my time and effort in the field of polling has been devoted to this problem.

The questions included in a national survey of public opinion should meet many tests: they must deal with the vital issues of the day, they must be worded in a way to get at the heart of these issues, they must be stated in language understandable to the least well educated, and finally, they must be strictly impartial in presenting the issue.

If any reader thinks this is easy, let him try to word questions on any present-day issue. It is a tough and trying mental task. And even years of experience do not make the problem less onerous.

One rule must always be followed. No question, no matter how simple, must reach the interviewing stage without first having gone through a thorough pretesting procedure. Many tests must be applied to see that each question meets required standards.

Every survey organization has its own methods of testing the wording of questions. Here it will suffice to describe in some detail how the Gallup Poll goes about this task.

Pretesting of questions dealing with complicated issues is carried on in the Interviewing Center maintained in Hopewell, New Jersey, by the Gallup organizations. Formerly, this center was a motion-picture theater. In the early 1950s it was converted into an interviewing center. The town of Hopewell is located in the middle of an area with a total population of 500,000—an area that includes the cities of Trenton and Princeton, suburban communities, small towns, and rural districts. Consequently, people from many walks of life are available for interviewing.

Pretesting procedures normally start with "in-depth" interviews with a dozen or more individuals invited to come to the center. The purpose of these interviews is to find out how much thought each participant has given to the issue under consideration, the level of his or her knowledge about the issue, and the important facets that must be probed. Most of the questions asked in these sessions are "open" questions—that is, questions which ask: "What do you know about the XX problem? What do you think about it? What should the government do about it?" and so forth.

In conversations evoked by questions of this type, it is possible, in an unhurried manner, to discover how much knowledge average persons have of a given issue, the range of views regarding it, and the special aspects of the issue that need to be probed if a series of questions is to be developed.

The next step is to try out the questions, devised at this first stage, on a new group of respondents, to see if the questions are understandable and convey the meaning intended. A simple test for this can be employed. After reading the question, the respondent is asked to "play back" what it says to him. The answer quickly reveals whether the person being interviewed understands the language used and whether he grasps the main point of the question. This approach can also reveal, to the trained interviewer, any unsuspected biases in the wording of the question. When the language in which a question is stated is not clear to the interviewee, his typical reaction is: "Will you read that question again?" If questions have to be repeated, this is unmistakable evidence that they should be worded in a simpler and more understandable manner.

Another procedure that has proved valuable in testing questions is the self-administered interview. The respondent, without the benefit of an interviewer, writes out the answers to the questions. The advantages of this procedure are many. Answers show whether the individual has given real thought to the issue and reveal, also, the degree of his interest. If he has no opinion, he will typically leave the question blank. If he has a keen interest in the issue, he will spell out his views in some detail. And if he is misinformed, this becomes apparent in what he writes.

Self-administered questionnaires can be filled out in one's own home, or privately in an interviewing center. Since the interviewer is not at hand, many issues, such as those dealing with sex, drug addiction, alcoholism, and other personal matters, can be covered in this manner. The interviewer's function is merely to drop off the questionnaire, and pick it up in a sealed envelope the next day—or the respondent can mail it directly to the Princeton office.

Even with all of these precautions, faulty question wordings do sometimes find their way onto the survey interviewing form. Checks for internal consistency, made when the ballots are returned and are tabulated, usually bring to light these shortcomings.

Most important, the reader himself must be the final judge. The Gallup Poll, from its establishment in 1935, has followed the practice of including the exact wording of questions, when this is important, in the report of the poll findings. The reader is thus in a position to decide whether the question is worded impartially and whether the interpretation of the results, based upon the question asked, is fair and objective.

A United States senator has brought up another point about questions:

How do pollsters like yourself determine what questions to ask from time to time? It seems to me that pollsters can affect public opinion simply by asking the question. The results could be pro or anti the president depending upon the questions asked and the president's relation to it.

To be sure, a series of questions could be asked that would prove awkward to the administration, even though worded impartially, and interpreted objectively. But this would be self-defeating because it would soon become apparent to readers and commentators that the survey organization was not engaged solely in fact-finding but was trying to promote a cause.

One way to prevent unintentional biases from creeping into survey operations is to have a staff that is composed of persons representing the different shades of political belief—from right to left. If not only the questions but also the written reports dealing with the results have to run this gamut—as is the practice in the Gallup office—the dangers of unintentional bias are decreased accordingly.

Still one more safeguard in dealing with biases of any type comes about through the financial support of a poll. If sponsors represent all shades of political belief, then economic pressures alone help to keep a poll on the straight and narrow path.

So much for bias in the wording and selection of questions. This still does not answer the question posed by some who wish to know what standards or practices are followed in deciding what issues to present to the public.

Since the chief aim of a modern public opinion poll is to assess public opinion on the important issues of the day and to chart the trend of sentiment, it follows that most subjects chosen for investigation must deal with current national and international issues, and particularly those that have an immediate concern for the typical citizen. Newspapers, magazine, and the broadcast media are all useful sources of ideas for polls. Suggestions for poll subjects come from individuals and institutions—from members of Congress, editors, public officials, and foundations. Every few weeks the public itself is questioned about the most important problems facing the nation, as they see them. Their answers to this question establish priorities, and provide an up-to-date list of areas to explore through polling.

A widely held assumption is that questions can be twisted to get any answer you want. In the words of one publisher: "If you word a question one way you get a result which may differ substantially from the result you get if you word the question in a different way."

It's not that easy. Questions can be worded in a manner to bring confusing and misleading results. But the loaded question is usually self-defeating because it is obvious that it is biased.

Hundreds of experiments with a research procedure known as the split-ballot technique (one-half the cross-section gets Question A, the other half Question B) have proved that even a wide variation in question wordings did not bring substantially different results if the basic meaning or substance of the question remained the same.

Change the basic meaning of the question, add or leave out an essential part, and the results will change accordingly, as they should. Were people insensitive to words—if they were unable to distinguish between one concept and another—then the whole *raison d'être* of polling would vanish.

Often the interpreters of poll findings draw inferences that are not warranted or make assumptions that a close reading of the question does not support. Consider, for example, these two questions:

"Do you feel the United States should have gotten involved in Vietnam in the first place?"

"Do you feel the United States should have helped South Vietnam to defend itself?"

While at first glance these questions seem to deal with the same point—America's involvement—actually they are probing widely different aspects of involvement. In the first case, the respondent can read in that we helped Vietnam "with our own troops"; in the second question, that our help would have been limited to materials. Many polls have shown that the American people are willing to give military supplies to almost any nation in the world that is endangered by the communists, but they are unwilling to send troops.

If the two questions cited above did not bring substantially different results, then all the other poll results dealing with this issue would be misleading.

Questions must be stated in words that everyone understands, and results are likely to be misleading to the extent that the words are not fully understood. Ask people whether they are disturbed about the amount of pornography in their magazines and newspapers and you will get one answer; if you talk about the amount of smut you will get another.

Word specialists may insist that every word in the language conveys a slightly different connotation to every individual. While this may be true, the world (and polls) must operate on the principle that commonly used words convey approximately the same meaning to the vast majority. And this fact can easily be established in the pretesting of questions. When a question is read to a respondent and he is then asked to "play it back" in his own words, it becomes quickly evident whether he has understood the words, and in fact, what they mean to him.

Some questions that pass this test can still be faulty. The sophisticated poll watcher should be on the alert for the "desirable goal" question. This type of question ties together a desirable goal with a proposal for reaching this end. The respondent typically reacts to the goal as well as to the means. Here are some examples of desirable goal questions:

"To win the war quickly in Vietnam, would you favor all-out bombing of North Vietnam?"

"To reduce crime in the cities, would you favor increasing jail and prison sentences?"

"In order to improve the quality of education in the United States, should teachers be paid higher salaries?"

These questions, which present widely accepted goals accompanied by the tacit assumption that the means suggested will bring about the desired end, produce results biased on the favorable side.

The more specific questions are, the better. One of the classic arguments between newspapers and television has centered around a question that asks the public: "Where do you get most of your news about what's going on in the world today—from the newspaper, or radio, or television, or magazines, or talking to people, or where?" The answers show TV ahead of daily newspapers. But when this question is asked in a way to differentiate between international news, and local and state news, TV wins on international news, but the daily newspaper has a big lead on local news. A simple explanation is that the phrase, "What is going on in the *world?*" is interpreted by the average citizen to mean in the faraway places—not his home city.

People are extremely literal minded. A farmer in Ontario, interviewed by the Canadian Gallup Poll, was asked at the close of the interview how long he had lived in the same house; specifically, the length of his residence there. The answer that came back was "Twenty-six feet and six inches."

Whenever it is possible, the questions asked should state both sides of the issue. Realistic alternatives should be offered, or implied.

Looking back through more than four decades of polling, this aspect of question wording warrants the greatest criticism. There is probably little need to state the other side, or offer an alternative, in a question such as this: "Should the voting age be lowered to include those eighteen years of age?" The alternative implied is to leave the situation as it is.

An excellent observation has been made by a political scientist on the faculty of a New England college:

> Somehow more realism must be introduced into polls. . . . People often affirm abstract principles but will not be willing to pay the price of their concrete application. For example, would you be willing to pay more for each box of soap you buy in order to reduce ground pollution—or $200 more for your next car in order to reduce air pollution, etc.?

This type of question is similar to the desirable goal question. The public wants to clear the slums, wants better medical care, improved racial relations, better schools, better housing. The real issue is one of priorities and costs. The role of the public opinion poll in this situation is to shed light on the public's concern about each major problem, establish priorities, and then discover whether the people are willing to foot the bill.

The well-informed person is likely to think of the costs involved by legislation that proposes to deal with these social problems. But to the typical citizen there is no immediate or direct relationship between legislation and the amount he has to pay in taxes. Congress usually tries to disguise costs by failing to tie taxes or costs to large appropriations, leaving John Doe with the impression that someone else will pay the bill.

Still another type of question that is suspect has to do with good intentions. Questions of this type have meaning only when controls are used and when the results are interpreted with a full understanding of their shortcomings.

Examples of questions that fall into this category are those asking people if they "plan to go to church," "read a book," "listen to good music," "vote in the coming election," and so forth.

To the typical American the word "intend" or "plan" connotes many things, such as "Do I think this is a good idea?" "Would I like to do it?" "Would it be good for me?" "Would it be good for other people?" These and similar questions of a prestige nature reveal attitudes, but they are a poor guide to action.

Behavior is always the best guide. The person who attended church last Sunday is likely to go next Sunday, if he says he plans to. The citizen who voted in the last election and whose name is now on the registration books is far more likely to vote than the person who hasn't bothered to vote or to register, even though he insists that he "plans" to do both.

Probably the most difficult of all questions to word is the type that offers the respondent several alternatives. Not only is it hard to find alternatives that are mutually exclusive; it is equally difficult to find a series that covers the entire range of opinions. Added to this is the problem of wording each alternative in a way that doesn't give it a special advantage. And finally, in any series of alternatives that ranges from one extreme of opinion to the other, the typical citizen has a strong inclination to choose one in the middle.

As a working principle it can be stated that the more words included in a question, either by way of explanation or in stating alternatives, the greater the possibilities that the question wording itself will influence answers.

A member of the editorial staff of a newsmagazine voiced a common reaction when he observed:

> On more than a few occasions I have found that I could not, were I asked, answer a poll with a "yes" or "no." More likely my answer would be "yes, but" or "yes, if." I wonder whether pollsters can't or just don't want to measure nuances of feeling.

Obviously it is the desire of a polling organization to produce a full and accurate account of the public's views on any given issue, nuances and all.

First, however, it should be pointed out that there are two main categories of questions serving two different purposes—one to *measure* public opinion, the other to *describe* public opinion. The first category has to do with the "referendum" type of question. Since the early years of polling, heavy emphasis has been placed upon this type of question, which serves in effect as an unofficial national referendum on a given issue, actually providing the same results, within a small margin of error, that an official nationwide referendum would if it were held at the same time and on the same issue.

At some point in the decision process, whether it be concerned with an important issue before Congress, a new law before the state legislature, or a school bond issue in Central City, the time comes for a simple "yes" or "no" vote. Fortunately, or unfortunately, there is no lever on a voting machine that permits the voter to register a "yes, if" or a "yes, but" vote. While discussion can and should proceed at length, the only way to determine majority opinion is by a simple count of noses.

If polling organizations limited themselves to the referendum type of question they would severely restrict their usefulness. They can and should use their machinery to reveal the many facets of public opinion of any issue, and to shed light on the reasons why the people hold the views they do; in short, to explore the "why" behind public opinion.

More and more attention is being paid to this diagnostic approach and the greatest improvements in the field of public opinion research in the future are likely to deal with this aspect of polling.

One of the important developments in question technique was the development in the late 1940s of a new kind of question design that permits the investigation of views on any issue of a complex nature.

This design, developed by the Gallup Poll, has been described as the "quintamensional approach" since it probes five aspects of opinion:

1. the respondent's awareness and general knowledge about it,
2. his overall opinions,
3. the reasons why he holds his views,
4. his specific views on specific aspects of the problem,
5. the intensity with which he hold his opinions.

This question design quickly sorts out those who have no knowledge of a given issue—an important function in successful public opinion polling. And it can even reveal the extent or level of knowledge of the interviewee about the issue.

This is how the system works. The first question put to the person being interviewed (on any problem or issue no matter how complex) is this: "Have you heard or read about the XXX problem (proposal or issue)?"

The person being interviewed can answer either "yes" or "no" to this question, or he can add, "I'm not sure." If he answers in the negative, experience covering many years indicates that he is being entirely truthful. If he answers "yes" or "I'm not sure" he is then asked: "Please tell me in your own words what the debate (or the proposal or issue) is about." At this point the person interviewed must produce evidence that reveals whether he has some knowledge of the problem or issue.

The reader might imagine himself in this interviewing situation. You are called upon by an interviewer and in the course of the interview are asked if you have "heard or read about the Bronson proposal to reorganize the Security Council of the United Nations." The answer is likely to be "no." Possibly you might say: "I seem to have heard about it somewhere." Or suppose that, just to impress the interviewer (something that rarely happens) you fall into the trap of saying "yes."

The next question puts you neatly and delicately on the spot. It asks you to describe in your own words what the Bronson proposal is. You have to admit at this point that you do not know, or come up with an answer that immediately indicates you do not know what it is.

At this stage the questioning can be expanded to discover just how well informed you are. If it is an issue or proposal, then you can be asked to give the main arguments for and the main arguments against the plan or issue. In short, by adding questions at this stage, the *level* of knowledge of the respondent can be determined.

The next question in the design is an "open" question that asks simply: "What do you think should be done about this proposal?" or "How do you think this issue should be resolved?" This type of question permits the person being interviewed to give his views without any specifics being mentioned. Answers, of course, are recorded by the interviewer as nearly as possible in the exact words of the respondent.

The third category of questions seeks to find out the "why" behind the respondent's views. This can be done with a simple question asking: "Why do you feel that way?" or variations of this, along with "nondirective" probes such as "What else?" or "Can you explain that in greater detail?"

The fourth category in the design poses specific issues that can be answered in "yes" or "no" fashion. At this fourth stage it is possible to go back to those who were excluded by the first two questions: those who said they had not heard or read about the issue in question or proved, after the second question, that they were uninformed.

By explaining in neutral language to this group what the problem or issue is and the specific proposals that have been made for dealing with it, the uninformed can voice their opinions, which later can be compared with those of the already informed group.

The fifth category attempts to get at the intensity with which opinions are held. How strongly does each side hold to its views? What action is each individual willing to take to see that his opinion prevails? What chance is there that he may change his mind?

This, then, is the quintamensional approach. And its special merit is that it can quickly sort out the informed from the uninformed. The views of the well informed can be compared not only with the less well informed but with those who are learning about the issue for the first time. Moreover, through cross-tabulations, it is possible to show how special kinds of knowledge are related to certain opinions.

The filtering process may screen out nearly all individuals in the sample because they are uninformed, but it is often of interest and importance to know how the few informed individuals divide on a complex issue. When the best informed individuals favor a proposal or issue, experience indicates that their view tends to be accepted by lower echelons as information and knowledge become more widespread.

But this is not the invariable pattern. In the case of Vietnam, it was the best educated and the best informed who reversed their views as the war went on. The least well educated were always more against the war in Vietnam.

It is now proper to ask why, with all of its obvious merits, this question design is not used more often. The answer is that polling organizations generally avoid technical and complex issues, preferring to deal with those on which the vast majority of Americans have knowledge and opinions. Often the design is shortened to embrace only the filter question that seeks to find out if the individual has read or heard about a given issue, and omits the other questions.

In the field of public opinion research, one finds two schools of thought: one is made up largely of those in academic circles who believe that research on public attitudes should be almost entirely descriptive or diagnostic; the other, made up largely of persons in political life or in journalism or allied fields, who want to know the "score." It is the task of the polling organization to satisfy both groups. And to do this, both categories of questions must be included in the surveys conducted at regular intervals.

The long experience of the Gallup Poll points to the importance of reporting trends of opinion on all the continuing problems, the beliefs, the wishes of the people.

In fact, about four out of every ten questions included in a typical survey are for the purpose of measuring trends. Simple "yes" and "no" questions are far better suited to this purpose than "open-ended" questions, and this accounts chiefly for the high percentage of this type of question in the field of polling.

INTERVIEWERS AND INTERVIEWING PROBLEMS

Since the reliability of poll results depends so much on the integrity of interviewers, polling organizations must go to great lengths to see that interviewers follow instructions conscientiously.

A professor at an Ivy League college sums up the problems that have to do with interviewers in this question: "How do you insure quality control over your interviewers, preventing them from either influencing the answers, mis-recording them, or filling in the forms themselves?"

Before these specific points are dealt with, the reader may wish to know who the interviewers are and how they are selected and trained.

Women make the best interviewers, not only in the United States but in virtually every nation where public opinion survey organizations are established. Generally, they are more conscientious and more likely to follow instructions than men. Perhaps the nature of the work makes interviewing more appealing to them. The fact that the work is part-time is another reason why women prefer it.

Most interviewers are women of middle age, with high-school or college education. Most are married and have children.

Very few interviewers devote full time to this work. In fact, this is not recommended. Interviewing is mentally exhausting and the interviewer who works day after day at this task is likely to lose her zeal, with a consequent drop in the quality of her work.

When an area is drawn for the national cross-section, the interviewing department of the polling organization finds a suitable person to serve as the interviewer in this particular district. All the usual methods of seeking individuals who can meet the requirements are utilized, including such sources as school superintendents, newspaper editors, members of the clergy, and the classified columns of the local press.

Training for this kind of work can be accomplished by means of an instruction manual, by a supervisor, or by training sessions. The best training consists of a kind of trial-by-fire process. The interviewer is given test interviews to do after she has completed her study of the instruction manual. The trial interviews prove whether she can do the work in a satisfactory manner; more important, making these interviews enables the interviewer to discover if she really likes this kind of work. Her interviews are carefully inspected and investigated. Telephone conversations often straighten out procedures and clear up any misunderstandings about them.

Special questions added to the interviewing form and internal checks on consistency can be used to detect dishonesty. Also, a regular program of contacting persons who have been interviewed—to see if they in fact have been interviewed—is commonly employed by the best survey organizations.

It would be foolhardy to insist that every case of dishonesty can be detected in this manner, but awareness of the existence of these many ways of checking honesty removes most if not all of the temptation for the interviewers to fill in the answers themselves.

Experience of many years indicates that the temptation to "fudge" answers is related to the size of the work load given to the interviewer. If too many interviews are required in too short a time, the interviewer may hurry through the assignment, being less careful than she otherwise would be and, on occasion, not above the temptation to fill in a last few details.

To lessen this pressure, the assignment of interviews given to Gallup Poll interviewers has been constantly reduced through the years. At the present time, an assignment consists of only five or six interviews, and assignments come at least a week apart. This policy increases the cost per interview but it also keeps the interviewer from being subjected to too great pressure.

In the case of open questions that require the interviewer to record the exact words of the respondent, the difficulties mount. The interviewer must attempt to record the main thought of the respondent as the respondent is talking, and usually without benefit of shorthand. The addition of "probe" questions to the original open-end questions helps to organize the response in a more meaningful way. In certain circumstances, the use of small tape recorders, carried by the interviewer, is highly recommended.

So much for the interviewer's side of this situation. What about the person being interviewed? How honest is he?

While there is no certain way of telling whether a given individual is answering truthfully, the evidence from thousands of surveys is that people are remarkably honest and frank when asked their views in a situation that is properly structured— that is, when the respondent knows the purpose of the interview and is told that his name will not be attached to any of the things he says, and when the questions are properly worded.

It is important to point out that persons reached in a public opinion survey normally do not know the interviewer personally. For this reason, there is little or no reason to try to impress her. And, contrary to a widely held view, people are not inclined to "sound off" on subjects they know little about. In fact, many persons entitled, on the basis of their knowledge, to hold an opinion about a given problem or issue often hesitate to do so. In the development of the quintamensional procedure, described earlier, it was discovered that the opening question could not be stated: "Have you *followed* the discussion about the XX issue?" Far too many said they hadn't. And for this reason the approach had to be changed to ask: "Have you *heard or read* about the XX issue?"

The interviewer is instructed to read the question exactly as it is worded, and not try to explain it or amplify it. If the interviewee says, "Would you repeat that?" (incidentally, this is always the mark of a bad question), the interviewer repeats the question, and if on the second reading the person does not understand or get the point of the question, the interviewer checks the "no opinion" box and goes on to the next question.

But don't people often change their minds? This is a question often asked of poll-takers. The answer is, "Of course." Interviewed on Saturday, some persons may have a different opinion on Sunday. But this is another instance when the law of averages comes to the rescue. Those who shift their views in one direction will almost certainly be counterbalanced by those who change in the opposite direction. The net result is to show no change in the overall results.

Polls can only reflect people as they are—sometimes inconsistent, often uninformed. Democracy, however, does not require that every individual, every voter, be a philosopher. Democracy requires only that the sum total of individual views—the collective judgment—add up to something that makes sense. Fortunately, there now exists some forty years of polling evidence to prove the soundness of the collective judgment of the people.

How many persons refuse to be interviewed? The percentage is very small, seldom more than 10% of all those contacted. Interestingly, this same figure is found in all the nations where public opinion polls are conducted. Refusals are chiefly a function of lack of interviewing skill. Top interviewers are rarely turned down. This does not mean that a man who must get back to work immediately or a woman who has a cake in the oven will take thirty to forty-five minutes to discuss issues of the day. These situations are to be avoided. And that is why the Time-Place interviewing plan was developed by the Gallup Poll.

Readers may wonder how polls allow for the possible embarrassment or guilty conscience factor that might figure in an interviewee's answers to some questions. For example, while a voter might be prepared to vote for a third-party candidate like George Wallace, he might be uneasy about saying so to a stranger sitting in his living room.

When interviews and the interviewing situation are properly structured, however, this does not happen. In the 1968 election campaign, to follow the same example, the Gallup Poll found Wallace receiving at one point as much as 19% of the total vote. Later his popularity declined. The final poll result showed him with 15% of the vote; he actually received 14%. If there had been any embarrassment about admitting being for Wallace, his vote would obviously have been under-estimated by a sizable amount.

Properly approached, people are not reluctant to discuss even personal matters—their private problems, their religion, sex. By using an interesting technique developed in Sweden, even the most revealing facts about the sex life of an individual can be obtained. And the same type of approach is found to be highly successful in finding out the extent of drug use by college students. Many studies about the religious beliefs of individuals have been conducted by the Gallup Poll without meeting interviewing difficulties.

The desire to have one's voice heard on issues of the day is almost universal. An interviewer called upon an elderly man and found him working in his garden. After he had offered his views on many subjects included in the poll, he called to the interviewer who had started for her car, and said: "You know, two of the most important things in my life have happened this week. First, I was asked to serve on a jury, and now I have been asked to give my views in a public opinion poll."

MEASURING INTENSITY

To the legislator or administrator the intensity with which certain voters or groups of voters hold their opinions has special significance. If people feel strongly enough about a given issue they will likely do something about it—write letters, work for a candidate who holds a contrary view, contribute money to a campaign, try to win other voters to their candidate. To cite an example: Citizens who oppose any kind of gun control laws, though constituting a minority of the public, feel so strongly about this issue that they will do anything they can to defeat such legislation. As a result, they have succeeded in keeping strict gun laws from being adopted in most states and by the federal government.

Since most legislation calls for more money, a practical measure of the intensity of feeling about a given piece of legislation is the willingness to have taxes increased to meet the costs.

One politician made this criticism of polling efforts: "Issue polling often fails to differentiate between hard and soft opinion. If the issue is national health insurance, then the real test is not whether the individual favors it but how much more per year he is willing to pay in taxes for such a program."

This is a merited criticism of polls and, as stated earlier, one that points to the need for greater attention on the part of polling organizations. The action that an individual is willing to take—the sacrifice he is willing to undergo—to see that his side of an issue prevails is one of the best ways of sorting out hard from soft opinion.

Questions put to respondents about "how strongly" they feel, "how important it is to them," and "how much they care" all yield added insights into the intensity of opinions held by the public. The fact, however, that they are used as seldom as they are in the regular polls, here and abroad, indicates that the added information gained does not compensate for the time and the difficulties encountered by the survey interviewer. Most attitude scales are, in fact, better suited to the classroom with students as captive subjects than to the face-to-face interviews undertaken by most survey organizations.

The best hope, in my opinion, lies in the development of new questions that are behavior- or action-oriented. Here, then, is an important area where both academicians and practitioners can work together in the improvement of present research procedures.

The specific complaint mentioned above—that of providing a more realistic presentation of an issue—can probably be dealt with best in the question wording, as noted earlier.

While verbal scales to measure intensity can be usefully employed in many situations, two nonverbal scales have gained wide acceptance and use throughout the world. Since they do not depend upon words, language is no barrier to their use in any nation. Moreover, they can be employed in normal interviewing situations, and on a host of problems.

The scales were devised by Jan Stapel of the Netherlands Institute of Public Opinion and by Hadley Cantril and a colleague, F. P. Kilpatrick. While the scales seem to be similar, each has its own special merits.

The Stapel scale consists of a column of ten boxes. The five at the top are white, the five at the bottom black.

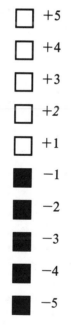

The boxes are numbered from +5 to −5. The interviewer carries a reproduction of this scale and at the appropriate time in the interview hands it to the respondent. The interviewer explains the scale in these or similar words: "You will notice that the boxes on this card go from the highest position of plus 5—something you like very much—all the way down to the lowest position of minus 5—or something you dislike very much. Now, how far up the scale, or how far down the scale, would you rate the following?"

After this explanation, the interviewer asks the respondent how far up or down the scale he would rate an individual, political party, product, company, proposal, or almost anything at issue. The person is told "put your finger on the box" that best represents his point of view; or, in other situations, to call off the number opposite the box. The interviewer duly records this number on his interviewing form.

One of the merits of the Stapel Scalometer is that it permits the person being interviewed to answer two questions with one response: whether he has a positive or a negative feeling toward the person or party or institution being rated, and at the same time the degree of his liking or disliking. By simply calling off a number he indicates that he has a favorable or unfavorable opinion of the F.B.I., of Jimmy Carter, or of the Equal Rights Amendment, and how much he likes or dislikes each. In actual use, researchers have found the extreme positions on the scale are most indicative and most sensitive to change. These are the +4 and +5 positions on the favorable side and the −4 and −5 positions on the negative side. Normally these two positions are combined to provide a "highly favorable" or a "highly unfavorable" rating.

Scale ratings thus obtained are remarkably consistent and remarkably reliable in ranking candidates and parties. In fact, the ratings given to the two major-party candidates have paralleled the relative standings of the candidates in elections, especially when the party ratings are averaged with the candidate ratings.

Cantril and Kilpatrick devised the "Self-Anchoring Scale."* Cantril and his associate, Lloyd Free, used this scale to measure the aspirations and fears of people in different nations of the world—both those living in highly developed countries and those in the least developed. They sought "to get an overall picture of the reality worlds in which people lived, a picture expressed by individuals in their own terms and to do this in such a way . . . as to enable meaningful comparisons to be made between different individuals, groups of individuals, and societies."

The Self-Anchoring scale is so simple that it can be used with illiterates and with people without any kind of formal education. A multination survey in which this measuring instrument was employed included nations as diverse in their educational and living standards as Nigeria, India, the United States, West Germany, Cuba, Israel, Japan, Poland, Panama, Yugoslavia, Philippines, Brazil, and the Dominican Republic.

---

*F. P. Kilpatrick and Hadley Cantril, "Self-Anchoring Scale." *Journal of Individual Psychology,* November 1960.

The scale makes use of a ladder device.

```
——— 10 ———
——— 9 ———
——— 8 ———
——— 7 ———
——— 6 ———
——— 5 ———
——— 4 ———
——— 3 ———
——— 2 ———
——— 1 ———
——— 0 ———
```

The person being interviewed describes his own wishes and hopes, the realization of which would constitute the best possible life. This is the top anchoring point of the scale. At the other extreme, the same individual describes his worries and fears embodied in the worst possible life he can imagine. With the use of this device, he is asked where he thinks he stands on the ladder today. Then he is asked where he thinks he stood in the past, and where he thinks he will stand in the future.

This same procedure was used by Albert Cantril and Charles Roll in a survey called *Hopes and Fears of the American People*—a revealing study of the mood of the American people in the spring of 1971.

Use of this scale would be extremely helpful in pursuing the goal set forth by Alvin Toffler in his book *Future Shock*. He writes:

> The time has come for a dramatic reassessment of the directions of change, a reassessment made not by the politicians or the sociologists or the clergy or the elitist revolutionaries, not by technicians or college presidents, but by the people themselves. We need, quite literally, to "go to the people" with a question that is almost never asked of them: *"What kind of a world do you want 10, 20, or 30 years from now?"* We need to initiate, in short, a continuing plebiscite on the future. Toffler points out that "the voter may be polled about specific issues, but not about the general shape of the preferable future."

This is true to a great extent. With the exception of the Cantril-Free studies, this area has been largely overlooked by polling organizations. Toffler advocates a continuing plebiscite in which millions of persons would participate. From a practical point of view, however, sampling offers the best opportunity to discover just what the public's ideas of the future are—and more particularly, the kind of world they want ten years, twenty years, or thirty years from now.

REPORTING AND INTERPRETING POLL FINDINGS

Public opinion polls throughout the world have been sponsored by the media of communication—newspapers, magazines, television, and radio. It is quite proper, therefore, to answer this question: "How well do the various media report and evaluate the results of a given poll?"

Since October 1935, Gallup Poll reports have appeared weekly in American newspapers in virtually all of the major cities. During this period, I am happy to report, no newspaper has changed the wording of poll releases sent to them to make the findings fit the newspaper's editorial or political views. Editors, however, are permitted to write their own headlines because of their own special type and format policies; they can shorten articles or, in fact, omit them if news columns are filled by other and more pressing material.

Since the funds for the Gallup Poll come from this source and since the sponsoring newspapers represent all shades of political belief, the need for strict objectivity in the writing and interpretation of poll results becomes an economic as well as a scientific necessity.

At various stages in the history of the Gallup Poll, charges have been made that the poll has a Republican bias, and at other times, a Democratic bias, largely dependent upon whether the political tide is swinging toward one side or the other. Even a cursory examination of the findings dealing with issues of the day, and of election survey results, will disprove this.

The Gallup Poll is a fact-finding organization, or looked at in another way, a kind of scorekeeper in the political world.

When poll findings are not to the liking of critics there is always a great temptation to try to discredit the poll by claiming that it is "biased," that it makes "secret adjustments" and that it manipulates the figures to suit its fancy, and that it is interfering with "democratic dialogue." Such charges were heard often in earlier years, but time has largely stilled this kind of attack on the poll's integrity.

Limitations of space, in the case of newspapers, and of time in the case of television and radio, impose restrictions on the amount of detail and analysis that can be included in any one report. The news media have a strong preference for "hard" news, the kind that reports the most recent score on candidate or party strength, or the division of opinion on highly controversial subjects. This type of news, it should be added, makes up the bulk of their news budgets.

These space and time requirements do require a different kind of poll report form from one that would be written to satisfy those who prefer a full and detailed description of public opinion.

A political writer for a large metropolitan newspaper has raised this point: "Is it not more accurate to report a point spread instead of a simple single figure? . . . If so, would it not be more responsible to state it that way, even though it would take away some of the sharpness in published reports?"

A degree of error is inherent in all sampling and it is important that this fact be understood by those who follow poll findings. The question is how best to achieve this end. One way, of course, is to educate the public to look at all survey results not as fixed realities or absolutes but as reliable estimates only.

The best examples, as noted earlier, are the monthly figures on unemployment and the cost of living. Should these be published showing a point spread or the margin of error? If they were, then the monthly index of unemployment, based as it is on a sample of 50,000, would read, at a given point in time, not 8.8%, but 8.5% to 9.1%. Reporting the cost of living index in such fashion would almost certainly cause trouble, since many labor contracts are based upon changes as small as 0.1%.

In reporting the trend of opinion, especially on issues, the inclusion of a point spread would make poll reports rather meaningless, particularly if the trend were not a sharp one. The character of the trend curve itself normally offers evidence of the variations due to sample size.

In the case of elections, the reporting of the margin of error can, on occasion, be misleading to the reader. The reason is that polling errors come from many sources, and often the least of these in importance is the size of the sample. Yet, the statistical margin of error relates solely to this one factor.

An example may help to shed light on this point. A telephone poll taken in a mayoralty race in a large eastern city, reported the standings of the candidates and added that they were accurate within "a possible error margin of 3.8%." In short, the newspaper in which the results were published and the polling organization assured readers that the results perforce had to be right within this margin, based upon the laws or probability. Actually, the poll figure was 14 percentage points short on the winning candidate. Factors other than the size of the sample were responsible for this wide deviation.

The best guide to a poll's accuracy is its record. If allowance is to be made for variation in the poll's reported figures, then perhaps the best suggestion, to be reasonably certain that the error will not exceed a stated amount in a national election, is to multiply by 2.5 the average deviation of the poll in its last three or four elections.

Still another way to remind readers and viewers of the presence of some degree of error in all survey findings is to find a word or words that convey this fact. A growing practice among statisticians in dealing with sampling data is to refer to results as "estimates." Unfortunately, this word conveys to some the impression that subjective judgments have entered into the process. A better word needs to be found that removes some of the certainty that is too often attached to poll percentages without, at the same time, erring in the opposite direction. The word "assessment" has been adopted by some survey researchers and it is hoped that it will come into general use in the future.

DESIGN OF THE SAMPLE

The design of the sample used in the Gallup Poll is that of a replicated probability sample down to the block level in the case of urban areas and to segments of townships in the case of rural areas.

After stratifying the nation geographically and by size of community in order to insure conformity of the sample with the latest available estimates by the Census Bureau of the distribution of the adult population, about 350 different sampling locations or areas are selected on a strictly random basis. The interviewers have no choice whatsoever concerning the part of the city or county in which they conduct their interviews.

Interviewers are given maps of the area to which they are assigned, with a starting point indicated, and are required to follow a specified direction. At each occupied dwelling unit, interviewers are instructed to select respondents by following a prescribed systematic method. This procedure is followed until the assigned number of interviews is completed. The standard sample size for most Gallup Polls is 1500 interviews. This is augmented in specific instances where greater survey accuracy is considered desirable.

Since this sampling procedure is designed to produce a sample that approximates the adult civilian population (18 and older) living in private households in the United States (that is, excluding those in prisons and hospitals, hotels, religious institutions, and on military reservations), the survey results can be applied to this population for the purpose of projecting percentages into numbers of people. The manner in which the sample is drawn also produces a sample that approximates the population of private households in the United States. Therefore, survey results also can be projected in terms of numbers of households when appropriate.

SAMPLING TOLERANCES

It should be remembered that all sample surveys are subject to sampling error; that is, the extent to which the results may differ from what would be obtained if the whole population surveyed had been interviewed. The size of such a sampling error depends largely on the number of interviews. Increasing the sample size lessens the magnitude of possible error and vice versa.

The following tables may be used in estimating sampling error. The computed allowances (the standard deviation) have taken into account the effect of the sample design upon sampling error. They may be interpreted as indicating the range (plus or minus the figure shown) within which the results of repeated samplings in the same time period could be expected to vary, 95 percent of the time (or at a confidence level of .5), assuming the same sampling procedure, the same interviewers, and the same questionnaire.

Table A shows how much allowance should be made for the sampling error of a percentage. The table would be used in the following manner: Say a reported percentage is 33 for a group that includes 1500 respondents. Go to the row "percentage near 30" in the table and then to the column headed "1500." The number at this point is three, which means that the 33 percent obtained in the sample is subject to a sampling error of plus or minus 3 points. Another way of saying it is that very probably (95 chances out of 100) the average of repeated samplings would be somewhere between 30 and 36, with the most likely figure being the 33 obtained.

In comparing survey results in two subsamples, such as men and woman, the question arises as to how large must a difference between them be before one can be reasonably sure that it reflects a statistically significant difference. In Table B and C, the number of points that must be allowed for, in such comparisons, is indicated.

For percentages near 20 or 80, use Table B; for those near 50, Table C. For percentages in between, the error to be allowed for is between that shown in the two tables.

Here is an example of how the tables should be used: Say 50 percent of men and 40 percent of women respond the same way to a question—a difference of 10 percentage points. Can it be said with any assurance that the ten-point difference reflects a significant difference between men and women on the question? (Samples, unless otherwise noted, contain approximately 750 men and 750 women.)

Because the percentages are near 50, consult Table C. Since the two samples are about 750 persons each, look for the place in the table where the column and row labeled "750" converge. The number six appears there. This means the allowance for error should be 6 points, and the conclusion that the percentage among men is somewhere between 4 and 16 points higher than the percentage among women would be wrong only about 5 percent of the time. In other words, there is a considerable likelihood that a difference exists in the direction observed and that it amounts to at least 4 percentage points.

If, in another case, male responses amount to 22 percent, and female to 24 percent, consult Table B because these percentages are near 20. The column and row labeled "750" converge on the number five. Obviously, then, the two-point difference is inconclusive.

TABLE A

Recommended Allowance for Sampling Error of a Percentage

In Percentage Points
(at 95 in 100 confidence level)*
Size of the Sample

	3000	1500	1000	750	600	400	200	100
Percentages near 10	2	2	2	3	4	4	5	7
Percentages near 20	2	3	3	4	4	5	7	9
Percentages near 30	2	3	4	4	4	6	8	10
Percentages near 40	3	3	4	4	5	6	9	11
Percentages near 50	3	3	4	4	5	6	9	11
Percentages near 60	3	3	4	4	5	6	9	11
Percentages near 70	2	3	4	4	4	6	8	10
Percentages near 80	2	3	3	4	4	5	7	9
Percentages near 90	2	2	2	3	4	4	5	7

*The chances are 95 in 100 that the sampling error is not larger than the figures shown.

TABLE B

Recommended Allowance for Sampling Error of the Difference Between Two Subsamples

In Percentage Points
(at 95 in 100 confidence level)*

Percentages near 20 or percentages near 80

	1500	750	600	400	200
Size of the Sample					
1500	3				
750	4	5			
600	5	6	6		
400	6	7	7	7	
200	8	8	8	9	10

TABLE C

Percentages near 50

	1500	750	600	400	200
Size of the Sample					
1500	4				
750	5	·6			
600	6	8	8		
400	7	8	8	9	
200	10	10	11	11	13

*The chances are 95 in 100 that the sampling error is not larger than the figures shown.

RECORD OF
GALLUP POLL ACCURACY

Year	Gallup Final Survey*		Election Result*	
1980	47.0%	Reagan	50.8%	Reagan
1978	55.0	Democratic	54.0	Democratic
1976	48.0	Carter	50.0	Carter
1974	60.0	Democratic	58.9	Democratic
1972	62.0	Nixon	61.8	Nixon
1970	53.0	Democratic	54.3	Democratic
1968	43.0	Nixon	43.5	Nixon
1966	52.5	Democratic	51.9	Democratic
1964	64.0	Johnson	61.3	Johnson
1962	55.5	Democratic	52.7	Democratic
1960	51.0	Kennedy	50.1	Kennedy
1958	57.0	Democratic	56.5	Democratic
1956	59.5	Eisenhower	57.8	Eisenhower
1954	51.5	Democratic	52.7	Democratic
1952	51.0	Eisenhower	55.4	Eisenhower
1950	51.0	Democratic	50.3	Democratic
1948	44.5	Truman	49.9	Truman
1946	58.0	Republican	54.3	Republican
1944	51.5	Roosevelt	53.3[2]	Roosevelt
1942	52.0	Democratic	48.0[1]	Democratic
1940	52.0	Roosevelt	55.0	Roosevelt
1938	54.0	Democratic	50.8	Democratic
1936	55.7	Roosevelt	62.5	Roosevelt

*The figure shown is the winner's percentage of the Democratic-Republican vote except in the elections of 1948, 1968, and 1976. Because the Thurmond and Wallace voters in 1948 were largely split-offs from the normally Democratic vote, they were made a part of the final Gallup Poll preelection

[1] Final report said Democrats would win control of the House, which they did even though the Republicans won a majority of the popular vote.
[2] Civilian vote 53.3, Roosevelt soldier vote 0.5 = 53.8% Roosevelt. Gallup final survey based on civilian vote.

estimate of the division of the vote. In 1968 Wallace's candidacy was supported by such a large minority that he was clearly a major candidate, and the 1968 percents are based on the total Nixon-Humphrey-Wallace vote. In 1976, because of interest in McCarthy's candidacy and its potential effect on the Carter vote, the final Gallup Poll estimate included Carter, Ford, McCarthy, and all other candidates as a group.

Average Deviation for 23
    National Elections . . . . 2.3 percentage points

Average Deviation for 16
    National Elections
    Since 1950, inclusive . . . . 1.6 percentage points

Trend in Deviation Reduction

Elections	Average Error
1936–48	4.0
1950–58	1.7
1960–68	1.5
1970–78	1.1
1970–80	1.5
1966–80	1.2

CHRONOLOGY

The chronology is provided to enable the reader to relate poll results to specific events or series of events that may have influenced public opinion.

1980

December 1   The Commerce Department reports that the economic index rose 0.9% in October, the smallest gain in four months.

December 3   Representatives Frank Thompson (D.–NJ) and John Murphy (D.–NY) are found guilty of charges stemming from the government's Abscam investigation into political corruption.

December 5   United States suspends $25 million in new economic and military aid to El Salvador following the killings of four American citizens in that country.

The Labor Department announces that the unemployment rate dropped in November from 7.6% to 7.3%.

December 8   The Chrysler Corporation informs the government that it needs $350 million in additional federal loan guarantees if it is to keep producing automobiles. This was to be in addition to the $800 million previously guaranteed.

Singer, composer, and ex-Beatle John Lennon is killed outside his apartment in New York City.

December 19   The prime lending rate increases to 20½%.

1981

January 5   The second round of draft registration begins with about 1.9 million men born in 1962 registering with the Selective Service System. In the previous registration period, 95% of those eligible registered.

January 16   President Jimmy Carter authorizes the emergency delivery of $5 million in combat equipment to aid the government of El Salvador in putting down the revolution. This decision was prompted by indications that the guerrillas had been receiving weapons from leftists in other countries.

               In his final State of the Union message to Congress, President Carter warns that the United States faces serious problems, deplores the Soviet threat to the integrity of Poland, and defends his SALT treaty with the Soviet Union.

January 20   Ronald Reagan becomes the fortieth president of the United States. At the age of sixty-nine he is the oldest man ever to be sworn in as president.

               Fifty-two Americans held hostage in Iran for 444 days are flown to freedom. The release was precipitated by a January 19 agreement between the United States and Iran in which this country agreed to return $8 billion in Iranian assets, which had been frozen following the November 1979 seizure of the hostages and the U.S. embassy in Tehran.

January 23   The Bureau of Labor Statistics releases a report on the consumer price index, which climbed 1.1% in December. The total rise to 12.4% marks the first time since World War I that there has been two consecutive years of double-digit inflation.

January 27   Alexander M. Haig, Jr., is sworn in as secretary of state.

January 28   President Ronald Reagan abolishes the remaining price and allocation controls on domestic oil and gasoline production.

February 17   In an attempt to curb lagging sales, General Motors and Ford announce that they will institute the largest rebate plans in their history.

February 18	President Reagan urges Congress to cut the size of the budget and proposes a $695.5-billion budget for fiscal year 1982, with a $45-billion deficit. The cuts would affect eighty-three major federal programs and provide an annual tax cut for individuals of about 10% over the next three years. Only the military budget is to be increased.
February 24	President Reagan reiterates his support for the El Salvador junta, although he says he has no intention of involving the United States.
February 25	The Labor Department announces that consumer prices rose 0.7% during January.
February 27	Chrysler reports a loss of $1.71 billion for 1980, the largest in American corporate history.
March 2	The U.S. State Department declares that it will expand military assistance to El Salvador by sending twenty additional military advisers and $25 million in military equipment to the Duarte government.
March 6	Producer prices rose 0.8% in February, while unemployment declined to 7.3%.
March 10	President Reagan arrives in Ottawa on his first foreign visit. In an address to Parliament, he deplores the Russian invasion of Afghanistan and pledges continuing friendship with Canada.
March 24	The consumer price index rose 1% during February.
March 27	The membership of the United Mine Workers union rejects a tentative agreement with the Bituminous Coal Operators Association and goes on strike.
March 30	President Reagan is shot as he walked to his limousine after addressing a labor meeting in Washington, DC. Also wounded were Presidential Press Secretary James Brady, a Secret Service agent, and a police officer. The alleged assailant, John Hinkley, Jr., was captured.
April 3	March unemployment remains at the same rate as that of February—7.3%.

April 6	The Reagan administration suggests easing or eliminating thirty-five air quality and safety regulations on automobiles. The proposal is designed to help the domestic auto industry fight Japanese imports.
April 7	The Justice Department announces that 30% of the nation's 80.6 million households were victimized by one or more crimes in 1980. Members of 14% of the households experienced personal larceny away from home.
April 12	The space shuttle *Columbia,* designed as a reusable cargo ship, roars into space from Cape Canaveral, Florida, with astronauts John Young and Robert Crippen aboard. Fifty-four and one-half hours later *Columbia* lands at Edwards Air Force Base in California.
April 24	President Reagan lifts the fifteen-month curb on exporting grain to the Soviet Union. He recognizes that the curb is ineffective and harmful to American farmers.
May 8	Producer prices increased only 0.8% in April, while the unemployment rate remained at 7.3% for the third consecutive month.
May 12	The Reagan administration announces details for a reduction in Social Security benefits that would sharply reduce the pensions of workers who retire before sixty-five. The president states that he has three goals—preserve the integrity of the Social Security Trust Fund, hold down taxes that support the system, and eliminate abuses within the system.
May 19	The Commerce Department announces that the gross national product had grown at an 8.4% annual rate in the first quarter of 1981. This was the strongest quarterly growth since spring 1978.
May 23	The Census Bureau reports that there are 25.5 million people over sixty-five years of age in the United States, representing an increase of 28% over the 1970 figure.
May 29	United Mine Workers leaders approve a new wage agreement, and on June 6 the miners themselves agree on a new contract, ending the seventy-two day strike.

June 5	Unemployment in May rose from 7.3% to 7.6%, the first significant increase in a year. The Labor Department also announces that prices of finished goods rose in May only 0.4%, an indication that inflation is slowing down.
June 21	Wayne Williams, a twenty-three-year-old black man, is taken into custody and questioned about the killings of twenty-eight young blacks in and around Atlanta, Georgia.
June 25	The U.S. Supreme Court rules that the Constitution permits Congress to limit draft registration to men.
July 1	The United Automobile Workers union rejoins the AFL-CIO, ending a thirteen-year separation.
July 7	President Reagan announces that he will nominate Sandra Day O'Connor for a seat on the U.S. Supreme Court. Mrs. O'Connor was confirmed by the Senate on September 21, thus becoming the first woman to serve on the Court.
July 29	The House of Representatives approves the administration's tax cut bill, a decisive victory for the president over the House Democratic majority.
August 3	Federal air traffic controllers begin an illegal nationwide strike after their union rejects the government's final offer for a new contract. President Reagan warns the strikers that if they do not return to work by 11 A.M., August 5, they will be fired. Most of the 13,000 controllers defy the president's order and the Federal Aviation Administration begins to dismiss the controllers.
August 6	President Reagan decides to go forward with the full production of neutron weapons.
August 7	The unemployment rate fell to 7% for July, the lowest since 1980.
August 8	Consumer prices rose 1.2% in July, the fastest pace for inflation in sixteen months.
August 19	Two navy jets shoot down two Libyan Soviet-built planes after the Libyan aircraft fired on the American planes. The battle

occurred during a U.S. naval exercise in the southern Mediterranean, with Libya claiming that the attack took place over its territorial waters and the United States stating that it regarded the area as international waters.

August 21   *Voyager II,* the unmanned spacecraft, begins sending photographs of Saturn back to Earth.

September 23   Defense Secretary Caspar Weinberger outlines a three-year, $13-billion defense budget cut.

September 29   For the first time in American history the Senate votes to raise the federal debt to exceed the $1-trillion mark.

October 1   American officials announce that the United States will almost triple the amount of grain that it will allow the Soviet Union to purchase during the next year.

October 2   The unemployment rate rose to 7.5% in September.

President Reagan rejects the plan for shuttling MX missiles among shelters in the western deserts of the United States. Rather than play a guessing game with a possible enemy as to which silos contain missiles, Reagan says he favors reinforcing existing silos.

October 6   President Anwar el-Sadat of Egypt is shot and killed by a group of men in uniform during a military parade in Nasser City outside of Cairo. The assassination will complicate U.S. efforts to maintain a Middle East peace.

November 12   President Reagan rejects Office of Management and Budget Director David Stockman's resignation over his remarks in the *Atlantic Monthly,* in which he expressed doubts concerning the effectiveness of Reagan's economic plan.

The Exxon Corporation announces that it will end all oil and gas production in Libya.

December 1   Most U.S. banks lower their prime interest rate to 15¾%.

December 12   Martial law is declared in Poland, further deteriorating U.S.-Soviet relations.

JANUARY 1
IDEAL FAMILY SIZE

Interviewing Date: 11/7–10/80
Survey #164-G

*What do you think is the ideal number of
children for a family to have?*

One	2%
Two	55
Three	20
Four	9
Five	1
Six or more	1
None	3
Don't know	9

Those Saying Four or More Children

By Sex

Male	11%
Female	12

By Education

College	8%
High school	11
Grade school	20

By Age

18–24 years	13%
25–29 years	7
30–49 years	8
50 years and over	16

By Religion

Protestants	11%
Catholics	15

Note: Clear evidence that large families are going out of style in the United States is seen in a recent Gallup survey that shows only 11% of Americans favoring families with four or more children, the lowest percentage recorded in forty-four years.

In 1936, when Gallup surveys on ideal family size were first undertaken, 34% of Americans said that they believed the ideal family should include four or more children. That percentage rose sharply from 41% in 1941 to a high of 49% in 1945, anticipating the postwar baby boom.

In the thirty-five years since the 1945 measurement was first taken, an overall downtrend has been recorded in the proportion favoring large families, although as recently as 1968 no fewer than 41% of Americans said the ideal family includes four or more children. From 1968 to the present, however, the number in favor of such large families has plunged 30 points.

The views of Americans regarding the ideal number of children more or less consistently have reflected actual population trends. The high cost of rearing children and uncertainty regarding the world situation are undoubtedly factors in the trend away from large families.

The decline since 1968 in the number favoring large families has been far more pronounced among Catholics than Protestants. In 1968, 50% of Catholics believed the ideal family included four or more children; today only 15% hold this view. Among Protestants, the decline over this same period has been less precipitous—from 37% to 11%.

Religion is not the only demographic characteristic for which significant differences in opinion are apparent. Persons who have had only a grade-school education are far more likely to prefer larger families than those with more formal education. Similarly, persons fifty years of age and older are more inclined toward larger families.

Percent Saying Four or More Is Ideal Number of Children

1981	11%
1980	16
1978	17
1977	13
1974	19
1973	20
1971	23
1968	41
1966	35
1963	42
1960	45
1957	38
1953	41
1947	47
1945	49
1941	41
1936	34

JANUARY 4
INFLATION AND UNEMPLOYMENT

Interviewing Date: 11/21–24/80
Survey #165-G

The current inflation rate is now about 13%. By the end of 1981, what do you think the inflation rate will be?

15% or more	35%
14%	6
13%	13
12%	5
11%	4
10%	11
9% or less	8
Don't know	18

Median estimate: 13.6%

By Education
College

15% or more	33%
14%	5
13%	15
12%	5
11%	5
10%	18
9% or less	10
Don't know	9

Median estimate: 13%

High School

15% or more	37%
14%	7
13%	13
12%	5
11%	3
10%	9
9% or less	6
Don't know	20

Median estimate: 14.1%

Grade School

15% or more	31%
14%	6
13%	11
12%	4
11%	3
10%	5
9% or less	8
Don't know	32

Median estimate: 14%

By Income
$15,000 and Over

15% or more	36%
14%	5
13%	14
12%	6
11%	4
10%	13
9% or less	9
Don't know	13

Median estimate: 13.4%

Under $15,000

15% or more	35%
14%	8
13%	12
12%	4
11%	3
10%	8

9% or less 6
Don't know 24
    Median estimate: 14.2%

The current unemployment rate is now 7.6%. By the end of 1981, what do you think the unemployment rate will be?

10% or more 15%
9% 9
8% 12
7% 17
6% 17
5% or less 15
Don't know 15
    Median estimate: 7.1%

By Education
College

10% or more 12%
9% 8
8% 13
7% 24
6% 20
5% or less 16
Don't know 7
    Median estimate: 6.9%

High School

10% or more 15%
9% 9
8% 14
7% 14
6% 16
5% or less 16
Don't know 16
    Median estimate: 7.2%

Grade School

10% or more 19%
9% 7
8% 6
7% 11
6% 13
5% or less 13
Don't know 31
    Median estimate: 7.3%

By Income
$15,000 and Over

10% or more 13%
9% 8
8% 14
7% 20
6% 19
5% or less 16
Don't know 10
    Median estimate: 7%

Under $15,000

10% or more 16%
9% 10
8% 11
7% 13
6% 15
5% or less 15
Don't know 20
    Median estimate: 7.3%

Note: The American public foresees little progress in the coming year in reducing inflation or unemployment. A recent Gallup survey shows the public forecasting a "misery index" —a combined inflation and unemployment rate—of 21% by the end of 1981. This index was invented by President Jimmy Carter's political strategists during the 1976 presidential campaign.

    While the Reagan administration appears to be highly vulnerable on the economic front, it also should be borne in mind that since Americans do not expect a dramatic improvement in the nation's economic health, they may allow the new president a longer than usual grace period.

    Interestingly, public expectations of the Reagan administration's likely impact on economic problems are in sharp contrast with the high hopes the public invested four years ago in the Carter administration. In a survey conducted by the Gallup Organization for *Newsweek* in January 1977, firm majorities expressed the belief that the Carter administration would reduce inflation (58%) and unemployment (69%). Carter lost much of his early high popularity when these economic expectations were not reached.

In the current survey, respondents were asked to estimate what the unemployment and inflation rates would be at the end of 1981, after being told the rates as of late 1980. On an average, the public believes that the inflation rate will be between 13% and 14% one year from now and unemployment 7%. The overall misery index was calculated by adding the two medians together.

A sizable segment of the public foresees inflation and unemployment worsening. About one in three respondents feel inflation will be 15% or higher, and close to one in four believes that the unemployment rate will be 9% or more. Fewer than one in ten forecasts an end to double-digit inflation in 1981.

America's business leaders are more optimistic than the public about the rate of inflation. In a recent *Wall Street Journal*/Gallup survey of the nation's top executives, the median expectation was an inflation rate of 10% by the end of 1981.

JANUARY 8
PRESIDENT CARTER

Interviewing Date: 12/5–8/80
Survey #166-G

> Do you approve or disapprove of the way Carter is handling his job as president?

Final Carter Popularity Rating

Approve............................34%
Disapprove 55
No opinion 11

By Sex
Male

Approve............................30%
Disapprove 61
No opinion 9

Female

Approve............................38%
Disapprove 50
No opinion 12

By Race
White

Approve............................31%
Disapprove 59
No opinion 10

Nonwhite

Approve............................55%
Disapprove 30
No opinion 15

By Education
College

Approve............................29%
Disapprove 66
No opinion 5

High School

Approve............................36%
Disapprove 52
No opinion 12

Grade School

Approve............................38%
Disapprove 45
No opinion 17

By Region
East

Approve............................28%
Disapprove 61
No opinion 11

Midwest

Approve............................35%
Disapprove 51
No opinion 14

South

Approve........................38%
Disapprove 53
No opinion 9

West

Approve........................36%
Disapprove 57
No opinion 7

By Age
18–24 Years

Approve........................48%
Disapprove 45
No opinion 7

25–29 Years

Approve........................35%
Disapprove 54
No opinion 11

30–49 Years

Approve........................29%
Disapprove 59
No opinion 12

50 Years and Over

Approve........................32%
Disapprove 57
No opinion 11

By Income
$15,000 and Over

Approve........................31%
Disapprove 60
No opinion 9

Under $15,000

Approve........................38%
Disapprove 50
No opinion 12

By Politics
Republicans

Approve........................14%
Disapprove 80
No opinion 6

Democrats

Approve........................49%
Disapprove 38
No opinion 13

Independents

Approve........................30%
Disapprove 60
No opinion 10

By Religion
Protestants

Approve........................36%
Disapprove 53
No opinion 11

Catholics

Approve........................34%
Disapprove 57
No opinion 9

By Occupation
Professional and Business

Approve........................29%
Disapprove 65
No opinion 6

Clerical and Sales

Approve........................36%
Disapprove 52
No opinion 12

Manual Workers

Approve........................32%
Disapprove 56
No opinion 12

Nonlabor Force

Approve............................36%
Disapprove 52
No opinion 12

By Community Size
One Million and Over

Approve............................35%
Disapprove 53
No opinion 12

500,000–999,999

Approve............................32%
Disapprove 59
No opinion 9

50,000–499,999

Approve............................35%
Disapprove 54
No opinion 11

2,500–49,999

Approve............................35%
Disapprove 56
No opinion 9

Under 2,500; Rural

Approve............................33%
Disapprove 56
No opinion 11

Labor Union Families Only

Approve............................32%
Disapprove 55
No opinion 13

Nonlabor Union Families Only

Approve............................35%
Disapprove 55
No opinion 10

How do you think Jimmy Carter will go down in history—as an outstanding president, above average, below average, or poor?

Outstanding......................... 3%
Above average 11
Average (volunteered)................37
Below average.......................31
Poor 15
No opinion 3

Comparable Evaluation for Gerald Ford Conducted December 10–13, 1976

Outstanding......................... 5%
Above average 20
Average (volunteered)................50
Below average.......................15
Poor 6
No opinion 4

Note: President Jimmy Carter consistently has won praise from the public throughout his four-year tenure as "a man of high moral principles," "a religious person," and as a person who is "sympathetic to the problems of the poor." At the same time, however, a recent Gallup Poll indicates that only 3% of Americans think history will regard Carter as an outstanding president.

President Carter also holds the unfortunate distinction of having received the lowest popularity rating given any president in the last four decades—21% in July 1980—and won only a 34% approval rating in the public's final assessment of his performance in office.

Further evidence of the president's lack of public approbation is seen in the fact that he failed to top the Gallup Poll's 1980 list of men most admired in the world; he led the list in the three previous years. With only a few exceptions incumbent presidents have been the most admired men during their tenure in annual audits conducted for more than three decades.

Yet while confidence in Carter's leadership began to falter as early as his second year in office, and this may have contributed to his loss to Ronald Reagan, trust and confidence in

Carter as a person has remained strong throughout his tenure. His supporters contend that few presidents have been confronted with problems as complex, including the seemingly intractable problem of inflation. Further, the Carter administration also had its successes: the ratification of the Panama Canal treaties, the establishment of diplomatic relations with the People's Republic of China, and the Camp David agreement between Israel and Egypt. And an even greater show of support followed the seizure of the U.S. hostages by Iran in November 1979.

In the final test of Carter's performance in office, conducted in early December, 34% expressed approval. This represents only a marginal gain over the 31% rating he received last November and is far below his overall average of 47% for his four years in office. President Carter's final rating is lower than that accorded his immediate predecessor, Gerald Ford, who was given a 53% performance rating as he completed his final weeks in office.

The evaluation of the Carter presidency compares poorly with that of Gerald Ford's. A Gallup Poll conducted in December 1976 showed 5% saying history would regard Ford as an outstanding president, 20% as above average, 50% as average, 15% as below average, and 6% as poor.

President Carter's wife, Rosalynn, was a big plus for her husband's presidency. In fact, a survey conducted in April 1979 showed six Americans in ten saying that they approved of the way Mrs. Carter was handling her job as First Lady. In addition, Mrs. Carter has topped the annual Gallup Poll audits of women most admired by the American people during all four years her husband was in office, including 1980.

The following is a summary of the public's assessment of the Carter presidency:

Carter Popularity

(Percent Who Approve)

Final (December 5–8, 1980) 34%
Average while in office 47
High point (March 1977) 75
Low point (July 1980) 21

Approval Ratings of Carter's Predecessors

	High	Low	Average
Gerald Ford	71%	37%	46%
Richard Nixon	68	24	48
Lyndon Johnson	80	35	54
John Kennedy	83	57	70
Dwight Eisenhower	79	49	66
Harry Truman	87	23	46
Franklin Roosevelt	84	54	68

JANUARY 11
PREDICTIONS FOR 1981

Interviewing Date: 11/7–10/80
Survey #164-G

As far as you are concerned, do you think that 1981 will be better or worse than 1980?

Better 49%
Worse 26
Same (volunteered) 19
Don't know 6

By Race
White

Better 53%
Worse 23
Same (volunteered) 20
Don't know 4

Nonwhite

Better 18%
Worse 48
Same (volunteered) 16
Don't know 18

By Education
College

Better 57%
Worse 23
Same (volunteered) 17
Don't know 3

High School

Better.............................48%
Worse.............................28
Same (volunteered) 18
Don't know 6

Grade School

Better.............................40%
Worse.............................23
Same (volunteered) 25
Don't know 12

By Age
18–24 Years

Better.............................50%
Worse.............................35
Same (volunteered) 11
Don't know 4

25–29 Years

Better.............................57%
Worse.............................28
Same (volunteered) 14
Don't know 1

30–49 Years

Better.............................46%
Worse.............................26
Same (volunteered) 20
Don't know 8

50 Years and Over

Better.............................50%
Worse.............................20
Same (volunteered) 23
Don't know 7

As far as you are concerned, do you think that 1981 will be a year of economic prosperity, economic difficulty, or remain the same?

Economic prosperity 18%
Economic difficulty 34
Remain the same 42
Don't know 6

By Race
White

Economic prosperity 20%
Economic difficulty 32
Remain the same 43
Don't know 5

Nonwhite

Economic prosperity 8%
Economic difficulty 48
Remain the same 33
Don't know 11

By Education
College

Economic prosperity 20%
Economic difficulty 32
Remain the same 45
Don't know 3

High School

Economic prosperity 19%
Economic difficulty 36
Remain the same 40
Don't know 5

Grade School

Economic prosperity 15%
Economic difficulty 31
Remain the same 41
Don't know 13

By Age
18–24 Years

Economic prosperity 19%
Economic difficulty 40
Remain the same 34
Don't know 7

25–29 Years

Economic prosperity 23%
Economic difficulty 32
Remain the same 43
Don't know 2

30–49 Years

Economic prosperity 16%
Economic difficulty 34
Remain the same 45
Don't know 5

50 Years and Over

Economic prosperity 19%
Economic difficulty 32
Remain the same 42
Don't know 7

Note: The American people are not only far more optimistic about the new year than they were at the start of 1979 and 1980, but they also hold a brighter outlook toward 1981 than do the publics of most of the twenty-eight other countries recently surveyed by the Gallup International Inc.

In the latest poll almost half the American public (49%) predict that 1981 will be better than 1980, compared with 26% who think it will be worse, 19% who see no change, and 6% who express no opinion. At the onset of 1979 and 1980 only a third of the U.S. population anticipated better times for the coming year—33% and 31%, respectively.

Of the more than 30,000 residents in the twenty-nine nations participating in the current study, only the citizens of Argentina (64%), Chile (41%), and Uruguay (49%) are as sanguine about 1981 as Americans. The Latin American nations have suffered such devastating economic woes, including runaway inflation and unemployment rates, that their people perhaps feel that almost anything that 1981 may bring would be an improvement over their current problems.

Other countries with above average expectations for 1981 include: Norway (44%), Mexico (43%), Venezuela (43%), Australia (42%), South Africa (40%), Greece (39%), and Brazil (38%).

Most pessimistic about the outlook for the immediate future are the citizens of most of the European nations surveyed, including Belgians (only 7% of whom feel 1981 will be better than

1980), West Germans (8%), Austrians (10%), Netherlanders (13%), Danes (14%), Luxembourgers (14%), and the French (15%).

Survey participants were also asked to name the top problem facing their nation. Except for isolated instances the twin economic problems of inflation and unemployment are the dominant concerns in each country. Energy shortages were cited as the most important problem facing the Japanese.

The survey results show a strong correlation between economic expectations and the overall outlook for 1981: residents of countries where the economic prospect appears dim are also more pessimistic about their general well-being. On the average, 48% of the citizens of all twenty-nine countries surveyed anticipate economic difficulties during 1981 and 30% expect this year will be better in general than 1980. Among the fifteen countries that are more optimistic about their economy, 33% expect their nation to experience financial problems and 37% foresee 1981 as worse than 1980. On the other hand, in the fourteen countries that are more pessimistic about their economy, 63% look for difficulties in this area, while only 22% are confident about the overall prospects for 1981.

JANUARY 15
MOST IMPORTANT PROBLEM

Interviewing Date: 11/7–10/80
Survey #164-G

In your opinion, what is the most important problem facing this country today?

High cost of living; inflation 53%
Unemployment 11
Crime; violence 4
Energy problems 4
International problems 4
Others 20
No opinion 4

Note: The twin economic problems of high inflation and unemployment loom large among the major concerns of the publics in virtually all of the twenty-one nations surveyed toward the end of 1980 by the Gallup International Inc. At the same time, however, such problems as energy and crime dominate the worries of those in other nations reached in the global study.

Inflation and the high cost of living are named as either the most serious or second most serious problem in all twenty-one nations. It is the number one problem in thirteen countries, with the greatest concern found in the Philippines (65%), Brazil (58%), and in the United States (53%).

In six of the twenty-one nations surveyed, unemployment is named as the top problem, especially by residents of Australia (66%), the Netherlands (65%), and Great Britain (59%). Energy related matters are cited as the primary problem by the Japanese (29%) and Swiss (16%), and receive the second greatest concern in Austria (22%) and in the Philippines (12%). And substantial percentages in almost all the nations surveyed named crime and violence. Crime is cited second most often by the Brazilians (12%) and third most often in Finland, France, India, Mexico, Norway, Switzerland, and the United States.

The following shows the three problems named most often in each nation surveyed:

Australia

Unemployment	66%
High cost of living; inflation	41
Strikes; labor unrest	13

Austria

High cost of living; inflation	40%
Energy problems	22
Unemployment	14

Brazil

High cost of living; inflation		58%
Crime; violence		12
Unemployment	} tie	8
Energy problems		8

Chile

Unemployment	28%
High cost of living; inflation	23
Relations with other nations	16

Finland

Unemployment	41%
High cost of living; inflation	28
Crime; violence	14

France

Unemployment	47%
High cost of living; inflation	21
Crime; violence	9

Great Britain

Unemployment	59%
High cost of living; inflation	18
Strikes; labor unrest	2
Peace; war	2

India

High cost of living; inflation	42%
Unemployment	32
Crime; violence	5

Japan

Energy problems	29%
High cost of living; inflation	25
Relations with other nations	9

Mexico

High cost of living; inflation		45%
Unemployment		26
Crime; violence	} tie	6
Dissatisfaction with government		6

Netherlands

Unemployment	65%
High cost of living; inflation	20
Energy problems	13

Norway

High cost of living; inflation 33%
Unemployment 15
Crime; violence 9

Peru

High cost of living; inflation 44%
Unemployment 42
Strikes; labor unrest 6

Philippines

High cost of living; inflation 65%
Energy problems 12
Unemployment 10

Portugal

High cost of living; inflation 42%
Unemployment 32
Social problems 4

South Africa

High cost of living; inflation 38%
Race relations; racism 31
Unemployment 7

Sweden

High cost of living; inflation 26%
Foreign debts 21
Unemployment 18

Switzerland

Energy problems 16%
High cost of living; inflation 14
Unemployment   } tie   9
Crime; violence   9

Venezuela

High cost of living; inflation 46%
Foreign policy; international relations . . . 22
Social problems 15

West Germany

High cost of living; inflation 27%
Unemployment 23
Energy problems 17

The following shows the trend since 1935 in the most important problem facing the United States:

1980	High cost of living; unemployment
1979	High cost of living; energy problems
1978	High cost of living; energy problems
1977	High cost of living; unemployment
1976	High cost of living; unemployment
1975	High cost of living; unemployment
1974	High cost of living; Watergate; energy crisis
1973	High cost of living; Watergate
1972	Vietnam
1971	Vietnam; high cost of living
1970	Vietnam
1969	Vietnam
1968	Vietnam
1967	Vietnam; high cost of living
1966	Vietnam
1965	Vietnam; race relations
1964	Vietnam; race relations
1963	Keeping peace; race relations
1962	Keeping peace
1961	Keeping peace
1960	Keeping peace
1959	Keeping peace
1958	Unemployment; keeping peace
1957	Race relations; keeping peace
1956	Keeping peace
1955	Keeping peace
1954	Keeping peace
1953	Keeping peace
1952	Korean War
1951	Korean War
1950	Labor unrest
1949	Labor unrest
1948	Keeping peace
1947	High cost of living; labor unrest
1946	High cost of living
1945	Winning war
1944	Winning war
1943	Winning war
1942	Winning war
1941	Keeping out of war; winning war
1940	Keeping out of war
1939	Keeping out of war
1938	Keeping out of war
1937	Unemployment

1936 Unemployment
1935 Unemployment

JANUARY 22
GUN CONTROL

Interviewing Date: 12/12–21/80
Special Telephone Survey

> *In general, do you feel that the laws cover-*
> *ing the sale of handguns should be made*
> *more strict, less strict, or kept as they are*
> *now?*

More strict 62%
Less strict 3
Kept same 24
No opinion 11

By Sex
Male

More strict 54%
Less strict 4
Kept same 35
No opinion 7

Female

More strict 69%
Less strict 2
Kept same 15
No opinion 14

By Education
College

More strict 67%
Less strict 2
Kept same 22
No opinion 9

High School

More strict 65%
Less strict 3
Kept same 24
No opinion 8

Grade School

More strict 53%
Less strict 5
Kept same 25
No opinion 17

By Region
East

More strict 67%
Less strict 3
Kept same 20
No opinion 10

Midwest

More strict 54%
Less strict 7
Kept same 24
No opinion 15

South

More strict 63%
Less strict 1
Kept same 29
No opinion 7

West

More strict 66%
Less strict 1
Kept same 21
No opinion 12

By Age
18–34 Years

More strict 64%
Less strict 4
Kept same 26
No opinion 6

35–49 Years

More strict 63%
Less strict 3
Kept same 24
No opinion 10

50 Years and Over

More strict 57%
Less strict 3
Kept same 23
No opinion 17

By Community Size
500,000 and Over

More strict 73%
Less strict 3
Kept same 18
No opinion 6

50,000–499,999

More strict 62%
Less strict 1
Kept same 23
No opinion 14

2,500–49,999

More strict 60%
Less strict 3
Kept same 21
No opinion 16

Under 2,500; Rural

More strict 52%
Less strict 6
Kept same 33
No opinion 9

Guns in Home
(All Types)

More strict 45%
Less strict 5
Kept same 38
No opinion 12

Handguns in Home

More strict 38%
Less strict 1
Kept same 53
No opinion 8

No Guns in Home

More strict 72%
Less strict 3
Kept same 15
No opinion 10

Do you think there should or should not be a law which would forbid the possession of handguns except by the police and other authorized persons?

Should 38%
Should not 51
No opinion 11

By Sex
Male

Should 31%
Should not 62
No opinion 7

Female

Should 44%
Should not 40
No opinion 16

By Education
College

Should 44%
Should not 55
No opinion 1

High School

Should 41%
Should not 49
No opinion 10

Grade School

Should 27%
Should not 51
No opinion 22

By Region

East

Should	53%
Should not	39
No opinion	8

Midwest

Should	33%
Should not	51
No opinion	16

South

Should	30%
Should not	59
No opinion	11

West

Should	34%
Should not	56
No opinion	10

By Age

18–34 Years

Should	43%
Should not	48
No opinion	9

35–49 Years

Should	39%
Should not	52
No opinion	9

50 Years and Over

Should	30%
Should not	54
No opinion	16

By Community Size

500,000 and Over

Should	47%
Should not	47
No opinion	6

50,000–499,999

Should	38%
Should not	48
No opinion	14

2,500–49,999

Should	32%
Should not	46
No opinion	22

Under 2,500; Rural

Should	32%
Should not	61
No opinion	7

Guns in Home

(All Types)

Should	19%
Should not	70
No opinion	11

Handguns in Home

Should	13%
Should not	81
No opinion	6

No Guns in Home

Should	50%
Should not	39
No opinion	11

Note: Six in ten Americans (62%) would like to see stricter laws covering the sale of handguns, but fewer (38%) favor an outright ban on the possession of handguns except by the police and other authorized persons. Support for a ban, however, has grown since an earlier survey conducted in November 1979, when 31% favored such a prohibition and 65% were opposed. Currently, 51% express opposition.

Indication that public pressure for greater controls on handguns is likely to grow during the 1980s is suggested by the fact that younger adults are more likely than their elders to favor both greater controls and legal strictures on possession. Furthermore, six in ten teen-agers, according to a recent Gallup Youth Survey, favor a ban on possession of handguns.

The perennial issue of gun control gained recent attention with the murder in December of former Beatle John Lennon, whose killer used a snub-nosed .38 caliber revolver.

Each year in this country 20,000 Americans are killed by handguns, half of them murders and accidents. It has been estimated that someone is murdered with a handgun in the United States every fifty minutes. Advocates of stronger laws dealing with handguns point out that during the seven peak years of the Vietnam War 40,000 Americans were killed in combat, while 50,000 were killed with handguns on the domestic front.

Those who oppose a ban on handguns feel that such a move would violate their constitutional rights and believe that a prohibition would not reduce the number of crimes committed, since a person who will violate laws against rape, robbery, or murder will not obey a gun law.

Supporters of a ban, however, counter that a large majority of the nation's gun victims (70% in some estimates) are shot not by burglars or other criminals but by people they know, who in a moment of passion or anger reach for a handgun rather than use some less deadly outlet for their aggression.

Some states now require proof of need or competence to obtain a handgun. Other states are adopting or considering laws similar to the Bartley-Fox Act that became law in Massachusetts in 1975. The law provides that a person who carries a handgun outside his home must have a license to do so and violators are given a mandatory sentence of one year in jail. According to David Bartley, one of the cosponsors of the bill, after the Massachusetts statute went into effect the death rate from gun-related incidents dropped. Nationwide Gallup surveys have shown the public consistently in support of both provisions of the Bartley-Fox law.

A measure similar to the Bartley-Fox Act was signed into law in New York by Governor Hugh L. Carey last June. It mandates a one-year prison term for anyone convicted of having a loaded, illegal handgun in public. But the New York statute provides that a judge may waive the penalty if he feels it is too harsh for the circumstances.

JANUARY 25
RELIGION

Interviewing Date: Seven surveys conducted during 1980

Did you, yourself, happen to attend church or synagogue in the last seven days?

	Yes
National	40%

By Region

East	40%
Midwest	45
South	42
West	29

By Age

18–29 years	31%
30–49 years	40
50 years and over	47

By Religion

Protestants	39%
Catholics	53
Jews	24*

*Figure is based on surveys conducted between 1975 and 1980.

Note: The following is the full trend since 1939. The audits from 1955 to 1980 were based on an average of the combined results of several surveys during each year. The figures prior to 1955 were based on a single annual survey:

Church and Synagogue Attendance

1980	40%
1979	40
1978	41
1977	41
1976	42

1975	40
1974	40
1973	40
1972	40
1971	40
1970	42
1969	42
1968	43
1967	43
1966	44
1965	44
1964	45
1963	46
1962	46
1961	47
1960	47
1959	47
1958	49***
1957	47
1956	46
1955	49***
1954	46
1950	39
1940	37**
1939	41

**Low point in attendance
***High point in attendance

Christian Church Attendance Only

	Protestants	Catholics
1980	39%	53%
1979	40	52
1978	40	52
1968	38	65
1958	44	74

Synagogue Attendance Only

1975–80	24%
1970–74	17
1965–69	20
1961–64	22
1955–56	23

Since 1958—a peak year for church attendance—the national rate of churchgoing has dropped 9 percentage points, from 49% to 40% in 1980, the same rate of attendance observed throughout the 1970s.

The decline has been sharpest among Catholics. Attendance at Mass fell 22 points—from 74% to 52%—between 1958 and 1978, and it currently stands at 53%. Catholic churchgoing has remained fairly stable since 1973.

Attendance among Protestants has changed very little, declining only 6 percentage points—from 44% to 38%—between 1958 and 1968 and has since remained at the 1964 level.

Mirroring the pattern of churchgoing among Protestants and Catholics, attendance at synagogue declined between the late 1950s and early 1970s, but since then it has shown an upturn. In surveys taken between 1975 and 1980, 24% of Jews attended synagogue in a typical week.

Sharp differences in church or synagogue attendance are found by age, with 31% of adults under thirty attending in a typical week in 1980, compared to 40% among persons thirty to forty-nine years old and 47% among those fifty and older. In 1958 the proportions in each age group were very similar, with about as many younger and older persons attending church or synagogue. Churchgoing among adults under thirty is 17 percentage points lower today than it was in 1958, while it has declined by 11 points among thirty to forty-nine years old and by only 1 point among those fifty and older.

Do you happen to be a member of a church or synagogue?

	Yes
National	69%

Trend in Church or Synagogue Membership

1980	69%
1979	68
1978	68
1977	70
1976	71
1975	71
1965	73
1952	73
1944	75
1942	74

```
1940................................75
1939................................75
1938................................75
1937................................75
1936................................77
```

Note: The forty-four-year downtrend in church and synagogue membership appears to have leveled out in 1980, with 69% of the adults surveyed saying they are members.

It is important to bear in mind that the percentages represent self-classifications: the proportions of people who say they are members of a church. Thus, they may include some who are not actually on the rolls of a local church. Furthermore, it should be noted that adherents of certain faiths, such as Roman Catholics and the Eastern Orthodox, are considered to be members at birth.

JANUARY 29
RELIGION

Interviewing Date: 11/21–24/80
Survey #165-G

Have you watched any religious television programs in the last twelve months?

	Yes
National	50%

Note: Among the 50% of adults who have watched religious programs on television during the twelve-month period tested, a high proportion are Protestants (particularly members of Baptist churches), older persons, women, nonwhites, and those living in the South.

Asked of those who replied in the affirmative: Would you say that religious television programs have increased your involvement in your local church and its activities over the last three years, or lessened your involvement?

Increased	27%
Lessened	7
No difference (volunteered)	65
Don't know	1

By Sex
Male

Increased	24%
Lessened	9
No difference (volunteered)	66
Don't know	1

Female

Increased	30%
Lessened	6
No difference (volunteered)	63
Don't know	1

By Race
White

Increased	23%
Lessened	7
No difference (volunteered)	69
Don't know	1

Nonwhite

Increased	50%
Lessened	5
No difference (volunteered)	43
Don't know	1

By Education
College

Increased	17%
Lessened	9
No difference (volunteered)	73
Don't know	1

High School

Increased	28%
Lessened	7
No difference (volunteered)	64
Don't know	1

Grade School

Increased	39%
Lessened	5
No difference (volunteered)	54
Don't know	2

By Region
East

Increased..............................20%
Lessened 7
No difference (volunteered) 72
Don't know .... *

Midwest

Increased..............................21%
Lessened 9
No difference (volunteered) 69
Don't know 1

South

Increased..............................37%
Lessened 6
No difference (volunteered) 55
Don't know 2

West

Increased..............................25%
Lessened 7
No difference (volunteered) 67
Don't know 1

By Age
18–24 Years

Increased..............................25%
Lessened 13
No difference (volunteered) 60
Don't know 2

25–29 Years

Increased..............................24%
Lessened 5
No difference (volunteered) 71
Don't know .... *

30–49 Years

Increased..............................26%
Lessened 6
No difference (volunteered) 67
Don't know 1

50 Years and Over

Increased..............................29%
Lessened 7
No difference (volunteered) 63
Don't know 1

By Income
$15,000 and Over

Increased..............................17%
Lessened 6
No difference (volunteered) 76
Don't know 1

Under $15,000

Increased..............................38%
Lessened 9
No difference (volunteered) 52
Don't know 1

By Politics
Republicans

Increased..............................25%
Lessened 5
No difference (volunteered) 68
Don't know 2

Democrats

Increased..............................33%
Lessened 5
No difference (volunteered) 61
Don't know 1

Independents

Increased..............................16%
Lessened 13
No difference (volunteered) 70
Don't know 1

By Religion
Protestants

Increased..............................30%
Lessened 6
No difference (volunteered) 63
Don't know 1

Catholics

Increased........................22%
Lessened 7
No difference (volunteered) 70
Don't know 1

Church Attenders Only

Increased........................34%
Lessened 2
No difference (volunteered) 63
Don't know 1

Nonchurch Attenders Only

Increased........................20%
Lessened 12
No difference (volunteered) 66
Don't know 2

Church Members Only

Increased........................29%
Lessened 6
No difference (volunteered) 64
Don't know 1

Nonchurch Members Only

Increased........................20%
Lessened 10
No difference (volunteered) 68
Don't know 2

Those Who Say Religion Is Very Important in Life

Increased........................32%
Lessened 5
No difference (volunteered) 62
Don't know 1

Those Who Say Religion Is Fairly Important in Life

Increased........................17%
Lessened 9
No difference (volunteered) 72
Don't know 2

Those Who Say Religion Is Not At All Important in Life

Increased........................ 2%
Lessened 25
No difference (volunteered) 72
Don't know 1

*Less than 1%

Note: Much controversy has surrounded the so-called "electronic church" and particularly those religious programs involving television and radio evangelists. The electronic church has proved to be one of the most remarkable developments in American religion, with an estimated 1,400 religious radio stations, 35 religious television stations, and 4 religious television networks currently in operation.

Some pastors have expressed concern that the electronic church will cause their members to decrease their involvement in local churches and will keep prospective members from joining a church. Others worry about the effects of the electronic media on the quality of Christian life and feel that such programs can make religion too easy and comfortable, encourage individualized religion, and undermine religious commitment. Still others object to what they consider the "show business" aspects of certain religious programs on radio and television.

Defenders of the electronic church, however, point out that religious programs on radio and television reach a vast number of people who might not be reached otherwise and, in fact, are the only way to contact many of the elderly, the infirm, and handicapped. Other supporters feel that such efforts raise the level of awareness of the unchurched* and make them more likely to become involved in the community of active believers. Some evangelists, including Drs. Billy Graham and Robert

*The unchurched were defined as those who were not members of a church or synagogue or who had not attended church or synagogue in the previous six months, other than weddings, funerals, or special holidays like Christmas, Easter, or Yom Kippur.

Schuller, actively encourage their listeners to participate in the life of local churches.

Findings from a study, *The Unchurched American,* conducted in 1978 by the Gallup Organization Inc. and the Princeton Religion Research Center for a coalition of thirty-one religious organizations, showed that in a thirty-day test period three in ten unchurched Americans said they had listened to or watched radio or television programs produced by a religious organization. As a result of watching or listening to these programs, one in seven said they considered becoming active in a church.

The findings from the current survey reveal that as many as one-third of those who watch religious television programs say that these programs have had an effect of one kind or another on their involvement in their local church and its activities over the last three years. And among these persons opinion is heavily on the side that religious television programs have increased rather then lessened their local involvement.

FEBRUARY 1
STATUS OF BLACKS IN AMERICA

Interviewing Date: 12/5–8/80
Survey #166-G

In your opinion, how well do you think blacks are treated in this community?

By Race
White

Same as whites	67%
Not very well	17
Badly	3
Don't know	13

Nonwhite

Same as whites	35%
Not very well	41
Badly	16
Don't know	8

Looking back over the last ten years, do you think the quality of life of blacks in the United States has gotten better, stayed about the same, or gotten worse?

By Race
White

Gotten better	80%
Stayed the same	11
Gotten worse	5
No opinion	4

Nonwhite

Gotten better	55%
Stayed the same	22
Gotten worse	18
No opinion	5

Note: To gain insight into the state of race relations at the beginning of the Reagan presidency, the Gallup Poll studied two key dimensions on the status of blacks in the United States: 1) how people of both races regard the treatment of blacks in their community, and 2) what changes, if any, whites and blacks perceive in the quality of life of blacks over the last ten years.

The results of this December 1980 poll found that whites and blacks hold widely divergent views on the treatment of blacks in their community. Furthermore, among blacks the proportion believing they are treated as well as whites has declined since the same question was last asked in a May 1980 Gallup survey. The results last May indicated somewhat more optimism than is apparent in the recent figures. In the May survey, 44% felt their treatment was the same as that accorded whites, and 31% said they were not treated very well.

Whites, in contrast, view the treatment of blacks quite differently, with 67% responding in December that the treatment of blacks in their community is the same as that of whites. Another 17% said blacks are not treated very well, 3% said badly, and 13% expressed no opinion. When compared with the May survey, virtually no change was found in the opinion of whites. In the earlier survey essentially the same percentage (68%) estimated that the treatment of blacks in their community was comparable to that of whites.

A further survey question reveals that an overwhelming majority of whites (80%) feels the quality of life of blacks in the United States has gotten better over the past ten years, while only 11% express the opinion that it has stayed the same. Blacks responded less optimistically, with 55% saying their lives have gotten better and 22% sensing little change over the preceding ten-year period.

One of the key challenges facing President Ronald Reagan during the next four years will be to increase his level of support and confidence among the nation's black population. That this will be no easy task is seen in the fact that: 1) only one black in ten voted for Reagan in the November presidential election; 2) only 16% of blacks think Reagan will make a great or a good president, compared to 43% of whites; 3) far fewer blacks (26%) than whites (48%) believe Reagan will be able to reduce inflation; and 4) only 31% of blacks, compared to 49% of whites, think Reagan can reduce unemployment.

FEBRUARY 5
SCHOOL BUSING

Interviewing Date: 12/5–8/80
Survey #166-G

Do you favor or oppose busing children to achieve a better racial balance in the schools?

Favor 22%
Oppose 72
Don't know 6

By Sex
Male

Favor 21%
Oppose 74
Don't know 5

Female

Favor 24%
Oppose 70
Don't know 6

By Race
White

Favor 17%
Oppose 78
Don't know 5

Northern White

Favor 17%
Oppose 77
Don't know 6

Southern White

Favor 17%
Oppose 80
Don't know 3

Black

Favor 59%
Oppose 31
Don't know 10

Northern Black

Favor 53%
Oppose 34
Don't know 13

Southern Black

Favor 73%
Oppose 22
Don't know 5

By Education
College

Favor 21%
Oppose 75
Don't know 4

High School

Favor 22%
Oppose 72
Don't know 6

Grade School

Favor 27%
Oppose 65
Don't know 8

By Region
East

Favor 23%
Oppose 69
Don't know 8

Midwest

Favor 18%
Oppose 76
Don't know 6

South

Favor 25%
Oppose 71
Don't know 4

West

Favor 24%
Oppose 70
Don't know 6

By Age
18–24 Years

Favor 33%
Oppose 58
Don't know 9

25–29 Years

Favor 28%
Oppose 68
Don't know 4

30–49 Years

Favor 21%
Oppose 75
Don't know 4

50 Years and Over

Favor 18%
Oppose 76
Don't know 6

By Income
$25,000 and Over

Favor 14%
Oppose 81
Don't know 5

$20,000–$24,999

Favor 20%
Oppose 77
Don't know 3

$15,000–$19,999

Favor 14%
Oppose 79
Don't know 7

$10,000–$14,999

Favor 29%
Oppose 65
Don't know 6

$5,000–$9,999

Favor 32%
Oppose 61
Don't know 7

Under $5,000

Favor 30%
Oppose 62
Don't know 8

By Politics
Republicans
Favor.............................15%
Oppose............................81
Don't know........................ 4

Democrats
Favor.............................28%
Oppose............................64
Don't know........................ 8

Independents
Favor.............................18%
Oppose............................78
Don't know........................ 4

By Religion
Protestants
Favor.............................23%
Oppose............................71
Don't know........................ 6

Catholics
Favor.............................18%
Oppose............................79
Don't know........................ 3

By Occupation
Professional and Business
Favor.............................19%
Oppose............................75
Don't know........................ 6

Clerical and Sales
Favor.............................23%
Oppose............................69
Don't know........................ 8

Manual Workers
Favor.............................22%
Oppose............................74
Don't know........................ 4

Nonlabor Force
Favor.............................23%
Oppose............................70
Don't know........................ 7

By Community Size
One Million and Over
Favor.............................24%
Oppose............................67
Don't know........................ 9

500,000–999,999
Favor.............................23%
Oppose............................73
Don't know........................ 4

50,000–499,999
Favor.............................24%
Oppose............................71
Don't know........................ 5

2,500–49,999
Favor.............................22%
Oppose............................73
Don't know........................ 5

Under 2,500; Rural
Favor.............................20%
Oppose............................74
Don't know........................ 6

Asked of white respondents with children in either grade school or high school (29% of the total sample): Would you, yourself, have any objection to sending your children to a school where a few of the children are black? If "no": Where half are black? If "no": Where more than half of the children are black?*

*Because the numbers of interviews in the individual demographic groups can be very small, the possible sampling error in some cases can be over 10 percentage points either way.

A few children are black 5%
Half of children are black 23
More than half of children are black 55

By Education
College

A few children are black 2%
Half of children are black 26
More than half of children are black 56

High School

A few children are black 6%
Half of children are black 22
More than half of children are black 56

Grade School

A few children are black 9%
Half of children are black 20
More than half of children are black 45

By Region
East

A few children are black 2%
Half of children are black 26
More than half of children are black 57

Midwest

A few children are black 7%
Half of children are black 22
More than half of children are black 49

South

A few children are black 5%
Half of children are black 27
More than half of children are black 66

West

A few children are black 5%
Half of children are black 27
More than half of children are black 66

By Age
18–29 Years

A few children are black 4%
Half of children are black 16
More than half of children are black 50

30–49 Years

A few children are black 6%
Half of children are black 25
More than half of children are black 57

50 Years and Over

A few children are black 3%
Half of children are black 18
More than half of children are black 49

By Income
$15,000 and Over

A few children are black 6%
Half of children are black 26
More than half of children are black 55

Under $15,000

A few children are black 4%
Half of children are black 18
More than half of children are black 57

By Community Size
500,000 and Over

A few children are black 7%
Half of children are black 33
More than half of children are black 65

50,000–499,999

A few children are black 3%
Half of children are black 22
More than half of children are black 46

2,500–49,999

A few children are black 5%
Half of children are black 19
More than half of children are black 59

Under 2,500; Rural

A few children are black.............. 5%
Half of children are black 18
More than half of children are black..... 52

Central City

A few children are black.............. 6%
Half of children are black 22
More than half of children are black..... 51

Suburbs

A few children are black.............. 4%
Half of children are black 32
More than half of children are black..... 60

Note: The wording of the survey question has varied slightly over the years, changing along with the language. In the five surveys between 1958 and 1966, white respondents were asked whether they had objections to sending their children to the same schools with children who are "colored." In 1969 and 1970 the term "Negroes" was used. In the surveys conducted since 1973, the question has been framed in terms of "blacks." Except for these individual words, the question wording has remained unchanged since it was first put to the public in the late 1950s.

The following survey findings represent the trend in the varying attitudes of white parents toward sending their children to a school attended by blacks:

Northern White Parents With Children in High School or Grade School

	Object to few black	Object to half black	Object to more than half black
1980	5%	22%	51%
1978	4	23	38
1975	3	24	47
1973	6	27	63
1970	6	24	51
1969	7	28	54
1966	6	32	60

1965	7	28	52
1963 10		33	53
1959	7	34	58
1958 13		39	58

Southern White Parents With Children in High School or Grade School

	Object to few black	Object to half black	Object to more than half black
1980	5%	27%	66%
1978	7	28	49
1975 15		38	61
1973 16		36	69
1970 16		43	69
1969 21		46	64
1966 24		49	62
1965 37		68	78
1963 61		78	86
1959 72		83	86
1958 72		81	84

The Reagan administration's position on the busing of students in order to achieve racial balance in the schools is in line with the views of the majority of white Americans. The latest survey shows opinion among whites four to one in opposition to busing, while blacks are two to one in favor.

Although the majority of whites oppose busing, factors other than racial prejudice underlie much of their opposition. For example, even among the 45% of white parents who say they have no objection to their children attending racially integrated schools, 78% are opposed to busing. Much of this opposition can be explained in the objection to the distance children have to be bused.

On November 17, 1980 the Senate passed a bill that would have prohibited the Justice Department from intervening in school desegregation cases involving busing. The Senate bill, which was never approved, would not actually outlaw busing but by requiring private parties to bring busing cases to court, it would have made it difficult and impractical for probusing groups to use busing as an effective antidiscrimination tool.

Since the 1954 case of *Brown* vs. *Board of Education,* when the Supreme Court ruled purposeful racial segregation in the public schools unconstitutional, the court has been involved in more than five hundred school desegregation cases.

In the immediate aftermath of the 1954 Supreme Court decision, the Gallup Poll designed the following question, which was asked at frequent intervals until 1961:

The U.S. Supreme Court has ruled that racial segregation in the public schools is illegal. This means that all children, no matter what their race, must be allowed to go to the same schools. Do you approve or disapprove of this decision?

Trend on Views Toward
U.S. Supreme Court Decision

	Approve	Disapprove	No opinion
May 1961	62%	33%	5%
May 1959	57	35	6
Sept. 1957	59	35	6
July 1957	58	36	6
Apr. 1957	62	32	6
Dec. 1956	63	31	6
Nov. 1955	59	37	4
Apr. 1955	56	38	6
May 1954	54	41	5

Not surprisingly, there was anything but regional and racial unanimity on approval of the high court's far-reaching decision. The November 1955 survey, for instance, revealed 16% approval among southern whites, compared to 71% among northern whites and 53% among southern blacks. A special Gallup survey conducted in the South two years later showed whites there intransigent, with only 15% approving, while southern blacks were moving toward a more overwhelming acceptance (69%) of the decision.

While nationally, but not in the South, there could be said to be approval of the Supreme Court decision in principle, in practice the speed with which the schools were to be integrated remained a hotly debated issue, as reflected by the following Gallup Poll questions:

(April 1956): The Supreme Court has ruled that racial segregation in the public schools is illegal. Which of these points of view comes nearest to your way of thinking about the problem of segregation? [Respondents were handed a card listing two viewpoints.]: 1) The government should try to bring about the integration of white and Negro children in public schools gradually, that is, over a long period of years, or 2) the government should do everything it can to see that white and Negro children in all parts of the country go to the same public schools within the coming year.

Integrate gradually	71%
Integrate immediately	18
No opinion	11

(December 1956): Do you think integration, that is, bringing Negro and white children together in the schools, should be brought about gradually, or do you think every means should be used to bring it about in the near future?

Gradually	69%
Near future	26
No opinion	5

(July 1958): A judge in Little Rock, Arkansas, has put off bringing Negro and white children together in the schools there for a period of two and one-half years. Do you approve or disapprove of this ruling?

Approve	46%
Disapprove	44
No opinion	10

(September 1958): In many communities in the Deep South states, the number of colored school children is greater than the number of white school children. Would you say that these communities in the South should be required to integrate schools immediately, should they be given

a few years to do this, should they be given a longer time such as ten to twenty years, or should they not be required to integrate at all?

Immediately 29%
In a few years 25
Ten to twenty years 8
Never 31
Uncertain........................... 7

(July 1969): What is your opinion—do you think the racial integration of schools in the United States is going too fast or not fast enough?

February/March 1970

Too fast............................ 48%
Not fast enough 17
About right (volunteered) 21
No opinion 14

July 1969

Too fast............................ 44%
Not fast enough 22
About right (volunteered) 25
No opinion 9

By 1958 the South was beginning to have a little experience with integrated schools, many of them unpleasant. As the numerous disturbances, such as those at Central High School in Little Rock, Arkansas, demonstrated, violence was often just below the surface. In August 1958 the Gallup Poll conducted a special survey in the South:

(August 1958): If the courts order the schools in your community to integrate immediately, do you think there would be violence, or not?

Yes................................ 62%
No................................. 15
Uncertain........................... 23

(August 1958): Are there any plans to integrate the schools in your community in the next year or two?

Yes................................ 3%
No................................. 74
Don't know 23

(August 1958): If the courts order the schools in your community to integrate immediately, would you favor or oppose this?

Favor.............................. 14%
Oppose............................. 75
No opinion 11

Where residential segregation and not deliberate government policy led to segregated schools, as was often the case in northern cities, court rulings emerged that called for busing in order to achieve racial balance in the public schools. Numerous Gallup surveys since 1970 have documented public opposition at the same time that a majority of Americans favors integrated schools.

Starting in March 1970, the following question was asked of respondents who said they had heard or read about school busing:

In general, do you favor or oppose the busing of Negro and white school children from one school district to another?

	Favor	Oppose	No opinion
October 1971	18%	76%	6%
August 1971	18	78	4
March 1970	11	86	3

In October and November 1970 the Gallup Poll conducted a special referendum of public opinion in four "barometer" counties around the country: New London County, Connecticut; Montgomery County, Illinois; Shelby County, Tennessee; and San Luis Obispo County, California. These four counties were chosen because their vote accurately had reflected that of their region in the 1956, 1960, 1964, and 1968 presidential elections. Furthermore, taken together their vote also reflected the national vote in the same four presidential elections. The busing question:

*Do you think children should be bused to school to achieve better racial balance?**

Should 22%
Should not 78

*Responses based on those who had heard or read about school busing.

In June 1972 a similar referendum was conducted in the same four counties, using the following busing question:

*Do you favor or oppose busing children to achieve a better racial balance in the schools?**

Favor 27%
Oppose 73

*Responses based on those who expressed an opinion.

And in August 1973 and September 1975 respondents were asked for their opinion on possible ways to integrate public schools:

Which, if any, of these ways [respondents were handed a card listing five alternatives] do you think would be best to achieve integration of public schools in terms of different economic and racial groups?

September 1975*

	Total	Whites only	Blacks only
Create more housing for low-income people in middle-income neighborhoods	18%	16%	32%
Change school boundaries to allow more persons from different economic and racial groups to attend same schools . . .	31	31	31
Bus school children from one school district to another	4	3	6
Do something other than above to integrate schools	19	20	16
Oppose integration of schools	17	19	5
No opinion	11	11	10

August 1973*

	Total	Whites only	Blacks only
Create more housing for low-income people in middle-income neighborhoods	22%	21%	32%
Change school boundaries to allow more persons from different economic and racial groups to attend same schools . . .	27	27	27
Bus school children from one school district to another	5	4	9
Do something other than above to integrate schools	22	23	15
Oppose integration of schools	18	19	9
No opinion	17	16	26

*Multiple responses were given.

The creation of low-income housing in middle-income neighborhoods, a means of reducing residential segregation, was chosen by a third of blacks in both surveys but by only one-fifth or less of whites. The most frequent answers among whites were to change school district boundaries and to do something other than integrate the schools. Interestingly, with the presentation of several alternatives the proportion in favor of busing was noticeably lower than in other surveys conducted around the same period.

In late October 1974, very close to the national election, a nationwide Gallup Poll referendum was carried out, making use of a special ballot on which respondents were asked to place a mark next to one statement in each of several pairs of statements on various issues:

Suppose that on election day, November 5, you could vote on key issues as well as candidates. Please tell me how you would vote on each of these issues.

When it came to busing, 35% were in favor and 65% opposed. The political heat that busing generated even led to proposals for a constitutional amendment to ban busing. Gallup asked the following question of respondents in a September–December 1974 national survey, financed by the Ford Foundation, on attitudes toward education:

Do you favor busing of school children for the purpose of racial integration or should busing for this purpose be prohibited through a constitutional amendment?

Favor busing........................18%
Prohibited through amendment 72
No opinion 10

FEBRUARY 8
ALCOHOLIC BEVERAGES

Interviewing Date: 1/9–12/81
Survey #167-G

Do you have occasion to use alcoholic beverages such as liquor, wine, or beer, or are you a total abstainer?

	Those who drink
National	70%

By Sex

Male	75%
Female	66

By Education

College	81%
High school	70
Grade school	52

By Region

East	77%
Midwest	75
South	58
West	72

By Age

18–29 years	76%
30–49 years	74
50 years and over	63

By Religion

Protestants	62%
Catholics	82

National Trend

	Those who drink
1981	70%
1976	71
1974	68
1966	65
1960	62
1958	55
1952	60
1947	63
1946	67
1939	58

Would you favor or oppose a law forbidding the sale of all liquor, wine, and beer throughout the nation?

Favor	17%
Oppose	80
Not sure	3

By Sex
Male

Favor	15%
Oppose	83
Not sure	2

Female

Favor	20%
Oppose	74
Not sure	6

By Education
College

Favor	9%
Oppose	90
Not sure	1

High School

Favor	18%
Oppose	79
Not sure	3

Grade School

Favor	28%
Oppose	66
Not sure	6

By Region
East

Favor	10%
Oppose	86
Not sure	4

Midwest

Favor	17%
Oppose	82
Not sure	1

South

Favor	25%
Oppose	71
Not sure	4

West

Favor	17%
Oppose	81
Not sure	2

By Age
18–29 Years

Favor	17%
Oppose	82
Not sure	1

30–49 Years

Favor	17%
Oppose	79
Not sure	4

50 Years and Over

Favor	17%
Oppose	80
Not sure	3

By Religion
Protestants

Favor	21%
Oppose	76
Not sure	3

Catholics

Favor	11%
Oppose	85
Not sure	4

National Trend

	Those who favor prohibition
1981	17%
1976	19
1966	22
1960	26
1957	28
1954	34
1948	38
1945	33
1944	37
1940	32
1936	38

Has liquor ever been a cause of trouble in your family?

	Yes
National	22%

By Education

College	17%
High school	23
Grade school	23

By Region

East	18%
Midwest	19
South	23
West	28

By Age

18–29 years	24%
30–49 years	22
50 years and over	19

By Income

$25,000 and over	17%
$20,000–$24,999	20
$15,000–$19,999	23
$10,000–$14,999	20
$5,000–$9,999	24
Under $5,000	29

By Occupation

Professional and business	17%
Clerical and sales	23
Manual workers	26
Nonlabor force	20

By Community Size

One million and over	22%
500,000–999,999	20
50,000–499,999	21
2,500–49,999	27
Under 2,500; rural	20

National Trend

	Alcohol-related problems
1981	22%
1978	22
1976	17
1974	12
1966	12
1950	14

Note: If your family has been adversely affected by alcohol-related problems, you have a lot of company, since one person in five reports that alcohol has been a cause of trouble in his or her family. Currently, 22% of adult Americans say their homes are troubled by alcohol-related problems, nearly double the 12% recorded in 1974.

In the latest survey, women are almost twice as likely to perceive family problems related to the use of alcohol as are men. Of particular concern is the fact that slightly more persons under thirty years of age said that alcohol had caused trouble in their families than did persons thirty and older.

A somewhat higher proportion of alcohol-related problems is reported by persons from blue-collar than from white-collar households. Survey participants whose formal education ended at the high-school level or earlier were also more apt to cite an alcohol-related family problem than the college-educated.

The latest nationwide audit of alcoholic beverage drinking shows 70% of adults, eighteen and older, saying they use liquor, wine, or beer, while 30% are total abstainers. This is about the same level recorded in 1976, 1978, and 1979. The lowest percentage of drinkers recorded during forty-two years of measurements was in 1958, when 55% said they used alcoholic beverages.

The highest proportion of drinkers today is found among men, younger persons, higher-income groups, those living outside the South, Catholics, professional and business people, and persons with a college background.

The latest survey shows that one person in six (17%) favors a return to prohibition, making the sale of all beer, wine, and liquor illegal throughout the nation. This is half the proportion favoring prohibition in the Gallup Poll's initial survey in 1936 and is the lowest ever recorded.

While no single group of Americans votes in favor of prohibition, there are some among whom favorable opinion is strong. Support for prohibition was highest in 1936 and again in 1948, when 38% favored a ban on the sale of alcoholic beverages. As might be expected, the demand for prohibition is considerably higher in the South (25%) than it is outside the South (14%).

Among those who say liquor has been a problem in their homes, 29% favor a return to prohibition. The comparable figure in homes unscarred by alcohol-related problems is 14%.

FEBRUARY 12
SPORTS

Interviewing Date: 1/9–12/81
Survey #167-G

What is your favorite sport to watch?

Football	38%
Baseball	16
Basketball	9
Bowling	3
Tennis	2
Golf	2
Other	16
None; don't know	14

By Sex
Male

Football	49%
Baseball	14
Basketball	7
Bowling	1
Tennis	1
Golf	2
Other	14
None; don't know	12

Female

Football	28%
Baseball	18
Basketball	10
Bowling	5
Tennis	4
Golf	2
Other	17
None; don't know	16

By Education
College

Football	44%
Baseball	11
Basketball	9
Bowling	1
Tennis	5
Golf	3
Other	18
None; don't know	9

High School

Football	40%
Baseball	16
Basketball	9
Bowling	3
Tennis	2
Golf	1
Other	15
None; don't know	14

Grade School

Football	20%
Baseball	27
Basketball	8
Bowling	5
Tennis	2
Golf	3
Other	12
None; don't know	23

By Age
18–29 Years

Football	41%
Baseball	10
Basketball	9
Bowling	2
Tennis	3
Golf	1
Other	21
None; don't know	13

30–49 Years

Football	41%
Baseball	15
Basketball	10
Bowling	2
Tennis	3
Golf	1
Other	17
None; don't know	11

50 Years and Over

Football 34%
Baseball 22
Basketball 7
Bowling 4
Tennis 2
Golf 4
Other 10
None; don't know 17

Note: In the more than four decades since the beginning of the Gallup surveys on sports, football and baseball have reversed their positions almost exactly as the first and second most favorite spectator sports of the American people, with basketball staying at about the same level.

In 1937 the American Institute of Public Opinion (as the Gallup Poll was then called) published the results of its initial nationwide sports poll. When Americans were asked what their favorite sport was to watch, baseball ranked first among 44% of men and 27% of women. Football followed with 28% and 23%, respectively. Although baseball was the overwhelming first choice of men, football led 44% to 23% over baseball with youths aged seventeen to twenty. Baseball resumed its lead, however, as the age level increased.

In 1948, when television was beginning to appear on the scene, a nationwide Gallup survey once again revealed that baseball outranked football (39% to 17%) as the sport Americans most enjoyed watching. But by the 1960 poll the margin between baseball and football had narrowed somewhat, with the former leading 34% to 21%. And finally the results of the 1972 survey indicated that football had pulled ahead to replace baseball as America's favorite sport, as reaffirmed in the latest Gallup poll.

The 1981 survey results show that although baseball and basketball are equally popular with both male and female spectators, football has a disproportionate appeal among men, 49% of whom claim it to be their favorite sport, compared with only 28% of women.

Football enjoys its greatest popularity among blacks, the college educated, upper-income families, and persons living in the South. Baseball, on the other hand, has a greater proportion of followers among whites, men and women aged fifty or over, lower-income groups, and those with less formal education. Baseball's appeal is somewhat lower in the South than in other regions of the country. And the distribution of basketball fans is remarkably even, with across-the-board appeal among different viewer groups. However, it is slightly more popular among women, blacks, and persons living in the South.

Aside from the big-three spectator sports, tennis continues to exhibit an uptrend, particularly among women. Two sports appearing in the top ten in popularity for the first time are gymnastics and soccer, each named by 2% of Americans as their favorite sport to watch.

Football's popularity with adults is almost matched by its 34% of teen-age partisans, according to the Gallup Youth Survey, with baseball 19% and basketball 16% in close contention for second place. Tennis is somewhat more popular with teen-age girls (12%) than it is with boys (2%).

FEBRUARY 12
OPINION POLLING AND THE REAGAN PRESIDENCY*

The Gallup Poll soon will be providing the percentage of Americans who approve of the way Ronald Reagan is handling his presidential duties. Other polls will tell us the percentage of the public who give the Reagan administration an excellent or good rating, or will report on the percentage who consider themselves supporters versus critics.

If the polls are true to form, the first public opinion surveys will show large percentages of the public saying favorable things about Reagan, since voters usually respond positively to a new

*This Gallup analysis was written by Andrew Kohut, president of the Gallup Organization Inc.

president. As a rule, at least a year is required for the public to have a really good sense of the new man in the Oval Office.

The following shows how the last four presidents fared with the public during the first twelve months:

Gallup Poll Approval Ratings

	High rating	Low rating	Difference in percentage points
Jimmy Carter			
1977	75%	51%	−24
Gerald Ford			
1974–75	71	37	−34
Richard Nixon			
1969	67	56	−11
Lyndon Johnson			
1963–64	80	73	−7

An exception to the rule was Gerald Ford's ratings, which plummeted as a result of the Nixon pardon just one month after he took office. The decline in Carter's ratings was not associated with any specific issue but rather with a growing feeling that he was not capable of doing the job. Richard Nixon and Lyndon Johnson maintained high levels of public support throughout their early years in office.

Johnson took his first serious tumble at the time of the Vietnam buildup in 1965, two and one-half years after being sworn in. Nixon lost considerable support as a consequence of the Cambodian invasion but did not fall below 50% approval until well into his third year in office.

The significance of the early polls will be their usefulness as gauges to assess trends in public reaction to the new administration over the first year. It should be kept in mind that Carter and Ford, who fell badly by the end of the first year, subsequently were not returned to office, but Johnson and Nixon, who succeeded in maintaining their popularity through the first years, were reelected.

The early polls also will be important for what they reveal about first impressions of the president, that is, how the public responds to the presidential manner or style and the extent to which public expectations are aroused by the new administration.

To date the Reagan administration appears to have the best of both worlds with regard to public anticipation. Surveys show that while the public is not expecting dramatic progress on what it considers its most important problem—the economy—there is a general mood of optimism about 1981. According to a twenty-nine-nation survey, the American people are expressing more personal optimism than are the publics of most other countries polled by the Gallup International Inc. At the same time, the American public does not expect the Reagan administration to make much progress in 1981 in curbing either inflation or unemployment.

This should be good news for President Reagan. What he must try to achieve is to impart in Americans both a sense of optimism about the future and realistic expectations about what he can do in a short period of time. The Carter administration paid a heavy toll in public support as a consequence of trying to fulfill a very high measure of public anticipation four years ago. In contrast, expectations of the Reagan administration are much more subdued.

The first year and how the public reacts to it takes on added significance in 1981 because of the widely accepted notion that the election of Reagan marked the beginning of a new conservative era. Pollsters and many political scientists disagree with this interpretation of the Reagan victory. Virtually all major polls show that voters have not changed their views on issues that are thought to divide liberals and conservatives. Attitudes toward gun control, abortion, the Equal Rights Amendment, and busing have not changed significantly over the last four years.

What may occur, however, is the proclamation of a new conservative era and the Reagan assumption of power may in fact lead to a change in the public's political ideology. To a certain extent the acceptance of the view that the country has turned to the right may become a self-fulfilling prophecy, but for this to happen the administration must prove successful. The American public is quite pragmatic. If Reagan's conservative leadership and policies seem to work, the public may well become more conservative.

FEBRUARY 15
WASTE OF TAX DOLLARS

Interviewing Date: 1/9–12/81
Survey #167-G

Of every tax dollar that goes to the federal government in Washington, DC, how many cents of each dollar would you say are wasted?

	Median average
National	48¢

By Education

College	41¢
High school	49
Grade school	38

By Region

East	40¢
Midwest	49
South	48
West	46

By Age

18–29 years	49¢
30–49 years	49
50 years and over	42

By Politics

Republicans	40¢
Democrats	48
Independents	49

By Community Size

One million and over	35¢
500,000–999,999	43
50,000–49,999	48
2,500–49,999	44
Under 2,500; rural	49

And how many cents of each tax dollar that goes to the government of this state would you say are wasted?

	Median average
National	29¢

By Education

College	25¢
High school	29
Grade school	27

By Region

East	31¢
Midwest	26
South	28
West	27

By Age

18–29 years	28¢
30–49 years	30
50 years and over	27

By Politics

Republicans	24¢
Democrats	29
Independents	30

By Community Size

One million and over	27¢
500,000–999,999	30
50,000–499,999	30
2,500–49,999	28
Under 2,500; rural	28

And how many cents of each tax dollar that goes to your local government would you say are wasted?

	Median average
National	23¢

By Education

College	24¢
High school	25
Grade school	22

By Region

East .... 31¢
Midwest 21
South 24
West 21

By Age

18–29 years .... 26¢
30–49 years 23
50 years and over.................... 22

By Politics

Republicans .... 20¢
Democrats 25
Independents 24

By Community Size

One million and over.................. 23¢
500,000–999,999 20
50,000–499,999 25
2,500–49,999........................ 24
Under 2,500; rural 22

Note: President Ronald Reagan undoubtedly struck a responsive chord with the American people in his recent television speech when he called for cuts in government waste and administrative overhead.

The public judgment today, according to a recent Gallup survey, is that about half (48¢) of every tax dollar that goes to the federal government in Washington is wasted. This survey finding suggests that much of the public's frustration and anger over government spending is directed not so much at the services those funds provide but at what is widely perceived to be wasted taxpayers' money.

President Reagan has an opportunity to improve on former President Jimmy Carter's record by convincing Americans that waste is being cut out of federal spending. The Carter administration made little headway in this respect. In surveys conducted in 1978 and 1979 the public believed that almost half (48¢) of every tax dollar that went to the federal government was wasted, the same figure recorded this year.

The closer government is to the people, the less money they believe is wasted. For example, when survey respondents were asked how many cents of each tax dollar received by their state government is wasted, the median average obtained is 29¢. And in the case of local government, the figure is 23¢. Again, little difference is found in responses since the earlier surveys.

FEBRUARY 18
PRESIDENT REAGAN

Interviewing Date: 12/5–8/80; 1/30–2/2/81
Survey #166-G; 168-G

Just your best impression at this point— What kind of president do you think Ronald Reagan will make—a great president, a good president, a fair president, or a poor president?

	Jan. 30–Feb. 2	Dec. 5–8
Great president......	8%	4%
Good president......	43	36
Fair president	32	35
Poor president.......	8	15
No opinion	9	10

Those Saying Reagan Will Make
Great or Good President

By Race

	Jan. 30–Feb. 2	Dec. 5–8
White	54%	43%
Nonwhite..........	23	21

By Region

	Jan. 30–Feb. 2	Dec. 5–8
East	47%	33%
Midwest...........	51	44
South	53	41
West..............	53	42

By Politics

	Jan. 30–Feb. 2	Dec. 5–8
Republicans........	76%	70%
Democrats.........	37	23
Independents.......	52	37

Note: President Ronald Reagan has registered a considerable gain in public favor during the transition period, among Democrats as well as Republicans. In an early December survey, 40% of adults surveyed thought that Reagan would make a great or good president, while 50% felt he would be only a fair or poor president. In the second survey, conducted shortly after Reagan took the oath of office on January 20, a total of 51% thought Reagan would make a great or good president, while a smaller proportion (40%) said fair or poor.

While Reagan's action during the transition period and his call on inauguration day for "an era of national renewal" have elicited a positive response among many key groups in the populace, he continues to face an uphill struggle to win the confidence of the nation's nonwhite population. At present only 23% of this group feel that Reagan will make a great or good president, statistically the same percentage as recorded in December.

FEBRUARY 22
MINIMUM WAGE FOR TEEN-AGERS

Interviewing Date: 1/9–12/81
Survey #167-G

Have you followed or read about the discussion regarding a lower minimum wage to provide work for more unemployed teen-agers? Asked of those who replied in the affirmative: What is the best reason for lowering the minimum wage, in your opinion? What is the best reason against lowering the minimum wage?

and

Asked of those who said they had followed the discussion and could give reasons for and/or against the proposal: How do you yourself feel? Do you favor or oppose lowering the minimum wage for teen-agers?

Favor.............................20%
Oppose...........................21
No opinion 3
                                   ——
                                   44%*

By Sex
Male

Favor.............................22%
Oppose...........................22
No opinion 3
                                   ——
                                   47%*

Female

Favor.............................19%
Oppose...........................19
No opinion 3
                                   ——
                                   41%*

By Race
White

Favor.............................22%
Oppose...........................20
No opinion 3
                                   ——
                                   45%*

Nonwhite

Favor............................. 7%
Oppose...........................26
No opinion 3
                                   ——
                                   36%*

By Education
College

Favor.............................31%
Oppose...........................24
No opinion 2
                                   ——
                                   57%*

High School

Favor.............................17%
Oppose...........................20
No opinion 4
                                   ——
                                   41%*

Grade School

Favor.............................13%
Oppose..........................16
No opinion 2
                                 31%*

By Region
East

Favor.............................20%
Oppose..........................22
No opinion 3
                                 45%*

Midwest

Favor.............................22%
Oppose..........................21
No opinion 2
                                 45%*

South

Favor.............................19%
Oppose..........................21
No opinion 4
                                 44%*

West

Favor.............................21%
Oppose..........................19
No opinion 3
                                 43%*

By Age
18–24 Years

Favor.............................13%
Oppose..........................21
No opinion 2
                                 36%*

25–29 Years

Favor.............................17%
Oppose..........................22
No opinion 4
                                 43%*

30–49 Years

Favor.............................21%
Oppose..........................21
No opinion 2
                                 44%*

50 Years and Over

Favor.............................24%
Oppose..........................20
No opinion 4
                                 48%*

By Income
$25,000 and Over

Favor.............................27%
Oppose..........................24
No opinion 4
                                 55%*

$20,000–$24,999

Favor.............................19%
Oppose..........................24
No opinion 4
                                 47%*

$15,000–$19,999

Favor.............................21%
Oppose..........................23
No opinion 2
                                 46%*

$10,000–$14,999

Favor.............................19%
Oppose..........................17
No opinion 4
                                 40%*

$5,000–$9,999

Favor.............................14%
Oppose..........................20
No opinion 1
                                 35%*

Under $5,000

Favor 12%
Oppose 14
No opinion . . . . <u>3</u>
29%*

By Politics
Republicans

Favor 33%
Oppose 17
No opinion . . . . <u>4</u>
54%*

Democrats

Favor 14%
Oppose 24
No opinion . . . . <u>3</u>
41%*

Independents

Favor 17%
Oppose 21
No opinion . . . . <u>3</u>
41%*

Labor Union Families Only

Favor 16%
Oppose 29
No opinion . . . . <u>4</u>
49%*

Nonlabor Union Families Only

Favor 22%
Oppose 18
No opinion . . . . <u>3</u>
43%*

*Percentage of total sample

Asked of the entire sample: Would you favor or oppose lowering the minimum wage to encourage employers to hire more physically or mentally handicapped persons who are not as productive as most workers because of their disability?

Favor 50%
Oppose 40
No opinion 10

By Sex
Male

Favor 51%
Oppose 40
No opinion 9

Female

Favor 49%
Oppose 41
No opinion 10

By Race
White

Favor 51%
Oppose 39
No opinion 10

Nonwhite

Favor 39%
Oppose 52
No opinion 9

By Education
College

Favor 49%
Oppose 44
No opinion 7

High School

Favor 50%
Oppose 42
No opinion 8

Grade School

Favor 52%
Oppose 29
No opinion 19

By Region

East

Favor 49%
Oppose 41
No opinion 10

Midwest

Favor 51%
Oppose 38
No opinion 11

South

Favor 51%
Oppose 39
No opinion 10

West

Favor 49%
Oppose 46
No opinion 5

By Age

18–29 Years

Favor 52%
Oppose 40
No opinion 8

30–49 Years

Favor 45%
Oppose 46
No opinion 9

50 Years and Over

Favor 53%
Oppose 36
No opinion 11

By Income

$25,000 and Over

Favor 49%
Oppose 43
No opinion 8

$20,000–$24,999

Favor 42%
Oppose 51
No opinion 7

$15,000–$19,999

Favor 49%
Oppose 42
No opinion 9

$10,000–$14,999

Favor 52%
Oppose 39
No opinion 9

$5,000–$9,999

Favor 55%
Oppose 34
No opinion 11

Under $5,000

Favor 49%
Oppose 32
No opinion 19

By Politics

Republicans

Favor 57%
Oppose 35
No opinion 8

Democrats

Favor 50%
Oppose 40
No opinion 10

Independents

Favor 44%
Oppose 46
No opinion 10

Labor Union Families Only

Favor 44%
Oppose 48
No opinion 8

Nonlabor Union Families Only

Favor 52%
Oppose 38
No opinion 10

Note: Those familiar with the proposal to lower the minimum wage in order to provide work for more teen-agers are evenly divided in their views. Among the 44% of the informed American public, 20% say they favor a lower wage for teens, while 21% are opposed and 3% are undecided. The current minimum wage is $3.35 per hour.

The key findings of this Gallup survey show that those groups most likely to favor the proposal include Republicans, the college educated, older persons, and those living in nonunion households. Conversely, greater opposition is found among those groups that might be more directly affected by a subminimum wage for teens: younger adults, blacks, and those with less formal education. In addition, members of labor union households, and Democrats and political independents voice greater opposition on ideological grounds.

Some social scientists support a two-tier minimum wage, arguing that the high rate of youth unemployment contributes to such problems as drug abuse and crime and that these problems put a serious drain on the financial resources of many communities. They maintain that positive action must be taken to provide work for young people who cannot find jobs because they are unskilled or undertrained.

Those who favor the proposal often argue from a social point of view, while those opposed to lowering the minimum wage for teens cite what they see as practical shortcomings of the plan. Among the key reasons given by opponents are: 1) a subminimum wage for teens would take jobs from older people and cause greater unemployment among adults, 2) teens should receive equal pay for equal work, and 3) companies would take advantage of the situation and exploit the teen-age job market.

All persons in the survey also were asked their opinion about a lower minimum wage to encourage employers to hire more physically or mentally handicapped persons. Although the public favors such a change by a 5-to-4 ratio, the fact that as many as four out of ten oppose the proposal suggests how deeply the idea of a single minimum wage is ingrained.

FEBRUARY 26
PRESIDENTIAL TERM OF OFFICE

Interviewing Date: 1/9–12/81
Survey #167-G

Would you favor changing the term of office of the president of the United States to one six-year term with no reelection?

Yes 30%
No 63
No opinion 7

By Education
College

Yes 35%
No 63
No opinion 2

High School

Yes 27%
No 66
No opinion 7

Grade School

Yes 29%
No 52
No opinion 19

By Region
East

Yes 24%
No 67
No opinion 9

Midwest

Yes 30%
No 64
No opinion 6

South

Yes...............................30%
No................................61
No opinion 9

West

Yes...............................36%
No................................60
No opinion 4

By Age
18–29 Years

Yes...............................20%
No................................74
No opinion 6

30–49 Years

Yes...............................33%
No................................62
No opinion 5

50 Years and Over

Yes...............................34%
No................................56
No opinion 10

By Politics
Republicans

Yes...............................31%
No................................63
No opinion 6

Democrats

Yes...............................31%
No................................61
No opinion 8

Independents

Yes...............................27%
No................................66
No opinion 7

National Trend on Views Toward Six-Year Presidential Term*

	Favor	Oppose	No opinion
1981	30%	63%	7%
1979	30	62	8
1973	28	64	8
1971	20	73	7
1969	18	75	7
1945	25	68	7
1943	29	59	12
1938	21	67	12
1936	26	74	*

*No opinion figures were allocated between favor and oppose and are not available.

Note: Although a proposal for a single six-year term for U.S. president has had the support of many presidents and a growing number of students of the American political system, it is clearly an idea whose time has not come as far as the American public is concerned.

In the latest Gallup Poll, conducted shortly before Ronald Reagan took office in January, 30% of the public favored changing the term of U.S. presidents to one six-year term with no reelection, with 63% opposed. The balance (7%) did not express an opinion.

Although a majority of Americans oppose the proposed change, public support has advanced somewhat since the Gallup Poll first studied the issue in 1936, when 26% of the public voted in favor of the single six-year presidential term. Almost the same degree of support or opposition to the proposal is found in all major population groups. For example, 63% of Republicans, 61% of Democrats, and 66% of political independents voice disapproval.

In a recent issue of the *New York Times Magazine,* former Secretary of State Cyrus Vance, who served in four administrations, summarized the basic arguments in favor of the one-term presidency:

.... One key proposal—which I support— would limit a President to one term of six years. The idea of a single, limited Presidential term

is not new. It was proposed, debated and initially adopted by the Committee of the Whole at the Constitutional Convention in 1787. The issue was later revived by Andrew Jackson, and many Presidents since him have publicly subscribed to the belief that the national interest would be better served by Presidents who are not intent on being re-elected. The virtues of a single, six-year term are that a President could devote his full attention to national needs, rather than spending much of his energy on trying to win re-election; the paralysis in decision-making that grips the executive branch during the long primary campaign could be eliminated; and a single-term President would be less inclined to use his office for the purpose of courting voters to win re-election.

Although the American people presently reject the idea of one six-year presidential term, their views shifted sharply on a similar issue—a two-term limit to the presidency. In the late 1930s, survey evidence showed that a majority of the public was opposed to a two-term limit. However, in 1943 majority opinion shifted in favor of this limit, with subsequent surveys continuing to show widespread support. The 22nd Amendment to the Constitution, limiting to two the number of terms a president may serve, was proposed by the Congress in 1947 and ratified in 1951.

In this century many proposals for six-year terms have been introduced in Congress, and once (in 1913) the Senate, but not the House, passed such a resolution. Interestingly, the constitution of the Confederacy during the Civil War provided for a six-year term and Jefferson Davis took office on that basis.

Although a majority of the American people oppose limiting the presidency to one six-year term, others have long favored other reforms in the electoral process, including: 1) abolishing the Electoral College and electing presidents by popular vote, 2) limiting the number of terms of U.S. representatives and senators, 3) substituting a single national primary for the present system of state primaries, and 4) shortening the campaign period.

MARCH 1
DEATH PENALTY

Interviewing Date: 1/30–2/2/81
Survey #168-G

Are you in favor of the death penalty for persons convicted of murder?

Yes 66%
No 25
Don't know 9

By Sex
Male

Yes 71%
No 22
Don't know 7

Female

Yes 62%
No 28
Don't know 10

By Race
White

Yes 70%
No 22
Don't know 8

Nonwhite

Yes 44%
No 44
Don't know 12

By Education
College

Yes 62%
No 32
Don't know 6

High School

Yes 72%
No 20
Don't know 8

Grade School

Yes...............................55%
No................................30
Don't know........................15

By Region
East

Yes...............................67%
No................................24
Don't know........................ 9

Midwest

Yes...............................65%
No................................25
Don't know........................10

South

Yes...............................65%
No................................26
Don't know........................ 9

West

Yes...............................70%
No................................25
Don't know........................ 5

By Age
18–29 Years

Yes...............................62%
No................................31
Don't know........................ 7

30–49 Years

Yes...............................68%
No................................24
Don't know........................ 8

50 Years and Over

Yes...............................68%
No................................22
Don't know........................10

By Community Size
One Million and Over

Yes...............................67%
No................................23
Don't know........................10

500,000–999,999

Yes...............................62%
No................................30
Don't know........................ 8

50,000–499,999

Yes...............................69%
No................................25
Don't know........................ 6

2,500–49,999

Yes...............................65%
No................................28
Don't know........................ 7

Under 2,500; Rural

Yes...............................67%
No................................21
Don't know........................12

Are you in favor of the death penalty for persons convicted of treason?

Yes...............................39%
No................................49
Don't know........................12

By Sex
Male

Yes...............................46%
No................................44
Don't know........................10

Female

Yes...............................33%
No................................52
Don't know........................15

By Race
White
Yes 41%
No 47
Don't know 12

Nonwhite
Yes 25%
No 61
Don't know 14

By Education
College
Yes 33%
No 58
Don't know 9

High School
Yes 43%
No 45
Don't know 12

Grade School
Yes 38%
No 43
Don't know 19

By Region
East
Yes 39%
No 48
Don't know 13

Midwest
Yes 39%
No 49
Don't know 12

South
Yes 39%
No 49
Don't know 12

West
Yes 38%
No 49
Don't know 13

By Age
18–29 Years
Yes 26%
No 65
Don't know 9

30–49 Years
Yes 42%
No 46
Don't know 12

50 Years and Over
Yes 45%
No 39
Don't know 16

By Community Size
One Million and Over
Yes 41%
No 46
Don't know 13

500,000–999,999
Yes 45%
No 45
Don't know 10

50,000–499,999
Yes 37%
No 52
Don't know 11

2,500–49,999
Yes 34%
No 55
Don't know 11

Under 2,500; Rural

Yes.....................................39%
No......................................45
Don't know.............................16

Are you in favor of the death penalty for persons convicted of rape?

Yes.....................................37%
No......................................53
Don't know.............................10

By Sex
Male

Yes.....................................40%
No......................................50
Don't know.............................10

Female

Yes.....................................34%
No......................................55
Don't know.............................11

By Race
White

Yes.....................................38%
No......................................52
Don't know.............................10

Nonwhite

Yes.....................................33%
No......................................57
Don't know.............................10

By Education
College

Yes.....................................29%
No......................................63
Don't know..............................8

High School

Yes.....................................41%
No......................................49
Don't know.............................10

Grade School

Yes.....................................37%
No......................................46
Don't know.............................17

By Region
East

Yes.....................................34%
No......................................57
Don't know..............................9

Midwest

Yes.....................................38%
No......................................54
Don't know..............................8

South

Yes.....................................41%
No......................................45
Don't know.............................14

West

Yes.....................................34%
No......................................56
Don't know.............................10

By Age
18–29 Years

Yes.....................................37%
No......................................56
Don't know..............................7

30–49 Years

Yes.....................................37%
No......................................53
Don't know.............................10

50 Years and Over

Yes.....................................37%
No......................................50
Don't know.............................13

By Community Size
One Million and Over

Yes 41%
No 49
Don't know 10

500,000–999,999

Yes 38%
No 56
Don't know 6

50,000–499,999

Yes 39%
No 51
Don't know 10

2,500–49,999

Yes 36%
No 52
Don't know 12

Under 2,500; Rural

Yes 33%
No 55
Don't know 12

Are you in favor of the death penalty for persons convicted of hijacking an airplane?

Yes 22%
No 68
Don't know 10

By Sex
Male

Yes 26%
No 65
Don't know 9

Female

Yes 19%
No 71
Don't know 10

By Race
White

Yes 23%
No 68
Don't know 9

Nonwhite

Yes 20%
No 67
Don't know 13

By Education
College

Yes 18%
No 76
Don't know 6

High School

Yes 24%
No 67
Don't know 9

Grade School

Yes 27%
No 55
Don't know 18

By Region
East

Yes 24%
No 67
Don't know 9

Midwest

Yes 21%
No 72
Don't know 7

South

Yes 24%
No 64
Don't know 12

West

Yes	21%
No	69
Don't know	10

By Age
18–29 Years

Yes	18%
No	77
Don't know	5

30–49 Years

Yes	19%
No	73
Don't know	8

50 Years and Over

Yes	28%
No	58
Don't know	14

By Community Size
One Million and Over

Yes	26%
No	63
Don't know	11

500,000–999,999

Yes	19%
No	75
Don't know	6

50,000–499,999

Yes	22%
No	68
Don't know	10

2,500–49,000

Yes	22%
No	70
Don't know	8

Under 2,500; Rural

Yes	23%
No	66
Don't know	11

Note: In this survey, 12% of the sample favor the death penalty for persons convicted of either murder, treason, rape, or hijacking an airplane, while 19% oppose the death penalty for these crimes.

Public support for the death penalty for murder has reached its highest point in twenty-eight years, as frustration mounts over the nation's inability to stem the tide of violent crime. Two Americans in every three (66%) currently favor the death penalty for persons convicted of murder, compared to 1971 when 49% of the public approved. The previous high in support was recorded in 1953 when the question was first asked. In that year 68% voted in favor of the death penalty for murder. The lowest point was the 42% recorded in 1966.

Public opinion on capital punishment is conditioned to a great extent by the type of crime involved as well as by the socioeconomic background of survey respondents. While a substantial majority of Americans nationwide favor the death penalty for murder, the weight of opinion is opposed to capital punishment for rape, hijacking, and treason.

Women are considerably less likely to favor the death penalty for all four crimes studied. Nonwhites are less apt than whites to support capital punishment for murder and treason, but the races hold similar views toward the death penalty in the cases of rape and hijacking.

Analysis of the reasons given by survey respondents both for and against the death penalty for murder indicates considerable ambivalence in public attitudes. For example, those in favor of capital punishment frequently cite these arguments: 1) the death penalty deters crime, 2) jail sentences are an economic burden on society, 3) criminals today get off too easily, 4) vengeance, and 5) jail is not rehabilitative.

Those opposed to capital punishment give these reasons: 1) religion forbids it; the Bible says: "Thou shalt not kill," 2) the death penalty is not a deterrent, 3) there should be life imprisonment with no parole, 4) people can be rehabilitated, 5) the legal system is not equitable, and 6) taking a second life will not solve anything.

MARCH 5
SPEED LIMIT

Interviewing Date: 2/13–16/81
Survey #169-G

Do you favor or oppose keeping the present 55-mile-per-hour speed limit on the highways of the nation?

Favor 75%
Oppose 23
No opinion 2

By Sex
Male

Favor 71%
Oppose 27
No opinion 2

Female

Favor 79%
Oppose 18
No opinion 3

By Education
College

Favor 74%
Oppose 25
No opinion 1

High School

Favor 74%
Oppose 24
No opinion 2

Grade School

Favor 82%
Oppose 15
No opinion 3

By Region
East

Favor 84%
Oppose 13
No opinion 3

Midwest

Favor 73%
Oppose 26
No opinion 1

South

Favor 71%
Oppose 27
No opinion 2

West

Favor 73%
Oppose 25
No opinion 2

By Age
18–29 Years

Favor 75%
Oppose 23
No opinion 2

30–49 Years

Favor 71%
Oppose 27
No opinion 2

50 Years and Over

Favor 80%
Oppose 18
No opinion 2

Those Who Obey 55-MPH Limit
All or Most of the Time

Favor 82%
Oppose 17
No opinion 1

Those Who Do Not Obey 55-MPH Limit Most of the Time Or Who Never Obey It

Favor 42%
Oppose 55
No opinion 3

Those Who Have Been Stopped By Police For Speeding

Favor 53%
Oppose 45
No opinion 2

Those Who Never Have Been Stopped By Police For Speeding

Favor 80%
Oppose 18
No opinion 2

Asked of drivers: Would you say that you, yourself, obey the 55-mile-per-hour speed limit all of the time, most of the time, not very often, or never?

All of the time 29%
Most of the time 48
Not very often 13
Never 3
Don't know 7

By Sex
Male

All of the time 24%
Most of the time 50
Not very often 19
Never 3
Don't know 4

Female

All of the time 33%
Most of the time 46
Not very often 8
Never 3
Don't know 10

By Education
College

All of the time 22%
Most of the time 55
Not very often 18
Never 3
Don't know 2

High School

All of the time 29%
Most of the time 49
Not very often 13
Never 3
Don't know 6

Grade School

All of the time 42%
Most of the time 30
Not very often 4
Never 3
Don't know 21

By Age
18–29 Years

All of the time 18%
Most of the time 53
Not very often 21
Never 3
Don't know 5

30–49 Years

All of the time 25%
Most of the time 53
Not very often 15
Never 3
Don't know 4

50 Years and Over

All of the time 42%
Most of the time 38
Not very often 6
Never 2
Don't know 12

Those Who Favor the 55-MPH Speed Limit

All of the time.........................34%
Most of the time......................49
Not very often.........................7
Never.................................2
Don't know............................8

Those Who Oppose the 55-MPH Speed Limit

All of the time.........................14%
Most of the time......................45
Not very often........................34
Never.................................5
Don't know............................2

Those Who Have Been Stopped By Police For Speeding

All of the time.........................11%
Most of the time......................53
Not very often........................31
Never.................................3
Don't know............................2

Those Who Never Have Been Stopped By Police For Speeding

All of the time.........................33%
Most of the time......................46
Not very often........................10
Never.................................3
Don't know............................8

Asked of drivers: Have you, yourself, ever been stopped by the police for exceeding the 55-mile-per-hour speed limit since the law was passed?

	Yes
National	18%

By Sex

Male	25%
Female	12

By Education

College	22%
High school	18
Grade school	8

By Age

18–29 years.........................25%
30–49 years.........................20
50 years and over....................11

Those who favor the
  55-mph speed limit................12%
Those who oppose the
  55-mph speed limit................36
Those who obey 55-mph limit
  all of the time.....................7
Those who obey 55-mph limit
  most of the time...................20
Those who do not obey 55-mph
  limit most of the time
  or who never obey it...............37

Asked of those who replied in the affirmative: How many times?*

Once...............................58%
Twice..............................22
Three or more......................17
Don't know.........................3

By Sex
Male

Once...............................53%
Twice..............................22
Three or more......................22
Don't know.........................3

Female

Once...............................69%
Twice..............................22
Three or more......................5
Don't know.........................4

By Education
College

Once...............................54%
Twice..............................27
Three or more......................15
Don't know.........................4

High School

Once............................61%
Twice............................16
Three or more....................20
Don't know....................... 3

Grade School**

By Age
18–29 Years

Once............................56%
Twice............................21
Three or more....................20
Don't know....................... 3

30–49 Years

Once............................59%
Twice............................19
Three or more....................18
Don't know....................... 4

50 Years and Over

Once............................63%
Twice............................28
Three or more.................... 5
Don't know....................... 4

*Because these results are based on only drivers answering in the affirmative, the margin of error is considerably larger.
**Too few cases to be meaningful.

Asked of the entire sample: From your own observations, would you say that most drivers obey the 55-mile-per-hour speed limit all of the time, most of the time, not very often, or never?

All of the time...................... 2%
Most of the time.....................42
Not very often.......................49
Never............................ 5
Don't know....................... 2

Note: Although by their own testimony a relatively small proportion of the nation's drivers observe the fifty-five-mile-per-hour speed limit at all times, three out of four Americans favor retaining this national law.

One of President Ronald Reagan's campaign promises called for abolishing the fifty-five-mph national speed limit and letting the states set their own maximum speeds. Criticism of the national limit has been particularly intense in many western states, and some states there and elsewhere are considering repeal legislation.

Nevertheless, 75% of the public nationwide now approves of the fifty-five-mile-per-hour limit, which is similar to the findings of Gallup surveys conducted periodically since the law went into effect in 1973. Since then large majorities of residents of every geographical region consistently have backed the fifty-five-mile-per-hour limit.

Most likely to observe the fifty-five-mile-per-hour limit most or all of the time are supporters of the law, but even among the opponents of the national maximum speed, well over half (59%) report frequently or always abiding by the law.

While a majority of the public admits to exceeding the fifty-five-mile-per-hour limit at least on occasion, this indiscretion is not without its penalties. As many as 18% say that they have been stopped by the police for speeding, and this figure doubles to 37% among drivers who seldom or never observe the fifty-five-mile-per-hour limit. Even among the majority who obey the legal limit all or most of the time, 15% say they have been stopped by the police for speeding.

Proponents favor retaining the fifty-five-mile-per-hour speed limit for three reasons. First, there has been a substantial reduction in auto fatalities since the law was enacted. Second, savings in petroleum are effected. (It has been estimated that consumption would increase by a quarter-million barrels a day if the speed limit were removed.) Finally, it costs drivers less money to run cars at lower than at higher speeds.

Opposition centers on the fact that not many people, especially those living in sparsely populated areas, often drive long distances on highways specifically designed for high-speed travel. Allowing higher maximum speed limits on these roads would save time and, because of their construction, constitute no more of a hazard than the use of poorly built roads at lower speeds. Critics of the fifty-five-mile-per-hour speed limit also argue that automotive vehicles can be engineered to drive efficiently at higher speeds.

MARCH 8
MOST IMPORTANT PROBLEM/
POLITICAL AFFILIATION

Interviewing Date: 1/30–2/2/81
Survey #168-G

What do you think is the most important problem facing this country today?

Inflation; high cost of living	73%
Unemployment; recession; depression	8
Energy problems	5
Defense; war	3
Crime	2
Dissatisfaction with government	2
Moral decline	2
International; foreign affairs	2
All others	6
Don't know	3
	106%*

*Total adds to more than 100% due to multiple responses.

Asked of those who named a problem: Which party—the Republican or the Democratic—do you think is better able to deal with the problem you just mentioned?

Republican	39%
Democratic	20
No difference	30
No opinion	11

Interviewing Date: 11/7/1980–2/16/1981
Various Surveys

*In politics, as of today, do you consider yourself a Republican, Democrat, or independent?**

Republican	27%
Democrat	42
Independent	31

*The percentage figures given exclude those who do not classify themselves as belonging to one of the three parties.

*People who are conservative in their political views are referred to as being right of center and people who are liberal in their political views are referred to as being left of center. [Survey respondents were handed a card listing eight categories.] Which one of these categories best describes your own political position?***

Right of center	34%
Middle of the road	47
Left of center	19

**Responses based on those who expressed an opinion.

Note: Nationwide Gallup surveys reveal that the public is placing new confidence in the Republican party:

1). Almost twice as many voters currently name the Republican (39%) as the Democratic party (20%) as better able to deal with the nation's top problems, the widest margin that the GOP has held over its rival party in national surveys conducted over the past thirty-six years. And three in four voters now name the high cost of living as the most important problem facing the nation, with unemployment 8% and energy problems 5%.

2). The number of voters who classify themselves as Republicans has increased during recent months, and in the latest surveys 27% identify themselves as Republicans. This is the highest level recorded since 1972 and 6 percentage points above the figure recorded one year ago. Nonetheless, a substantially higher percentage of the electorate (42%) continues to claim allegiance to the Democratic party, and 31% say they are political independents.

While recent surveys offer encouragement for the Republicans, these trends do not seem to reflect any major shift toward the conservative viewpoint. The proportion of Americans who place themselves to the right of center on a 9-point liberal-conservative scale varies little from that found in earlier surveys.

The question arises as to whether recent gains for the GOP—in terms of public confidence in the ability of the party to handle the nation's top problems and in terms of party affiliation—can be sustained in the months ahead, or whether they are merely a temporary manifestation of the public's goodwill at the start of the Reagan presidency.

In the period immediately following President Dwight Eisenhower's landslide victory in the 1952 presidential election, sharp increases were noted, both in confidence in the Republican party and in GOP party affiliation. In subsequent months, however, this dissipated.

MARCH 12
COST OF LIVING

Interviewing Date: 1/30–2/2; 2/13–16/81
Survey #168-G; #169-G

On the average, about how much does your family spend on food, including milk, each week?

	Median average
National	$62*

By Education

College	$64
High school	$63
Grade school	$52

By Region

East	$69
Midwest	$59
South	$61
West	$68

By Community Size

One million and over	$76
500,000–999,999	$62
50,000–499,999	$62
2,500–49,999	$54
Under 2,500; rural	$60

By Income

$25,000 and over	$77
$20,000–$24,999	$67
$15,000–$19,999	$65
$10,000–$14,999	$54
$5,000–$9,999	$51
Under $5,000	$48

By Occupation

Professional and business	$72
Clerical and sales	$61
Manual workers	$70
Nonlabor force	$49

By Size of Household

Single person	$34
Two-person family	$52
Three-person family	$64
Four-person family	$77
Five-person-or-more family	$98

*Farm families were excluded from the survey since many farmers raise their own food.

Note: The 1981 Gallup Poll audit of weekly food expenditures shows the median amount spent by a representative (nonfarm) U.S. household is now $62 per week, the highest figure since the Gallup Poll began charting food expenditures in 1937 and almost six times the $11 recorded in the initial audit. The latest figure represents a $3 increase over the $59 median amount reported last year.

During the twenty-year period between 1949 and 1969, the figure grew from $25 per week to $33 per week, an increase of only 32%. However, during the 1970s the increase was a dramatic 56%—from $34 in 1970 to $53 in 1979.

In the past, food costs have taken a bigger

bite out of the family budget of easterners than of people living in other regions. But last year the West, previously a relatively inexpensive region in terms of food costs, caught up with the eastern median, with food bills skyrocketing from $51 per week to $62.

The following is the trend since the inception of the cost-of-living survey in 1937:

Weekly Food Expenditures**

	Median average
1981	$62
1980	$59
1979	$53
1978	$50
1975	$47
1973	$37
1970	$34
1966	$29
1964	$27
1959	$29
1954	$25
1953	$25
1949	$25
1948	$25
1947	$21
1946	$17
1942	$11
1937	$11

**Nonfarm families

MARCH 15
COST OF LIVING

Interviewing Date: 1/30–2/2; 2/13–16/81
Survey #168-G; #169-G

What is the smallest amount of money a family of four (husband, wife, and two children) needs each week to get along in this community?

	Median average
National	$277*

By Education

College	$300
High school	$252
Grade school	$202

By Region

East	$298
Midwest	$251
South	$252
West	$300

By Community Size

One million and over	$301
500,000–999,999	$300
50,000–499,999	$298
2,500–49,999	$249
Under 2,500; rural	$250

By Income

$25,000 and over	$301
$20,000–$24,999	$299
$15,000–$19,999	$274
$10,000–$14,999	$251
$5,000–$9,999	$225
Under $5,000	$249

By Occupation

Professional and business	$300
Clerical and sales	$275
Manual workers	$252
Nonlabor force	$250

What is the smallest amount of money your family needs each week to get along in this community?

	Median average
National	$248*

By Education

College	$298
High school	$219
Grade school	$151

By Region

East	$250
Midwest	$202
South	$202
West	$250

By Community Size

One million and over	$276
500,000–999,999	$249
50,000–499,999	$249
2,500–49,999	$200
Under 2,500; rural	$202

By Size of Household

Single person	$127
Two-person family	$200
Three-person family	$250
Four-person family	$299
Five-person-or-more family	$301

*Farm families were excluded from both the above surveys since many farmers raise their own food.

Note: The American people now believe it takes at least $277 per week for a husband, wife, and two children to make ends meet. This record high median amount represents a $27 increase, almost 11% higher than the 1980 figure of $250.

According to the Consumer Price Index (CPI), since 1980 the cost of living rose 12.5%. Similarly, the public's 1980 estimate of the minimum amount needed for a four-person family to get by was 12% higher than the $223 recorded in 1979, compared to a 13% increase as measured by the CPI.

Whether the Reagan administration's controversial "supply-side" economic program will accomplish its desired goal of stemming the inflationary spiral remains to be seen. Earlier Gallup surveys have indicated that the public is hopeful but somewhat skeptical whether this can be done.

That inflation looms large as one of the primary concerns of the American people is evidenced by the fact that 73% of the public currently cite inflation and the high cost of living

as the most important problem facing the nation. This is the highest proportion since the Gallup Poll began these measurements thirty-five years ago. Unemployment, the national problem mentioned second most often after inflation, is named by only 8% of the public.

In 1937, when the Gallup Poll first surveyed Americans' perceptions of weekly living costs for a family of four, the median response was $30. After World War II in 1947, the figure climbed to $43, but it did not hit three-digit proportions until 1967, when the median estimate was $101.

The recent survey findings indicate that inflation has hit home in varying degrees in the different sections of the country. In the Midwest and South the median estimates are $251 and $252, respectively, practically unchanged since 1980. On the other hand, easterners and westerners feel it takes approximately $300 to subsist from week to week, up roughly 20% since last year.

The type of community in which Americans live also contributes to their perceptions of living costs. Residents of the nation's central cities say it takes $242 a week to keep a family of four going. People living in the generally wealthier suburban areas report that a family requires $301 weekly. And for those who live in rural areas the median estimate is $250.

Highlights of the national trend since the inception of the cost-of-living survey in 1937 are as follows:

Minimum Amount Needed for a Family of Four*

1981	$277
1980	$250
1979	$223
1978	$201
1977	$199
1976	$177
1975	$161
1973	$149
1970	$126
1967	$101
1964	$81

1961	$84
1957	$72
1953	$60
1950	$50
1947	$43
1937	$30

*Nonfarm families

And the following figures show the rapid growth since 1977 in the weekly minimum amount needed for respondents' own family expenditures:

Minimum Amount Needed for Own Family*

	Median average
1981	$248
1980	$203
1979	$199
1978	$198
1977	$152

*Nonfarm families

MARCH 17
PRESIDENT REAGAN

Interviewing Date: 3/13–16/81
Survey #170-G

Do you approve or disapprove of the way Reagan is handling his job as president?

Approve.............................. 60%
Disapprove 24
No opinion 16

By Sex
Male

Approve.............................. 65%
Disapprove 22
No opinion 13

Female

Approve.............................. 55%
Disapprove 26
No opinion 19

By Race
White

Approve.............................. 65%
Disapprove 21
No opinion 14

Nonwhite

Approve.............................. 22%
Disapprove 49
No opinion 29

By Education
College

Approve.............................. 68%
Disapprove 21
No opinion 11

High School

Approve.............................. 60%
Disapprove 22
No opinion 18

Grade School

Approve.............................. 40%
Disapprove 39
No opinion 21

By Region
East

Approve.............................. 55%
Disapprove 24
No opinion 21

Midwest

Approve.............................. 61%
Disapprove 22
No opinion 17

South

Approve	63%
Disapprove	23
No opinion	14

West

Approve	58%
Disapprove	29
No opinion	13

By Age
18–29 Years

Approve	56%
Disapprove	28
No opinion	16

30–49 Years

Approve	63%
Disapprove	22
No opinion	15

50 Years and Over

Approve	58%
Disapprove	24
No opinion	18

By Income
$25,000 and Over

Approve	71%
Disapprove	18
No opinion	11

$20,000–$24,999

Approve	69%
Disapprove	16
No opinion	15

$15,000–$19,999

Approve	61%
Disapprove	26
No opinion	13

$10,000–$14,999

Approve	56%
Disapprove	27
No opinion	17

$5,000–$9,999

Approve	45%
Disapprove	33
No opinion	22

Under $5,000

Approve	37%
Disapprove	38
No opinion	25

By Politics
Republicans

Approve	87%
Disapprove	5
No opinion	8

Democrats

Approve	41%
Disapprove	39
No opinion	20

Independents

Approve	61%
Disapprove	22
No opinion	17

By Religion
Protestants

Approve	62%
Disapprove	24
No opinion	14

Catholics

Approve	58%
Disapprove	22
No opinion	20

By Occupation

Professional and Business

Approve.............................69%
Disapprove 21
No opinion 10

Clerical and Sales

Approve.............................49%
Disapprove 32
No opinion 19

Manual Workers

Approve.............................57%
Disapprove 25
No opinion 18

Nonlabor Force

Approve.............................56%
Disapprove 24
No opinion 20

By Community Size

One Million and Over

Approve.............................53%
Disapprove 30
No opinion 17

500,000–999,999

Approve.............................51%
Disapprove 28
No opinion 21

50,000–499,999

Approve.............................58%
Disapprove 26
No opinion 16

2,500–49,999

Approve.............................64%
Disapprove 22
No opinion 14

Under 2,500; Rural

Approve.............................66%
Disapprove 18
No opinion 16

Note: Despite generally broad public support for his economic proposals, President Ronald Reagan receives only a modest vote of confidence from his fellow Americans, with 60% now approving of his handling of his presidential duties, compared to 24% who disapprove and 16% undecided.

This rating is lower than those given other elected chief executives two months after they took office. For example, greater proportions of Americans approved of Jimmy Carter (75%), Richard Nixon (65%), John Kennedy (73%), and Dwight Eisenhower (67%) two months after their inauguration, compared to President Reagan's current ratings. Presidents Gerald Ford, Lyndon Johnson, and Harry Truman were excluded from this analysis because they assumed the presidency under unusual circumstances.

Not only does President Reagan's approval rating suffer by comparison with his predecessors but also the proportion of the public who disapproves of his job performance has grown at a faster rate than his approval rating. In the Gallup Poll's first assessment of Reagan's popularity, conducted ten days after inauguration day, a scant 51% majority of the public approved of his performance in office, while 13% disapproved and 36% withheld judgment. Two weeks later, shortly before the February 18 announcement of his plan for revitalizing the nation's economy, the president's approval rating had climbed to 55%, but the number of those who disapproved (18%) also rose.

Thus, from the initial Gallup measurement in late January–early February to the current mid-March assessment, Reagan's popularity has risen 9 percentage points. The proportion of the public, however, who disapproves of his actions has grown by 11 points, with a concomitant decline of 20 points in the undecided vote.

Understandably, the voter groups that heavily

supported Reagan in last November's presidential election tend to be those in which higher levels of job approval are now found. For example, the Gallup Poll's postelection analysis showed that proportionately more men than women voted for Reagan and his current approval rating among men is significantly higher than it is among women.

Similarly, the college-educated segment of the electorate backed Reagan to a greater extent than did persons with less formal education, and the president's current approval rating stands at 68% among persons who attended college, compared to 40% approval from those whose education ended at the grade-school level.

However, proportionately more westerners gave Reagan their vote than now voice confidence in his stewardship of the country. On the other hand, comparatively few voters under thirty years of age backed President Reagan at the polls, while his approval rating among this group exactly matches the national figure.

A comparison of Reagan's current standing among persons claiming affiliation with one of the three major political entities with Carter's approval ratings in mid-March 1977 shows that Reagan has far less support from Democrats and independents than President Carter did from Republicans and independents.

Presidential Approval Ratings

	Reagan	Carter
Republicans	87%	60%
Democrats	41	84
Independents	61	73

MARCH 19
RELIGION/PERSONAL HAPPINESS

Interviewing Date: 1/30–2/2/81
Survey #168-G

Do you believe that religion can answer all or most of today's problems, or that religion is largely old-fashioned and out of date?

Can answer problems 65%
Out of date 15
No opinion 20

By Sex
Male

Can answer problems 58%
Out of date 20
No opinion 22

Female

Can answer problems 71%
Out of date 10
No opinion 19

By Race
White

Can answer problems 64%
Out of date 15
No opinion 21

Nonwhite

Can answer problems 71%
Out of date 13
No opinion 16

By Education
College

Can answer problems 57%
Out of date 15
No opinion 28

High School

Can answer problems 67%
Out of date 16
No opinion 17

Grade School

Can answer problems 73%
Out of date 13
No opinion 14

By Age

18–24 Years

Can answer problems 62%
Out of date 18
No opinion 20

25–29 Years

Can answer problems 56%
Out of date 20
No opinion 24

30–49 Years

Can answer problems 60%
Out of date 18
No opinion 22

50 Years and Over

Can answer problems 73%
Out of date 10
No opinion 17

By Income

$15,000 and Over

Can answer problems 62%
Out of date 15
No opinion 23

Under $15,000

Can answer problems 69%
Out of date 15
No opinion 16

By Religion

Protestants

Can answer problems 72%
Out of date 8
No opinion 20

Catholics

Can answer problems 64%
Out of date 17
No opinion 19

Note: The following table compares the percentages in various population groups who currently believe religion can answer today's problems, along with the percentages who held this opinion in 1957 and 1974:

Those Who Say Religion Can Answer Problems

	1981	1974	1957
National	65%	62%	81%

By Sex

Male	58	54	75
Female	71	70	86

By Education

College	57	52	78
High school	67	63	83
Grade school	73	73	79

By Age

18–29 years.	58	55	84
30–49 years.	60	64	80
50 years and over	73	66	79

By Religion

Protestants	72	70	83
Catholics	64	58	83

Generally speaking, how happy would you say you are: very happy, fairly happy, or not too happy?

Very happy 46%
Fairly happy 45
Not too happy. 8
Not sure. 1

By Sex

Male

Very happy 44%
Fairly happy 47
Not too happy. 8
Not sure. 1

Female

Very happy	47%
Fairly happy	44
Not too happy	8
Not sure	1

By Race

White

Very happy	47%
Fairly happy	44
Not too happy	8
Not sure	1

Nonwhite

Very happy	32%
Fairly happy	51
Not too happy	14
Not sure	3

By Education

College

Very happy	49%
Fairly happy	46
Not too happy	4
Not sure	1

High School

Very happy	44%
Fairly happy	46
Not too happy	9
Not sure	1

Grade School

Very happy	44%
Fairly happy	41
Not too happy	13
Not sure	2

By Age

18–24 Years

Very happy	45%
Fairly happy	48
Not too happy	6
Not sure	1

25–29 Years

Very happy	40%
Fairly happy	49
Not too happy	10
Not sure	1

30–49 Years

Very happy	42%
Fairly happy	49
Not too happy	8
Not sure	1

50 Years and Over

Very happy	51%
Fairly happy	39
Not too happy	9
Not sure	1

By Income

$15,000 and Over

Very happy	49%
Fairly happy	46
Not too happy	5
Not sure	*

Under $15,000

Very happy	41%
Fairly happy	44
Not too happy	13
Not sure	2

By Religion

Protestants

Very happy	48%
Fairly happy	42
Not too happy	9
Not sure	1

Catholics

Very happy	40%
Fairly happy	54
Not too happy	6
Not sure	*

Those Who Say Religion
Can Answer Problems

Very happy 49%
Fairly happy 43
Not too happy. 8
Not sure . . . . *

Those Who Say Religion
Is Out of Date

Very happy 31%
Fairly happy 56
Not too happy. 12
Not sure 1

*Less than 1%

Note: Two out of three Americans (65%) believe that religion can answer all or most of today's problems, while only one person in seven (15%) clearly doubts the relevance of religion in the modern world and 20% do not express an opinion.

When this question was first asked in 1957, 81% of the public expressed faith in religion's ability to provide answers for contemporary problems, while only 7% felt it was out of date. The proportion of believers dropped sharply to 62% in a 1974 survey. Thus the current findings indicate that public opinion on the relevance of religion has at least leveled since 1974.

This general period also saw other key indicators of religious behavior and attitudes register declines. For example, the proportion of Americans who claimed to be members of a church or synagogue dropped from 73% in the late 1950s to 68% in 1976. And the percentage saying they regularly attend religious services declined from the 50% level to around 40%.

Women, persons with a high-school education or less, and residents of the Midwest and South have been more likely to believe in religion's relevance, according to each of the three Gallup surveys in which this question was asked. The modest national upturn in belief since 1974 has been more pronounced among easterners (up 8 percentage points), nonwhites (up 8 points), older persons (up 7 points), and Roman Catholics (up 6 points).

Gallup findings also show that persons who feel religion can answer today's problems are more likely to say they are very happy than are those who believe religion is outmoded.

MARCH 26
EL SALVADOR SITUATION

Interviewing Date: 3/13–16/81
Survey #170-G

Have you heard or read about the situation in El Salvador?

Yes 84%
No 14
Not sure 2

From what you know about the situation, which side is the United States backing— the government of El Salvador, or those who are opposed to the government?

Government of El Salvador (correct) 74%
Those opposed to the government 8
Not sure 18

Asked of those who had heard or read about the situation in El Salvador and who knew that the United States is supporting the government of El Salvador (62% of the sample): How likely do you think it is that the U.S. involvement in El Salvador could turn into a situation like Vietnam—that is, that the United States would become more and more deeply involved as time goes on? Would you say this is very likely, fairly likely, not very likely, or not at all likely?

Very likely. 19%
Fairly likely. 19
Not very likely 15
Not at all likely. 7
Don't know 2
                                        62%*

By Education
College

Very likely	18%
Fairly likely	25
Not very likely	22
Not at all likely	11
Don't know	1
	77%*

High School

Very likely	20%
Fairly likely	17
Not very likely	12
Not at all likely	6
Don't know	2
	57%*

Grade School

Very likely	19%
Fairly likely	13
Not very likely	10
Not at all likely	5
Don't know	3
	50%*

By Age
18–24 Years

Very likely	15%
Fairly likely	19
Not very likely	15
Not at all likely	3
Don't know	1
	53%*

25–29 Years

Very likely	22%
Fairly likely	25
Not very likely	14
Not at all likely	4
Don't know	**
	65%*

30–49 Years

Very likely	20%
Fairly likely	19
Not very likely	16
Not at all likely	8
Don't know	1
	64%*

50 Years and Over

Very likely	20%
Fairly likely	16
Not very likely	15
Not at all likely	9
Don't know	3
	63%*

By Politics
Republicans

Very likely	9%
Fairly likely	20
Not very likely	25
Not at all likely	13
Don't know	2
	69%*

Democrats

Very likely	23%
Fairly likely	18
Not very likely	9
Not at all likely	6
Don't know	2
	58%*

Independents

Very likely	23%
Fairly likely	20
Not very likely	14
Not at all likely	5
Don't know	2
	64%*

Those Who Voted for Carter in 1980

Very likely	24%
Fairly likely	20

Not very likely 10
Not at all likely 4
Don't know 2
                                              60%*

Those Who Voted for Reagan in 1980

Very likely 15%
Fairly likely 18
Not very likely 22
Not at all likely 14
Don't know 2
                                              71%*

Those Who Voted for Anderson in 1980

Very likely 15%
Fairly likely 35
Not very likely 11
Not at all likely 3
Don't know 1
                                              65%*

Those Who Approve of the Way Reagan Is Handling His Job As President

Very likely 16%
Fairly likely 19
Not very likely 20
Not at all likely 9
Don't know 2
                                              66%*

Those Who Disapprove of the Way Reagan Is Handling His Job As President

Very likely 27%
Fairly likely 21
Not very likely 6
Not at all likely 2
Don't know 2
                                              58%*

*Those who had heard or read about the situation in El Salvador.
**Less than 1%

Also asked of those who had heard or read about the situation in El Salvador and who knew that the United States is supporting the government of El Salvador (62% of the sample): Do you think the United States should help the current government in El Salvador, or stay completely out of the situation?

Help the government 27%
Stay completely out 29
Don't know 6
                                              62%*

By Education
College

Help the government 38%
Stay completely out 32
Don't know 7
                                              77%*

High School

Help the government 23%
Stay completely out 29
Don't know 5
                                              57%*

Grade School

Help the government 22%
Stay completely out 25
Don't know 3
                                              50%*

By Age
18–24 Years

Help the government 22%
Stay completely out 26
Don't know 5
                                              53%*

25–29 Years

Help the government 29%
Stay completely out 30
Don't know 6
                                              65%*

30–49 Years

Help the government 26%
Stay completely out 32
Don't know 6
                                                    64%*

50 Years and Over

Help the government 30%
Stay completely out 28
Don't know 5
                                                    63%*

By Politics
Republicans

Help the government 44%
Stay completely out 19
Don't know 6
                                                    69%*

Democrats

Help the government 19%
Stay completely out 33
Don't know 6
                                                    58%*

Independents

Help the government 25%
Stay completely out 34
Don't know 5
                                                    64%*

Those Who Voted for Carter in 1980

Help the government 21%
Stay completely out 34
Don't know 6
                                                    60%*

Those Who Voted for Reagan in 1980

Help the government 41%
Stay completely out 25
Don't know 6
                                                    72%*

Those Who Voted for Anderson in 1980

Help the government 22%
Stay completely out 39
Don't know 4
                                                    65%*

Those Who Approve of the Way Reagan Is Handling His Job As President

Help the government 35%
Stay completely out 26
Don't know 6
                                                    67%*

Those Who Disapprove of the Way Reagan Is Handling His Job As President

Help the government 11%
Stay completely out 42
Don't know 4
                                                    57%*

*Those who had heard or read about the situation in El Salvador.

Asked of the informed group who thought that the United States should help the government of El Salvador (27% of the total sample): Which of these types of aid [respondents were handed a card with options listed] do you think the United States should provide to the government of El Salvador?

Economic aid 19%
Military advisers 16
Military supplies 18
American troops 2
Don't know . . . . **
                                                    55%***

**Less than 1%
***Total adds to more than 27% due to multiple responses.

Note: Two out of every three informed American fears that the situation in El Salvador will develop into another Vietnam, with about equal numbers saying it is very or fairly likely that the United States will become more deeply involved as times goes on.

The United States is officially supporting the current Salvador regime of President José Napoleón Duarte, providing both substantial economic aid as well as military supplies and advisers. According to testimony by Secretary of State Alexander Haig on Capitol Hill last week, El Salvador is the second of four countries on a Communist "hit list" of Central American nations targeted for subversion.

MARCH 27
EL SALVADOR SITUATION

Interviewing Date: 3/13–16/81
Survey #170-G

Asked of those who had heard or read about the situation in El Salvador and who knew that the United States is supporting the government of El Salvador (62% of the sample): Do you approve or disapprove of the way Reagan is handling the situation in El Salvador?

Approve............................27%
Disapprove 25
No opinion 10
                                   62%*

By Education
College

Approve............................34%
Disapprove 34
No opinion 10
                                   78%*

High School

Approve............................24%
Disapprove 22
No opinion 10
                                   56%*

Grade School

Approve............................24%
Disapprove 19
No opinion 7
                                   50%*

By Age
18–24 Years

Approve............................17%
Disapprove 26
No opinion 9
                                   52%*

25–29 Years

Approve............................24%
Disapprove 33
No opinion 7
                                   64%*

30–49 Years

Approve............................29%
Disapprove 25
No opinion 10
                                   64%*

50 Years and Over

Approve............................30%
Disapprove 23
No opinion 10
                                   63%*

By Politics
Republicans

Approve............................44%
Disapprove 13
No opinion 12
                                   69%*

Democrats

Approve............................20%
Disapprove 27
No opinion 11
                                   58%*

Independents

Approve...........................22%
Disapprove 35
No opinion 7
                                   64%*

Those Who Voted for Carter in 1980

Approve...........................18%
Disapprove 33
No opinion 9
                                   60%*

Those Who Voted for Reagan in 1980

Approve...........................42%
Disapprove 16
No opinion 13
                                   71%*

Those Who Voted for Anderson in 1980

Approve...........................13%
Disapprove 48
No opinion 3
                                   64%*

Those Who Approve of the Way Reagan Is Handling His Job As President

Approve...........................36%
Disapprove 21
No opinion 10
                                   67%*

Those Who Disapprove of the Way Reagan Is Handling His Job As President

Approve...........................10%
Disapprove 40
No opinion 7
                                   57%*

*Those who had heard or read about the situation in El Salvador.

Also asked of those who had heard or read about the situation in El Salvador and who knew that the United States is supporting the government of El Salvador (62% of the sample): Do you, yourself, agree or disagree with the U.S. position?

Agree.............................29%
Disagree...........................25
No opinion 8
                                   62%*

By Education
College

Agree.............................37%
Disagree...........................30
No opinion 11
                                   78%*

High School

Agree.............................26%
Disagree...........................23
No opinion 7
                                   56%*

Grade School

Agree.............................25%
Disagree...........................17
No opinion 8
                                   50%*

By Age
18–24 Years

Agree.............................22%
Disagree...........................25
No opinion 5
                                   52%*

25–29 Years

Agree.............................26%
Disagree...........................31
No opinion 7
                                   64%*

30–49 Years

Agree.............................28%
Disagree...........................27
No opinion 9
                            64%*

50 Years and Over

Agree.............................34%
Disagree...........................20
No opinion 9
                            63%*

By Politics
Republicans

Agree.............................48%
Disagree...........................13
No opinion 8
                            69%*

Democrats

Agree.............................24%
Disagree...........................26
No opinion 8
                            58%*

Independents

Agree.............................22%
Disagree...........................33
No opinion 9
                            64%*

Those Who Voted for Carter in 1980

Agree.............................20%
Disagree...........................31
No opinion 9
                            60%*

Those Who Voted for Reagan in 1980

Agree.............................46%
Disagree...........................17
No opinion 8
                            71%*

Those Who Voted for Anderson in 1980

Agree.............................17%
Disagree...........................38
No opinion 9
                            64%*

Those Who Approve of the Way Reagan Is Handling His Job As President

Agree.............................38%
Disagree...........................21
No opinion 8
                            67%*

Those Who Disapprove of the Way Reagan Is Handling His Job As President

Agree.............................14%
Disagree...........................37
No opinion 6
                            57%*

*Those who had heard or read about the situation in El Salvador.

Note: Americans are sharply divided on all three facets of the situation in El Salvador: U.S. involvement in El Salvador, President Reagan's handling of the situation, and American policy regarding that nation. Currently, 29% of the public believes that the United States should stay out of the El Salvador situation, 27% think we should help that nation's government, and 6% express no opinion. The balance (38%) are uninformed.

Most likely to agree with the current U.S. policy on El Salvador and to approve of Reagan's handling of the situation are Republicans, those who voted for Reagan, and persons aged fifty and over. Least supportive are the young (under thirty), Democrats, and Anderson voters.

On this issue there is also a sharp split between the sexes. Among men approval of Reagan's handling of El Salvador is 37% compared to 20% for women. Men are likewise more inclined toward agreement with U.S. policy toward the Central American nation.

These differences are not surprising in light of the fact that men voted overwhelmingly for Reagan in the 1980 election, whereas among women the president's margin was much narrower.

APRIL 4
CRIME

Interviewing Date: 1/9–12/81
Survey #167-G

Is there more crime in this area than there was a year ago, or less?

More 54%
Less 8
Same (volunteered) 29
No opinion 9

By Sex
Male

More 51%
Less 9
Same (volunteered) 30
No opinion 10

Female

More 56%
Less 7
Same (volunteered) 28
No opinion 9

By Race
White

More 54%
Less 8
Same (volunteered) 29
No opinion 9

Nonwhite

More 48%
Less 12
Same (volunteered) 26
No opinion 14

By Age
18–29 Years

More 47%
Less 11
Same (volunteered) 31
No opinion 11

30–49 Years

More 54%
Less 8
Same (volunteered) 28
No opinion 10

50 Years and Over

More 58%
Less 6
Same (volunteered) 28
No opinion 8

By Community Size
One Million and Over

More 51%
Less 7
Same (volunteered) 30
No opinion 12

500,000–999,999

More 44%
Less 13
Same (volunteered) 32
No opinion 11

50,000–499,999

More 53%
Less 9
Same (volunteered) 29
No opinion 9

2,500–49,999

More 65%
Less 8
Same (volunteered) 18
No opinion 9

Under 2,500; Rural

More	54%
Less	7
Same (volunteered)	32
No opinion	7

Is there any area right around here—that is, within a mile—where you would be afraid to walk alone at night?

	Yes
National	45%

By Sex

Male	28%
Female	62

By Race

White	45%
Nonwhite	52

By Age

18–29 years	43%
30–49 years	42
50 years and over	50

By Community Size

One million and over	55%
500,000–999,999	49
50,000–499,999	52
2,500–49,999	43
Under 2,500; rural	33

How about at home at night—do you feel safe and secure, or not?

	Unsafe and unsecure
National	16%

By Sex

Male	12%
Female	19

By Race

White	15%
Nonwhite	20

By Age

18–29 years	17%
30–49 years	16
50 years and over	16

By Community Size

One million and over	21%
500,000–999,999	10
50,000–499,999	16
2,500–49,999	16
Under 2,500; rural	14

During the last twelve months have any of these happened to you? [Respondents were handed a card listing various crimes.]

	Yes
Money or property stolen	11%
Property vandalized	11
Home broken into or attempt made	7
Car stolen	2
Assaulted or mugged; money or property taken by force or threat of force	3

By Sex
Male

Money or property stolen	13%
Property vandalized	11
Home broken into or attempt made	7
Car stolen	3
Assaulted or mugged; money or property taken by force or threat of force	2

Female

Money or property stolen	10%
Property vandalized	10
Home broken into or attempt made	8
Car stolen	1
Assaulted or mugged; money or property taken by force or threat of force	4

By Race
White

Money or property stolen	12%
Property vandalized	11
Home broken into or attempt made	7

Car stolen 2
Assaulted or mugged; money or property
   taken by force or threat of force 3

Nonwhite

Money or property stolen 8%
Property vandalized 6
Home broken into or attempt made 7
Car stolen 2
Assaulted or mugged; money or property
   taken by force or threat of force 3

By Age
18–29 Years

Money or property stolen 16%
Property vandalized 13
Home broken into or attempt made 11
Car stolen 3
Assaulted or mugged; money or property
   taken by force or threat of force 3

30–49 Years

Money or property stolen 13%
Property vandalized 15
Home broken into or attempt made 7
Car stolen 2
Assaulted or mugged; money or property
   taken by force or threat of force 3

50 Years and Over

Money or property stolen 6%
Property vandalized 6
Home broken into or attempt made 5
Car stolen 1
Assaulted or mugged; money or property
   taken by force or threat of force 3

By Community Size
One Million and Over

Money or property stolen 11%
Property vandalized 10
Home broken into or attempt made 9
Car stolen 3
Assaulted or mugged; money or property
   taken by force or threat of force 4

500,000–999,999

Money or property stolen 16%
Property vandalized 13
Home broken into or attempt made 5
Car stolen 1
Assaulted or mugged; money or property
   taken by force or threat of force 5

50,000–499,999

Money or property stolen 12%
Property vandalized 12
Home broken into or attempt made 9
Car stolen 2
Assaulted or mugged; money or property
   taken by force or threat of force 4

2,500–49,999

Money or property stolen 11%
Property vandalized 14
Home broken into or attempt made 7
Car stolen 2
Assaulted or mugged; money or property
   taken by force or threat of force 1

Under 2,500; Rural

Money or property stolen 9%
Property vandalized 8
Home broken into or attempt made 6
Car stolen 1
Assaulted or mugged; money or property
   taken by force or threat of force 1

Total of Sample Victimized At Least Once

National 23%

By Sex

Male 24%
Female 22

By Education

College 26%
High school 24
Grade school 12

By Region

East 25%
Midwest 19
South 21
West 31

By Age

18–29 years 30%
30–49 years 26
50 years and over 15

By Income

$25,000 and over 28%
$20,000–$24,999 25
$15,000–$19,999 21
$10,000–$14,999 21
$5,000–$9,999 22
Under $5,000 19

By Community Location

Central cities 28%
Suburbs 23
Rural areas 19

Asked of those who have been victimized during the last twelve months: Did you report this to the police, or not?

	Crime incidence	Reported to police
Money or property stolen...	11	6%
Property vandalized	11	7
Home broken into or attempt made	7	6
Car stolen	2	2
Assaulted or mugged; money or property taken by force or threat of force	3	2

Asked of the entire sample: Listed on this card are some things people do because of their concern over crime. Please tell me which, if any, of these things you, yourself, do or have done.

Lock residence at night 84%
Let neighbors know if absent 55

Keep residence lights on 46
Keep a dog for protection 20
Walk only with others in neighborhood
   at night 20
Bought gun for protection of residence
   or person 16
Had special locks installed 13
Carry weapon or other instrument
   for defense 11
Carry Mace or other repellent 7
Had burglar alarm installed 5
Carry whistle on person or in car 5
Belong to neighborhood crime watch 5
Other measures 8
                              295%*

*Total adds to more than 92% due to multiple responses.

Note: Even before the March 30 assassination attempt on President Ronald Reagan, the American people were deeply concerned about violence and crime in our society. A recent nationwide Gallup survey highlights this concern:

1. A 54% majority of Americans say there is more crime in their communities or neighborhoods than a year ago, with this perception common to each region of the nation and cities of all sizes. This represents a dramatic increase from four years ago when 43% reported a rise in crime in the area where they live. The sharpest jump recorded between the 1977 and 1981 surveys was in the West—from 44% to 63%.

Americans also see a change in the nature of crime. In a recent Gallup survey conducted for *Newsweek*, three out of four respondents expressed the belief that criminals today are more violent than they were five years ago.

2. A Gallup survey conducted for the National League of Cities showed crime to be uppermost in the minds of urban residents asked to name the top problem facing their neighborhoods. Twenty-five years ago crime was not even among the top ten problems named.

3. Fear of crime has grown, with 45% now saying that they are afraid to walk alone at night in their neighborhoods. The growth in fear is

most pronounced among residents of smaller communities, with 33% of persons living in small towns and villages or in rural areas saying they are afraid to venture out after dark in their neighborhoods. In addition, no fewer than one person in six admits to being fearful even behind the locked doors of his or her own home.

4. One U.S. household in four has been hit by crime at least once in the last twelve months, with either property stolen or a household member the victim of a physical assault. This represents an increase in victimization since the 1979 Gallup survey, when the proportion was closer to one in five. Most likely to have been victimized during the past year were younger adults, the college educated, those from higher-income families, persons living in the eastern and western regions of the nation, and residents of central cities.

That the actual crime situation in this country is more serious than FBI statistics indicate is reflected in these Gallup crime audits, since they measure not only reported crimes but also those that have not been reported to the police.

5. The vast majority of Americans now take crime preventive measures. People avoid going out alone at night and when they do they walk with friends. They stay away from dangerous areas even in the daytime. They carry all manner of weapons, including Mace or other forms of chemical repellent, and many keep a whistle on their person or in their cars. And 5% of the nation's adults, or a projected 8 million people, already have joined a neighborhood crime watch group, with 31% saying they would be willing to do so.

APRIL 6
CRIME

Interviewing Date: 1/9–12/81
Survey #167-G

> Asked of the 54% who said there is more crime than there was a year ago: In your opinion, why is there more crime in this area than there was a year ago?

Unemployment	21%
High cost of living	16
Lack of money; poverty	6
Judges too lenient	15
Inadequate police protection	11
Drugs; alcohol	18
Lack of parental guidance, discipline	12
Decline in morality; permissiveness	9
Dissatisfaction with life	2
Attitudes in our society (general)	2
Population increase; overcrowding	11
Other responses	6
Don't know	7
	136%*

*Total adds to more than 100% due to multiple responses.

Note: At no time in the nation's recent history have Americans been more concerned about the rising tide of crime and violence. Yet the Gallup Poll found no public consensus about the underlying reasons for this unprecedented surge in crime.

While the public has no panacea for stemming the crime rate, its perceptions of the causes seem to fall into four general classifications: 1) economic problems, 2) inadequate legal system, 3) general breakdown in public morality, and 4) demographic factors. There probably is no one dominant reason for today's alarming crime incidence. More likely it represents a coming together of many of these forces at one unfortunate time in the nation's history.

As reported, a 54% majority of Americans say there is more crime in their community than there was a year ago, a dramatic increase from a 1977 survey. Fear of crime has grown to the point that 45% of the public now say they are afraid to walk alone at night near where they live and as many as one in six admits being fearful even while at home.

An increase in victimization also has occurred, with almost one-fourth of Americans the victims of a serious crime. Virtually all survey participants (92%) report having taken some step to protect themselves from criminals—from the simple expedient of making sure the doors are locked (84%) to buying a gun for protection (16%).

First among the perceived causes for the wave of lawlessness are the many economic problems facing the nation, including the lack of jobs (particularly for young people), the country's general economic climate, and, simply, perpetrators' need for money. Second is the legal system and the failure of the police to detect crime and enforce the laws. Too many criminals get off without punishment and those who are sentenced receive punishment that is not severe enough. Third is the widely perceived breakdown of traditional moral standards and the absence of parental guidelines or discipline. Fourth, a considerable amount of responsibility for the crime upsurge is laid on the use of drugs and alcohol. Finally, at least some of the blame falls on demographic factors such as the nation's increased population, the housing shortage, and consequent overcrowding.

APRIL 12
ECONOMIC SITUATION

Interviewing Date: 3/13–16/81
Survey #170-G

The current inflation rate is now about 12%. By the end of 1981, what do you think the inflation rate will be?

15% or more........................ 35%
14% 10
13% 6
12% 15
11% 4
10% 12
9% or less 7
Don't know 11
    Median estimate: 13.5%

The current unemployment rate is now 7.3%. By the end of 1981, what do you think the unemployment rate will be?

10% or more........................ 28%
9% 13
8% 17

7% 15
6% 11
5% or less 7
Don't know 9
    Median estimate: 8.2%

Do you approve or disapprove of the way Reagan is dealing with inflation?

Approve............................ 56%
Disapprove 30
No opinion 14

By Sex
Male

Approve............................ 60%
Disapprove 27
No opinion 13

Female

Approve............................ 52%
Disapprove 32
No opinion 16

By Race
White

Approve............................ 61%
Disapprove 25
No opinion 14

Nonwhite

Approve............................ 22%
Disapprove 61
No opinion 17

By Education
College

Approve............................ 64%
Disapprove 24
No opinion 12

High School

Approve............................ 57%
Disapprove 31
No opinion 12

Grade School

Approve............................36%
Disapprove 37
No opinion 27

By Income
$25,000 and Over

Approve............................71%
Disapprove 21
No opinion 8

$20,000–$24,999

Approve............................59%
Disapprove 26
No opinion 15

$15,000–$19,999

Approve............................58%
Disapprove 30
No opinion 12

$10,000–$14,999

Approve............................49%
Disapprove 33
No opinion 18

$5,000–$9,999

Approve............................40%
Disapprove 37
No opinion 23

Under $5,000

Approve............................36%
Disapprove 47
No opinion 17

By Occupation
Professional and Business

Approve............................66%
Disapprove 27
No opinion 7

Clerical and Sales

Approve............................54%
Disapprove 36
No opinion 10

Manual Workers

Approve............................52%
Disapprove 33
No opinion 15

Nonlabor Force

Approve............................49%
Disapprove 25
No opinion 26

Do you approve or disapprove of the way Reagan is dealing with unemployment?

Approve............................40%
Disapprove 37
No opinion 23

By Sex
Male

Approve............................44%
Disapprove 34
No opinion 22

Female

Approve............................37%
Disapprove 39
No opinion 24

By Race
White

Approve............................44%
Disapprove 32
No opinion 24

Nonwhite

Approve............................15%
Disapprove 70
No opinion 15

By Education
College
Approve..43%
Disapprove 33
No opinion 24

High School
Approve..41%
Disapprove 37
No opinion 22

Grade School
Approve..31%
Disapprove 41
No opinion 28

By Age
18–24 Years
Approve..33%
Disapprove 47
No opinion 20

25–29 Years
Approve..35%
Disapprove 42
No opinion 23

30–49 Years
Approve..43%
Disapprove 36
No opinion 21

50 Years and Over
Approve..42%
Disapprove 31
No opinion 27

By Income
$25,000 and Over
Approve..51%
Disapprove 29
No opinion 20

$20,000–$24,999
Approve..46%
Disapprove 30
No opinion 24

$15,000–$19,999
Approve..40%
Disapprove 33
No opinion 27

$10,000–$14,999
Approve..33%
Disapprove 43
No opinion 24

$5,000–$9,999
Approve..31%
Disapprove 46
No opinion 23

Under $5,000
Approve..26%
Disapprove 52
No opinion 22

By Occupation
Professional and Business
Approve..44%
Disapprove 34
No opinion 22

Clerical and Sales
Approve..36%
Disapprove 49
No opinion 15

Manual Workers
Approve..38%
Disapprove 40
No opinion 22

Nonlabor Force

Approve............................38%
Disapprove 28
No opinion 34

Labor Union Families Only

Approve............................38%
Disapprove 41
No opinion 21

Nonlabor Union Families Only

Approve............................41%
Disapprove 35
No opinion 24

Do you approve or disapprove of the way Reagan is dealing with the energy situation?

Approve............................37%
Disapprove 39
No opinion 24

By Region

East

Approve............................35%
Disapprove 39
No opinion 26

Midwest

Approve............................41%
Disapprove 38
No opinion 21

South

Approve............................39%
Disapprove 36
No opinion 25

West

Approve............................32%
Disapprove 42
No opinion 26

Note: The misery index—the public's perceptions of what the inflation and unemployment rates will be at the end of this year—remains unchanged despite President Ronald Reagan's February 18 announcement of his administration's program for revitalizing the nation's economy.

In a mid-March Gallup Poll the public's estimate of the year-end inflation figure was 13.5%, virtually identical to the 13.6% recorded in a late-November survey. In contrast, Americans now predict that the unemployment situation will worsen by the end of 1981; their unemployment estimate now stands at 8.2% compared to 7.1% in November.

The Reagan economic program is seen by some economists as the only effective way to combat inflation, but the latest survey shows that Americans are skeptical. The luke-warm public reaction to Reagan's proposals suggests that any anticipation of a long-term reduction in inflation may have been offset by the immediate effect on consumers of the January decontrol of domestic crude oil prices, which led to sharply higher retail gasoline prices within a week.

Another factor may be public expectations that the unemployment rate will rise once the Reagan budget cuts are put into effect. Many economists believe that is one of the probable immediate consequences of the program.

Other evidence from the latest survey, conducted before the March 30 assassination attempt on President Reagan, shows that while Americans only moderately approve of the president's efforts to deal with inflation, he won even lower marks for his handling of the unemployment and energy situations.

The misery index was created in 1976 by presidential candidate Jimmy Carter to dramatize the failure of the Ford administration to improve the economy. Reagan, in turn, found the index an effective political weapon to use against President Carter during the 1980 campaign.

In the current survey, respondents were asked to estimate what the unemployment and inflation rates would be at the end of 1981 after being told the rates as of March. On the average, the public believes that the inflation rate will be between 13% and 14% and unemployment around 8%. The overall misery index was calculated by adding the two medians together.

A comparison of the November and March findings shows that increases in the unemployment rate are perceived by all major demographic groups, but they are most pronounced among nonwhites. The median response of this group in November was 7.6%, compared to 7% for whites. In the latest survey the median figure for nonwhites rose to 9.8%, while the comparable median for whites was 8.5%.

APRIL 13
THE FRAGILE MANDATE*

The public opinion polls are detecting troublesome signs for the Reagan administration: economic expectations are declining, the public seems increasingly uneasy about the Reagan economic program, and there is evidence that cutting the size of government and deregulating prices may have some unpopular consequences. A close reading of a recent poll suggests that the much-revered Reagan mandate may be more fragile than previously thought.

The president's popularity, when last measured by the *Washington Post*/ABC Poll just after the assassination attempt, showed him commanding a 73% approval rating. However, prior to the shooting the March Gallup Poll showed that increasing numbers of Americans were voicing disapproval of Reagan's job performance and his rating was significantly below those of other newly elected presidents two months after taking office.

To a certain extent the assassination attempt seems to have forestalled what was beginning to appear to be a declining curve in the president's popularity. While personal sympathy will fade as he recovers, it seems likely that the pre-assassination criticism and reservations may endure, if not grow, according to survey findings.

*This Gallup analysis was written by Andrew Kohut, president of the Gallup Organization Inc.

The Gallup Poll and the *Washington Post*/ABC Poll both showed that Americans have become more pessimistic about the economy since the president unveiled his package. As compared to a November survey, a recent Gallup Poll found no improvement in the public forecast of the inflation rate, and it also showed that the public has become much more pessimistic about unemployment.

The *Washington Post*/ABC Poll also found an even more pronounced decline in economic expectations, and it uncovered a sharp falloff in the percentage of Americans who feel that Reagan's tax reduction in the government spending program will lead to a decline in inflation. Only 49% expressed the view that the Reagan program will help end inflation, compared to 64% a month before.

Declining confidence in the ability of the president's program to deal with inflation could bring to a head public reservations about cutting government spending. One of the anomalies of public opinion about the program has been that while the public heartily endorsed the general idea of cutting government spending and agreed with Reagan and Office of Management and Budget Director David Stockman that government spending is the principal culprit in the spiraling inflation rate, almost all polls showed that when it came to many specific government programs the public wanted more, not less, government spending.

The *Newsweek* Poll tested the opinion of ten government spending programs and found that for only one program—food stamps—did a majority feel that the government spends too much money. And in only two others was the balance of opinion that the government spends too much, not too little. For the other spending programs the view was that the government spends either too little or the right amount.

The CBS/*New York Times* Poll asked a similar series of questions. Again, food stamps was the only program clearly defined as over-budgeted. On the other hand, the balance of opinion was that spending should be kept the same or increased for pollution control, defense, mass transit, and Social Security cost-of-living benefits. The public supports the principle of cutting government spending, but when it considers reductions on a program-by-program basis the public is reluctant to support cuts.

Reaction to possible cuts in popular programs undoubtedly had some bearing on increased disapproval of Reagan over the past few months. Gallup connected the president's popularity problems to a lower rate of approval among Democrats and Democratic groups who are most concerned about the proposed cuts. As compared to past presidents, the loyal opposition is opposing faster and harder than ever before.

Gallup findings also showed over 39% of the public disapproving of the president's energy policies and only 37% approving. This is an astonishingly low rating for a new president on any aspect of his job performance and suggests extreme public dissatisfaction with rising gasoline prices as an immediate consequence of price deregulation. The same poll showed Reagan's approval rating for handling the unemployment problem only at 40%.

An overall reading of these polls suggests that the Reagan mandate is beginning to be put into some perspective. The president continues to have the goodwill of the American people, but he certainly does not have the carte blanche support for his leadership policies that was assumed earlier by the administration and even by many Democrats.

Part of this logic was the view that the country had made a sharp ideological shift to the right with the election of Reagan. There has been no evidence of this, and it is now becoming quite clear that there is no ideological underpinning to promote support for the Reagan programs when they begin to personally affect voters. How the administration fares with the public in the immediate future will be dependent upon the extent to which these fears and concerns can be allayed, combined with a sense that the administration continues to have momentum in its attempt to deal with inflation through its economic program. The public's anxiety over changes in Washington can be mitigated by the feeling that something positive is being accomplished.

APRIL 16
ANTI-SEMITISM

Interviewing Date: 3/13–16/81
Survey #170-G

You will notice that the ten boxes on this card go from the highest position of +5 for someone or something you have a very favorable opinion of all the way down to the lowest position of −5 for someone or something you have a very unfavorable opinion of. How far up or how far down the scale would you rate Jews?

	Highly favorable (+5, +4)	Highly unfavorable (−4, −5)
National	39%	3%

By Sex

Male	37%	3%
Female	41	2

By Race

White	39%	2%
Nonwhite	44	6

By Education

College	35%	2%
High school	41	3
Grade school	41	2

By Region

East	44%	2%
Midwest	36	2
South	42	4
West	32	3

By Age

18–29 years	35%	3%
30–49 years	38	3
50 years and over	44	2

By Income

$25,000 and over	38%	1%
$20,000–$24,999	37	3
$15,000–$19,999	44	5

$10,000–$14,999	39	2
$5,000–$9,999	41	3
Under $5,000	38	3

By Religion

Protestants	39%	2%
Catholics.	46	2

By Occupation

Professional and business	40%	1%
Clerical and sales	39	3
Manual workers.	40	3
Nonlabor force.	38	2

By Community Size

One million and over . . .	36%	1%
500,000–999,999	39	5
50,000–499,999	44	2
2,500–49,999	43	4
Under 2,500; rural	36	2

Note: The recent rash of anti-Semitic incidents in various parts of the nation does not appear to be symptomatic of increased prejudice toward Jews in the United States. On the contrary, positive attitudes have shown a marked increase in recent years, according to a variety of Gallup Poll measurements.

Further evidence of increased religious tolerance is seen from earlier Gallup Poll findings that show steady and marked declines in the proportions of persons who have feelings of animosity toward Jews. For example, the percentage of both Catholics and Protestants who say they have had unpleasant experiences that caused them to dislike Jews was on a steady downtrend between 1952 and 1979, the last time the measurement was taken. In addition, a decline was found in the percentage of both Catholics and Protestants who feel Jews are becoming too powerful in the United States.

Results of further survey questions show the trend in attitudes of Protestants and Catholics toward Jews:

Have you or your family ever had any unpleasant personal experiences that might have made you dislike Jews?

Views of Protestants

	Yes
1979.	2%
1965.	5
1952.	8

Views of Catholics

1979.	2%
1965.	5
1952.	6

Do you think the Jews are trying to get too much power in the United States, or not?

Views of Protestants

	Yes
1979.	12%
1965.	14
1952.	35

Views of Catholics

1979.	13%
1965.	12
1952.	33

Further evidence that American society is becoming more tolerant, or accepting, in recent decades can be seen in the changing attitudes toward interfaith marriages. Between 1968 and 1978 the proportion of Americans who said they approve of marriages between Jews and non-Jews rose from 59% to 69%.

Gallup surveys also have shown that the climate for Jews seeking political leadership roles has never been more favorable than it is at the present time. The percentage who said they would vote for a Jew for president was 46% in the first survey in 1937, compared to 82% in 1978.

One of the key factors in the growth of religious tolerance in U.S. society has been the increase in the proportion of the populace with college training. This proportion has more than tripled since the Gallup Poll was founded in

1935. The college-educated segment in each survey consistently has been found to be more tolerant than those with less formal education.

Despite the reported cumulative survey evidence, which shows an increase in goodwill toward Jews on a broad national basis, random anti-Semitic incidents (as well as acts directed against Christian churches and cemeteries) may be growing in numbers.

APRIL 19
URBAN PROBLEMS

Interviewing Date: November–December 1980
Special Survey*

Asked in cities containing more than 50,000 inhabitants: If you had the chance, would you like to move away from this city, or not?

Yes................................36%
No.................................55
Not sure........................... 9

By Race
White

Yes................................37%
No.................................56
Not sure........................... 7

Nonwhite

Yes................................30%
No.................................51
Not sure..........................19

By Education
College

Yes................................36%
No.................................56
Not sure........................... 8

High School

Yes................................37%
No.................................54
Not sure........................... 9

Grade School

Yes................................30%
No.................................58
Not sure..........................12

By Region
East

Yes................................37%
No.................................53
Not sure..........................10

Midwest

Yes................................37%
No.................................51
Not sure..........................12

South

Yes................................32%
No.................................60
Not sure........................... 8

West

Yes................................37%
No.................................59
Not sure........................... 4

By Age
18–34 Years

Yes................................46%
No.................................44
Not sure..........................10

35–49 Years

Yes................................35%
No.................................58
Not sure........................... 7

50 Years and Over

Yes................................46%
No.................................44
Not sure..........................10

*This study was sponsored by the Charles F. Kettering and Charles Stewart Mott Foundations and the National League of Cities.

Asked of those who replied in the affirmative: Why do you want to move away from this city—that is, what things about this city make you want to move away?

High crime rate.......................24%
Overcrowding........................16
Unemployment.......................12
Bad climate..........................11
Pollution 8
Housing 7
Traffic congestion.................... 7
Poor schools 6
High taxes........................... 6
Noise 6

Note: If America's urban residents had their wish, more than one-third would move away from the city in which they live. And the most frequently mentioned reason for wanting to relocate is crime, cited by almost half the residents of cities with a population of one million and over.

Underscoring the statistic that many of the nation's city dwellers would like to move away is that only 15% of the residents of communities under 50,000 population express the desire to move.

Since a 1977 survey little change has occurred in the proportion of urban residents reporting they would like to move. Nor was any major change noted in the demographic background of those wishing to leave.

Those residents expressing a desire to leave their city represent essentially the same socio-economic groups who have been moving away for the last three decades and whom the cities can least afford to lose. These are the younger, better educated, and more affluent residents, who provide the largest share of tax revenue, as well as most of the people needed to fill public and private leadership roles. Conversely, those least likely to want to move are the older, less well educated, less affluent population segments, including the so-called public-service dependent groups such as the retired and the unemployed.

The following shows the proportions of urban residents who in two previous surveys cited crime and overcrowding as reasons for wanting to move:

	Crime	Overcrowding
Urban Residents		
1980	24%	16%
1977	18	25
Central City Residents		
1980	30%	13%
1977	20	25
Suburban Residents		
1980	14%	21%
1977	14	23

Undoubtedly contributing to the desire to leave the cities is the feeling that they have declined as desirable places to live and are not likely to improve in the future. Again, it is in the nation's largest cities, those experiencing the biggest problems, in which residents are most apt to perceive a decline.

When the residents of large cities were asked to rate their own city as a place to live, on a scale from zero to ten, the figures did not vary significantly from those recorded in the 1977 study:

City Ratings—One Million and Over

	1980	1977
Five years ago	6.3%	6.4%
Today	5.6	5.8
Five years from now	5.6	5.4

APRIL 23
GUN CONTROL

Interviewing Date: 4/3–6/81
Survey #171-G

In Massachusetts a law requires that a person who carries a gun outside his home must have a license to do so. Would you approve or disapprove of having such a law in your state?

Approve..............................81%
Disapprove 17
Don't know.......................... 2

By Sex
Male
Approve..........................77%
Disapprove 21
Don't know 2

Female
Approve..........................84%
Disapprove 13
Don't know 3

By Race
White
Approve..........................80%
Disapprove 17
Don't know 3

Nonwhite
Approve..........................86%
Disapprove 12
Don't know 2

By Education
College
Approve..........................81%
Disapprove 18
Don't know 1

High School
Approve..........................81%
Disapprove 16
Don't know 3

Grade School
Approve..........................80%
Disapprove 17
Don't know 3

By Region
East
Approve..........................88%
Disapprove 8
Don't know 4

Midwest
Approve..........................81%
Disapprove 17
Don't know 2

South
Approve..........................76%
Disapprove 21
Don't know 3

West
Approve..........................77%
Disapprove 22
Don't know 1

By Age
18–29 Years
Approve..........................85%
Disapprove 13
Don't know 2

30–49 Years
Approve..........................77%
Disapprove 21
Don't know 2

50 Years and Over
Approve..........................81%
Disapprove 16
Don't know 3

By Community Size
One Million and Over
Approve..........................87%
Disapprove 10
Don't know 3

500,000–999,999
Approve..........................85%
Disapprove 12
Don't know 3

50,000–499,999

Approve................................82%
Disapprove 16
Don't know 2

2,500–49,999

Approve................................77%
Disapprove 20
Don't know 3

Under 2,500; Rural

Approve................................75%
Disapprove 23
Don't know 2

National Trend

	Approve	Disapprove	Don't know
1980........	75%	20%	5%
1975........	77	19	4

Asked of those who responded in the affirmative (81%): Under the Massachusetts law, anyone who is convicted of carrying a gun outside his home without having obtained a license is sentenced to a mandatory year in jail. Would you approve or disapprove of this?

Approve................................62%
Disapprove 17
Don't know 2

National Trend

	Approve	Disapprove	Don't know
1980........	50%	21%	4%
1975........	53	21	3

Asked of the entire sample: In general, do you feel that the laws covering the sale of handguns should be made more strict, less strict, or kept as they are now?

More strict 65%
Less strict 3
Kept same........................... 30
Don't know 2

By Community Size
One Million and Over

More strict 74%
Less strict 4
Kept same........................... 19
Don't know 3

500,000–999,999

More strict 70%
Less strict 2
Kept same........................... 28
Don't know .... *

50,000–499,999

More strict 68%
Less strict 3
Kept same........................... 28
Don't know 1

2,500–49,999

More strict 56%
Less strict 2
Kept same........................... 37
Don't know 5

Under 2,500; Rural

More strict 56%
Less strict 3
Kept same........................... 39
Don't know 2

*Less than 1%

National Trend

	More strict	Less strict	Kept same	Don't know
Jan. 1980	59%	6%	29%	6%
Dec. 1980........	62	3	24	11

Also asked of the entire sample: Do you think there should or should not be a law which would forbid the possession of handguns except by the police or other authorized persons?

Should 39%
Should not 58
Don't know 3

By Community Size

One Million and Over

Should 67%
Should not 31
Don't know 2

500,000–999,999

Should 37%
Should not 61
Don't know 2

50,000–499,999

Should 37%
Should not 61
Don't know 2

2,500–49,999

Should 30%
Should not 65
Don't know 5

Under 2,500; Rural

Should 28%
Should not 69
Don't know 3

National Trend

	Should	Should not	Don't know
Jan. 1980	31%	65%	4%
Dec. 1980	38	51	11

Note: Public support for tough gun legislation, similar to the Bartley-Fox law now in effect in Massachusetts, has increased sharply since 1980, with 62% of Americans now favoring adoption of a similar law in their own states.

The Bartley-Fox law has two provisions: 1) persons must have a license to carry handguns outside their homes, and 2) persons convicted of carrying guns without a license are given a mandatory sentence of one year in jail.

Among the fifty states only Massachusetts and New York impose mandatory sentences for persons carrying an unlicensed handgun regardless of whether or not they are involved in the commission of a felony. Backers of the Massachusetts statute maintain it has been effective in preventing violent crimes in the six years since it was enacted. The New York law was approved only last summer.

Although support has grown for tough gun laws, such as those in Massachusetts and New York, and large majorities still favor stricter laws covering the sale of handguns, the public continues to vote against an outright ban, with 58% of Americans opposed to a law that would forbid the possession of handguns except by the police and other authorized persons. At present only Washington, DC, has a law banning the private possession of handguns.

One possible explanation for the apparent inconsistency between support for stricter gun laws and opposition to a ban on handguns is that the growing fear of crime has caused many people to believe they need a gun for self-protection, which is a false security measure in the opinion of many experts.

Recent national Gallup surveys highlight the concern over violence and crime in our society:

1. A majority of the public now takes crime prevention measures, with 16% saying they have bought a gun for protection.

2. Crime was uppermost in the minds of urban residents asked last year to name the top problem facing their cities and neighborhoods. In contrast, twenty-five years ago crime was not even among the top ten problems named.

3. A 54% majority of Americans say there is more crime in their communities than a year ago, with this perception common to every region of the nation and in cities of all sizes; in 1977, 43% reported a rise in crime where they live.

4. Fear of crime has grown, with 45% now saying they are afraid to walk alone at night in their neighborhood.

5. One household in four, compared to one in five in 1979, has been hit by crime at least once in the last twelve months, with either property

stolen or a household member the victim of a physical assault.

APRIL 26
PRESIDENT REAGAN

Interviewing Date: 4/3–6/81
Survey #171-G

This card lists some things the president is sometimes criticized for. Some of these criticisms will reflect how you, yourself, feel and some will not. Would you read off all of the items, if any, which worry or bother you about Ronald Reagan, even if they worry you only a little bit?

Would cut needed social programs 44%
Might get United States into war 41
Sides with big business and special
  interests 37
Puts foot in mouth; impulsive 23
Too old for job 22
Not sympathetic to minorities 21
Wants to increase defense spending
  substantially 19
His stand on the Equal Rights
  Amendment 19
His stand on abortion 19
Not tough enough with Russia 15
Has poor advisers. 15
Country is drifting; little sense of
  direction 10
None; no answer 14

Those Who Approve of the Way Reagan Is Handling His Job As President*

Would cut needed social programs 34%
Might get United States into war 34
Sides with big business and special
  interests 30
Puts foot in mouth; impulsive 18
Too old for job 15
Not sympathetic to minorities 12
Wants to increase defense spending
  substantially 14
His stand on the Equal Rights
  Amendment 15

His stand on abortion 14
Not tough enough with Russia 14
Has poor advisers. 12
Country is drifting; little sense of
  direction 8
None; no answer 17

National Trend

	April 1981	Sept. 1980	Point change
Puts foot in mouth; impulsive	23%	46%	−23
Too old for job	22	42	−20
Might get United States into war	41	37	+ 4
Sides with big business and special interests	37	29	+ 8
Would cut needed social programs	44	27	+17
Not sympathetic to minorities.	21	24	− 3

*67% of the sample

Note: President Ronald Reagan has succeeded in allaying some of the worries and doubts held by the public before last November's election, but criticism of other aspects of his presidency has increased sharply.

Preelection fears that, if elected, Reagan would side with big business and special interest groups and that he would cut back on needed social programs have intensified greatly since last fall. And concerns that he would not be sympathetic to the problems of blacks and other minorities and that he might get the country into a "shooting war" have persisted at about the same high levels recorded before the election.

Last September the leading concern about Reagan was that he was prone to say things without considering the consequences, cited by 46% of the public; today that figure has dropped to 23%. The other major worry last fall was that Reagan was too old to handle the strains and stresses of the presidency, named by 42%. Perhaps due to the resilience that the president has shown in recovering from his wound in the March 30 assassination attempt, his age causes concern among only 22% of the public.

Other key findings of Gallup Poll results indicate that compared with the current survey, in September the public was more worried about Reagan's personal characteristics—his impulsiveness and his age—than about the substantive aspects of his programs.

APRIL 27
PRESIDENT REAGAN

Interviewing Date: 4/3–6/81
Survey #171-G

Do you approve or disapprove of the way Reagan is handling his job as president?

Approve............................67%
Disapprove 18
No opinion 15

By Sex
Male

Approve............................70%
Disapprove 16
No opinion 14

Female

Approve............................63%
Disapprove 21
No opinion 16

By Race
White

Approve............................73%
Disapprove 12
No opinion 15

Nonwhite

Approve............................25%
Disapprove 59
No opinion 16

By Education
College

Approve............................71%
Disapprove 18
No opinion 11

High School

Approve............................69%
Disapprove 16
No opinion 15

Grade School

Approve............................50%
Disapprove 27
No opinion 23

By Region
East

Approve............................63%
Disapprove 22
No opinion 15

Midwest

Approve............................66%
Disapprove 19
No opinion 15

South

Approve............................72%
Disapprove 13
No opinion 15

West

Approve............................66%
Disapprove 20
No opinion 14

By Age
18–29 Years

Approve............................63%
Disapprove 23
No opinion 14

30–49 Years

Approve............................ 70%
Disapprove 18
No opinion 12

50 Years and Over

Approve............................ 67%
Disapprove 15
No opinion 18

By Income
$25,000 and Over

Approve............................ 79%
Disapprove 9
No opinion 12

$20,000–$24,999

Approve............................ 74%
Disapprove 13
No opinion 13

$15,000–$19,999

Approve............................ 72%
Disapprove 13
No opinion 15

$10,000–$14,999

Approve............................ 60%
Disapprove 23
No opinion 17

$5,000–$9,999

Approve............................ 53%
Disapprove 28
No opinion 19

Under $5,000

Approve............................ 52%
Disapprove 32
No opinion 16

By Politics
Republicans

Approve............................ 87%
Disapprove 5
No opinion 8

Democrats

Approve............................ 52%
Disapprove 29
No opinion 19

Independents

Approve............................ 69%
Disapprove 16
No opinion 15

By Religion
Protestants

Approve............................ 69%
Disapprove 17
No opinion 14

Catholics

Approve............................ 69%
Disapprove 16
No opinion 15

By Occupation
Professional and Business

Approve............................ 79%
Disapprove 10
No opinion 11

Clerical and Sales

Approve............................ 60%
Disapprove 18
No opinion 22

Manual Workers

Approve............................ 62%
Disapprove 23
No opinion 15

Nonlabor Force

Approve...........................62%
Disapprove 22
No opinion 16

Labor Union Families Only

Approve...........................62%
Disapprove 24
No opinion 14

Nonlabor Union Families Only

Approve...........................68%
Disapprove 17
No opinion 15

Do you approve or disapprove of the way Reagan is handling our relations with Russia?

Approve...........................56%
Disapprove 17
No opinion 27

By Sex
Male

Approve...........................63%
Disapprove 16
No opinion 21

Female

Approve...........................50%
Disapprove 17
No opinion 33

By Race
White

Approve...........................60%
Disapprove 14
No opinion 26

Nonwhite

Approve...........................30%
Disapprove 34
No opinion 36

By Education
College

Approve...........................62%
Disapprove 18
No opinion 20

High School

Approve...........................56%
Disapprove 16
No opinion 28

Grade School

Approve...........................44%
Disapprove 15
No opinion 41

By Region
East

Approve...........................56%
Disapprove 17
No opinion 27

Midwest

Approve...........................56%
Disapprove 18
No opinion 26

South

Approve...........................56%
Disapprove 13
No opinion 31

West

Approve...........................57%
Disapprove 20
No opinion 23

By Age
18–29 Years

Approve...........................48%
Disapprove 23
No opinion 29

30–49 Years

Approve..............................62%
Disapprove 14
No opinion 24

50 Years and Over

Approve..............................57%
Disapprove 14
No opinion 29

By Politics
Republicans

Approve..............................72%
Disapprove 8
No opinion 20

Democrats

Approve..............................49%
Disapprove 23
No opinion 28

Independents

Approve..............................53%
Disapprove 17
No opinion 30

Those Who Approve of Reagan

Approve..............................70%
Disapprove 9
No opinion 21

Do you approve or disapprove of the way Reagan is handling the situation in El Salvador?

Approve..............................39%
Disapprove 30
No opinion 31

By Education
College

Approve..............................34%
Disapprove 43
No opinion 23

High School

Approve..............................43%
Disapprove 25
No opinion 32

Grade School

Approve..............................34%
Disapprove 26
No opinion 40

By Region
East

Approve..............................37%
Disapprove 35
No opinion 28

Midwest

Approve..............................33%
Disapprove 34
No opinion 33

South

Approve..............................46%
Disapprove 21
No opinion 33

West

Approve..............................40%
Disapprove 33
No opinion 27

By Age
18–29 Years

Approve..............................31%
Disapprove 36
No opinion 33

30–49 Years

Approve..............................47%
Disapprove 26
No opinion 27

50 Years and Over

Approve............................38%
Disapprove 30
No opinion 32

Those Who Approve of Reagan

Approve............................49%
Disapprove 25
No opinion 26

Do you approve or disapprove of the way Reagan is dealing with inflation?

Approve............................58%
Disapprove 28
No opinion 14

By Sex
Male

Approve............................60%
Disapprove 25
No opinion 15

Female

Approve............................55%
Disapprove 31
No opinion 14

By Race
White

Approve............................63%
Disapprove 22
No opinion 15

Nonwhite

Approve............................23%
Disapprove 67
No opinion 10

By Region
East

Approve............................54%
Disapprove 29
No opinion 17

Midwest

Approve............................58%
Disapprove 31
No opinion 11

South

Approve............................62%
Disapprove 23
No opinion 15

West

Approve............................55%
Disapprove 30
No opinion 15

By Age
18–29 Years

Approve............................50%
Disapprove 37
No opinion 13

30–49 Years

Approve............................62%
Disapprove 25
No opinion 13

50 Years and Over

Approve............................59%
Disapprove 24
No opinion 17

By Income
$25,000 and Over

Approve............................72%
Disapprove 17
No opinion 11

$20,000–$24,999

Approve............................65%
Disapprove 22
No opinion 13

$15,000–$19,999

Approve............................63%
Disapprove 22
No opinion 15

$10,000–$14,999

Approve............................51%
Disapprove 33
No opinion 16

$5,000–$9,999

Approve............................43%
Disapprove 40
No opinion 17

Under $5,000

Approve............................37%
Disapprove 46
No opinion 17

Labor Union Families Only

Approve............................55%
Disapprove 31
No opinion 14

Nonlabor Union Families Only

Approve............................58%
Disapprove 27
No opinion 15

Those Who Approve of Reagan

Approve............................77%
Disapprove 13
No opinion 10

Do you approve or disapprove of the way Reagan is dealing with unemployment?

Approve............................43%
Disapprove 34
No opinion 23

By Sex
Male

Approve............................46%
Disapprove 34
No opinion 20

Female

Approve............................39%
Disapprove 35
No opinion 26

By Race
White

Approve............................48%
Disapprove 28
No opinion 24

Nonwhite

Approve............................11%
Disapprove 72
No opinion 17

By Region
East

Approve............................38%
Disapprove 37
No opinion 25

Midwest

Approve............................42%
Disapprove 37
No opinion 21

South

Approve............................47%
Disapprove 28
No opinion 25

West

Approve............................42%
Disapprove 37
No opinion 21

By Age

18–29 Years

Approve............................36%
Disapprove 42
No opinion 22

30–49 Years

Approve............................47%
Disapprove 33
No opinion 20

50 Years and Over

Approve............................44%
Disapprove 29
No opinion 27

By Income

$25,000 and Over

Approve............................52%
Disapprove 26
No opinion 22

$20,000–$24,999

Approve............................50%
Disapprove 28
No opinion 22

$15,000–$19,999

Approve............................44%
Disapprove 35
No opinion 21

$10,000–$14,999

Approve............................38%
Disapprove 40
No opinion 22

$5,000–$9,999

Approve............................35%
Disapprove 38
No opinion 27

Under $5,000

Approve............................28%
Disapprove 49
No opinion 23

Labor Union Families Only

Approve............................38%
Disapprove 41
No opinion 21

Nonlabor Union Families Only

Approve............................44%
Disapprove 32
No opinion 24

Those Who Approve of Reagan

Approve............................57%
Disapprove 21
No opinion 22

Do you approve or disapprove of the way Reagan is dealing with the energy situation?

Approve............................42%
Disapprove 34
No opinion 24

By Education

College

Approve............................39%
Disapprove 37
No opinion 24

High School

Approve............................45%
Disapprove 31
No opinion 24

Grade School

Approve............................35%
Disapprove 38
No opinion 27

Those Who Approve of Reagan

Approve............................54%
Disapprove 26
No opinion 20

Note: President Ronald Reagan receives a high popularity rating from the public at this time, with 67% of Americans approving of the way he is handling his duties as chief executive. This overall approval rating is higher than the ratings given Reagan for his handling of specific issues, reflecting sympathy accorded him because of the March 30 assassination attempt.

The current survey, for example, shows 58% of the public approving of the way Reagan is dealing with inflation, while 56% have a favorable outlook toward his handling of our relations with Russia. He draws less than majority support, however, on his performance in dealing with unemployment (43%), the energy situation (42%), and the situation in El Salvador (39%).

If the president's complex economic program for curbing inflation does not live up to the public's expectations, his overall performance rating could suffer regardless of his perceived competence in other areas.

A special analysis of the relative importance of each of these five issues with which the Reagan administration must deal indicates that inflation is of considerably more importance to the public. The figures suggest that a shift from approval to disapproval on the inflation issue would be more than twice as damaging to Reagan as the loss of support that would be associated with a shift from approval to disapproval on his handling of the energy situation.

Similarly, while the president scores rather poorly on energy, unemployment, and El Salvador, a shift from approval to disapproval on these issues would not affect his overall performance rating to nearly the same extent as would a shift on inflation.

Relative Importance of Reagan's Approval Ratings

	Percent approval	Relative importance on scale of 100
Inflation	58%	43%
Energy situation	42	18
Unemployment	43	16
El Salvador	39	12
Relations with Russia	56	11

MAY 3
PARTY BEST FOR PEACE AND PROSPERITY

Interviewing Date: 4/10–13/81
Survey #172-G

Which political party do you think would be more likely to keep the United States out of World War III—the Republican party or the Democratic party?

Republican	26%
Democratic	39
No difference (volunteered)	22
No opinion	13

Which political party—the Republican party or the Democratic party—do you think will do a better job of keeping the country prosperous?

Republican	41%
Democratic	28
No difference (volunteered)	18
No opinion	13

Note: Since July of last year there has been a major turnaround in the way the public perceives the relative ability of the two major political parties to deal with the key issues of peace and prosperity. The Democratic party, which has virtually "owned" the prosperity issue since these Gallup measurements were initiated three decades ago, has relinquished the lead for the first time to the Republican party and, in fact, now trails by 13 percentage points—41% for the Republicans to 28% for the Democrats.

The GOP, on the other hand, which consistently has been thought of by voters as the party of peace, has now fallen behind its Democratic rivals. The Democratic party is considered by 39% of the public to be better for peace, with 26% naming the GOP.

The GOP's continued lead as the party of prosperity will depend in considerable measure upon the success of President Ronald Reagan's economic program in reducing inflation. If the Reagan administration's economic program proves effective, the current GOP margin over the Democratic party as the party of prosperity could be sustained. These gains could even lead to a major political realignment in this nation, which has been solidly Democratic since New Deal days. The extent of Democratic control in the United States over the last half century is seen in the fact that in only two years of this period Republicans have been in control of both the executive and legislative branches of government.

Thus, if the Republican gains on the economic issue are sustained, the current period could become a major political watershed and ensure Republican domination of Congress. Between the Civil War and the Great Depression, the Republican party was dominant in the minds of voters on key issues, including prosperity. Since the New Deal, however, the nation has been essentially Democratic.

The Republican party's strong showing as the party of prosperity could be offset by the Democratic party's almost as impressive gain as the party of peace. The Democratic party currently enjoys a wide margin over the GOP as the party seen by voters as better able to keep peace. In the previous survey both parties were in a virtual tie, 32% of the Democrats and 30% for the Republicans. Throughout the 1950s and early 1960s the GOP held an advantage over the Democratic party on this issue. However, the Democrats took the lead in the mid-1960s only to relinquish it later in the decade and finally to challenge again in the late 1970s.

The decline of the GOP as the party of peace may reflect public concern about the Reagan administration's outspoken stance on this issue. A recent Gallup survey showed as many as four voters in ten express concern that Reagan might get the United States into a shooting war.

By comparison, the following shows the percentages of survey respondents ascribing which of the two major political parties they feel is better able to deal with the key issues of peace and prosperity. The no difference and no opinion figures have been omitted:

Keeping United States Out of War

	Republican	Democratic
June 1980	28%	32%
March 1978	25	31
August 1976	29	32
September 1974	21	29
March 1974	24	33
September 1972	32	28

Keeping Prosperity

	Republican	Democratic
June 1980	31%	37%
March 1978	23	41
August 1976	23	47
September 1974	17	47
March 1974	19	49
September 1972	38	35

MAY 7
MILITARY SPENDING

Interviewing Date: 4/3–6/81
Survey #171-G

Of every tax dollar spent by the federal government for defense purposes, how many cents would you say are wasted?

	Median average
National	25¢

By Education

College	26¢
High school	24¢
Grade school	24¢

By Region

East	27¢
Midwest	23¢
South	23¢
West	26¢

By Politics

Republicans	23¢
Democrats	25¢
Independents	26¢

Those who approve of Reagan . . . . 23¢
Those who disapprove of Reagan . . . . 28¢

Interviewing Date: 1/30–2/2/81
Survey #168-G

*There is much discussion as to the amount
of money the government in Washington
should spend for national defense and
military purposes. How do you feel about
this? Do you think we are spending too
little, too much, or about the right amount?*

Too little 51%
Too much 15
About right 22
No opinion 12

By Education
College

Too little 50%
Too much 19
About right 24
No opinion 7

High School

Too little 53%
Too much 13
About right 23
No opinion 11

Grade School

Too little 42%
Too much 20
About right 16
No opinion 22

By Region
East

Too little 44%
Too much 15
About right 27
No opinion 14

Midwest

Too little 52%
Too much 17
About right 22
No opinion 9

South

Too little 53%
Too much 16
About right 16
No opinion 15

West

Too little 54%
Too much 12
About right 27
No opinion 7

By Politics
Republicans

Too little 53%
Too much 12
About right 23
No opinion 12

Democrats

Too little 49%
Too much 15
About right 24
No opinion 12

Independents

Too little 51%
Too much 19
About right 21
No opinion 9

National Trend*

	Too little	Too much
1981	51%	15%
1980	49	14
1979	34	21
1977	27	23
1976	22	36
1974	12	44

1973	8	42
1971	11	49
1969	8	52

*Figures for the about right and no opinion have been omitted.

Note: Despite public support for increased defense spending, there is a widespread belief that much of the government's military expenditure is wasted. When the Gallup Poll recently asked Americans to estimate how much of every tax dollar spent for defense purposes is wasted, the median response was 25¢. The estimate was about the same in every major population group, including Republicans, Democrats, and political independents.

This is not to say, however, that the public perceived nondefense expenditures to be more efficient than defense spending, for the national estimate from the same survey is that 32¢ of every tax dollar spent in nondefense areas is wasted.

With the current fiscal 1981 military budget of $159 billion, the public's estimated waste figure of 25% would translate to almost $40 billion. If the estimate is applied to the Reagan administration's fiscal 1982 military spending request of $188.8 billion, the projected amount becomes $47 billion, a sum closely approximating the total cuts in spending for social programs advocated by President Reagan. In fact, in the administration's 1982 budget only three individual items—income security, health, and debt services—are larger than the amount of waste in military spending perceived by the public.

Obviously, if effective measures can be taken to reduce waste in defense spending, the saving could go far to alleviate the nation's pressing social problems as well as providing greater efficiency in military spending itself.

In its most recent survey on the subject, the Gallup Poll found the highest level of public support (51%) for increased defense spending in over a decade. This was the first time that a majority said they believed the military budget was inadequate. By comparison, in 1969 only 8% of the public supported increased defense spending, while a 52% majority called for a reduction. At that time this may have reflected criticism of U.S. military involvement in the Vietnam War.

Among those who have been critical of excessive military spending is Elmer Staats, who recently retired as U.S. comptroller general. Staats told the Pentagon that it could save at least $4 billion a year by economies in fifteen specific areas of defense spending.

Also, Deputy Secretary of Defense Frank Carlucci said recently that he had ordered the Pentagon "to make major changes both in acquisition philosophy and the acquisition process itself." Although Carlucci said he could not estimate the possible savings if all his decisions were carried out, he testified before a House Armed Services subcommittee that: ". . . The Administration is going to exert every possible effort to improve its stewardship of monies expended through the acquisition process."

MAY 10
RELOCATION OF URBAN POOR

Interviewing Date: 4/10–13/81
Survey #172-G

A plan has been proposed to invite welfare families now living in ghetto areas of large cities to move to areas of the nation where living conditions and job opportunities are better. The government would pay the costs of moving as well as living costs until these families found jobs. Would you favor or oppose such a plan?

Favor	44%
Oppose	48
No opinion	8

By Race
White

Favor	40%
Oppose	52
No opinion	8

Nonwhite

Favor............................67%
Oppose...........................22
No opinion 11

By Education
College

Favor............................37%
Oppose...........................55
No opinion 8

High School

Favor............................44%
Oppose...........................48
No opinion 8

Grade School

Favor............................57%
Oppose...........................32
No opinion 11

By Age
18–29 Years

Favor............................48%
Oppose...........................44
No opinion 8

30–49 Years

Favor............................42%
Oppose...........................49
No opinion 9

50 Years and Over

Favor............................43%
Oppose...........................50
No opinion 7

By Income
$15,000 and Over

Favor............................38%
Oppose...........................55
No opinion 7

Under $15,000

Favor............................51%
Oppose...........................39
No opinion 10

By Occupation
White-Collar Households

Favor............................35%
Oppose...........................57
No opinion 8

Blue-Collar Households

Favor............................52%
Oppose...........................42
No opinion 6

By Community Location
Central City

Favor............................49%
Oppose...........................41
No opinion 10

Suburbs

Favor............................39%
Oppose...........................52
No opinion 9

Nonmetropolitan Areas

Favor............................43%
Oppose...........................51
No opinion 6

*Asked of those who expressed an opinion:
Why do you feel this way?*

Reasons for Favoring

Opportunity for betterment..........20%
More jobs.........................10
Less cost for welfare and crime 10
Better living conditions 4
Other positive reasons 1

Reasons for Opposing

Oppose welfare and government
   handouts......................12%
Would cost too much..............11

Poor should help themselves 8
People on welfare will not work 8
No guarantee of jobs 7
Would destroy initiative . . . . 4'
Would create new ghettos 3
Other negative reasons 4
Don't know; no answer 11

113%*

*Total adds to more than 100% due to multiple responses.

Note: A plan to move poor families, on a voluntary basis, out of big city ghettos into areas of the nation where living conditions and job opportunities are better finds substantial support in urban areas and among low-income groups. The results of a nationwide Gallup Poll show public opinion to be closely divided (44% in favor, 48% opposed), with residents of the central cities voting 49% to 41% in favor.

Among the group that would be directly affected if the relocation plan were implemented—persons from lower-income households in the nation's central cities—approval outweighs disapproval by almost a 2-to-1 ratio.

Specifically, the plan would invite urban welfare families to move to areas where there are more job opportunities and where the quality of life is better than in the inner cities. The federal government would assume the expense of moving these families as well as their living costs until they found jobs. In view of the fact that the cost of maintaining welfare families in big cities in much higher than in the nation as a whole, the cost of relocating these families would be largely offset by savings in welfare outlays.

Urban specialists point out that many large cities cannot cope with their large dependent populations and that the poor do not have much hope of improving their future as long as they are concentrated in financially distressed cities. They also contend that the much publicized "urban renaissance"—the back-to-the-city movement of the middle- and upper-income families—is largely an illusion, since the concentration of minorities and poverty-level families in the central cities continues to increase.

A crucial factor behind the voluntary relocation plan is recognition that the labor force mobility is essential to the health of the American economy. While one solution to the problem of ghettos is to bring new businesses into center city areas, many planners have reached the conclusion that it is better to move people to jobs than jobs to people.

A presidential commission noted that "many Federal programs encourage people to stay put in the older cities, removing any incentive they might have to seek jobs elsewhere." The panel also noted that it may be desirable to disperse the urban poor to a "healthier environment" so that the slums do not aggravate their "multiple afflictions."

The plan has greater acceptance among non-whites, persons in blue-collar households, those with only a grade-school education, lower-income families, younger adults, and central city residents.

To answer those surveyed who worry about costs, urban experts favoring relocation point out that while the cost of moving people to new communities would be considerable, it would be offset by savings in such federal expenditures as custodial institutions, remedial education, welfare, and drug rehabilitation centers. In fact, relocation proponents argue that the savings could be so substantial the federal government could afford not only to pay the actual moving costs but also could give a family an income supplement until they were settled in their new environment.

MAY 14
CONGRESSIONAL TERM OF OFFICE

Interviewing Date: 4/3–6/81
Survey #171-G

How would you feel about changing the term of members of the House of Representatives from two years to four years? Would you favor or oppose this?

Favor 51%
Oppose 37
No opinion 12

By Education
College

Favor 54%
Oppose 37
No opinion 9

High School

Favor 50%
Oppose 38
No opinion 12

Grade School

Favor 48%
Oppose 31
No opinion 21

By Region
East

Favor 50%
Oppose 38
No opinion 12

Midwest

Favor 54%
Oppose 34
No opinion 12

South

Favor 50%
Oppose 38
No opinion 12

West

Favor 51%
Oppose 36
No opinion 13

By Age
18–29 Years

Favor 46%
Oppose 40
No opinion 14

30–49 Years

Favor 54%
Oppose 37
No opinion 9

50 Years and Over

Favor 53%
Oppose 33
No opinion 14

By Politics
Republicans

Favor 54%
Oppose 38
No opinion 8

Democrats

Favor 51%
Oppose 34
No opinion 15

Independents

Favor 49%
Oppose 38
No opinion 13

Note: A constant complaint of members of the House of Representatives, who are elected for a two-year term, is that they have to start campaigning for the next election the day after they take office.

A majority of the public (51%) agrees that the term of office of members of the House should be lengthened, compared to 37% who disagree and 12% who express no opinion. These survey findings are similar to those found in a 1961 study, when 51% approved and 34% disapproved of a constitutional amendment that would extend the term of office from two to four years. Since 1961 approval of extending the two-year term has outweighed disapproval, except in 1973 when the vote was even.

Those who favor a four-year congressional term are found in every educational and income category as well as in every section of the nation. Little difference is found on the basis of political identity: Republicans favor the proposal by a 16-point margin, Democrats by 17 points, and independents by 11 points.

It has been pointed out that the reason why the Founding Fathers wrote a two-year term into the Constitution no longer exists. In those days poor transportation and poor communication forced many congressmen to spend virtually all of their time in Washington. By limiting their terms to two years, they were forced to go back to familiarize themselves with the problems of their districts. Today they can be in constant contact with their constituents.

In addition to citing the time that must be spent in campaigning, members of the House in support of a four-year term also point to today's high cost of running for office. An effective campaign can cost well over $100,000. To raise this amount, even from special interest groups, is difficult, especially if a congressman must go back to these same campaign contributors every two years.

MAY 17
CONGRESSIONAL TERM OF OFFICE

Interviewing Date: 4/3–6/81
Survey #171-G

A law has been proposed which would limit a member of the House of Representatives to three terms of four years apiece, or a total of twelve years. Would you favor or oppose such a law?

Favor...............................59%
Oppose..............................32
No opinion 9

By Education
College

Favor...............................60%
Oppose..............................34
No opinion 6

High School

Favor...............................59%
Oppose..............................33
No opinion 8

Grade School

Favor...............................59%
Oppose..............................26
No opinion 15

By Region
East

Favor...............................56%
Oppose..............................38
No opinion 6

Midwest

Favor...............................61%
Oppose..............................30
No opinion 9

South

Favor...............................59%
Oppose..............................31
No opinion 10

West

Favor...............................62%
Oppose..............................28
No opinion 10

By Age
18–29 Years

Favor...............................56%
Oppose..............................32
No opinion 12

30–49 Years

Favor................................63%
Oppose..............................30
No opinion 7

50 Years and Over

Favor................................59%
Oppose..............................33
No opinion 8

By Politics
Republicans

Favor................................62%
Oppose..............................34
No opinion 4

Democrats

Favor................................58%
Oppose..............................32
No opinion 10

Independents

Favor................................59%
Oppose..............................30
No opinion 11

National Trend

	Favor	Oppose	No opinion
1977	59%	31%	10%
1964	48	37	15

A law has been proposed which would limit a senator to two terms, or a total of twelve years in office. Would you favor or oppose such a law?

Favor................................61%
Oppose..............................32
No opinion 7

By Education
College

Favor................................62%
Oppose..............................34
No opinion 4

High School

Favor................................61%
Oppose..............................33
No opinion 6

Grade School

Favor................................59%
Oppose..............................26
No opinion 15

By Region
East

Favor................................58%
Oppose..............................36
No opinion 6

Midwest

Favor................................63%
Oppose..............................30
No opinion 7

South

Favor................................59%
Oppose..............................33
No opinion 8

West

Favor................................65%
Oppose..............................28
No opinion 7

By Age
18–29 Years

Favor................................58%
Oppose..............................34
No opinion 8

30–49 Years

Favor................................65%
Oppose..............................30
No opinion 5

50 Years and Over

Favor 60%
Oppose 33
No opinion 7

By Politics

Republicans

Favor 63%
Oppose 34
No opinion 3

Democrats

Favor 61%
Oppose 31
No opinion 8

Independents

Favor 60%
Oppose 32
No opinion 8

National Trend

	Favor	Oppose	No opinion
1977	60%	30%	10%
1971	48	39	13
1966	50	38	12
1964	49	38	13

Note: American voters believe that holding high political office should represent a period of service to the public and not a career. When the Gallup Poll recently offered two proposals that would limit to twelve years the tenure of U.S. senators and representatives, it found 2-to-1 support.

Specifically, a proposal for limiting senators to two six-year terms receives the approval of 61%, with 32% disapproving. A proposal for restricting service in the House of Representatives to three terms of four years each is favored by 59% of the public, with 32% opposed.

These two proposals were last put to the public for a vote in 1977. Despite dramatic changes in the political composition of both houses of Congress, with the Republicans now holding a majority in the Senate and picking up forty-eight House seats in last November's election, public opinion has not varied significantly since 1977 and remains at a high level.

The same degree of support for these proposals is found in all population groups, including partisans of the major political entities. For example, 63% of Republicans, 61% of Democrats, and 60% of independents vote in favor of the Senate limitation. Similarly, the opinions of college-educated persons are the same as those of respondents with less formal education.

The plan to limit senators to two terms of six years each has been advocated by at least two presidents—Harry Truman and Dwight Eisenhower. Eisenhower stated the case for the two-term limitation as follows:

If Senators were limited to two terms of six years, each man so serving would tend to think of his congressional career as an important and exciting interlude in his life, a period dedicated to the entire public, rather than as a way of making a living, or making a career of exercising continuous political power. Possibly, each would spend less time keeping his eyes on the next election, and more in centering them on the good of the nation. A more rapid turnover in the membership of both Houses, with its constant infusion of new blood, would largely eliminate the "career politician" in Congress.

The chief opposition to a two-term limitation comes from those who feel that this plan would shorten the tenure of many senators who have had distinguished careers in government, and that government today is so complex that it takes many years for a senator to familiarize himself with the legislative process.

Although Americans consistently have rejected the idea of one six-year term for U.S. president, their views on a two-term limit shifted sharply. In the late 1930s survey evidence showed that a majority of the public was opposed to a two-term limit. However, in 1943 majority opinion shifted in favor of this limit, with subsequent surveys continuing to show widespread support.

The 22nd Amendment to the Constitution, which limits to two the number of terms a president may serve, was proposed by the Congress in 1947 and ratified in 1951.

MAY 18
THE SOMBER MOOD OF BLACK AMERICA*

In December, when the Gallup Poll sent its interviewers out for its annual end-of-the-year poll, they encountered substantial optimism, at least among white respondents. Fifty-five percent of whites said they expected 1981 to be better for them personally. Those who interviewed blacks, however, received different answers. Only 18% expected a better year, while 48% expected a worse year. This was the first of several polls that pointed to substantial discontent among the nation's black population.

Small wonder that recent public opinion polls that studied black attitudes reveal pessimism. Consider what blacks have experienced in the past twelve months: the systematic murder of blacks in Atlanta and Buffalo; rising crime and unemployment rates, which take their greatest toll on blacks; the election of Ronald Reagan (opposed by 90% of black voters); and most recently the passage of a Reagan budget that assures either the dismantling or the significant weakening of many programs designed to help black people.

Recent polls also demonstrate the extent to which blacks are aware that the focus of American consciousness and politics has turned away from their particular problems. In a February Newsweek Poll conducted by the Gallup Organization Inc., 52% of blacks expected that things would get worse for them during Reagan's

*This Gallup analysis was written by Andrew Kohut, president of the Gallup Organization Inc.

presidency, while only 8% felt things would improve.

Similar views were echoed in a *Washington Post*/ABC Poll, which extensively surveyed blacks in late February–early March. Fifty-one percent expected the Reagan administration to do less for blacks than did the Carter administration.

Recent attitudes stand in stark contrast to how blacks felt about their situation a decade ago. In the late 1960s and early 1970s when blacks experienced seemingly rapid social advancement, polls of blacks registered a significant sense of progress. In the late 1970s these feelings waned, and today blacks are divided as to whether their race has made gains in the recent past.

As shown by a series of *Newsweek* polls, blacks have had second thoughts about their situation. Between March 1980 and February 1981 the percentage of blacks who feel progress has been made by their race has tumbled by 19 percentage points, as shown below:

Situation for Blacks Improved During Past Five Years

	Blacks saying Yes
1981	30%
1980	49
1969	70

Although blacks continue to see racial prejudice as an important cause of many of their social and economic problems, whites are now less often seen as standing in the way of black progress compared to a decade ago. In 1969 a *Newsweek* Poll found a plurality of blacks (46%) believed that most whites wanted to keep them from advancing. The February 1981 *Newsweek* Poll showed only 32% subscribing to this view.

From these survey results it is evident that the two races view the problem of blacks in very different ways. Whites consistently see blacks as better off than blacks see themselves, and far fewer whites than blacks view racial discrimination as an issue in the problems of blacks.

The troubles in black America mostly parallel those in white America. The *Washington Post*/ABC Poll showed that the races broadly agree on the most important problems facing the nation—inflation, unemployment, and crime—except that blacks put more emphasis on the latter two than do whites. Despite the spread of crime to suburbia and the Sun Belt states, the greatest concern about crime and reports of victimization are evident among blacks.

The decline in the quality of life of blacks as a result of rising inflation, unemployment, and crime plays a large part in the mood of black Americans. However, the changing political and social environment of the 1980s also intensifies the pessimism of black people. Politically, blacks believe that the federal government has made an overall positive impact on their lives, particularly in the areas of healthcare, education, and housing. As such, blacks have been the harshest critics of the Reagan administration.

In April, while whites gave Reagan a 74% rating, only 25% of blacks approved. This is one of the largest differences in black/white attitudes toward a political figure ever recorded. Blacks also have expressed the most resentment over the idea of a wholesale reduction in the size of government, a reduction that they believe is directed at them personally.

Polls on black opinion show few optimistic readings except for some signs of improved black attitudes toward whites. Still these same surveys show significant potential for racial violence. The *Washington Post*/ABC Poll found only the slightest majority of blacks (51%) rejecting violent protest as a means of accomplishing goals and two-thirds agreeing that the federal government seems to pay attention to blacks only when they resort to violence.

The debate in Congress over the renewal of the Voting Rights Act undoubtedly will be followed closely by blacks. It is an issue that has great symbolic meaning and should it not be renewed, it may represent yet another signal that the nation has turned away from concern about black problems.

MAY 21
AFFIRMATIVE ACTION

Interviewing Date: 12/5–8/80
Survey #166-G

Some people say that to make up for past discrimination, women and members of minority groups should be given preferential treatment in getting jobs and places in college. Others say that ability, as determined by test scores, should be the main consideration. Which point of view comes closest to how you feel on this subject?

Preferential treatment 10%
Ability 83
No opinion 7

By Sex
Male

Preferential treatment 9%
Ability 85
No opinion 6

Female

Preferential treatment 11%
Ability 82
No opinion 7

By Race
White

Preferential treatment 7%
Ability 87
No opinion 6

Nonwhite

Preferential treatment 29%
Ability 57
No opinion 14

By Education
College

Preferential treatment 10%
Ability 86
No opinion 4

High School

Preferential treatment 9%
Ability 84
No opinion 7

Grade School

Preferential treatment 13%
Ability 76
No opinion 11

By Region
East

Preferential treatment 10%
Ability 84
No opinion 6

Midwest

Preferential treatment 8%
Ability 85
No opinion 7

South

Preferential treatment 11%
Ability 79
No opinion 10

West

Preferential treatment 10%
Ability 87
No opinion 3

By Age
18–29 Years

Preferential treatment 11%
Ability 81
No opinion 8

30–49 Years

Preferential treatment 11%
Ability 83
No opinion 6

50 Years and Over

Preferential treatment 8%
Ability 86
No opinion 6

By Politics
Republicans

Preferential treatment 6%
Ability 92
No opinion 2

Democrats

Preferential treatment 14%
Ability 78
No opinion 8

Independents

Preferential treatment 8%
Ability 86
No opinion 6

Note: In the opinion of a large majority of Americans, including people of all races and both sexes, ability and not preferential treatment should be the basic criterion for placement in jobs and colleges.

The principle of affirmative action—called by its critics "reverse discrimination"—gained new currency when Senator Orrin Hatch opened Senate subcommittee hearings on a constitutional amendment proposed by the Utah Republican that would forbid the federal government to make distinctions on account of race, color, or national origin.

Among women and nonwhites, the two groups most directly affected by affirmative action, the results were conclusive: women chose ability (82%) over reparative preference (11%), while nonwhites voted for ability over special treatment, 57% to 29%.

While the concept of preferential treatment to compensate for past discrimination is unacceptable to most people, when the issue is narrowed to whether qualified blacks should receive preference over equally qualified whites, black opinion divides much more evenly. According to a recent *Newsweek* Poll, conducted by the Gallup Organization Inc., 45% of blacks believe members of their race should receive preference under these circumstances, while 47% believe they should not.

Rarely is public opinion, particularly on such a controversial issue, as united as it is over this question. Attitudes are similar in all regions, among all age groups, and by education. Democrats are only slightly more disposed to preferential treatment than are Republicans and independents. All groups back objective data such as test scores as the main qualification for jobs and college entrance.

Opponents of affirmative action programs maintain that ability alone should determine who is hired or admitted to colleges and professional schools, thereby ensuring the highest standards. These same people say those who are innocent of past discrimination should not be made to pay now, and that affirmative action programs will ultimately dilute the market value of other competent people who achieved their status on the basis of objective criteria.

Opponents also argue that preferential treatment places a stigma on minority professionals, saying in effect that a black lawyer or doctor is less qualified than a white one, while proponents of affirmative action counter that without it blacks and women will never participate fully in American society.

Aside from the issue of compensation for past discrimination, supporters maintain that without quotas, many institutions and professions will not be representative of the publics they serve. Backers of affirmative action also reason that tests are often discriminatory because of the inferior education minority group members have received in the past. They also point out that de facto affirmative action already exists for such groups as athletes, alumni sons and daughters, and, in the case of employment, for those who are fortunate enough to count a labor union business agent among their friends.

MAY 24
VOTING ON IMPORTANT ISSUES

Interviewing Date: 4/10–13/81
Survey #172-G

Asked of nonvoters in the 1980 presidential election: Would you be more likely or less likely to vote in national elections if you could vote on important national issues as well as candidates, or wouldn't it make any difference?

More likely 48%
Less likely 2
No difference (volunteered) 43
No opinion 7

By Age
18–29 Years

More likely 56%
Less likely 3
No difference (volunteered) 36
No opinion 5

30–49 Years

More likely 43%
Less likely 2
No difference (volunteered) 46
No opinion 9

50 Years and Over

More likely 41%
Less likely 1
No difference (volunteered) 50
No opinion 8

Asked of the entire sample: The U.S. Senate will consider a proposal that would require a national vote—that is, a referendum—on any issue when 3% of all voters who voted in the most recent presidential election sign petitions asking for such a nationwide vote. Do you favor or oppose such a plan?

Favor 52%
Oppose 23
No opinion 25

By Age

18–29 Years

Favor.............................59%
Oppose............................19
No opinion 22

30–49 Years

Favor.............................51%
Oppose............................25
No opinion 24

50 Years and Over

Favor.............................48%
Oppose............................23
No opinion 29

By Politics

Republicans

Favor.............................51%
Oppose............................26
No opinion 23

Democrats

Favor.............................49%
Oppose............................20
No opinion 31

Independents

Favor.............................58%
Oppose............................23
No opinion 19

Those Who Voted in 1980 Election

Favor.............................53%
Oppose............................25
No opinion 22

Those Who Did Not Vote in 1980 Election

Favor.............................50%
Oppose............................19
No opinion 31

Note: If Americans could vote on major issues facing the nation as well as on candidates, voter turnout in national elections, currently the worst of any major democracy in the world, could improve substantially. This conclusion is based on the results of a recent Gallup Poll in which national samples of those who voted in the 1980 presidential election and those who failed to vote were questioned about two related proposals that have been offered as ways of increasing turnout in national elections. Turnout in the 1980 presidential election was the lowest in thirty-two years. In fact only 54% of those eligible took the trouble to vote.

When nonvoters were asked if they would be more or less likely to vote in national elections if they could vote on important national issues as well as candidates, 48% said they would be more likely to do so. The implications of these findings are far-reaching: if half the nonvoters who say they would be more likely to vote actually did so, turnout would increase to almost 80%, a level equal to that found in other major democratic nations.

As the survey results indicate, measures that would provide the public with avenues for direct expression of their views might well enhance their participation in candidate elections. This may have particular application in election years similar to 1980, when many prospective voters were less than enthusiastic about the major party nominees.

Further evidence of the appeal of voting on issues as well as on candidates is seen in the results of a survey on the Voter Initiative Amendment. According to this constitutional amendment, a national referendum would be held on any issue when 3% of all voters in the previous presidential election signed petitions demanding such a vote. This amendment is favored by a 2-to-1 margin among all persons interviewed, with voters and nonvoters in last fall's election holding similar views.

A recent report by the Committee for the Study of the American Electorate indicated that most conventional proposals for increasing voter turnout have had little effect. Participation was not notably higher in states that used postcard registration or allowed voters to register at the polls on election day. These current survey results lend support to the proponents' view that offering citizens an opportunity to vote on major issues of the day would encourage voter participation by giving them a greater voice in national affairs.

MAY 28
PRESIDENT REAGAN

Interviewing Date: 5/8–11/81
Survey #173-G

Do you approve or disapprove of the way Reagan is handling his job as president?

Approve....................................68%
Disapprove 21
No opinion 11

By Sex
Male

Approve.............................70%
Disapprove 20
No opinion 10

Female

Approve.............................65%
Disapprove 22
No opinion 13

By Race
White

Approve.............................73%
Disapprove 16
No opinion 11

Nonwhite

Approve.............................31%
Disapprove 51
No opinion 18

By Education
College

Approve.............................72%
Disapprove 21
No opinion 7

High School

Approve............................68%
Disapprove 20
No opinion 12

Grade School

Approve............................55%
Disapprove 25
No opinion 20

By Region
East

Approve............................64%
Disapprove 21
No opinion 15

Midwest

Approve............................70%
Disapprove 22
No opinion 8

South

Approve............................69%
Disapprove 21
No opinion 10

West

Approve............................68%
Disapprove 19
No opinion 13

By Age
18–24 Years

Approve............................65%
Disapprove 29
No opinion 6

25–29 Years

Approve............................66%
Disapprove 25
No opinion 9

30–49 Years

Approve...........................72%
Disapprove 18
No opinion 10

50 Years and Over

Approve...........................65%
Disapprove 19
No opinion 16

By Income
$25,000 and Over

Approve...........................80%
Disapprove 13
No opinion 7

$20,000–$24,999

Approve...........................74%
Disapprove 15
No opinion 11

$15,000–$19,999

Approve...........................68%
Disapprove 20
No opinion 12

$10,000–$14,999

Approve...........................68%
Disapprove 22
No opinion 10

$5,000–$9,999

Approve...........................55%
Disapprove 26
No opinion 19

Under $5,000

Approve...........................40%
Disapprove 42
No opinion 18

By Politics
Republicans

Approve...........................92%
Disapprove 4
No opinion 4

Democrats

Approve...........................51%
Disapprove 35
No opinion 14

Independents

Approve...........................70%
Disapprove 17
No opinion 13

Note: After holding office for approximately four months, President Ronald Reagan receives a favorable rating from two out of three Americans (68%) for his handling of his presidential duties. Twenty-one percent of the public expressed disapproval and 11% were undecided. These ratings are very close to those accorded Jimmy Carter at a similar point in 1977, when 66% of Americans approved of Carter's handling of the presidency, 19% disapproved, and 15% withheld judgment.

The following figures compare Reagan's latest ratings with those of his elected predecessors:

Presidential Approval Ratings After Four Months in Office

	Approve	Dis-approve	No opinion
Reagan—1981	68%	21%	11%
Carter—1977	66	19	15
Nixon—1969	62	15	23
Kennedy—1961	77	9	14
Eisenhower—1953	74	10	16

The public usually grants incoming presidents the benefit of the doubt for a brief period after they assume office, the so-called honeymoon period. For example, in early 1953

Eisenhower was given a 68% approval with only 7% disapproval; John Kennedy in early 1961 was acclaimed by 72% with 6% dissenting; Richard Nixon earned a 60% positive rating with 5% disapproving in February 1969; and Jimmy Carter had a popularity rating of 66% with 8% negative shortly after he took office in 1977.

The mid-February announcement of Reagan's economic plan had two immediate political consequences. First, it was a dramatic proposal with far-reaching implications that effectively cut short the honeymoon period. Second, it was seen as depriving many low-income families of social benefits, the Reagan "safety net" notwithstanding.

The twin results were: 1) Reagan's approval rating of 60% after the announcement of his economic program was not as high as his predecessors' had been, and 2) his disapproval figure of 24% was substantially higher. Shortly after the March 30 assassination attempt, 67% of Americans approved of Reagan's handling of his presidential duties, a level that has persisted throughout the latest measurement.

Although Reagan's current popularity tends to be higher among voter groups who supported him in the 1980 presidential election—men, whites, the college educated, and Republicans—his approval ratings have improved among all voter groups since the mid-March survey, including those who most strongly opposed Reagan in the November election. Even among nonwhites, few of whom voted for President Reagan and many of whom are apprehensive about the effects of Reagan's economic program, his approval rating has grown from 22% to 31%. However, Reagan's present rating among nonwhites still ranks among the lowest recorded at comparable periods during past presidencies.

Since March, President Reagan's rating among Democrats has improved by 10 percentage points, to 51% approval. This present level is only slightly below the 54% popularity rating accorded Carter by Republicans at this time in 1977. Reagan's current popularity at 70% among political independents is marginally higher than Carter's 62% in the 1977 survey.

MAY 31
ABORTION

Interviewing Date: 5/8–11/81
Survey #173-G

The U.S. Supreme Court has ruled that a woman may go to a doctor to end pregnancy at any time during the first three months of pregnancy. Do you favor or oppose this ruling?

Favor............................... 45%
Oppose.............................. 46
No opinion 9

By Sex
Male

Favor............................... 47%
Oppose.............................. 44
No opinion 9

Female

Favor............................... 43%
Oppose.............................. 49
No opinion 8

By Race
White

Favor............................... 46%
Oppose.............................. 46
No opinion 8

Nonwhite

Favor............................... 38%
Oppose.............................. 51
No opinion 11

By Education
College

Favor............................... 58%
Oppose.............................. 35
No opinion 7

High School

Favor.............................41%
Oppose............................49
No opinion 10

Grade School

Favor.............................33%
Oppose............................59
No opinion 8

By Region
East

Favor.............................51%
Oppose............................38
No opinion 11

Midwest

Favor.............................37%
Oppose............................54
No opinion 9

South

Favor.............................40%
Oppose............................52
No opinion 8

West

Favor.............................57%
Oppose............................37
No opinion 6

By Age
18–24 Years

Favor.............................44%
Oppose............................46
No opinion 10

25–29 Years

Favor.............................48%
Oppose............................43
No opinion 9

30–49 Years

Favor.............................50%
Oppose............................43
No opinion 7

50 Years and Over

Favor.............................40%
Oppose............................51
No opinion 9

By Politics
Republicans

Favor.............................47%
Oppose............................45
No opinion 8

Democrats

Favor.............................41%
Oppose............................50
No opinion 9

Independents

Favor.............................39%
Oppose............................55
No opinion 6

By Religion
Protestants

Favor.............................45%
Oppose............................46
No opinion 9

Catholics

Favor.............................37%
Oppose............................56
No opinion 7

Evangelicals

Favor.............................30%
Oppose............................60
No opinion 10

Non-Evangelicals

Favor 51%
Oppose 41
No opinion 8

Those Who Say Life Begins At Conception

Favor 27%
Oppose 66
No opinion 7

Those Who Say Life Begins At Birth

Favor 73%
Oppose 20
No opinion 7

Some people feel that human life begins at the moment of conception. Others feel that human life does not begin until the baby is actually born. Do you, yourself, feel that human life begins at conception, at the time of birth, or at some point in between?

At conception 54%
At birth 17
In between 22
No opinion 7

By Sex
Male

At conception 49%
At birth 21
In between 22
No opinion 8

Female

At conception 59%
At birth 14
In between 22
No opinion 5

By Race
White

At conception 54%
At birth 16
In between 23
No opinion 7

Nonwhite

At conception 53%
At birth 22
In between 18
No opinion 7

By Education
College

At conception 48%
At birth 19
In between 27
No opinion 6

High School

At conception 56%
At birth 16
In between 22
No opinion 6

Grade School

At conception 59%
At birth 18
In between 13
No opinion 10

By Region
East

At conception 49%
At birth 21
In between 22
No opinion 8

Midwest

At conception 59%
At birth 15
In between 20
No opinion 6

South

At conception 57%
At birth 15
In between 20
No opinion 8

West

At conception........................49%
At birth 19
In between........................27
No opinion 5

By Age
18–24 Years

At conception........................57%
At birth 17
In between........................20
No opinion 6

25–29 Years

At conception........................58%
At birth 15
In between........................22
No opinion 5

30–49 Years

At conception........................53%
At birth 18
In between........................23
No opinion 6

50 Years and Over

At conception........................52%
At birth 17
In between........................22
No opinion 9

By Politics
Republicans

At conception........................53%
At birth 18
In between........................23
No opinion 6

Democrats

At conception........................55%
At birth 17
In between........................22
No opinion 6

Independents

At conception........................54%
At birth 17
In between........................21
No opinion 8

By Religion
Protestants

At conception........................52%
At birth 16
In between........................26
No opinion 6

Catholics

At conception........................66%
At birth 13
In between........................14
No opinion 7

Evangelicals

At conception........................68%
At birth 11
In between........................18
No opinion 3

Non-Evangelicals

At conception........................48%
At birth 20
In between........................24
No opinion 8

Those Who Favor Supreme Court Decision

At conception........................32%
At birth 28
In between........................34
No opinion 6

Those Who Oppose Supreme Court Decision

At conception........................77%
At birth 7
In between........................10
No opinion 6

Do you think abortions should be legal under any circumstances, legal under only certain circumstances, or illegal in all circumstances?

Legal, any circumstances 23%
Legal, certain circumstances 52
Illegal, all circumstances 21
No opinion 4

By Sex
Male

Legal, any circumstances 22%
Legal, certain circumstances 54
Illegal, all circumstances............. 19
No opinion 5

Female

Legal, any circumstances 23%
Legal, certain circumstances 50
Illegal, all circumstances............. 24
No opinion 3

By Race
White

Legal, any circumstances 24%
Legal, certain circumstances 53
Illegal, all circumstances............. 20
No opinion 3

Nonwhite

Legal, any circumstances 18%
Legal, certain circumstances 47
Illegal, all circumstances............. 29
No opinion 6

By Education
College

Legal, any circumstances 35%
Legal, certain circumstances 50
Illegal, all circumstances............. 14
No opinion 1

High School

Legal, any circumstances 19%
Legal, certain circumstances 55
Illegal, all circumstances............. 22
No opinion 4

Grade School

Legal, any circumstances 12%
Legal, certain circumstances 42
Illegal, all circumstances............. 37
No opinion 9

By Region
East

Legal, any circumstances 29%
Legal, certain circumstances 53
Illegal, all circumstances............. 14
No opinion 4

Midwest

Legal, any circumstances 16%
Legal, certain circumstances 57
Illegal, all circumstances............. 23
No opinion 4

South

Legal, any circumstances 20%
Legal, certain circumstances 48
Illegal, all circumstances............. 28
No opinion 4

West

Legal, any circumstances 30%
Legal, certain circumstances 49
Illegal, all circumstances............. 19
No opinion 2

By Age
18–24 Years

Legal, any circumstances 20%
Legal, certain circumstances 59
Illegal, all circumstances............. 18
No opinion 3

25–29 Years

Legal, any circumstances	30%
Legal, certain circumstances	52
Illegal, all circumstances	16
No opinion	2

30–49 Years

Legal, any circumstances	28%
Legal, certain circumstances	49
Illegal, all circumstances	20
No opinion	3

50 Years and Over

Legal, any circumstances	17%
Legal, certain circumstances	51
Illegal, all circumstances	26
No opinion	6

By Politics
Republicans

Legal, any circumstances	24%
Legal, certain circumstances	55
Illegal, all circumstances	19
No opinion	2

Democrats

Legal, any circumstances	21%
Legal, certain circumstances	49
Illegal, all circumstances	25
No opinion	5

Independents

Legal, any circumstances	26%
Legal, certain circumstances	52
Illegal, all circumstances	19
No opinion	3

By Religion
Protestants

Legal, any circumstances	20%
Legal, certain circumstances	55
Illegal, all circumstances	22
No opinion	3

Catholics

Legal, any circumstances	21%
Legal, certain circumstances	49
Illegal, all circumstances	25
No opinion	5

Those Who Say Life Begins At Conception

Legal, any circumstances	11%
Legal, certain circumstances	56
Illegal, all circumstances	30
No opinion	3

Those Who Say Life Begins At Birth

Legal, any circumstances	44%
Legal, certain circumstances	39
Illegal, all circumstances	13
No opinion	4

The following table shows current attitudes on abortion closely parallel those recorded in earlier surveys:

Trend on Views Toward Abortion

	1981	1980	1979	1977	1975
Legal, any circumstances	23%	25%	22%	22%	21%
Legal, certain circumstances	52	53	54	55	54
Illegal, all circumstances	21	18	19	19	22
No opinion	4	4	5	4	3

Note: The American public is closely divided—45% in favor and 46% opposed—on the U.S. Supreme Court ruling that permits a woman to obtain an abortion during the first three months of pregnancy. Senator Jesse Helms (R-North Carolina) and others have been pressing for action on a bill that would circumvent the Supreme Court's decision by stating that human life begins at conception.

The current survey sought to determine public attitudes on the question of when human life begins and to see how these attitudes relate to views on the Supreme Court ruling. The results indicate that while American opinion as a whole is evenly divided on the court decision, the public's views depend in considerable measure on when they believe life begins.

Among those who think that human life begins at conception, only 27% favor the U.S. Supreme Court ruling, while 66% are opposed. In contrast, among those who believe human life does not begin until the baby is actually born opinion is almost the reverse, with 73% in favor of the court ruling and 20% opposed.

Senator Helms speaks for many Evangelicals. The current survey indicates that persons who can be broadly classified as Evangelicals are overwhelmingly opposed to the U.S. Supreme Court ruling. In addition, they are far more inclined than non-Evangelicals to believe that human life begins at conception.

A further survey to determine what change, if any, has come about in the proportions of Americans who believe abortions should be legal under any circumstances and those who hold the belief that abortions should be illegal under all circumstances shows little change since 1975. About equal proportions (one in five) take each of the extreme positions, with the weight of opinion between these two. Fifty-two percent believe that abortions should be legal under certain circumstances.

JUNE 4
PRESIDENT REAGAN

Interviewing Date: 5/8–11/81
Survey #173-G

Do you approve or disapprove of the way Reagan is handling his job as president?

Approve............................68%
Disapprove 21
No opinion 11

Do you approve or disapprove of the way Reagan is handling our relations with Russia?

Approve............................53%
Disapprove 23
No opinion 24

Do you approve or disapprove of the way Reagan is handling the situation in El Salvador?

Approve............................30%
Disapprove 38
No opinion 32

Do you approve or disapprove of the way Reagan is dealing with inflation?

Approve............................56%
Disapprove 30
No opinion 14

Do you approve or disapprove of the way Reagan is dealing with unemployment?

Approve............................42%
Disapprove 34
No opinion 24

Do you approve or disapprove of the way Reagan is dealing with the energy situation?

Approve............................44%
Disapprove 31
No opinion 25

Do you approve or disapprove of the way Reagan is handling our national defense?

Approve............................62%
Disapprove 20
No opinion 18

Do you approve or disapprove of the way Reagan is dealing with economic conditions in this country?

Approve............................58%
Disapprove 31
No opinion 11

Note: Eleven percent of the sample surveyed approve of the way President Ronald Reagan is handling his job and of the way he is handling each of the above problems, while 15% disapprove. These percentages indicate that more Americans approve of Reagan's general performance in office than have favorable opinions about his handling of seven specific foreign and domestic issues.

Recent survey findings suggest that while the public generally admires Reagan for his personal attributes, for example, his resilience in recovering from the March 30 assassination attempt and his willingness to take a sometimes unpopular leadership role in addressing the economic problems of the nation, many people are either dubious or downright skeptical about the effectiveness of the president's approaches to these problems.

In the latest Gallup Poll two out of three citizens (68%) express confidence in Reagan's overall discharge of his presidential duties. Yet approval of his handling of specific problems ranges from a high of 62% for his efforts to improve our national defense to a low of 30% for the way he is dealing with the situation in El Salvador.

Between these extremes the president receives favorable ratings of 58% for handling economic conditions in the United States, 56% for dealing with inflation, and 53% for the way he is handling U.S.-Soviet relations. Reagan gets less than majority support from the public for his approach to energy problems (44%) and for dealing with unemployment (42%).

The president's overall popularity rating has increased by 8 percentage points since a survey completed two weeks before the attempt on his life. However with one exception during this interim there have been no significant increases in the positive ratings accorded Reagan for his handling of specific problems facing the country. The single exception is a 7-point improvement in favorable public attitudes of the president's handling of the energy situation, from 37% approval in the March survey to 44% at present. Ironically, this may be a reflection of lower retail gasoline prices, a product not of Reagan's making but of the present world oversupply of oil.

An analysis of the relative importance of President Reagan's handling of specific issues indicates that inflation is by far the most important. The analysis suggests that a shift from public approval to disapproval on the inflation issue would be more than twice as damaging to the president as the loss of support on any other single issue.

JUNE 7
REAGAN'S ECONOMIC PLAN

Interviewing Date: 5/8–11/81
Survey #173-G

Now, let's talk about the Reagan administration's economic policies. What effect do you think that these policies will have on your own and your family's financial situation? Do you feel your financial situation will be much better, somewhat better, somewhat worse, or much worse as a result of the Reagan economic policies?

Much better. 7%
Somewhat better. 41
Somewhat worse 28
Much worse. 9
No opinion 15

By Race
White

Much better. 8%
Somewhat better. 44
Somewhat worse 27
Much worse. 7
No opinion 14

Nonwhite

Much better. 6%
Somewhat better. 24
Somewhat worse 34
Much worse. 20
No opinion 16

By Education
College

Much better. 8%
Somewhat better. 47
Somewhat worse 29
Much worse. 7
No opinion 9

High School

Much better	7%
Somewhat better	43
Somewhat worse	26
Much worse	9
No opinion	15

Grade School

Much better	7%
Somewhat better	22
Somewhat worse	35
Much worse	12
No opinion	24

By Region
East

Much better	7%
Somewhat better	39
Somewhat worse	31
Much worse	10
No opinion	13

Midwest

Much better	5%
Somewhat better	41
Somewhat worse	29
Much worse	9
No opinion	16

South

Much better	11%
Somewhat better	40
Somewhat worse	25
Much worse	7
No opinion	17

West

Much better	8%
Somewhat better	46
Somewhat worse	27
Much worse	9
No opinion	10

By Age
18–29 Years

Much better	7%
Somewhat better	47
Somewhat worse	23
Much worse	11
No opinion	12

30–49 Years

Much better	9%
Somewhat better	45
Somewhat worse	25
Much worse	9
No opinion	12

50 Years and Over

Much better	7%
Somewhat better	32
Somewhat worse	35
Much worse	7
No opinion	19

By Income
$25,000 and Over

Much better	7%
Somewhat better	50
Somewhat worse	26
Much worse	5
No opinion	12

$20,000–$24,999

Much better	6%
Somewhat better	51
Somewhat worse	21
Much worse	7
No opinion	15

$15,000–$19,999

Much better	9%
Somewhat better	44
Somewhat worse	25
Much worse	7
No opinion	15

$10,000–$14,999

Much better 9%
Somewhat better 38
Somewhat worse 29
Much worse 8
No opinion 16

$5,000–$9,999

Much better 8%
Somewhat better 35
Somewhat worse 32
Much worse 10
No opinion 15

Under $5,000

Much better 4%
Somewhat better 16
Somewhat worse 33
Much worse 27
No opinion 20

By Politics
Republicans

Much better 10%
Somewhat better 55
Somewhat worse 21
Much worse 2
No opinion 12

Democrats

Much better 5%
Somewhat better 32
Somewhat worse 33
Much worse 14
No opinion 16

Independents

Much better 7%
Somewhat better 43
Somewhat worse 27
Much worse 8
No opinion 15

By Occupation
Professional and Business

Much better 8%
Somewhat better 50
Somewhat worse 28
Much worse 8
No opinion 6

Clerical and Sales

Much better 9%
Somewhat better 45
Somewhat worse 25
Much worse 11
No opinion 10

Manual Workers

Much better 7%
Somewhat better 43
Somewhat worse 28
Much worse 9
No opinion 13

Nonlabor Force

Much better 5%
Somewhat better 36
Somewhat worse 32
Much worse 7
No opinion 20

Labor Union Families Only

Much better 3%
Somewhat better 45
Somewhat worse 31
Much worse 10
No opinion 11

Nonlabor Union Families Only

Much better 9%
Somewhat better 40
Somewhat worse 27
Much worse 9
No opinion 15

The 11% of the Sample That Approves of the Way Reagan Is Handling His Job and of the Way He Is Handling Major Domestic and Foreign Problems

Much better. 20%
Somewhat better. 57
Somewhat worse 12
Much worse. 1
No opinion 10

The 15% of the Sample That Disapproves of the Way Reagan Is Handling His Job and of the Way He Is Handling Major Domestic and Foreign Problems

Much better. 4%
Somewhat better. 10
Somewhat worse 36
Much worse. 31
No opinion 19

Do you expect the cuts in federal government spending may hurt you or your family's financial situation in any of the ways shown on this card? [Respondents were handed a card listing twelve possible effects of government spending cuts.]

Will have an effect on me or my family 64%
  Reduced payments from government
    (e.g. Social Security, food stamps,
    welfare, student loans, etc.). . . 50%
  Will have to pay more for
    goods and/or services. 26
  Might lose job. 8
                       84%*
Will not have an effect on me
  or my family. 33
No opinion 3

By Race
White

Will have an effect on me or my family 63%
  Reduced payments from government
    (e.g. Social Security, food stamps,
    welfare, student loans, etc.). . . 48%

  Will have to pay more for
    goods and/or services. 25
  Might lose job. 7
                       80%*
Will not have an effect on me
  or my family. 35
No opinion 2

Nonwhite

Will have an effect on me or my family 76%
  Reduced payments from government
    (e.g. Social Security, food stamps,
    welfare, student loans, etc.). . . 62%
  Will have to pay more for
    goods and/or services. 29
  Might lose job. 12
                      103%*
Will not have an effect on me
  or my family. 18
No opinion 6

By Income
$15,000 and Over

Will have an effect on me or my family 59%
  Reduced payments from government
    (e.g. Social Security, food stamps,
    welfare, student loans, etc.). . . 42%
  Will have to pay more for
    goods and/or services. 27
  Might lose job. 6
                      75%*
Will not have an effect on me
  or my family. 40
No opinion 1

Under $15,000

Will have an effect on me or my family 71%
  Reduced payments from government
    (e.g. Social Security, food stamps,
    welfare, student loans, etc.). . . 60%
  Will have to pay more for
    goods and/or services. 24
  Might lose job. 10
                      94%*

Will not have an effect on me
  or my family 24
No opinion 5

*Multiple responses were given.

Note: The American people are generally optimistic about the Reagan administration's economic policies, even though as many as half believe the planned spending cuts may mean some loss of income for them. Even those who feel the projected budget cuts will affect them are divided over President Ronald Reagan's economic package, with roughly equal proportions saying their personal economic situation will be improved or made worse.

Recent findings show that 58% of Americans approve of the way President Reagan is dealing with economic conditions and a similar proportion approve of the administration's handling of inflation. Moreover, 60% of the public believe that the Reagan administration will be successful in reducing inflation, which surveys consistently have shown to be the nation's most important problem.

Almost half (48%) of Americans are of the opinion that the overall Reagan economic package will make their personal financial situation better. Slightly under two in five (37%) think just the opposite, while 15% offer no opinion.

Optimism about the beneficial effects of the Reagan program is especially widespread among college-educated respondents (55% of whom think the economic package will make their personal financial situation better), upper-income households (57%), and those in the professions and business (58%). Expecting to be hurt by the Reagan program are nonwhites (54% of whom foresee a worsening of their personal finances), low-income households (49%), respondents with only a grade-school background (47%), and those fifty years of age and over (42%).

Close to two-thirds of Americans report that the spending cuts may affect them either directly or indirectly, while half expect reductions in payments they are receiving from the government, such as Social Security, food stamps, and welfare. Twenty-six percent expect to have to pay more for certain goods and services as a result and 8% are fearful of losing their job.

A three-quarters majority of those who feel that their economic situation will improve approve of Reagan's handling of the economy and inflation. On the other hand, those who foresee a worsening of personal finances lean toward disapproval. Nonetheless, of those who report they stand to lose from Reagan's economic package, as many as one-third approve of the president's handling of the economy in general and inflation in specific.

The fact that a considerable proportion of Americans who expect the Reagan economic policies to worsen their personal finances approve of the program reflects the degree of success that the administration has had in convincing voters of the necessity—and efficacy— of its proposed measures.

Similarly, respondents who say the projected budget cuts may affect them are roughly equally divided as to whether the Reagan economic package will help or hurt their personal economic situation, with only slightly fewer (40%) believing it will improve their personal finances rather than worsen them (48%). This stands in sharp contrast to those respondents who say the Reagan budget ax will have no effect on them, 67% of whom feel they will be better off once the Reagan policies are implemented.

JUNE 8
REAGAN'S ECONOMIC PLAN

Interviewing Date: 5/8–11/81
Survey #173-G

The Reagan administration's budget has called for cuts in federal government spending in a number of areas. Do you feel that the total amount of spending cuts that the Reagan administration wants to make is too high, too low, or about the right amount?

Too high 34%
Too low 12
About right 46
No opinion 8

By Race
White

Too high 30%
Too low 13
About right 49
No opinion 8

Nonwhite

Too high 64%
Too low 3
About right 25
No opinion 8

By Education
College

Too high 30%
Too low 16
About right 48
No opinion 6

High School

Too high 34%
Too low 10
About right 48
No opinion 8

Grade School

Too high 44%
Too low 6
About right 36
No opinion 14

By Region
East

Too high 42%
Too low 10
About right 39
No opinion 9

Midwest

Too high 27%
Too low 14
About right 51
No opinion 8

South

Too high 34%
Too low 10
About right 47
No opinion 9

West

Too high 34%
Too low 13
About right 47
No opinion 6

By Age
18–29 Years

Too high 42%
Too low 9
About right 45
No opinion 4

30–49 Years

Too high 28%
Too low 16
About right 49
No opinion 7

50 Years and Over

Too high 35%
Too low 9
About right 44
No opinion 12

By Income
$25,000 and Over

Too high 25%
Too low 17
About right 53
No opinion 5

$20,000–$24,999

Too high 26%
Too low 13
About right 57
No opinion 4

$15,000–$19,999

Too high 33%
Too low 11
About right 49
No opinion 7

$10,000–$14,999

Too high 36%
Too low 9
About right 47
No opinion 8

$5,000–$9,999

Too high 42%
Too low 7
About right 39
No opinion 12

Under $5,000

Too high 53%
Too low 7
About right 23
No opinion 17

By Politics
Republicans

Too high 15%
Too low 16
About right 63
No opinion 6

Democrats

Too high 50%
Too low 7
About right 34
No opinion 9

Independents

Too high 29%
Too low 13
About right 49
No opinion 9

By Occupation
Professional and Business

Too high 28%
Too low 20
About right 47
No opinion 5

Clerical and Sales

Too high 31%
Too low 14
About right 43
No opinion 12

Manual Workers

Too high 38%
Too low 9
About right 46
No opinion 7

Nonlabor Force

Too high 40%
Too low 9
About right 38
No opinion 13

By Community Location
Central Cities

Too high 42%
Too low 11
About right 39
No opinion 8

Suburbs

Too high 35%
Too low 12
About right 47
No opinion 6

Nonmetropolitan Areas

Too high 28%
Too low 12
About right 50
No opinion 10

Labor Union Families Only

Too high 39%
Too low 13
About right 42
No opinion 6

Nonlabor Union Families Only

Too high 33%
Too low 11
About right 47
No opinion 9

In general, are there any specific cuts being made in federal government spending that you disapprove of?

Yes.................................. 48%
No................................... 41
Don't know 11

Asked of those who responded in the affirmative: Which spending cuts do you disapprove?

Social Security....................... 17%
Federal aid to education 8
Welfare 8
Aid to the elderly 6
Social programs (general)............. 5
Food stamps 5
Medicare/Medicaid 4
CETA job programs 4
Financial aid to college students 3
Veterans' benefits.................... 2
School lunches 2
Fuel/rent/utility subsidies............. 2
Other programs...................... 9
Don't know 2
                                    ─────
                                    77%*

*Total adds to more than 48% due to multiple responses.

*Asked of the entire sample: President Reagan has proposed that federal income tax rates be reduced by 10% in each of the next three years, for a total reduction in tax rates of 30%. Just your best guess, what do you think is most likely—will federal income tax rates be cut by the full 30%, or will there be a smaller cut, or will there be no cut at all?***

Full 30% cut......................... 17%
Smaller cut 61
No cut at all 13
Don't know 9

**President Reagan's tax cut proposals were enacted into law on August 12, 1981.

Note: The budget cuts proposed by the Reagan administration have the broad approval of the American public, with only 34% saying that the projected cutbacks are too high. In contrast, just under half of Americans (46%) think that the budget cuts are about the right amount, 12% are of the opinion they are too low, and 8% offer no opinion.

Most likely to think the proposed cuts are too high are nonwhites (64%), Democrats (50%), low-income households (46%), respondents with only a grade-school education (44%), easterners (42%), and residents of the nation's central cities (42%). The opinion that the cuts are about right is most widespread among Republicans (63%), upper-income households (54%), midwesterners (51%), and residents of nonmetropolitan areas (50%).

The same groups who are most likely to feel the budget cuts are too high also mention opposition to specific cuts more frequently. For instance, 60% of Democrats object to cuts in one or more areas, against 33% of Republicans. Like Democrats, nonwhites (66%), easterners (53%), urban residents (53%), and low-income households (52%) object most often to specific cuts.

As reported, more Americans think that the Reagan economic policies will improve their personal financial situation (48%) than hurt them (37%). Among those who believe that the

Reagan spending cuts are too high, on the other hand, only 28% feel their economic situation will be improved by the administration's package, while 60% think things will worsen for them personally.

While the budget battle largely has been won by the Reagan forces on Capitol Hill, a fight is brewing over the second part of the Reagan economic package, a plan to cut federal income tax rates by 10% a year over the next three years for a total reduction of 30%. Opponents of the Reagan proposal contend it is inflationary and have come up with several counterproposals that would decrease both the overall cut in tax rates and the length of time over which the rate cuts would be spread.

Respondents in the recent Gallup survey overwhelmingly expect a tax cut, albeit a smaller one than the president originally backed. Fewer than one in five expect the full 30% cut in federal income tax rates, and fewer still believe there will be no cut at all.

JUNE 14
REAGAN CAMPAIGN PROMISES

Interviewing Date: 11/21–24/80; 5/8–11/81
Survey #165-G; #173-G

Do you think the Reagan administration will or will not be able to reduce inflation?

	May 1981	November 1980
Will	60%	46%
Will not	28	38
Don't know	12	16

Do you think the Reagan administration will or will not be able to reduce unemployment?

	May 1981	November 1980
Will	48%	47%
Will not	36	37
Don't know	16	16

Do you think the Reagan administration will or will not be able to reduce the size of government?

	May 1981	November 1980
Will	66%	52%
Will not	23	32
Don't know	11	16

Do you think the Reagan administration will or will not be able to balance the budget?

	May 1981	November 1980
Will	41%	30%
Will not	46	55
Don't know	13	15

Do you think the Reagan administration will or will not be able to increase respect for the United States abroad?

	May 1981	November 1980
Will	68%	62%
Will not	19	24
Don't know	13	14

By Politics
Republicans

		Point change since Nov. 1980
Will reduce inflation	82%	+8
Will reduce unemployment	68	+6
Will reduce size of government	84	+16
Will balance budget	57	+9
Will increase respect for United States	89	+4

Democrats

Will reduce inflation	46%	+17
Will reduce unemployment	38	+7
Will reduce size of government	60	+17
Will balance budget	34	+12
Will increase respect for United States	54	+7

Independents

Will reduce inflation	63%	+15
Will reduce unemployment	46	−2

Will reduce size of
    government 62   +8
Will balance budget 39   +12
Will increase respect for
    United States 70   +5

Note: The public's confidence in President Ronald Reagan's ability to make good on three important campaign pledges—roll back inflation, reduce the size of the federal government, and increase respect for the United States abroad—has grown markedly since last November, with solid majorities now believing he will be successful in these efforts. In fact, President Reagan's continued high level of popularity may be largely due to these perceptions.

Six Americans in ten now believe Reagan will be able to reduce inflation. In addition, a majority of the public thinks that the Reagan administration's economic plan will work and only one-third believes the budget cuts that the plan entails are too drastic.

In a Gallup Poll conducted three weeks after Reagan's victory last November, only 46% of Americans thought he would be able to reduce inflation in contrast to 60% at present. Public expectations that the president will be able to increase world respect for the United States also have grown, from 62% in November to the current 68%.

Between the two surveys the number of Americans holding the belief that Reagan will be able to reduce the size of the federal government has grown from 52% to 66%. And although a plurality still thinks President Reagan will not be able to balance the budget, optimism in this area has increased as well, with 41% now anticipating a balanced budget compared to merely 30% who held this view in November. And on the issue of reducing unemployment, no change in the public's expectations has been found, with 47% and 48% in the November and May surveys, respectively.

Many Democrats still harbor doubts about Reagan's chances of success in the areas measured. However, the increase in positive attitudes among Democrats is one of the most dramatic found in any population group. For example, in November 1980, only 29% of Democrats believed that Reagan would be able to reduce inflation; currently a 46% plurality holds that opinion—a 17-point increase. Similarly, optimism among Democrats has grown by 17 points on the issue of reducing the size of the government. An increase of 12 points is recorded on balancing the budget, 7 points on increasing respect for the United States abroad, and 7 points on reducing unemployment.

JUNE 18
POLITICAL AFFILIATION

Interviewing Date: January–May 1981
Various Surveys

In politics, as of today, do you consider yourself a Republican, a Democrat, or an independent?*

Republican 28%
Democrat. 41
Independent 31

*Persons who say they belong to other parties or have no party allegiance have been excluded.

The following table shows the political affiliation of major population groups from late January through May 1981. The figures in the right-hand column indicate the shift to the Republican party since the period April–June 1980. The groups are ranked in order of Republican strength. (Persons who say they belong to other parties or who have no party allegiance have been excluded.)

Political Affiliation
Late January–May 1981

	Republicans	Democrats	Independents	Swing to Republicans since 1980
Farmers	42%	29%	29%	+15
$25,000 and over income.	35	33	32	+12

Group			
Professional and business	35	31	34	+11
College education	34	32	34	+12
Protestants	32	40	28	+10
Under 2,500 population	32	38	30	+10
50 years and over	31	47	22	+8
White	30	37	33	+10
West	30	42	28	+7
Nonlabor union families	30	39	31	+11
$20,000–$24,999 income	29	37	34	+17
National	28	41	31	+11
Women	28	44	28	+9
East	28	41	31	+10
Midwest	28	36	36	+11
Nonlabor force	28	50	22	+5
2,500–49,999 population	28	41	31	+4
Men	27	38	35	+10
30–49 years	27	40	33	+10
50,000–499,999 population	27	41	32	+16
High-school education	26	42	32	+10
$15,000–$19,999 income	26	41	33	+4
South	25	47	28	+8
18–24 years	25	34	41	+11
Clerical and sales	25	43	32	+10
One million and over population	25	46	29	+9
$10,000–$14,999 income	24	44	32	+9
Skilled workers	24	39	37	+14
$5,000–$9,999 income	23	49	28	+5
500,000–999,999 population	23	42	35	+5
25–29 years	22	38	40	+11
Catholics	22	45	33	+12
Labor union families	21	48	31	+10
Grade-school education	20	58	22	+2
Unskilled workers	20	48	32	+8
Under $5,000 income	18	57	25	+2
Jews	17	57	26	+16
Nonwhite	8	74	18	0

The following percentages represent the trend in political affiliation since 1946:

	Republicans	Democrats	Independents
1981 (Jan.–May)	28%	41%	31%
1980 (Oct.–Dec.)	26	44	30
1980 (July–Sept.)	25	48	27
1980 (Apr.–June)	23	47	30
1980 (Jan.–Mar.)	21	47	32
1979	22	45	33
1975	22	45	33
1972	28	43	29
1968	27	46	27
1964	25	53	22
1960	30	47	23
1954	34	46	20
1950	33	45	22
1946	40	39	21

Note: A greater proportion of Americans currently regard themselves as Republicans than at any time since 1972. Conversely, there are proportionately fewer Democrats in the adult population than has been the case since 1946. GOP affiliation, in fact, is now at a level last seen during the administrations of both Presidents Richard Nixon and Dwight Eisenhower.

In national in-person Gallup surveys conducted since President Ronald Reagan's inauguration, a total of 28% of the public claims allegiance to the Republican party, 41% are Democrats, and 31% say they are political independents. The comparable figures for the 1980 April-June quarter were: Republicans 23%, Democrats 47%, and independents 30%.

Not only has there been a significant nationwide increase in Republican strength but also the GOP has registered major gains among such traditionally Democratic groups as Jews, skilled workers, Catholics, and labor union households. Important gains also have been recorded in Republican strongholds such as farmers, upper-income families, persons from professional and managerial occupational backgrounds, and the college educated. In fact, the GOP has made headway against the Democrats in every major population group, with the sole exception of nonwhites.

Other signs of the burgeoning strength of the GOP are seen in these recent Gallup Poll findings: 1) more Americans consider the Republican party to be better able than the Democrats to handle the nation's most urgent problems than at any time since 1972; and 2) the Republican party is rated more favorably by the public, without regard to issues, than has been the case since the 1960s.

JUNE 19
PRESIDENT REAGAN

Interviewing Date: 6/5–8/81
Survey #174-G

Do you approve or disapprove of the way Reagan is handling his job as president?

Approve.............................59%
Disapprove 28
No opinion 13

Asked of those who expressed an opinion: How strongly would you say you approve/ disapprove—very strongly, or not so strongly?

Approve very strongly.................31%
Approve not so strongly 26
Disapprove very strongly 17
Disapprove not so strongly............ 10
No opinion 3
87%*

By Sex
Male

Approve very strongly.................33%
Approve not so strongly 26
Disapprove very strongly 16
Disapprove not so strongly............ 11
No opinion 2
88%*

Female

Approve very strongly.................30%
Approve not so strongly 25
Disapprove very strongly 18
Disapprove not so strongly............ 10
No opinion 2
85%*

By Race
White

Approve very strongly.................35%
Approve not so strongly 28
Disapprove very strongly 13
Disapprove not so strongly............ 10
No opinion 2
88%*

Nonwhite

Approve very strongly................. 4%
Approve not so strongly 15
Disapprove very strongly 45
Disapprove not so strongly............ 13
No opinion 3
80%*

By Education
College

Approve very strongly.................38%
Approve not so strongly 28
Disapprove very strongly 14
Disapprove not so strongly............ 9
No opinion 1
90%*

High School

Approve very strongly.................31%
Approve not so strongly 26
Disapprove very strongly 17
Disapprove not so strongly............ 11
No opinion 2
87%*

Grade School

Approve very strongly 18%
Approve not so strongly 18
Disapprove very strongly 24
Disapprove not so strongly 12
No opinion 6
                                               78%*

By Region
East

Approve very strongly 31%
Approve not so strongly 27
Disapprove very strongly 17
Disapprove not so strongly 10
No opinion 1
                                               86%*

Midwest

Approve very strongly 32%
Approve not so strongly 27
Disapprove very strongly 16
Disapprove not so strongly 10
No opinion 3
                                               88%*

South

Approve very strongly 35%
Approve not so strongly 21
Disapprove very strongly 17
Disapprove not so strongly 10
No opinion 2
                                               85%*

West

Approve very strongly 24%
Approve not so strongly 31
Disapprove very strongly 20
Disapprove not so strongly 13
No opinion 2
                                               90%*

By Age
18–29 Years

Approve very strongly 24%
Approve not so strongly 33
Disapprove very strongly 19
Disapprove not so strongly 11
No opinion 3
                                               90%*

30–49 Years

Approve very strongly 34%
Approve not so strongly 27
Disapprove very strongly 15
Disapprove not so strongly 10
No opinion 2
                                               88%*

50 Years and Over

Approve very strongly 35%
Approve not so strongly 19
Disapprove very strongly 17
Disapprove not so strongly 11
No opinion 2
                                               84%*

By Income
$25,000 and Over

Approve very strongly 40%
Approve not so strongly 30
Disapprove very strongly 12
Disapprove not so strongly 9
No opinion 2
                                               93%*

$15,000 and Over

Approve very strongly 36%
Approve not so strongly 29
Disapprove very strongly 14
Disapprove not so strongly 10
No opinion 1
                                               90%*

Under $15,000

Approve very strongly................25%
Approve not so strongly 22
Disapprove very strongly 21
Disapprove not so strongly............11
No opinion ....<u> 3</u>
                                    82%*

By Politics
Republicans

Approve very strongly................62%
Approve not so strongly 23
Disapprove very strongly 3
Disapprove not so strongly............ 3
No opinion ....<u> 2</u>
                                    93%*

Democrats

Approve very strongly................15%
Approve not so strongly 28
Disapprove very strongly 28
Disapprove not so strongly............16
No opinion ....<u> 2</u>
                                    89%*

Independents

Approve very strongly................28%
Approve not so strongly 27
Disapprove very strongly 15
Disapprove not so strongly............10
No opinion ....<u> 3</u>
                                    83%*

*Percentage of respondents who expressed an opinion.

Also asked of those who expressed an opinion on approval or disapproval of the way Reagan is handling his job as president (87% of the sample): Why do you feel this way?

Approval
Deserves credit for trying (general) . . . 26%
Approve of economic plan and
   budget cuts 19

Leadership qualities; like him........16
Needed a change of leadership.......11
Reducing government size and
   waste ....<u> 6</u>
                                    78%*

Disapproval
Dislike economic plan and budget
   cuts 44%
Reducing Social Security benefits 24
Helps business and rich people.......22
Has not done anything positive....... 8
Outspoken military posture..........<u> 7</u>
                                    105%*

*Multiple responses were given.

Note: President Ronald Reagan's job performance rating has dropped sharply, with 59% now approving of Reagan's handling of his presidential duties, 28% disapproving, and 13% undecided. This rating shows a 9-percentage point decrease from a mid-May survey, when his positive rating stood at 68%.

This decline in approval is nearly matched by a 7-point increase (from 21% to 28%) in those who disapprove of the president's job performance—the highest level of disapproval noted during Reagan's brief tenure and higher than that recorded for any other president at this point in his administration.

By comparison, Presidents Jimmy Carter and Richard Nixon not only had slightly higher approval ratings at similar points in 1977 and 1969, respectively, but also significantly fewer people disapproved of their stewardship.

Analysis of the intensity with which the public holds its views of President Reagan's job performance shows that about half of those who approve do so very strongly and the other half not so strongly. Conversely, strong disapproval outweighs moderate disapproval by a 3-to-2 ratio. This pattern of disapproval is unlike that usually found in these measurements, in which moderate exceeds strong disapproval.

Recent Gallup surveys showed President Reagan to be personally more popular than his handling of specific problems. The current study, however, suggests that concern over the cuts in social programs, dissatisfaction with the proposed reductions in Social Security benefits, and criticism of the tax cuts are now being reflected in the president's lower overall performance ratings.

Although the Reagan economic and Social Security proposals have been viewed by some to have a disproportionate effect on the less advantaged segments of the population and on the elderly, the president's decline in popularity has occurred almost equally in all demographic groups. For example, Reagan lost 6 points among Americans under 30 years old, 10 points among 30 to 49 year olds, and 9 points among those over 50. Similarly, the president's popularity fell by 8 points among individuals whose family income is $15,000 or more and by 9 points among those with incomes of less than $15,000. And President Reagan suffered a loss of popularity not only among Democrats (7 points) but also Republicans (5 points) and independents (12 points).

JUNE 21
NUCLEAR DISARMAMENT

Interviewing Date: 5/8–11/81
Survey #173-G

Would you like to have the United Nations call for a referendum to be held in every nation of the world to permit the people of that nation to vote on the question of nuclear disarmament?

Favor 68%
Oppose 19
No opinion 13

If such a referendum were held in the United States, how would you vote—for or against nuclear disarmament?

For 59%
Against 29
No opinion 12

By Sex
Male

For 63%
Against 30
No opinion 7

Female

For 55%
Against 29
No opinion 16

By Education
College

For 64%
Against 30
No opinion 6

High School

For 56%
Against 31
No opinion 13

Grade School

For 56%
Against 24
No opinion 20

By Region
East

For 64%
Against 25
No opinion 11

Midwest

For 65%
Against 29
No opinion 6

South

For 49%
Against 33
No opinion 18

West

For......................................57%
Against...................................31
No opinion.................................12

By Age
18–29 Years

For......................................63%
Against...................................27
No opinion.................................10

30–49 Years

For......................................61%
Against...................................29
No opinion.................................10

50 Years and Over

For......................................53%
Against...................................32
No opinion.................................15

By Politics
Republicans

For......................................55%
Against...................................34
No opinion.................................11

Democrats

For......................................61%
Against...................................27
No opinion.................................12

Independents

For......................................59%
Against...................................28
No opinion.................................13

Do you think the United States should or should not meet with the Soviet Union this year to try to reach an agreement on nuclear disarmament?

Should....................................80%
Should not.................................13
No opinion..................................7

Would you favor or oppose an agreement between the United States and the Soviet Union not to build any more nuclear weapons in the future?

Favor.....................................72%
Oppose....................................20
No opinion.................................8

By Sex
Male

Favor.....................................72%
Oppose....................................22
No opinion.................................6

Female

Favor.....................................72%
Oppose....................................18
No opinion.................................10

By Education
College

Favor.....................................75%
Oppose....................................20
No opinion.................................5

High School

Favor.....................................72%
Oppose....................................20
No opinion.................................8

Grade School

Favor.....................................65%
Oppose....................................21
No opinion.................................14

By Region
East

Favor.....................................78%
Oppose....................................14
No opinion.................................8

Midwest

Favor.............................76%
Oppose............................19
No opinion 5

South

Favor.............................63%
Oppose............................26
No opinion 11

West

Favor.............................71%
Oppose............................21
No opinion 8

By Age
18–29 Years

Favor.............................75%
Oppose............................20
No opinion 5

30–49 Years

Favor.............................71%
Oppose............................22
No opinion 7

50 Years and Over

Favor.............................70%
Oppose............................19
No opinion 11

By Politics
Republicans

Favor.............................72%
Oppose............................21
No opinion 7

Democrats

Favor.............................72%
Oppose............................18
No opinion 10

Independents

Favor.............................72%
Oppose............................22
No opinion 6

How likely do you think the Soviet Union would be to abide by such an agreement—very likely, fairly likely, or not at all likely?

Very likely........................ 6%
Fairly likely.......................27
Not at all likely....................60
No opinion 7

Would you favor or oppose an agreement between the United States and the Soviet Union to destroy all nuclear weapons that already have been built?

Favor.............................47%
Oppose............................44
No opinion 9

By Sex
Male

Favor.............................48%
Oppose............................46
No opinion 6

Female

Favor.............................46%
Oppose............................41
No opinion 13

By Education
College

Favor.............................46%
Oppose............................47
No opinion 7

High School

Favor.............................48%
Oppose............................43
No opinion 9

Grade School

Favor...............................44%
Oppose..............................40
No opinion 16

By Region
East

Favor...............................51%
Oppose..............................40
No opinion 9

Midwest

Favor...............................48%
Oppose..............................44
No opinion 8

South

Favor...............................42%
Oppose..............................46
No opinion 12

West

Favor...............................47%
Oppose..............................46
No opinion 7

By Age
18–29 Years

Favor...............................52%
Oppose..............................39
No opinion 9

30–49 Years

Favor...............................44%
Oppose..............................49
No opinion 7

50 Years and Over

Favor...............................46%
Oppose..............................42
No opinion 12

By Politics
Republicans

Favor...............................42%
Oppose..............................49
No opinion 9

Democrats

Favor...............................49%
Oppose..............................41
No opinion 10

Independents

Favor...............................49%
Oppose..............................42
No opinion 9

How likely do you think the Soviet Union would be to abide by such an agreement—very likely, fairly likely, or not at all likely?

Very likely.........................4%
Fairly likely.......................16
Not at all likely...................73
No opinion 7

Note: A two-thirds majority of Americans would like the United Nations to conduct a referendum in every nation of the world in order to assess international public opinion on nuclear disarmament. According to a recent Gallup Poll, if such a referendum were held here the American public would vote in favor of nuclear disarmament by a 2-to-1 margin.

The survey also shows overwhelming support among all population groups (the percentage in any group does not fall below 73%) to hold a meeting between the United States and the Soviet Union this year to discuss nuclear disarmament. The two countries recently agreed to begin preparatory talks on limiting medium-range nuclear missiles in Europe.

If and when such a meeting between the two superpowers is held, most Americans (72% to 20%) would favor an agreement that would go beyond limitations on the building or deployment of nuclear weapons to include a total ban on their construction in the future. In fact, as many as 47% would prefer to see an accord between the United States and the Soviet Union, calling for the destruction of all nuclear weapons that already have been built.

Further evidence of the U.S. public's desire to stop the spread of nuclear arms is evidenced by the fact that most Americans would like the United States and the Soviet Union to agree to end future construction of these weapons, despite widespread skepticism about Soviet willingness to comply with the agreements. For example, 65% of those who think Russia would be not at all likely to abide by an agreement not to build any more nuclear weapons nonetheless favor such a pact. And 44% of those who doubt Russia's compliance favor an agreement to destroy existing nuclear weapons.

JUNE 28
SATISFACTION INDEX

Interviewing Date: 6/5–8/81
Survey #174-G

In general, are you satisfied or dissatisfied with the way things are going in the United States at this time?

Satisfied............................33%
Dissatisfied........................61
No opinion 6

By Sex
Male

Satisfied............................37%
Dissatisfied........................57
No opinion 6

Female

Satisfied............................29%
Dissatisfied........................65
No opinion 6

By Race
White

Satisfied............................35%
Dissatisfied........................59
No opinion 6

Nonwhite

Satisfied............................20%
Dissatisfied........................74
No opinion 6

By Education
College

Satisfied............................39%
Dissatisfied........................55
No opinion 6

High School

Satisfied............................30%
Dissatisfied........................64
No opinion 6

Grade School

Satisfied............................28%
Dissatisfied........................64
No opinion 8

By Region
East

Satisfied............................31%
Dissatisfied........................61
No opinion 8

Midwest

Satisfied............................31%
Dissatisfied........................64
No opinion 5

South

Satisfied............................39%
Dissatisfied........................54
No opinion 7

West

Satisfied...........................28%
Dissatisfied.......................67
No opinion 5

By Age
18–29 Years

Satisfied...........................36%
Dissatisfied.......................58
No opinion 6

30–49 Years

Satisfied...........................32%
Dissatisfied.......................62
No opinion 6

50 Years and Over

Satisfied...........................31%
Dissatisfied.......................63
No opinion 6

By Politics
Republicans

Satisfied...........................47%
Dissatisfied.......................48
No opinion 5

Democrats

Satisfied...........................23%
Dissatisfied.......................69
No opinion 8

Independents

Satisfied...........................33%
Dissatisfied.......................62
No opinion 5

Those Who Approve of Reagan

Satisfied...........................44%
Dissatisfied.......................51
No opinion 5

Those Who Disapprove of Reagan

Satisfied...........................13%
Dissatisfied.......................81
No opinion 6

National Trend on Views Toward United States

	Satisfied	Dissatisfied	No opinion
June 5–8, 1981	33%	61%	6%
January 1981	17	78	5
November 1979	19	77	4
February 1979	26	69	5

In general, are you satisfied or dissatisfied with the way things are going in your own personal life?

Satisfied...........................81%
Dissatisfied.......................16
No opinion 3

By Sex
Male

Satisfied...........................80%
Dissatisfied.......................17
No opinion 3

Female

Satisfied...........................83%
Dissatisfied.......................14
No opinion 3

By Race
White

Satisfied...........................84%
Dissatisfied.......................13
No opinion 3

Nonwhite

Satisfied...........................66%
Dissatisfied.......................31
No opinion 3

By Education
College

Satisfied...........................85%
Dissatisfied.......................13
No opinion 2

High School
Satisfied............................80%
Dissatisfied.........................16
No opinion 4

Grade School
Satisfied............................78%
Dissatisfied.........................19
No opinion 3

By Region
East
Satisfied............................84%
Dissatisfied.........................13
No opinion 3

Midwest
Satisfied............................82%
Dissatisfied.........................14
No opinion 4

South
Satisfied............................79%
Dissatisfied.........................18
No opinion 3

West
Satisfied............................80%
Dissatisfied.........................18
No opinion 2

By Age
18–29 Years
Satisfied............................79%
Dissatisfied.........................18
No opinion 3

30–49 Years
Satisfied............................80%
Dissatisfied.........................17
No opinion 3

50 Years and Over
Satisfied............................85%
Dissatisfied.........................12
No opinion 3

By Politics
Republicans
Satisfied............................89%
Dissatisfied......................... 9
No opinion 2

Democrats
Satisfied............................78%
Dissatisfied.........................18
No opinion 4

Independents
Satisfied............................79%
Dissatisfied.........................17
No opinion 4

Those Who Approve of Reagan
Satisfied............................85%
Dissatisfied.........................12
No opinion 3

Those Who Disapprove of Reagan
Satisfied............................74%
Dissatisfied.........................23
No opinion 3

National Trend on Views Toward Personal Life

	Satisfied	Dissatisfied	No opinion
June 5–8, 1981	81%	16%	3%
January 1981	81	17	2
November 1979	79	19	2
February 1979	77	21	2

Note: The mood of Americans is considerably brighter today than at the start of the year, with 33% saying they are satisfied with developments in the nation, compared to only 17% in

January. The current level of satisfaction is the highest recorded since February 1979. In contrast, a reduced but sizable majority (61%) expresses dissatisfaction.

Satisfaction with developments in the country has grown sharply among all major population groups with the notable exception of nonwhites. The current level of satisfaction among this group is only 20%.

This improved outlook has strong political overtones. In early January almost equal proportions of Republicans (18%) and Democrats (17%) expressed satisfaction; today the percentages are 47% and 23%, respectively. Further evidence of the political inclination of the nation's mood is found among those who approve of President Reagan's job performance. Forty-four percent express satisfaction with the national outlook, while among those who disapprove of Reagan's performance only 13% say they are satisfied.

Although only one-third of Americans express satisfaction with the way things are going in the nation, as many as eight in ten say they are satisfied with their personal lives, an interesting dichotomy that has been found in previous surveys.

The latest survey also reveals that nationally 13% can be classified as being dissatisfied both with the way things are going in the country and in their own personal lives. A profile of this group reveals that almost three in ten nonwhites (27%) express dissatisfaction at both levels, compared with only 10% of whites.

JULY 1
THE REAGAN/THATCHER MIRROR*

Special Survey

A nation plagued by inflation and sagging industrial vitality elects a conservative leader to put things right again. Cutting government

*This Gallup analysis was written by Andrew Kohut, president of the Gallup Organization Inc.

spending, which had grown steadily for decades under the opposition, and restoring the free enterprise system are the prime objectives of the new leadership. The voter mandate is not ideological but rather an attempt to take a different approach to some formidable economic problems.

The new leader in the above situation can read Ronald Reagan or Margaret Thatcher. Both came to office under remarkably similar circumstances and are dealing with common problems. Now it appears that there are also some distinct parallels between early British reaction to Thatcher and early American reaction to Reagan.

Although the problems of Britain are different from those of the United States, it is mostly in degree and not character. The British economy has been on a far longer and deeper economic skid than the American economy. Many times the inflation rate has broken 20% in the United Kingdom and in 1980 averaged about 17%. The proportional size and scope of government after decades of control by the Labour party is far greater than that envisioned by even the most liberal of Democrats. The tax burden is another common problem, which is more extremely felt in Britain as a consequence of heavy spending on social programs.

Obviously each country has its unique problems, but the new conservatives in Washington and London had to confront primarily the same dominant issues as they came to power. More importantly, both conservative leaders have had to deal with these problems in societies whose political orientation for decades had been to the left of the new leadership.

As a consequence, Thatcher and Reagan evoked significant amounts of public disapproval very early in the game. According to British Gallup Poll findings, Thatcher experienced the shortest honeymoon period with the British public in the political history of that country. After winning a May 1979 election by 7 percentage points (compared to Reagan's 10 percentage points), the Conservative party was trailing the Labour party by 10% in public support by December of that same year. The following is the trend in support for Thatcher's Conservative party since she took office:

Party Support in the United Kingdom

	Conservative	Labour	Liberal	Other
Share of votes in May 1979 general election	45%	38%	14%	3%
Gallup Poll June 1981	30	38	18	4
December 1980	33	49	15	3
December 1979	36	45	16	3

Nothing as dramatic as what happened in Great Britain has occurred in the United States during Reagan's first five months in office, but the June Gallup Poll, which showed Reagan's approval far below past presidents at a comparable period and disapproval at an all-time high for a new president, suggests that the Reagan honeymoon may be coming to a rapid close. The trend in Reagan popularity implies that the March 30 shooting suspended a great deal of criticism of the president's policies during his recovery period. However, this has reemerged according to the latest Gallup survey.

Despite this parallel, the American president has something going for him that Mrs. Thatcher does not—great personal appeal. President Reagan is consistently seen as more attractive than his programs. Margaret Thatcher has not had the benefit of personal popularity to aid her in the face of the towering economic problems that have beset her since taking office.

Unemployment in the United Kingdom has skyrocketed, forcing the Conservatives to put off cuts in government spending on which they had campaigned. Thatcher did manage a cut in personal income taxes, but its effect was offset by increases in other types of taxation and by the fact that British workers generally moved into higher income tax brackets as a result of inflated wages.

Ironically, the Conservatives have succeeded in taming inflation somewhat. For years the British Gallup Poll had shown inflation as the top concern of its public. In 1980 that changed abruptly. By December of that year only 10% of Britons named the 15% inflation rate as the country's worst problem, compared to 65% who believed that way about the 11% unemployment rate.

The economic consequences of Reaganomics have yet to be seen. If the president's program is successful, the parallels with Thatcher will break down. If it is not, or is only partially successful, Reagan may be judged as harshly by Americans as the English are now judging Thatcher. The Achilles' heel of both Republican Reagan and Conservative Thatcher is that they lead parties associated with the business and upper socioeconomic interests of their societies. This is the problem that most concerns British Conservative political strategists at the moment.

The British Gallup Poll shows that the percentage of those who believe that Thatcher is further dividing the country recently has risen to 70%. Similarly, throughout the spring a growing concern about Reagan has been that he sides too much with business interests (up 8 percentage points since the fall campaign). Support for Reagan and his programs divides more sharply along economic lines than has been the case for past presidents.

American Democrats should not take too much solace from this since their situation mirrors that of the Labour party in Britain. Evicted from power in 1979, the British Labour party really has not been able to capitalize on Thatcher's problems to a great extent because it has been perceived as a divided party without positive policies to deal with the economy. A new center party has emerged that severely handicaps the Labour party's opposition. The likelihood of this happening in the United States is not great, but the important point is that the Democrats may not be the automatic beneficiaries of Republican problems should they emerge.

Comparisons between American and British

politics can only extend so far, and the public jury is still largely out on Reagan as it is not in Thatcher's case. Nonetheless, in examining their own political scene, Americans too often ignore the politics of other Western democracies. In many cases, they provide insights and provocative parallels with what is happening in the United States. Nowhere is this more evident than in Great Britain.

JULY 2
WAGE AND PRICE CONTROLS

Interviewing Date: 6/5–8/81
Survey #174-G

Would you favor or oppose having the government bring back wage and price controls?

Favor.............................50%
Oppose.............................38
No opinion 12

By Region
East

Favor.............................57%
Oppose.............................31
No opinion 12

Midwest

Favor.............................49%
Oppose.............................41
No opinion 10

South

Favor.............................49%
Oppose.............................39
No opinion 12

West

Favor.............................41%
Oppose.............................46
No opinion 13

By Politics
Republicans

Favor.............................44%
Oppose.............................46
No opinion 10

Democrats

Favor.............................53%
Oppose.............................35
No opinion 12

Independents

Favor.............................51%
Oppose.............................38
No opinion 11

Labor Union Households Only

Favor.............................48%
Oppose.............................41
No opinion 11

Nonunion Households Only

Favor.............................50%
Oppose.............................38
No opinion 12

Note: President Ronald Reagan's economic plan to reduce inflation has not lessened the belief of most Americans for the need for wage and price controls. The weight of public opinion in the latest Gallup Poll is in support of controls, with 50% in favor of having the government take this action and 38% opposed. In the previous survey (conducted in early January prior to President Reagan's inauguration), the results were virtually the same, with 49% in favor and 40% opposed.

In contrast to the public as a whole, business and labor leaders traditionally have opposed controls. Labor leaders believe wage controls unfairly penalize union workers, while business people want the opportunity to raise prices and fear that controls will cause shortages in some commodities.

Proponents, however, point to the example of three European nations—the Netherlands, Switzerland, and West Germany—each of which has made great headway in controlling inflation and at the same time follows an incomes policy. Management and labor in each nation meet regularly to review the economic scene and jointly set the level of wage increases.

For almost forty years the public has approved wage and price controls during wars or periods of severe inflation. Fifteen years ago in 1966 opinion was evenly divided between those who favored and those who opposed wage-price curbs. But as inflationary pressures built during the latter half of the 1960s, opinion began to shift in favor of controls.

In a survey conducted shortly before President Richard Nixon's 1971 imposition of a wage-price freeze, public support for controls had reached its highest point since the Korean War. Just after Nixon froze wages and prices, a Gallup Poll showed Americans supported the move by a 5-to-1 ratio. Furthermore, surveys conducted at regular intervals during the three phases of Nixon's economic program consistently showed that the public favored stricter as opposed to less strict controls.

JULY 5
NATIONAL SERVICE

Interviewing Date: 6/5–8/81
Survey #174-G

Would you favor or oppose requiring all young men to give one year of service to the nation—either in the military forces or in nonmilitary work here, or abroad, such as work in hospitals or with elderly people?

Favor 71%
Oppose 24
No opinion 5

By Sex
Male

Favor 71%
Oppose 25
No opinion 4

Female

Favor 70%
Oppose 24
No opinion 6

By Race
White

Favor 71%
Oppose 25
No opinion 4

Nonwhite

Favor 71%
Oppose 18
No opinion 11

By Education
College

Favor 68%
Oppose 29
No opinion 3

High School

Favor 71%
Oppose 25
No opinion 4

Grade School

Favor 77%
Oppose 14
No opinion 9

By Region
East

Favor 70%
Oppose 26
No opinion 4

Midwest

Favor...............................70%
Oppose............................27
No opinion 3

South

Favor...............................69%
Oppose............................24
No opinion 7

West

Favor...............................77%
Oppose............................19
No opinion 4

By Age
18–24 Years

Favor...............................58%
Oppose............................37
No opinion 5

25–29 Years

Favor...............................64%
Oppose............................34
No opinion 2

30–49 Years

Favor...............................75%
Oppose............................21
No opinion 4

50 Years and Over

Favor...............................76%
Oppose............................18
No opinion 6

By Politics
Republicans

Favor...............................75%
Oppose............................22
No opinion 3

Democrats

Favor...............................72%
Oppose............................22
No opinion 6

Independents

Favor...............................69%
Oppose............................27
No opinion 4

Would you favor or oppose such a program for young women?

Favor...............................54%
Oppose............................40
No opinion 6

By Sex
Male

Favor...............................52%
Oppose............................41
No opinion 7

Female

Favor...............................56%
Oppose............................39
No opinion 5

By Race
White

Favor...............................54%
Oppose............................40
No opinion 6

Nonwhite

Favor...............................55%
Oppose............................38
No opinion 7

By Education
College

Favor...............................56%
Oppose............................39
No opinion 5

High School

Favor.................................54%
Oppose.................................40
No opinion 6

Grade School

Favor.................................51%
Oppose.................................40
No opinion 9

By Region
East

Favor.................................57%
Oppose.................................38
No opinion 5

Midwest

Favor.................................53%
Oppose.................................41
No opinion 6

South

Favor.................................47%
Oppose.................................45
No opinion 8

West

Favor.................................63%
Oppose.................................31
No opinion 6

By Age
18–24 Years

Favor.................................48%
Oppose.................................46
No opinion 6

25–29 Years

Favor.................................49%
Oppose.................................47
No opinion 4

30–49 Years

Favor.................................61%
Oppose.................................34
No opinion 5

50 Years and Over

Favor.................................52%
Oppose.................................40
No opinion 8

By Politics
Republicans

Favor.................................58%
Oppose.................................38
No opinion 4

Democrats

Favor.................................52%
Oppose.................................41
No opinion 7

Independents

Favor.................................54%
Oppose.................................39
No opinion 7

Suppose all young men were required to give one year of service, which would you prefer—military or nonmilitary?

Military...............................50%
Nonmilitary............................36
No opinion 14

By Sex
Male

Military...............................59%
Nonmilitary............................30
No opinion 11

Female

Military...............................42%
Nonmilitary............................41
No opinion 17

By Age
18–24 Years

Military 40%
Nonmilitary. 52
No opinion 8

25–29 Years

Military 39%
Nonmilitary. 46
No opinion 15

30–49 Years

Military 52%
Nonmilitary. 32
No opinion 16

50 Years and Over

Military 57%
Nonmilitary. 28
No opinion 15

Suppose all young women were required to give one year of service, which would you prefer—military or nonmilitary?

Military 18%
Nonmilitary. 67
No opinion 15

By Sex
Male

Military 20%
Nonmilitary. 65
No opinion 15

Female

Military 17%
Nonmilitary. 68
No opinion 15

By Age
18–24 Years

Military 12%
Nonmilitary. 78
No opinion 10

25–29 Years

Military 18%
Nonmilitary. 68
No opinion 14

30–49 Years

Military 22%
Nonmilitary. 62
No opinion 16

50 Years and Over

Military 19%
Nonmilitary. 65
No opinion 16

Note: A dramatic rise in support is recorded for a compulsory program of national service for young men and women, which could take the form of either military or nonmilitary duties, such as working in hospitals or helping the elderly.

Public backing for requiring young men to serve the nation for one year doing military or civilian work has jumped from 60% in 1979 to 71% in the latest survey. The current figure is higher than at any time since 1969 when these measurements began. However, far fewer favor such a plan for young women, but here too a sharp gain is recorded—from 40% two years ago to 54% today.

Support has grown among all major population groups but is most pronounced among eighteen to twenty-four year olds, who would be directly affected if a national service law were enacted. A total of 58% in this age group like the idea of national service for men, while 48% favor the concept for women.

Factors that may have contributed significantly to the gain in support for compulsory service are: 1) media reports of the failure of the all-volunteer armed forces to attract a sufficient number of competent recruits; 2) continuing concern over the seemingly intractable problem of youth unemployment and its attendant problems; and 3) a growing desire on the part of the public for greater military preparedness. This desire is reflected in the current survey results, which show a significantly greater proportion of the public today than in 1979 saying they would favor military over nonmilitary service for men if a compulsory national service plan were to go into effect. Similar to earlier survey findings, the public clearly opts for nonmilitary rather than military duties for women.

Public interest in national service probably has never been greater. The armed forces have been criticized both for the quantity and quality of their volunteer recruits. Youth unemployment, particularly among minority groups, is a serious and chronic problem. One result is that the armed services have become the "employer of last resort." At the same time, many young people have jobs that offer little promise for either upward mobility or self-fulfillment. Another problem that a compulsory national service program might help alleviate is the sense of drift or lack of purpose on the part of today's youth.

Proponents of national service point to successful examples abroad. With the exception of Great Britain, all countries in the European Economic Community have some form of compulsory national service. Here at home the Civilian Conservation Corps operated successfully during the Great Depression of the 1930s and, more recently, the Peace Corps and VISTA have enabled many young people to perform meaningful voluntary service to the nation.

Many opponents of compulsory national youth service see it as a precursor of military conscription, while others object to involuntary service on libertarian grounds. It is also argued that universal mandatory national service would present formidable practical problems, mainly financial.

JULY 9
PRESIDENT REAGAN/CONGRESS

Interviewing Date: 6/19–22/81
Survey #175-G

Do you approve or disapprove of the way Reagan is handling his job as president?

Approve. 59%
Disapprove 29
No opinion 12

By Sex
Male

Approve. 66%
Disapprove 23
No opinion 11

Female

Approve. 52%
Disapprove 34
No opinion 14

By Race
White

Approve. 65%
Disapprove 23
No opinion 12

Nonwhite

Approve. 19%
Disapprove 66
No opinion 15

By Education
College

Approve. 70%
Disapprove 23
No opinion 7

High School

Approve. 58%
Disapprove 28
No opinion 14

Grade School

Approve. 38%
Disapprove 42
No opinion 20

By Region
East
Approve.............................56%
Disapprove 29
No opinion 15

Midwest
Approve.............................58%
Disapprove 30
No opinion 12

South
Approve.............................62%
Disapprove 26
No opinion 12

West
Approve.............................60%
Disapprove 29
No opinion 11

By Age
18–29 Years
Approve.............................59%
Disapprove 29
No opinion 12

30–49 Years
Approve.............................64%
Disapprove 26
No opinion 10

50 Years and Over
Approve.............................54%
Disapprove 30
No opinion 16

By Politics
Republicans
Approve.............................85%
Disapprove 8
No opinion 7

Democrats
Approve.............................41%
Disapprove 43
No opinion 16

Independents
Approve.............................62%
Disapprove 27
No opinion 11

Do you approve or disapprove of the way Congress is handling its job?

Approve.............................38%
Disapprove 40
No opinion 22

By Sex
Male
Approve.............................37%
Disapprove 46
No opinion 17

Female
Approve.............................38%
Disapprove 35
No opinion 27

By Race
White
Approve.............................38%
Disapprove 40
No opinion 22

Nonwhite
Approve.............................36%
Disapprove 40
No opinion 24

By Education
College
Approve.............................41%
Disapprove 49
No opinion 10

High School

Approve.........................37%
Disapprove 38
No opinion 25

Grade School

Approve.........................34%
Disapprove 33
No opinion 33

By Region
East

Approve.........................36%
Disapprove 37
No opinion 27

Midwest

Approve.........................39%
Disapprove 43
No opinion 18

South

Approve.........................37%
Disapprove 41
No opinion 22

West

Approve.........................38%
Disapprove 41
No opinion 21

By Age
18–29 Years

Approve.........................38%
Disapprove 40
No opinion 22

30–49 Years

Approve.........................41%
Disapprove 43
No opinion 16

50 Years and Over

Approve.........................34%
Disapprove 39
No opinion 27

By Politics
Republicans

Approve.........................42%
Disapprove 40
No opinion 18

Democrats

Approve.........................40%
Disapprove 38
No opinion 22

Independents

Approve.........................32%
Disapprove 47
No opinion 21

Those Who Approve of Reagan

Approve.........................45%
Disapprove 39
No opinion 16

Those Who Disapprove of Reagan

Approve.........................28%
Disapprove 52
No opinion 20

Note: President Ronald Reagan's current approval rating of 59%, unchanged since early June, is substantially higher than the 38% positive rating the public accords Congress for the way it is handling its job.

Although Congress's present rating appears low in comparison to Reagan's, one must go back to the early days of the Carter administration to find a similar level of congressional approval. In May 1977, 40% of the public rated Congress positively, while 64% approved of Carter's performance. Two years later in June 1979, President Carter was at loggerheads with

Congress for its refusal to enact his energy legislation and for opposing his efforts to deal with inflation. At that time the approval scores for Carter and Congress stood at 29% and 19%, respectively.

Analysis of the latest survey findings shows that while Reagan enjoys disproportionately higher ratings among men, whites, the college educated, and Republicans, the profile of congressional approval is remarkably even. Proportionately as many nonwhites as whites give the Congress favorable marks for its performance. Similarly, congressional approval is about the same among Republicans as it is among Democrats.

JULY 12
GUN CONTROL

Interviewing Date: 6/19–22/81
Survey #175-G

> *Do you think there should or should not be a law which would forbid the possession of handguns except by the police and other authorized persons?*

Should 41%
Should not........................... 54
No opinion 5

By Sex
Male

Should 34%
Should not........................... 62
No opinion 4

Female

Should 48%
Should not........................... 46
No opinion 6

By Race
White

Should 40%
Should not........................... 55
No opinion 5

Nonwhite

Should 46%
Should not........................... 46
No opinion 8

By Education
College

Should 47%
Should not........................... 49
No opinion 4

High School

Should 37%
Should not........................... 57
No opinion 6

Grade School

Should 45%
Should not........................... 49
No opinion 6

By Region
East

Should 60%
Should not........................... 36
No opinion 4

Midwest

Should 37%
Should not........................... 57
No opinion 6

South

Should 30%
Should not........................... 64
No opinion 6

West

Should 37%
Should not........................... 59
No opinion 4

By Age

18–29 Years

Should 46%
Should not 49
No opinion 5

30–49 Years

Should 38%
Should not 57
No opinion 5

50 Years and Over

Should 40%
Should not 54
No opinion 6

By Politics

Republicans

Should 32%
Should not 62
No opinion 6

Democrats

Should 46%
Should not 48
No opinion 6

Independents

Should 42%
Should not 55
No opinion 3

Would you favor or oppose a law which would make it illegal to import gun parts from other nations?

Favor 49%
Oppose 37
No opinion 14

By Sex

Male

Favor 47%
Oppose 41
No opinion 12

Female

Favor 50%
Oppose 33
No opinion 17

By Race

White

Favor 48%
Oppose 37
No opinion 15

Nonwhite

Favor 50%
Oppose 34
No opinion 16

By Education

College

Favor 51%
Oppose 36
No opinion 13

High School

Favor 48%
Oppose 38
No opinion 14

Grade School

Favor 49%
Oppose 33
No opinion 18

By Region

East

Favor 61%
Oppose 27
No opinion 12

Midwest

Favor 48%
Oppose 40
No opinion 12

South

Favor.............................39%
Oppose............................43
No opinion 18

West

Favor.............................46%
Oppose............................38
No opinion 16

By Age
18–29 Years

Favor.............................49%
Oppose............................36
No opinion 15

30–49 Years

Favor.............................47%
Oppose............................40
No opinion 13

50 Years and Over

Favor.............................50%
Oppose............................35
No opinion 15

By Politics
Republicans

Favor.............................45%
Oppose............................38
No opinion 17

Democrats

Favor.............................51%
Oppose............................35
No opinion 14

Independents

Favor.............................49%
Oppose............................39
No opinion 12

Would you favor or oppose a twenty-one-day waiting period before a gun can be purchased in order to give authorities time to check to see if the prospective owner has

a criminal record or has been in a mental institution?

Favor.............................91%
Oppose............................ 6
No opinion 3

Those Who Favor a Ban On Handgun Possession

Favor.............................94%
Oppose............................ 4
No opinion 2

Those Who Oppose a Ban On Handgun Possession

Favor.............................89%
Oppose............................ 9
No opinion 2

Note: The American people continue to hold sharply divergent views on banning the possession of handguns, but on one issue they are in almost total agreement: requiring a twenty-one-day waiting period before a gun can be purchased in order to give authorities time to check whether the prospective owner has a criminal record or has been in a mental institution.

A remarkable 91% of adults say they favor such a law, a level of support that rarely has been found for any proposed legislation in the nearly fifty years of Gallup Polls. Both those who favor and those who oppose a ban on handgun possession overwhelmingly back the waiting period provision contained in a measure sponsored by Senator Edward Kennedy of Massachusetts and Representative Peter Rodino of New Jersey.

At present, many states require only that a gun buyer show a driver's license at the time of purchase. Although a few states require thorough background checks before issuing a gun purchase permit, the disparity in laws makes it possible for residents of restrictive states to buy handguns elsewhere.

According to present laws, gun dealers are prohibited from selling guns to minors (under twenty-one), convicted felons, fugitives, drug addicts, mental defectives, alcoholics, or residents of other states. But since no prior check is required, there is no way for dealers to know whether or not customers are legally qualified to own guns.

Paradoxically, both those who favor and oppose a ban on the ownership of handguns cite the prevalence of crime as a basis for their position on this issue. Those who want a ban believe that the ready availability and proliferation of handguns contributes to violence in American society. In view of the recent upsurge in crime, those who oppose a ban say they need guns for protection.

If the American people were voting in a referendum, however, large majorities would favor the following laws dealing with the possession of handguns:

1. Requirement of a twenty-one-day waiting period before a gun can be purchased to allow time for a check into the prospective buyer's background;

2. More severe penalties for use of handguns in the commission of crimes. A recent *Newsweek* survey conducted by the Gallup Organization Inc. showed that 51% of the public advocated adding five to ten years to the sentence of gun-carrying criminals, while 15% would go as far as to sentence those criminals to life imprisonment. Only 20% believed that gun possession should not be a factor in sentencing; and

3. A law similar to the Bartley-Fox Act in Massachusetts, which calls for a mandatory one-year jail sentence for carrying a gun outside one's home without a license.

Further reflecting the public's desire for tougher gun legislation is its support for a law that would make it illegal to import parts for handguns.

JULY 16
POLITICAL AFFILIATION/ CONGRESSIONAL ELECTIONS

Interviewing Date: Political Affiliation, March–June 1981; Congressional Elections, 6/19–22/81

Political Affiliation, Various Surveys; Congressional Elections, Survey #175-G

In politics, as of today, do you consider yourself a Republican, Democrat, or independent?

Republican	42%*
Democrat	28
Independent	30

*These figures exclude those who do not classify themselves as belonging to one of the three categories.

Note: A greater proportion of Americans currently regard themselves as Republicans than at any time since 1972. Conversely, there are proportionately fewer Democrats in the adult population than has been the case since 1946. Republican affiliation, in fact, is now at a level last seen during the Nixon and Eisenhower administrations.

Further evidence of Republican gains is found in terms of key voter issues. Twice as many voters now name the Republican rather than the Democratic party as better able to deal with the nation's top problems. This is the widest margin that the Republicans have held in national surveys conducted over the past thirty-five years. In addition, a major turnabout is noted in the way the public perceives the two major political parties' relative ability to deal with the key issues of peace and prosperity, a development that favors the Republicans because economic issues are now foremost in the minds of voters.

The Democratic party, which virtually has "owned" the prosperity issue since these Gallup measurements were initiated three decades ago, has relinquished the lead for the first time to the Republicans and, in fact, now trails by 13 percentage points: 42% for the Republicans to 28% for the Democrats. On the other hand, the Republicans, who consistently have been thought of by voters as the party of peace, have now fallen behind their Democratic rivals on this issue. The Democratic party is considered by 39% of the public to be better for maintaining peace, with 26% naming the Republicans.

Another source of encouragement for the Republicans is the fact that independent voters, who currently account for nearly one-third of the electorate, are now almost as likely to say they lean toward the Republican party as the Democratic party. By comparison, independents leaned heavily toward the Democratic party throughout 1976.

Asked of registered voters: If the elections for Congress were being held today, which party would you like to see win in this congressional district—the Democratic party or the Republican party? [Those who were undecided were asked: As of today, do you lean more to the Democratic party or to the Republican party?]

Democratic	49%
Republican	45
Other	1
Undecided	5

Republican Preference in Congressional Elections

	June 1981	June 1980	Point change
Nationwide	45%	39%	+6
By Sex			
Male	48%	41%	+7
Female	42	37	+5
By Race			
White	49%	42%	+7
Nonwhite	11	9	+2
By Education			
College	53%	45%	+8
High school	45	39	+6
Grade school	27	24	+3
By Region			
East	40%	43%	−3
Midwest	48	43	+5
South	48	36	+12
West	43	31	+12
By Age			
18–29 years	45%	39%	+6
30–49 years	49	39	+10
50 years and over	41	39	+2

By Politics			
Republicans	94%	89%	+5
Democrats	10	10	0
Southern Democrats	14	5	+9
Northern Democrats	8	12	−4
Independents	48	49	−1
By Religion			
Protestants	50%	45%	+5
Catholics	39	29	+10
By Union Membership			
Labor union families	37%	34%	+3
Nonlabor union families	47	40	+7

Note: Evidence of the growing appeal of the Republican party is found in the latest Gallup survey findings on congressional choices. Forty-nine percent of registered voters nationwide say they would like the Democratic party to win in their congressional district, while 45% say the Republicans. Last September, prior to the elections, the margin was a wide 51% to 41% in favor of the Democrats.

The current level of support for Republican congressional candidates is the high point to date in steady gains for the Republican party over the last year and one-half. Whereas today only 4 percentage points separate the two major parties, the difference was 16 points in February/March 1980.

The current results suggest that the traditional loss of seats in off-year elections for the party in control of the White House could be somewhat blunted if present Republican gains are sustained. At the same time, however, the findings provide little basis for believing that the Democratic party will lose control of the House of Representatives in next year's congressional elections.

Not since 1934 has a party that has just won the White House made gains in the House at midterm. Typically, a "political bounceback" develops that aids the party out of power. In that year the one exception in two generations—President Franklin Roosevelt's New Deal—was still gathering momentum, and the Democrats registered gains in that fall's congressional elections.

JULY 19
PRESIDENT REAGAN

Interviewing Date: 6/26–29/81
Survey #176-G

Do you approve or disapprove of the way Reagan is handling his job as president?

Approve............................58%
Disapprove 30
No opinion 12

By Sex
Male

Approve............................63%
Disapprove 28
No opinion 9

Female

Approve............................53%
Disapprove 32
No opinion 15

By Race
White

Approve............................64%
Disapprove 24
No opinion 12

Nonwhite

Approve............................21%
Disapprove 66
No opinion 13

By Education
College

Approve............................67%
Disapprove 25
No opinion 8

High School

Approve............................57%
Disapprove 30
No opinion 13

Grade School

Approve............................42%
Disapprove 40
No opinion 18

By Region
East

Approve............................53%
Disapprove 34
No opinion 13

Midwest

Approve............................58%
Disapprove 32
No opinion 10

South

Approve............................60%
Disapprove 25
No opinion 15

West

Approve............................61%
Disapprove 30
No opinion 9

By Age
18–29 Years

Approve............................59%
Disapprove 29
No opinion 12

30–49 Years

Approve............................59%
Disapprove 32
No opinion 9

50 Years and Over

Approve.............................56%
Disapprove 29
No opinion 15

By Income
$15,000 and Over

Approve.............................68%
Disapprove 23
No opinion 9

Under $15,000

Approve.............................44%
Disapprove 40
No opinion 16

By Religion
Protestants

Approve.............................61%
Disapprove 28
No opinion 11

Catholics

Approve.............................55%
Disapprove 32
No opinion 13

By Occupation
Professional and Business

Approve.............................63%
Disapprove 28
No opinion 9

Clerical and Sales

Approve.............................67%
Disapprove 24
No opinion 9

Manual Workers

Approve.............................57%
Disapprove 33
No opinion 10

Nonlabor Force

Approve.............................53%
Disapprove 31
No opinion 16

Labor Union Families Only

Approve.............................53%
Disapprove 38
No opinion 9

Nonlabor Union Families Only

Approve.............................59%
Disapprove 28
No opinion 13

Do you approve or disapprove of the way Reagan is handling our national defense?

Approve.............................57%
Disapprove 26
No opinion 17

Do you approve or disapprove of the way Reagan is dealing with inflation?

Approve.............................53%
Disapprove 35
No opinion 12

Do you approve or disapprove of the way Reagan is dealing with economic conditions in this country?

Approve.............................51%
Disapprove 40
No opinion 9

Do you approve or disapprove of the way Reagan is handling our relations with Russia?

Approve.............................48%
Disapprove 25
No opinion 27

Do you approve or disapprove of the way Reagan is dealing with the energy situation?

Approve..............................43%
Disapprove 35
No opinion 22

Do you approve or disapprove of the way Reagan is dealing with environmental issues?

Approve..............................39%
Disapprove 33
No opinion 28

Do you approve or disapprove of the way Reagan is dealing with unemployment?

Approve..............................39%
Disapprove 40
No opinion 21

Note: President Ronald Reagan's overall performance rating is holding steady, with six out of ten Americans (58%) expressing confidence in his handling of the presidency, the same level recorded in the two previous surveys. But a longer view shows that the president has lost some of the popularity he enjoyed for two months following the March 30 attempt on his life. In addition, public approval of Reagan's handling of key foreign and domestic issues has eroded steadily during this period.

At the same time, however, approval substantially outweighs disapproval on four of the specific issues tested. Approval ratings range from a high of 57% for his efforts to improve our national defense to a low of 39% for both his dealing with the unemployment situation and his handling of environmental problems.

The president's overall rating is higher than the rating given him for his handling of the issues tested, reflecting the importance of his personal attributes. It is also important to note that while Reagan receives relatively poor marks on his handling of unemployment, environmental issues, and energy problems, the effect of these ratings on his overall popularity is offset by his higher score on dealing with inflation. Analysis of the relative importance of President Reagan's handling of specific issues indicates that inflation is far more important than the others. The

analysis suggests that a shift from public approval to disapproval on the inflation issue would be more damaging to the president than the loss of support on any other single issue.

One person in eight nationwide (12%) expresses unqualified approval of Reagan, giving him a vote of confidence for his overall performance in office and for all seven specific issues tested. Slightly fewer (7%) express unqualified disapproval. Most inclined to do so are blacks, with 25%.

JULY 23
ARMS SALES BAN

Interviewing Date: 6/19–22/81
Survey #175-G

Would you approve or disapprove of having the United Nations pass a resolution that would request all nations not to give or sell arms to other nations?

Approve..............................52%
Disapprove 37
No opinion 11

By Sex
Male

Approve..............................48%
Disapprove 44
No opinion 8

Female

Approve..............................56%
Disapprove 31
No opinion 13

By Education
College

Approve..............................51%
Disapprove 45
No opinion 4

High School

Approve...........................53%
Disapprove 35
No opinion 12

Grade School

Approve...........................52%
Disapprove 30
No opinion 18

By Age
18–29 Years

Approve...........................55%
Disapprove 35
No opinion 10

30–49 Years

Approve...........................56%
Disapprove 36
No opinion 8

50 Years and Over

Approve...........................46%
Disapprove 40
No opinion 14

By Politics
Republicans

Approve...........................46%
Disapprove 42
No opinion 12

Democrats

Approve...........................56%
Disapprove 32
No opinion 12

Independents

Approve...........................53%
Disapprove 39
No opinion 8

Note: International debate on the arms issue gained new urgency in the wake of Israel's destruction of an Iraqi nuclear reactor last month, prompting the Reagan administration to suspend shipment of four F-16 fighter-bombers scheduled for delivery to Israel. And recently the administration also announced a new policy on arms sales that would relax some of the restrictions established by President Carter. Reagan officials claim the new guidelines will give U.S. foreign policy greater flexibility and that each weapons sale will be weighed on its own merits.

By a 52% to 37% margin, the American people would like the United Nations to pass a resolution requesting all nations not to give or sell arms to other countries. The survey also showed overwhelming support in favor of a meeting between the United States and the Soviet Union this year to discuss nuclear disarmament. The two countries recently agreed to begin preparatory talks on limiting medium-range nuclear missiles in Europe.

If and when such a meeting between the two superpowers is held, most Americans would like to see any resulting agreement go beyond limitations on the building or deployment of nuclear weapons to include a total ban on their construction in the future. By a one-sided 72% to 20% vote, Americans would favor such a prohibition. In fact, as many as half the U.S. public (47%) would like to see an accord between the United States and the Soviet Union, calling for the destruction of all existing nuclear weapons.

JULY 26
PRESIDENT REAGAN

Interviewing Date: 7/17–20/81
Survey #177-G

Do you approve or disapprove of the way Reagan is handling his job as president? Asked of the 89% who said they either approved or disapproved: How strongly would you say you approve/disapprove—very strongly, or not so strongly?

Approve very strongly................33%
Approve not so strongly 26
Disapprove not so strongly............11
Disapprove very strongly 17
No opinion 2
                                      89%

*Apart from whether you approve or dis-
approve of the way Reagan is handling his
job as president, what do you think of
Reagan as a person? Would you say you
approve or disapprove of him?*

Approve.............................78%
Disapprove 13
Don't know 9

By Sex
Male

Approve.............................80%
Disapprove 13
Don't know 7

Female

Approve.............................77%
Disapprove 13
Don't know 10

By Race
White

Approve.............................82%
Disapprove 10
Don't know 8

Nonwhite

Approve.............................50%
Disapprove 33
Don't know 17

By Education
College

Approve.............................83%
Disapprove 10
Don't know 7

High School

Approve.............................77%
Disapprove 14
Don't know 9

Grade School

Approve.............................75%
Disapprove 14
Don't know 11

By Region
East

Approve.............................79%
Disapprove 11
Don't know 10

Midwest

Approve.............................83%
Disapprove 10
Don't know 7

South

Approve.............................75%
Disapprove 16
Don't know 9

West

Approve.............................76%
Disapprove 14
Don't know 10

By Age
18–29 Years

Approve.............................75%
Disapprove 17
Don't know 8

30–49 Years

Approve.............................82%
Disapprove 10
Don't know 8

50 Years and Over

Approve............................77%
Disapprove 13
Don't know 10

Those Who Disapprove of Reagan's Job Performance*

Rating as a person
  Approve..........................53%
  Disapprove 32
  No opinion........................15

Those Who Strongly Disapprove of Reagan's Job Performance**

Rating as a person
  Approve..........................42%
  Disapprove........................42
  No opinion........................16

*29% of sample
**17% of sample

Note: As President Ronald Reagan rounds out his first six months in office, 59% of Americans approve of the way he is handling his presidential duties, while 28% disapprove. Consistent with earlier survey results, Reagan receives generally lower marks for his performance in office from Democrats, women, persons with little formal education, and blacks, than he does from other segments of the population.

The president's positions on ERA and abortion and his generally "hawkish" military stance have bothered some women. Democrats and socially disadvantaged groups, including many blacks, are fearful about the effects of the Reagan administration's proposed cuts in social programs and the perceived inequities of the planned tax reductions.

Yet the latest findings show President Reagan to be disproportionately popular as a person, not only among groups who generally approve of his overall job performance but also among those who have been more critical. Currently, eight in ten Americans (78%) say they approve of Reagan personally, an 18-point improvement over his 59% competency rating. The greatest disparities between the personal and the performance ratings are recorded for women (22 points), Democrats (28), the grade-school educated (30), and blacks (28).

Although three times more blacks express positive attitudes about Reagan as a person than approve of his performance in office, they remain the only demographic group in which less than a majority approves of Reagan, the man.

JULY 30
PERSONAL FINANCIAL SITUATION/ TAX RATES

Interviewing Date: 6/26–29; 7/17–20/81
Survey #176-G; Special Survey

President Reagan proposed that federal income tax rates be reduced by 10% in each of the next three years, for a total tax rate cut of 30% over the next three years. If tax rates were cut by 30% over the next three years, do you think that would increase inflation, reduce inflation, or not have much effect on inflation?

Increase inflation 16%
Reduce inflation 25
Not much effect 39
No opinion 20

If federal income tax rates were cut by 30% over the next three years, do you think that would increase business investment and employment, reduce business investment and employment, or not have much effect on business investment and employment?

Increase investment/employment 37%
Reduce investment/employment 9
Not much effect 35
Increase one, reduce the other
  (volunteered) 2
No opinion 17

*These surveys were conducted for the U.S. Chamber of Commerce, July 17–20, 1981.

We are interested in how people's financial situation may have changed. Would you say that you are financially better off now than you were a year ago, or are you financially worse off now?

Better now........................33%
Worse now 35
Same 30
No opinion 2

Now looking ahead—do you expect that this time next year you will be financially better off than now, or worse off than now?

Better............................44%
Worse.............................25
Same 23
No opinion 8

By Sex
Male

Better............................49%
Worse.............................21
Same 22
No opinion 8

Female

Better............................39%
Worse.............................29
Same 23
No opinion 9

By Race
White

Better............................45%
Worse.............................24
Same 23
No opinion 8

Nonwhite

Better............................34%
Worse.............................36
Same 18
No opinion 12

By Education
College

Better............................53%
Worse.............................21
Same 20
No opinion 6

High School

Better............................46%
Worse.............................23
Same 22
No opinion 9

Grade School

Better............................14%
Worse.............................44
Same 32
No opinion 10

By Region
East

Better............................41%
Worse.............................27
Same 25
No opinion 7

Midwest

Better............................41%
Worse.............................29
Same 22
No opinion 8

South

Better............................45%
Worse.............................21
Same 24
No opinion 10

West

Better............................51%
Worse.............................23
Same 17
No opinion 9

By Age

18–29 Years

Better	60%
Worse	20
Same	13
No opinion	7

30–49 Years

Better	52%
Worse	21
Same	20
No opinion	7

50 Years and Over

Better	24%
Worse	33
Same	33
No opinion	10

By Income

$20,000 and Over

Better	58%
Worse	16
Same	21
No opinion	5

$10,000–$19,999

Better	44%
Worse	24
Same	23
No opinion	9

Under $10,000

Better	24%
Worse	40
Same	23
No opinion	13

By Politics

Republicans

Better	50%
Worse	20
Same	24
No opinion	6

Democrats

Better	36%
Worse	31
Same	23
No opinion	10

Independents

Better	48%
Worse	23
Same	22
No opinion	7

Note: The American people are optimistic about the prospects for the economy if taxes are cut substantially. Critics of the Reagan administration's plan to cut federal personal income taxes by 25% to 30% over the coming three years have argued that such a cut would increase inflation, but relatively few Americans (16%) agree. Furthermore, one-third of the public concurs with the administration's assessment that a reduction in tax rates will foster increased business investment and employment.

President Ronald Reagan's primary goal in cutting taxes is to increase business investment as part of his "supply side" economic program. While the president's original proposal to cut taxes by 30% over the coming three years is unlikely to be enacted in its entirety, 37% of respondents say the originally planned cut would spur investment and employment, while 35% think that the tax cut would have little effect. Only a very small minority (9%) believe that the tax cut would reduce business investment.

The compromises being worked out on both sides of the political fence make it almost certain that taxes will be cut by less than 30%, which blunts opponents' criticism. Some economists argue that a smaller cut in tax rates will reduce the chances of an inflationary effect. Recently the differences between the two versions of the tax cut bill, one supported by House Democrats led by Ways and Means Committee Chairman Daniel Rostenkowski of Illinois and the other by the White House, have been reduced considerably.

The Democrats were after a 15% tax cut over two years, with an additional 10% tax reduction in the third year, dependent on the economy's performance according to administration estimates. The administration was pushing for a 25% tax cut over three years with no conditions attached and had added some "sweeteners" to its proposed bill in order to win the votes of congressional Democrats from conservative districts in which the president is highly popular.

Findings from a late June Gallup survey showed that 44% of Americans expect their economic situation to be better a year from now, against 25% who foresee an exacerbation of their personal finances. This perhaps reflects the slowdown in the inflation rate—8.8% annually according to the federal government's Consumer Price Index—as well as the public's belief that the proposed tax cuts will help them personally. A May Gallup survey showed that respondents who believe that there will be a tax cut, regardless of its size, think they will be better off as a result of the Reagan administration's economic policies.

Most likely to say that things will improve financially during the coming twelve months are respondents who have attended college, Westerners, persons under thirty years of age, those with incomes of $20,000 or more, and Republicans. To some extent this may reflect what analysts see as a bias in the president's proposed across-the-board tax rate reduction in favor of the more affluent segments of the population.

When asked if their financial situation had improved since a year ago, respondents were about equally divided between whether it had gotten worse or better in the interim, with another 30% reporting that things had stayed about the same between 1980 and 1981. The same groups that expressed the opinion that

things will get better in the coming year were also more likely to report that there had been financial improvement in the past year.

AUGUST 2
NUCLEAR WAR

Interviewing Date: 6/19–22/81
Survey #175-G

If we should happen to get into an all-out nuclear war, what do you think your own chances would be of living through it—very good, poor, or just 50-50?

Very good	5%
Poor	60
Just 50-50	32
No opinion	3

By Region
East

Very good	3%
Poor	66
Just 50-50	29
No opinion	2

Midwest

Very good	5%
Poor	58
Just 50-50	33
No opinion	4

South

Very good	5%
Poor	56
Just 50-50	37
No opinion	2

West

Very good	6%
Poor	58
Just 50-50	32
No opinion	4

By Community Size
One Million and Over

Very good 4%
Poor 70
Just 50-50 23
No opinion 3

500,000–999,999

Very good 4%
Poor 65
Just 50-50 29
No opinion 2

50,000–499,999

Very good 5%
Poor 56
Just 50-50 37
No opinion 2

2,500–49,999

Very good 5%
Poor 52
Just 50-50 41
No opinion 2

Under 2,500; Rural

Very good 5%
Poor 58
Just 50-50 33
No opinion 4

How likely do you think we are to get into a nuclear war within the next ten years— very likely, fairly likely, fairly unlikely, or very unlikely?

Very likely 19%
Fairly likely 28
Fairly unlikely 26
Very unlikely 23
No opinion 4

By Education
College

Very likely 13%
Fairly likely 25
Fairly unlikely 36
Very unlikely 24
No opinion 2

High School

Very likely 20%
Fairly likely 31
Fairly unlikely 23
Very unlikely 22
No opinion 4

Grade School

Very likely 26%
Fairly likely 24
Fairly unlikely 18
Very unlikely 23
No opinion 9

By Region
East

Very likely 16%
Fairly likely 26
Fairly unlikely 26
Very unlikely 27
No opinion 5

Midwest

Very likely 17%
Fairly likely 27
Fairly unlikely 29
Very unlikely 23
No opinion 4

South

Very likely 27%
Fairly likely 25
Fairly unlikely 23
Very unlikely 20
No opinion 5

West

Very likely	13%
Fairly likely	35
Fairly unlikely	25
Very unlikely	23
No opinion	4

By Community Size
One Million and Over

Very likely	16%
Fairly likely	22
Fairly unlikely	25
Very unlikely	31
No opinion	6

500,000–999,999

Very likely	14%
Fairly likely	37
Fairly unlikely	27
Very unlikely	18
No opinion	4

50,000–499,999

Very likely	22%
Fairly likely	29
Fairly unlikely	25
Very unlikely	21
No opinion	3

2,500–49,999

Very likely	16%
Fairly likely	29
Fairly unlikely	29
Very unlikely	24
No opinion	2

Under 2,500; Rural

Very likely	22%
Fairly likely	27
Fairly unlikely	24
Very unlikely	22
No opinion	5

Note: The American people clearly do not see eye to eye with those military strategists who maintain that a nuclear war is "winnable." In fact, only 5% of persons interviewed in a recent nationwide Gallup survey believe that their chances of surviving an all-out nuclear war are very good.

Pessimism has grown since 1961, as seen in the following table:

Chances of Surviving

	1981	1963	1961
Very good	5%	5%	9%
Poor	60	52	43
Just 50-50	32	37	40
No opinion	3	6	8

Remarkably little difference in views is found on the basis of age, sex, and level of education. Nor do the views of persons who live in the more densely populated areas of the nation differ to any marked degree from those who live in sparsely settled areas. This stark finding also emerged from the current survey in which 19% of Americans believe that the United States is very likely to get into an all-out nuclear war in the next ten years.

Differences in opinion on the basis of the age and sex of respondents are not great. Persons with a college background, however, are less apt to think that a nuclear war is very likely (13%) than are those with less formal education (20%).

AUGUST 3
CIVIL DEFENSE

Interviewing Date: 6/19–22/81
Survey #175-G

> Some people say that we should spend some of the money now being spent for national defense and military purposes on protecting the public. Do you agree or disagree?

Agree	50%
Disagree	39
No opinion	11

By Education

College

Agree 45%
Disagree 45
No opinion 10

High School

Agree 49%
Disagree 40
No opinion 11

Grade School

Agree 59%
Disagree 24
No opinion 17

By Region

East

Agree 61%
Disagree 29
No opinion 10

Midwest

Agree 43%
Disagree 45
No opinion 12

South

Agree 46%
Disagree 43
No opinion 11

West

Agree 48%
Disagree 38
No opinion 4

By Age

18–29 Years

Agree 55%
Disagree 35
No opinion 10

30–49 Years

Agree 48%
Disagree 42
No opinion 10

50 Years and Over

Agree 48%
Disagree 38
No opinion 14

By Community Size

One Million and Over

Agree 64%
Disagree 25
No opinion 11

500,000–999,999

Agree 44%
Disagree 40
No opinion 16

50,000–499,999

Agree 45%
Disagree 46
No opinion 9

2,500–49,999

Agree 48%
Disagree 40
No opinion 12

Under 2,500; Rural

Agree 46%
Disagree 42
No opinion 12

Russia is said to be spending many times as much protecting its people from nuclear attack as the United States is spending. Do you think we should do more than we are now doing, do less, or do you think our present efforts are about right?

Do more 53%
Do less........................... 4
About right 33
No opinion 10

By Education
College

Do more 49%
Do less........................... 7
About right 38
No opinion 6

High School

Do more 56%
Do less........................... 2
About right 33
No opinion 9

Grade School

Do more 52%
Do less........................... 2
About right 25
No opinion 21

By Region
East

Do more 53%
Do less........................... 4
About right 33
No opinion 10

Midwest

Do more 51%
Do less........................... 3
About right 36
No opinion 10

South

Do more 57%
Do less........................... 3
About right 30
No opinion 10

West

Do more 53%
Do less........................... 4
About right 35
No opinion 8

By Age
18–29 Years

Do more 56%
Do less........................... 6
About right 32
No opinion 6

30–49 Years

Do more 55%
Do less........................... 3
About right 34
No opinion 8

50 Years and Over

Do more 50%
Do less........................... 3
About right 33
No opinion 14

By Community Size
One Million and Over

Do more 51%
Do less........................... 3
About right 34
No opinion 12

500,000–999,999

Do more 49%
Do less........................... 5
About right 36
No opinion 10

50,000–499,999

Do more 55%
Do less........................... 5
About right 32
No opinion 8

2,500–49,999

Do more 54%
Do less............................. 2
About right 34
No opinion 10

Under 2,500; Rural

Do more 55%
Do less............................. 3
About right 32
No opinion 10

National Trend

	1981	1978	1976
Do more	53%	52%	44%
Do less	4	7	9
About right	33	30	37
No opinion	10	11	10

It has been proposed that every new house built in the United States be required to have a bomb shelter, with the federal government paying most of the costs. Would you favor or oppose such a plan?

Favor............................... 35%
Oppose............................. 58
No opinion 7

By Education
College

Favor............................... 20%
Oppose............................. 75
No opinion 5

High School

Favor............................... 40%
Oppose............................. 53
No opinion 7

Grade School

Favor............................... 44%
Oppose............................. 45
No opinion 11

By Region
East

Favor............................... 36%
Oppose............................. 58
No opinion 6

Midwest

Favor............................... 31%
Oppose............................. 62
No opinion 7

South

Favor............................... 38%
Oppose............................. 55
No opinion 7

West

Favor............................... 33%
Oppose............................. 58
No opinion 9

By Age
18–29 Years

Favor............................... 47%
Oppose............................. 46
No opinion 7

30–49 Years

Favor............................... 32%
Oppose............................. 63
No opinion 5

50 Years and Over

Favor............................... 27%
Oppose............................. 63
No opinion 10

By Community Size
One Million and Over

Favor............................... 40%
Oppose............................. 50
No opinion 10

500,000–999,999

Favor	27%
Oppose	66
No opinion	7

50,000–499,999

Favor	37%
Oppose	59
No opinion	4

2,500–49,999

Favor	30%
Oppose	61
No opinion	9

Under 2,500; Rural

Favor	35%
Oppose	58
No opinion	7

National Trend

	1981	1978	1976
Favor	35%	35%	37%
Oppose	58	56	56
No opinion	7	9	7

Do you happen to know where the nearest public bomb shelter is?

	Yes
National	20%

By Community Size

One million and over	12%
500,000–999,999	24
50,000–499,999	19
2,500–49,999	31
Under 2,500; rural	18

Note: The American public, by a vote of 50% to 39%, would like to see some of the money now being used for national defense and military purposes spent on civil defense. Furthermore, when reminded or informed that the Soviet Union is spending many times more than the United States on protecting its people from nuclear attack, 53% said we should do more toward this effort.

As further evidence of Americans' desire for protection, as many as one-third of the persons interviewed (35%) said they favor a proposal that would require every new house in the United States to have a bomb shelter, with the federal government paying most of the costs of shelter construction. In certain nations such measures are now standard policy. For example, it is reported that 5.3% of the defense budget of Switzerland is allocated for civil defense, and the Swiss government provides a 50% subsidy for private home bomb shelter construction.

As might be expected, those who share the opinion that we are very or fairly likely to get into a nuclear war are considerably more inclined to say that the United States should increase its efforts to protect the public than are those who believe the opposite view. For example, 65% of those who think war is very likely would like the United States to step up its efforts to protect the populace, while 59% of this group would prefer to allocate part of the defense budget to civil defense. And a similar percentage would favor the nation instituting a home bomb shelter program.

While many Americans, particularly those who believe that nuclear war is likely within the next ten years, call for greater protection of the populace, relatively few (20%) know where to find the nearest bomb shelter. Views on one's chances for survival also condition attitudes on the need for protection. The pessimistic segment of the public is more inclined to favor new measures to protect Americans from nuclear attack than those who are less pessimistic.

Some civil defense experts concerned over indications that the Soviet Union is conducting a massive program to protect its people and industry in the event of a nuclear attack believe the United States has no alternative but to undertake an all-out civil defense program of its own. Experts believe that the Russians have been building underground facilities since 1952 in an attempt to provide protection for virtually their entire population. Every industrial worker in Russia is required to take a twenty-hour course in civil defense procedures. Russian outlays for such procedures are believed to be many times the amount that the United States presently budgets for protecting its population.

According to an article in the *New York Times,* the Swiss government recently reported that in a war 90% of its country's 6.5 million population would have an opportunity for nuclear protection. By 1990 the goal of shelter space will be reached for everyone. Modern Swiss shelters offer protection against nuclear radiation, chemical weapons, and near hits by conventional weapons. According to civil defense engineers, they can withstand the blast and heat waves of any nuclear explosion except a direct hit and offer complete protection from primary and secondary radiation. The occupants are able to remain in shelter for fourteen days until the fallout danger has decreased.

AUGUST 6
ABORTION—PUBLIC OPINION MIRED IN THE MIDDLE GROUND: AN ANALYSIS*

Special Survey

Senator Robert Dole of Kansas, in commenting on the national debate on abortion, declared there is "no middle ground." This may well be the case when one considers the positions of the pro- and antiabortion groups who lobby the Congress and anyone else who will listen. But recent public opinion polls indicate that when it comes to the views of the American public on abortion, it is mostly middle ground.

When the Gallup Poll asked: *Do you favor or oppose the Supreme Court's ruling which enables a woman to end a pregnancy at any time during the first three months,* it found equal numbers favoring (45%) and opposing (46%) the abortion ruling. Surveys also show that the number of people who take extreme positions on abortion is about even—23% believe abortion

*This Gallup analysis was written by Andrew Kohut, president of Gallup Organization Inc.

should be legal under any circumstances and 21% say it should be illegal under all circumstances. The majority of the public takes the middle position—the legality of abortion should depend on the circumstance.

The extent to which people have conflicting views about abortion is seen in the way they respond to different polling questions. For example, the ABC/*Washington Post* Poll recently asked its respondents to agree or disagree that "a woman should be able to get an abortion if she decides she wants one no matter what the reason." This poll found a majority (59%) disagreeing. But when a similar question was asked in a slightly different way by the CBS/*New York Times* Poll, the results were just the opposite—63% said a woman should be allowed to have an abortion "if the woman wants to have it and the doctor agrees."

Both questions are fair and objective, but each focuses on different aspects of the issue. In the first question the public disapproved of the notion of abortion on demand, while in the second question the doctor's concurrence gives the abortion a legitimacy not evident in the first. The disparity in the results is indicative of how sensitive approval of abortion is to varying circumstances and values.

In an extensive survey, the ABC/*Washington Post* Poll tested approval of abortion in a wide range of circumstances. It found that the vast majority of the public believes abortion should be legal when the woman's life is endangered (87%), when pregnancy is a result of rape or incest (81%), and when the mother might suffer severe physical health damage (83%). Majorities also approved in circumstances when there is a chance that the baby might be deformed (69%) or when the woman's mental health is endangered (72%), but in these cases almost three in 10 disapproved.

Disapproval is greatest when abortion is viewed as a form of family planning. Fifty-one percent in the ABC/*Washington Post* Poll thought abortion should not be legal in the case where a family cannot afford to have the child. The Gallup Poll also found a majority (55%) of the public saying they would advise against an abortion in the case of a fifteen-year-old unmarried girl becoming pregnant.

These polls seem to suggest that for many people abortion is viewed as an undesirable alternative to be used only when the consequences of not having the operation affects the physical or psychological well-being of the pregnant woman. Disapproval of abortion is greatest when it is seen or portrayed as a last resort for birth control.

It is difficult to judge public opinion on the cases that fall between the extremes. For example, had Gallup changed the scenario for the unwed fifteen-year-old by making her emotionally incapable of dealing with a pregnancy or a potential drain on the taxpayers, it might well have changed the advice respondents would have given.

Views on when life begins are highly correlated with views on abortion. Certainly, a large part of the ambiguous yet intense feelings people express about abortion stems from the fact that it deals with basic human values and attitudes toward life itself. Gallup found half the public saying that human life begins at conception, while 17% said it occurs at birth. Only one in five believed life occurred somewhere in between.

However, Gallup's analysis showed that among those who favor the Supreme Court's ruling, which allows abortion in the first three months, a substantial number believe that life begins in that period. The table below shows that 41% of those who approve of the ruling think that life begins within the first three months. So it is not only an issue of when life begins but also of how one views unborn life.

Opinion of Supreme Court's Ruling Allowing Abortion in the First Three Months

Life begins	Favor	Oppose
At conception	32%	77%
In first two or three months	9	2
Later in pregnancy	25	8
At birth	28	7
Don't know	6	6

The most ironic aspect of opinion about abortion is that despite the years of campaigning by pro-life versus pro-choice groups, it all appears to have had little effect on American attitudes. Currently, Gallup shows no change whatsoever in basic attitudes toward abortion since it first measured opinion in response to the Supreme Court ruling in 1973. The vast majority of the public seems unwilling to respond to the pressures of either side. Whether abortion is right or wrong in any given circumstance is a highly personal moral decision that apparently is not easily influenced.

AUGUST 9
EQUAL RIGHTS AMENDMENT

Interviewing Date: 7/17–20/81
Survey #177-G

Have you heard or read about the Equal Rights Amendment to the U.S. Constitution which would prohibit discrimination on the basis of sex?

Yes*

National 88%

*The screening question asked in earlier surveys to determine awareness of the ERA was worded as follows: *Have you heard or read about the Equal Rights Amendment to the U.S. Constitution which would give women equal rights and equal responsibilities?* A split sample of the two variant wordings showed no significant differences in either awareness of or attitudes toward the ERA.

Asked of those who replied in the affirmative: Do you favor or oppose this amendment?

Favor 63%
Oppose 32
No opinion 5

By Sex

Male

Favor...............................63%
Oppose............................32
No opinion 5

Female

Favor...............................63%
Oppose............................32
No opinion 5

By Race

White

Favor...............................61%
Oppose............................34
No opinion 5

Nonwhite

Favor...............................78%
Oppose............................17
No opinion 5

By Education

College

Favor...............................61%
Oppose............................35
No opinion 4

High School

Favor...............................64%
Oppose............................31
No opinion 5

Grade School

Favor...............................60%
Oppose............................31
No opinion 9

By Region

East

Favor...............................69%
Oppose............................26
No opinion 5

Midwest

Favor...............................58%
Oppose............................35
No opinion 7

South

Favor...............................57%
Oppose............................40
No opinion 3

West

Favor...............................69%
Oppose............................25
No opinion 6

By Age

18–24 Years

Favor...............................68%
Oppose............................28
No opinion 4

25–29 Years

Favor...............................66%
Oppose............................28
No opinion 6

30–49 Years

Favor...............................65%
Oppose............................30
No opinion 5

50 Years and Over

Favor...............................57%
Oppose............................37
No opinion 6

By Income

$25,000 and Over

Favor...............................66%
Oppose............................30
No opinion 4

$15,000–$24,999

Favor 57%
Oppose 38
No opinion 5

Under $15,000

Favor 65%
Oppose 29
No opinion 6

By Politics
Republicans

Favor 55%
Oppose 41
No opinion 4

Democrats

Favor 67%
Oppose 26
No opinion 7

Independents

Favor 66%
Oppose 29
No opinion 5

Liberals

Favor 75%
Oppose 21
No opinion 4

Moderates

Favor 63%
Oppose 30
No opinion 7

Conservatives

Favor 58%
Oppose 38
No opinion 4

By Religion
Protestants

Favor 58%
Oppose 36
No opinion 6

Catholics

Favor 68%
Oppose 28
No opinion 4

By Occupation
Professional and Business

Favor 58%
Oppose 39
No opinion 3

Clerical and Sales

Favor 72%
Oppose 24
No opinion 4

Manual Workers

Favor 65%
Oppose 29
No opinion 6

Nonlabor Force

Favor 60%
Oppose 34
No opinion 6

By Community Size
One Million and Over

Favor 71%
Oppose 25
No opinion 4

500,000–999,999

Favor 65%
Oppose 26
No opinion 9

50,000–499,999

Favor..............................62%
Oppose............................34
No opinion 4

2,500–49,999

Favor..............................62%
Oppose............................33
No opinion 5

Under 2,500; Rural

Favor..............................57%
Oppose............................38
No opinion 5

Women Only

	Favor
National	63%

By Race

White..............................61%
Nonwhite...........................76

By Education

College............................64%
High school........................64
Grade school.......................55

By Region

East 72%
Midwest............................59
South 58
West...............................63

By Age

18–24 years 64%
25–29 years........................69
30–49 years........................67
50 years and over..................57

By Income

$15,000 and over...................62%
Under $15,000......................64

By Politics

Republicans 53%
Democrats..........................67
Independents.......................68

By Religion

Protestants 58%
Catholics..........................68

Note: The proposed Equal Rights Amendment states that "equality of rights under the law shall not be denied or abridged by the United States or by any state on account of sex." President Ronald Reagan has said that he favors equal rights for women but opposes the ERA because he believes such rights should be a matter of law and not part of the Constitution.

Although opposed by the Reagan administration, passage of the ERA now has greater public support than ever before, with 63% of Americans who have heard or read about the amendment voting in favor of it and 32% opposed. In surveys conducted regularly since 1975 support has never exceeded 58%. This upturn in public backing is primarily due to an increase in favorable attitudes toward the ERA by women. Men and women now equally support the amendment, where in each of four earlier surveys women were less inclined than men to favor the ERA.

National Trend
(*Based on Those Aware of ERA*)

	Favor	Oppose	No opinion
July 17–20, 1981	63%	32%	5%
1980	58	31	11
1978	58	31	11
1976	57	24	19
1975	58	24	18

Notwithstanding the 2-to-1 public support for ratification of the ERA, its chances of becoming the 27th amendment to the U.S. Constitution do not seem good. To date thirty-five states have ratified the amendment, but approval by thirty-eight states is required before it can become law. Of the fifteen states that have not endorsed the ERA, none appears close to approving it. In fact, more than four years have elapsed since any state voted for ratification, and five states that ratified the ERA have subsequently tried to rescind their action. When the ERA failed to win approval of the necessary thirty-eght states within the seven years provided by the Constitution, Congress extended the deadline for ratification by three years. The extension expires June 30, 1982.

Although there is majority support for the ERA in all major population groups, somewhat greater opposition is found among Republicans, persons living in the Midwest and South, and older Americans. Conversely, greater backing for the amendment is expressed by nonwhites, Democrats and independents, and persons living in the eastern and western regions of the country. In addition, those who consider themselves liberals support the ERA by a 3-to-1 margin, whereas a much closer 3-to-2 favorable vote is recorded among conservatives.

The greatest increases in support for the ERA since 1980 are found among women, persons with a grade-school education, Republicans and independents, persons under thirty years of age, those with annual family incomes of less than $15,000, and residents of the East and West. In most instances the greater disparities were between population groups in the 1980 survey than in the current poll. Of particular interest is the fact that no significant differences in attitudes toward the amendment are recorded between working women and those not employed outside the home.

Opposition to the ERA centers around the beliefs that ratification would mean increased competition between men and women for jobs and that de facto equality between the sexes already exists. A small minority of those opposed to the amendment contend that "a woman's place is in the home" and still fewer associate ratification with making women eligible for the military draft.

AUGUST 9
JUSTICE SANDRA O'CONNOR

Interviewing Date: 7/17–20/81
Survey #177-G

President Reagan has nominated a woman, Sandra Day O'Connor, to be an associate justice of the U.S. Supreme Court. Do you approve or disapprove of a woman serving on the Supreme Court?

Approve............................86%
Disapprove 8
No opinion 6

From what you have heard or read about Mrs. O'Connor, do you feel she is or is not qualified to serve on the Supreme Court?

Yes, she is..........................69%
No, she is not 4
No opinion 27

Note: Judge Sandra Day O'Connor, President Ronald Reagan's nominee for the first vacancy to occur on the U.S. Supreme Court during his brief tenure, is thought by 69% of Americans to be qualified for the position, with only 4% dissenting. In no population group, including persons who call themselves conservatives, does disapproval of Mrs. O'Connor's nomination reach as high as 10%.

Among the small minority who say Mrs. O'Connor is not qualified to be the nation's first woman justice, her perceived stand on abortion ranks behind the criticism that she is a woman and lacks experience.

AUGUST 13
UNDERDEVELOPED COUNTRIES

Interviewing Date: 5/8–11/81
Survey #173-G

Do you feel that the problems of the underdeveloped countries of the world are their own responsibility, or do you feel that the developed countries must share in this responsibility?

Underdeveloped are responsible 33%
Developed countries must share 61
No opinion 6

*Do you feel that the United States should
or should not increase aid to underdeveloped countries to assist them to become
more self-sufficient in the future?*

Should 32%
Should not 60
No opinion 8

By Education
College

Should 37%
Should not 56
No opinion 7

High School

Should 30%
Should not 63
No opinion 7

Grade School

Should 29%
Should not 59
. No opinion 12

By Age
18–29 Years

Should 38%
Should not 54
No opinion 8

30–49 Years

Should 30%
Should not 63
No opinion 7

50 Years and Over

Should 29%
Should not 62
No opinion 9

Regular Church Attenders Only

Should 39%
Should not 52
No opinion 9

Nonchurch Attenders Only

Should 26%
Should not 67
No opinion 7

Those Who Think Underdeveloped
Countries Need External Aid

Should 45%
Should not 48
No opinion 7

Those Who Think Underdeveloped
Countries Must Help Themselves

Should 8%
Should not 88
No opinion 4

Note: The weight of public opinion in the industrialized nations of the world is that these
countries must participate in the development of
the emerging nations. There is a sharp division
of opinion, however, in the extent to which their
publics believe these countries should increase
foreign aid to assist the Third World in becoming self-sufficient. In a recent survey conducted by Gallup International Research Institutes, the United States stood in the midrange
of twelve countries with 61% of Americans
stating that the developed nations must share
responsibility for the emerging nations' problems and 33% saying they must solve their own
problems.

Perhaps partly as a consequence of the
Reagan administration's cutbacks in domestic
programs, however, 60% of Americans are
unwilling to increase aid to Third World countries. Of the eight nations responding to this
question, only Austrians stood lower than Americans (32%) in their readiness to provide more
foreign aid.

Among Americans favoring increased foreign aid, the three types of assistance most often

selected (from a list of six) were: providing funding for local people to study ways and means of helping them to solve their own problems (49%), providing free technological knowhow (36%), and sending U.S. experts to make recommendations for development (33%).

The Reagan administration's foreign economic policy is broadly reflective of U.S. public opinion in that it favors measures that would assist the emerging nations to develop their own resources but opposes large increases in foreign aid.

The Third World wants the industrialized nations to provide foreign aid of at least 0.7% of their gross national product, which would require the United States to more than double its present $8.2 billion outlay. Third World proposals presented at an international conference earlier this month in Mexico were characterized by a U.S. State Department spokesman as "instruments for getting resources out of the rich for the so-called poor."

AUGUST 16
SPECIAL-INTEREST GROUPS

Interviewing Date: 6/26–29/81
Survey #176-G

> *To which of these groups, if any, have you contributed money in the past twelve months? Which, if any, of these are you, yourself, a member? [Respondents were handed a card listing various interest groups.]*

Gave money 23%
Member 13
Either/both 26

By Sex
Male

Gave money 25%
Member 15
Either/both 28

Female

Gave money 20%
Member 10
Either/both 23

By Education
College

Gave money 34%
Member 21
Either/both 38

High School

Gave money 21%
Member 11
Either/both 24

Grade School

Gave money 4%
Member 2
Either/both 5

By Region
East

Gave money 21%
Member 12
Either/both 23

Midwest

Gave money 23%
Member 12
Either/both 27

South

Gave money 21%
Member 12
Either/both 24

West

Gave money 27%
Member 15
Either/both 31

By Age
18–29 Years

Gave money 24%
Member 16
Either/both 29

30–49 Years

Gave money 27%
Member 15
Either/both 29

50 Years and Over

Gave money 17%
Member 8
Either/both 20

By Income
$25,000 and Over

Gave money 32%
Member 22
Either/both 38

$15,000–$24,999

Gave money 25%
Member 12
Either/both 27

Under $15,000

Gave money 15%
Member 7
Either/both 17

By Politics
Republicans

Gave money 23%
Member 13
Either/both 26

Democrats

Gave money 20%
Member 10
Either/both 23

Independents

Gave money 24%
Member 14
Either/both 28

Special-Interest Groups
(Type of Participation)

	Gave money	Member	Either/both
Protect wildlife	10%	4%	11%
Conservation; environment	6	2	7
Vietnam veterans	4	2	4
Antiabortion	3	1	4
Antigun control	3	2	4
Blacks' rights	3	1	4

Of which, if any, would you like to be a member?

Protect wildlife 20%
Conservation; environment 10
Tax reduction 10
Pro-gun control 8
Vietnam veterans 8
Free enterprise 7
Women's rights 7
Antiabortion 6
Antigun control 6
Antinuclear power 5
Blacks' rights 5
Pro-birth control 5
Antiwar 4
Pro-abortion 3
Homosexuals' rights 2
Pro-nuclear power 2
One or more of these 39

Note: Special-interest politics is commonly thought to comprise small, well-organized groups that wield disproportionately great influence on Congress and hence on the policies of the federal government. Contrary to this belief, the Gallup Poll recently found that as many as 20 million Americans are members of special-interest organizations; another 20 million have given money to these groups during the past year. These projections may understate public participation in groups formed to defend or promote single-issue interests, since the survey covered only a selected list of sixteen types of groups.

For the United States as a whole, the survey showed that 13% of the adult population claimed membership in one or more of these groups, while 23% said they had given money. About one-fourth of the public (26%) reported donations, membership, or both. In addition, 39% said they would like to become members of one or more of these organizations.

Although involvement in special interests was found in all major population groups, the survey findings indicate greater participation among those who are presumably better able to donate time or money to causes they support: the college-educated and upper-income persons employed in business or the professions.

Young adults (18 to 29 years old) are just as likely to have participated as those 30 to 49, with persons 50 years of age and older falling below the national norm. Men were found to be involved to a greater extent than women, but no differences existed by race. And geographically westerners belong to or gave money to organizations to a greater extent than did those living elsewhere in the country.

Surprisingly, persons who describe themselves as political independents claimed slightly greater participation in the groups studied than did Democrats and were tied with Republicans. On the average, independents typically have been less involved in the political process than persons claiming affiliation with one of the major parties. However, independents also tend to be younger than either Democrats or Republicans, which may account in part for their more active role in special-interest politics. In terms of education and income, independents fall between Democrats and Republicans.

AUGUST 20
TREATMENT BY REAGAN ADMINISTRATION

Interviewing Date: 7/24–7/27/81
Survey #178-G

Which of these groups, if any, do you think are being unfairly treated by the Reagan administration? [Respondents were handed a card listing twelve groups.]

Comparisons During Reagan and Carter Presidencies*

	Reagan	Carter
Senior citizens.............	45%	18%
People on welfare..........	25	10
Unemployed people........	23	14
Small business people	22	16
People like yourself	18	14
Farmers	13	12
Blacks....................	12	7
Women	10	7
Labor union members	8	4
Corporation executives	2	3
Jews	2	1
Catholics	2	1
None of these groups; don't know.............	30	42

*Totals in this and the following tables add to more than 100% due to multiple responses.

By Sex
Male

	Reagan	Carter
Senior citizens.............	44%	18%
People on welfare..........	25	9
Unemployed people........	22	13
Small business people	23	19
People like yourself	17	14
Farmers	14	12
Blacks....................	13	7
Women	9	4
Labor union members	11	6
Corporation executives	2	3

	Reagan	Carter
Jews	3	1
Catholics	2	1
None of these groups; don't know	29	40

Female

	Reagan	Carter
Senior citizens	46%	17%
People on welfare	26	11
Unemployed people	24	15
Small business people	21	13
People like yourself	19	13
Farmers	12	12
Blacks	11	7
Women	11	8
Labor union members	6	3
Corporation executives	1	3
Jews	1	1
Catholics	1	1
None of these groups; don't know	32	44

By Race
White

	Reagan	Carter
Senior citizens	45%	17%
People on welfare	21	8
Unemployed people	19	12
Small business people	21	17
People like yourself	16	14
Farmers	12	13
Blacks	9	4
Women	9	6
Labor union members	7	4
Corporation executives	1	3
Jews	1	1
Catholics	1	1
None of these groups; don't know	32	42

Nonwhite

	Reagan	Carter
Senior citizens	51%	18%
People on welfare	51	20
Unemployed people	45	24
Small business people	24	11
People like yourself	29	14
Farmers	16	5
Blacks	35	28
Women	16	10
Labor union members	14	7
Corporation executives	2	1
Jews	6	3
Catholics	4	1
None of these groups; don't know	18	37

By Education
College

	Reagan	Carter
Senior citizens	49%	19%
People on welfare	29	15
Unemployed people	26	11
Small business people	24	21
People like yourself	14	15
Farmers	11	12
Blacks	19	7
Women	18	10
Labor union members	8	3
Corporation executives	1	6
Jews	1	2
Catholics	2	1
None of these groups; don't know	29	40

High School

	Reagan	Carter
Senior citizens	45%	19%
People on welfare	22	10
Unemployed people	21	15
Small business people	22	14
People like yourself	19	14
Farmers	13	12
Blacks	9	6
Women	5	6
Labor union members	8	4
Corporation executives	2	2
Jews	2	1
Catholics	1	1
None of these groups; don't know	31	41

Grade School

	Reagan	Carter
Senior citizens............	41%	12%
People on welfare.........	31	13
Unemployed people.......	25	14
Small business people	16	11
People like yourself	24	13
Farmers.................	18	11
Blacks..................	10	11
Women	9	4
Labor union members	10	5
Corporation executives	**	1
Jews	4	2
Catholics	3	1
None of these groups; don't know	32	49

**Less than 1%

Note: The American public believes certain major population groups are being unfairly treated by the Reagan administration. At the same time, however, the president's popularity remains solid, testifying to the public's willingness to give his new economic program a chance.

A just completed Gallup survey shows seven out of every ten persons asked to choose from a list of twelve groups were able to single out at least one that they think is being treated unfairly. Nearly half of all persons interviewed (45%) said senior citizens are not being dealt with in a fair manner by the Reagan administration, while substantial proportions hold this view about welfare recipients (25%), the unemployed (23%), and small business people (22%).

Although a large majority of Americans cite at least one group they think is not getting a fair deal from the administration, many of these same people give the president a vote of approval for his performance in office. Key factors in his continuing high job rating appear to be his personal attributes and favorable reaction to his activist approach to economic and other problems.

President Jimmy Carter was under far less heat than Reagan at a similar time during his presidency. A July 1977 survey showed four in ten saying they felt no group was being unfairly treated, and the levels of criticism were far lower for most of the groups tested. For example, whereas 45% of Americans today believe that senior citizens are being treated unfairly by the Reagan administration, only 18% expressed this view about the Carter administration.

Although the Carter administration came off better on its treatment of various segments of the population after six months in office, the situation changed sharply one year later. In the case of virtually all groups tested, the proportions had grown by August 1978. During the same period President Carter's popularity declined from 66% in July 1977 to 41% in August 1978.

AUGUST 23
MILITARY DRAFT

Interviewing Date: 7/31–8/3/81
Survey #180-G

Do you think we should return to the military draft at this time, or not?

Should	48%
Should not	45
No opinion	7

By Sex
Male

Should	53%
Should not	42
No opinion	5

Female

Should	43%
Should not	49
No opinion	8

By Race
White

Should	50%
Should not	44
No opinion	6

Nonwhite

Should 33%
Should not 55
No opinion 12

By Education
College

Should 46%
Should not 51
No opinion 3

High School

Should 49%
Should not 44
No opinion 7

Grade School

Should 46%
Should not 39
No opinion 15

By Region
East

Should 45%
Should not 47
No opinion 8

Midwest

Should 51%
Should not 43
No opinion 6

South

Should 46%
Should not 46
No opinion 8

West

Should 49%
Should not 46
No opinion 5

By Age
18–24 Years

Should 27%
Should not 67
No opinion 6

25–29 Years

Should 43%
Should not 56
No opinion 1

30–49 Years

Should 53%
Should not 42
No opinion 5

50 Years and Over

Should 55%
Should not 35
No opinion 10

Do you approve or disapprove of the Supreme Court ruling that women cannot be drafted?

Approve.............................. 59%
Disapprove 36
No opinion 5

By Sex
Male

Approve.............................. 53%
Disapprove 43
No opinion 4

Female

Approve.............................. 64%
Disapprove 29
No opinion 7

By Race
White

Approve.............................. 58%
Disapprove 37
No opinion 5

Nonwhite

Approve...........................65%
Disapprove........................25
No opinion........................10

By Education
College

Approve...........................54%
Disapprove........................43
No opinion.........................3

High School

Approve...........................61%
Disapprove........................33
No opinion.........................6

Grade School

Approve...........................63%
Disapprove........................31
No opinion.........................6

By Region
East

Approve...........................60%
Disapprove........................34
No opinion.........................6

Midwest

Approve...........................57%
Disapprove........................36
No opinion.........................7

South

Approve...........................64%
Disapprove........................32
No opinion.........................4

West

Approve...........................52%
Disapprove........................43
No opinion.........................5

By Age
18–24 Years

Approve...........................61%
Disapprove........................35
No opinion.........................4

25–29 Years

Approve...........................51%
Disapprove........................47
No opinion.........................2

30–49 Years

Approve...........................59%
Disapprove........................35
No opinion.........................6

50 Years and Over

Approve...........................60%
Disapprove........................33
No opinion.........................7

Note: The possibility of a return to the draft has renewed discussion of a compulsory national service program. Gallup surveys over the last three decades consistently have shown a large majority of the American people to favor a proposal requiring every young man, eighteen and older, to give one year of service to the country, either in military or nonmilitary work. Survey findings also reveal that young people would be more likely to sign up for nonmilitary work under such a plan, but the evidence indicates enough youths would still opt for military service to more than fill the manpower needs of the armed forces.

As the White House turns its attention toward the nation's military manpower needs, a current Gallup Poll shows that 48% of Americans are in favor of reviving the draft and 45% opposed. The proconscription sentiment represents a sharp decline from one year ago, when 58% voted in favor of reinstating the draft and 34% in opposition.

The even division of opinion nationwide obscures the sharp differences found in key groups in the population. For example, men favor a return to the draft by a 53% to 42% vote but women are opposed 49% to 43%. Persons thirty and older indicate support for the draft, but young adults are more than 2 to 1 in opposition. In addition, another sharp division is found between the views of whites and nonwhites, with the former leaning in support of a draft and the latter substantially opposed.

The latest survey also shows 59% of all persons interviewed approving of the recent Supreme Court ruling that women cannot be drafted and 36% expressing disapproval. This represents a shift in opinion from one year ago, when by a vote of 49% to 47% Americans said that young women as well as young men should be required to participate if a draft were to become necessary.

Last month President Ronald Reagan appointed a commission to study military manpower and to make recommendations on whether or not the draft should be revived. Until recently the military services have experienced difficulty in recruiting new servicemen and women and in retaining experienced personnel. However, increases in military pay and high civilian unemployment have slowed the exodus from the armed services.

Over the longer run the contingent of young men of military age is projected to drop steadily until the mid-1980s. The Supreme Court's ruling that women may not be drafted further reduces the pool of young people who might be available for military service.

Although both President Reagan and Defense Secretary Caspar Weinberger have indicated their opposition to conscription, the administration apparently has not ruled out a return to the draft as a means of acquiring the 200,000 men and women reported to be needed by the armed forces.

AUGUST 27
POLITICAL IDEOLOGY

Interviewing Date: 6/19–22/81
Survey #175-G

People who are conservative in their political views are referred to as being right of center and people who are liberal in their political views are referred to as being left of center. Which one of these categories best describes Ronald Reagan's political position? Your own? [Respondents were handed a card listing eight categories.]

	Reagan	Public
Far right.	10%	4%
Substantially right of center . . .	17	8
Moderately right of center	22	20
Just slightly right of center	13	18
Middle of the road (volunteered)	6	10
Just slightly left of center	6	12
Moderately left of center.	8	10
Substantially left of center	2	5
Far left.	3	4
Don't know .	13	9

When these categories are combined into broader ones, the results are as follows:

	Reagan	Public
Right of center .	49%	32%
Middle of the road.	25	40
Left of center .	13	19
Don't know.	13	9

Note: Despite President Ronald Reagan's high popularity rating, he continues to be perceived by the electorate as considerably to the right of how they view themselves. This fact could possibly erode the president's standing with the public if the policies of the Reagan administration fail to yield results. Historically, a president or presidential candidate is on the most solid ground when the public's perceptions of his political philosophy closely match their self perceptions. Reagan, however, was able to overcome this handicap in his election victory last fall, despite the fact that the ideological fit between President Jimmy Carter and the voters was closer than between Reagan and the electorate.

Despite speculation that a profound shift to the right or to a conservative philosophy has occurred among the electorate in recent months, the Gallup trend on political ideology shows relatively little movement over the last five years, a period in which nineteen measurements were taken.

AUGUST 30
CIGARETTE SMOKING

Interviewing Date: 6/26–29/81
Survey #176-G

Have you, yourself, smoked any cigarettes in the past week?

	Yes
National	35%

By Sex

Male	38%
Female	33

By Education

College	29%
High school	41
Grade school	25

By Region

East	36%
Midwest	35
South	34
West	36

By Age

18–24 years	39%
25–29 years	30
30–49 years	46
50 years and over	25

National Trend

	Yes
1981	35%
1978	36
1977	38
1974	40
1973	40
1972	43
1971	42
1969	40

1958	45
1957	42
1954	45
1949	44
1944	41

Asked of those who replied in the affirmative: About how many cigarettes do you smoke each day?

Less than one pack	38%
One to two packs	59
More than two packs	2
Don't know	1

By Sex
Male

Less than one pack	32%
One to two packs	64
More than two packs	3
Don't know	1

Female

Less than one pack	45%
One to two packs	52
More than two packs	2
Don't know	1

By Age
18–24 Years

Less than one pack	56%
One to two packs	39
More than two packs	3
Don't know	2

25–29 Years

Less than one pack	35%
One to two packs	60
More than two packs	5
Don't know	*

*Less than 1%

30–49 Years

Less than one pack	36%
One to two packs	61
More than two packs	2
Don't know	1

50 Years and Over

Less than one pack	30%
One to two packs	67
More than two packs	2
Don't know	1

National Trend

	1981	1978	1977
Less than one pack	38%	34%	41%
One to two packs	59	61	45
More than two packs	2	4	13
Don't know	1	1	1

Asked of smokers: All things considered, would you like to give up smoking, or not?

	Yes
National	66%

By Sex

Male	64%
Female	69

By Education

College	70%
High school	66
Grade school	62

By Age

18–24 years	76%
25–29 years	69
30–49 years	63
50 years and over	64

Asked of smokers: Have you ever given up smoking for at least one day?

	Yes
National	83%

By Sex

Male	82%
Female	84

By Education

College	83%
High school	83
Grade school	88

By Age

18–24 years	81%
25–29 years	84
30–49 years	85
50 years and over	81

Asked of smokers who said they had once given up smoking for a minimum of one day: Thinking only of the last time you gave up smoking, what is the total length of time you went without a cigarette?

Up to and including one week	29%
Between one week and one month	11
One month to six months	20
Six months to one year	9
One year or more	13
Don't remember	1
	83%

Note: The percentage of smokers in the United States today is the lowest recorded in thirty-seven years of regular Gallup Poll audits. Currently, 35% say they have smoked within the past week, statistically little change from the previous 1978 audit but reflecting a continuing downtrend since 1972 when 43% of adults were classified as smokers. The decline in the proportion of smokers has been most pronounced among younger adults eighteen to twenty-nine years old, down 17 points since 1972.

Other highlights from the survey include:

1. The proportion who smoke more than two packs a day has declined from 13% in 1977 to 2%.

2. Sixty-six percent in the current survey say they would like to quit, the same number as recorded in the 1978 survey.

3. One-third of the 65% of American adults who do not presently smoke did so at one point in their lives.

4. Eight in ten current smokers have tried to quit, but almost one-third went back to smoking after one week.

5. Only one-fourth of those who smoke and attempted to quit managed to last six months or more without smoking.

According to the latest Gallup Youth Survey, one teen-ager in five (22%) is a smoker (defined as those who have smoked any cigarettes in the preceding week.) This is the same ratio found in surveys conducted in 1977 and 1979. As in the 1979 audit, slightly more girls (24%) than boys (20%) smoke cigarettes. On the whole, by adult standards teen-agers are light smokers, with about two out of three smoking half a package of cigarettes a day or less, and one out of three smoking more than half a pack.

AUGUST 31
CIGARETTE SMOKING

Interviewing Date: 6/26–29/81
Survey #176-G

Do you think that cigarette smoking is or is not harmful to your health?

Is.................................90%
Is not 7
No opinion 3

By Education
College

Is.................................94%
Is not 4
No opinion 2

High School

Is.................................89%
Is not 9
No opinion 2

Grade School

Is.................................87%
Is not 8
No opinion 5

Smokers Only

Is.................................80%
Is not 17
No opinion 3

Nonsmokers Only

Is.................................96%
Is not 2
No opinion 2

Do you think that cigarette smoking is or is not one of the causes of lung cancer?

Is.................................83%
Is not 10
No opinion 7

By Education
College

Is.................................93%
Is not 4
No opinion 3

High School

Is.................................81%
Is not 11
No opinion 8

Grade School

Is.................................71%
Is not 15
No opinion 14

Smokers Only

Is.................................69%
Is not 21
No opinion 10

Nonsmokers Only

Is.................................91%
Is not 4
No opinion 5

Do you think that cigarette smoking is or is not one of the causes of heart disease?

Is.................................74%
Is not 14
No opinion 12

By Education
College

Is.................................85%
Is not 7
No opinion 8

High School

Is.................................70%
Is not 17
No opinion 13

Grade School

Is.................................66%
Is not 19
No opinion 15

Smokers Only

Is.................................59%
Is not 25
No opinion 16

Nonsmokers Only

Is.................................82%
Is not 9
No opinion 9

Do you think that cigarette smoking is or is not one of the causes of cancer of the throat?

Is.................................81%
Is not 10
No opinion 9

By Education
College

Is.................................88%
Is not 6
No opinion 6

High School

Is.................................78%
Is not 11
No opinion 11

Grade School

Is.................................74%
Is not 15
No opinion 11

Smokers Only

Is.................................69%
Is not 19
No opinion 12

Nonsmokers Only

Is.................................87%
Is not 5
No opinion 8

Do you think that cigarette smoking is or is not one of the causes of birth defects?

Is.................................53%
Is not 23
No opinion 24

By Education
College

Is.................................55%
Is not 19
No opinion 26

High School

Is.................................53%
Is not 26
No opinion 21

Grade School

Is..54%
Is not 20
No opinion 26

Smokers Only

Is..34%
Is not 39
No opinion 27

Nonsmokers Only

Is..64%
Is not 14
No opinion 22

Do you think federal and state taxes on cigarettes should or should not be increased?

Should 46%
Should not......................................46
No opinion 8

Smokers Only

Should 23%
Should not......................................73
No opinion 4

Nonsmokers Only

Should 59%
Should not......................................32
No opinion 9

Do you think there should or should not be a complete ban on cigarette advertising?

Should 43%
Should not......................................51
No opinion 6

Smokers Only

Should 27%
Should not......................................68
No opinion 5

Nonsmokers Only

Should 53%
Should not......................................41
No opinion 6

Do you think the sale of cigarettes should or should not be banned completely?

Should 20%
Should not......................................74
No opinion 6

Smokers Only

Should 10%
Should not......................................89
No opinion 1

Nonsmokers Only

Should 26%
Should not......................................66
No opinion 8

Note: Cigarette smoking in the United States has declined during the last decade, apparently because growing numbers of Americans have become convinced that there is a causal relationship between smoking and such diseases as lung cancer, heart disease, and birth defects.

As the smoking level has trended downward—8 points nationally since 1972—an upward trend has been recorded in the proportion of Americans who see a link between smoking and lung cancer and other health problems. For example, the number who believe smoking to be a cause of heart disease has increased from 60% in 1969, to 68% in 1977, and to 74% in the current survey. And the percentage who perceive smoking as a cause of lung cancer has grown from 71% to 83% since 1971.

Over the last four years the proportion who favor stronger measures to discourage cigarette smoking has increased. Forty-six percent of all persons surveyed think federal and state taxes on cigarettes should be increased, compared to 38% who held this view in 1977. And 43% say there should be a complete ban on cigarette advertising, compared to 36% four years ago.

At the same time, however, similar majorities in both the 1977 and 1981 surveys oppose a complete ban on the sale of cigarettes.

SEPTEMBER 6
PRESIDENT REAGAN

Interviewing Date: 8/14–17/81
Survey #181-G

Do you approve or disapprove of the way Reagan is handling his job as president?

Approve.............................60%
Disapprove 29
No opinion 11

By Sex
Male

Approve.............................66%
Disapprove 27
No opinion 7

Female

Approve.............................54%
Disapprove 32
No opinion 14

By Race
White

Approve.............................66%
Disapprove 23
No opinion 11

Nonwhite

Approve.............................18%
Disapprove 70
No opinion 12

By Education
College

Approve.............................69%
Disapprove 25
No opinion 6

High School

Approve.............................59%
Disapprove 30
No opinion 11

Grade School

Approve.............................44%
Disapprove 37
No opinion 19

By Region
East

Approve.............................57%
Disapprove 31
No opinion 12

Midwest

Approve.............................63%
Disapprove 26
No opinion 11

South

Approve.............................59%
Disapprove 30
No opinion 11

West

Approve.............................59%
Disapprove 33
No opinion 8

By Age
18–24 Years

Approve.............................59%
Disapprove 34
No opinion 7

25–29 Years

Approve.............................62%
Disapprove 28
No opinion 10

30–49 Years

Approve............................61%
Disapprove 28
No opinion 11

50 Years and Over

Approve............................59%
Disapprove 29
No opinion 12

President Reagan has two main jobs. One concerns problems outside this country, the other concerns problems here in the United States. Do you approve or disapprove of the way Reagan is handling our domestic problems—that is, our problems here at home?

Approve............................55%
Disapprove 34
No opinion 11

By Sex
Male

Approve............................59%
Disapprove 33
No opinion 8

Female

Approve............................53%
Disapprove 34
No opinion 13

By Race
White

Approve............................62%
Disapprove 28
No opinion 10

Nonwhite

Approve............................17%
Disapprove 70
No opinion 13

By Education
College

Approve............................64%
Disapprove 30
No opinion 6

High School

Approve............................54%
Disapprove 34
No opinion 12

Grade School

Approve............................41%
Disapprove 41
No opinion 18

By Region
East

Approve............................53%
Disapprove 35
No opinion 12

Midwest

Approve............................58%
Disapprove 32
No opinion 10

South

Approve............................56%
Disapprove 34
No opinion 10

West

Approve............................55%
Disapprove 35
No opinion 10

By Age
18–24 Years

Approve............................54%
Disapprove 34
No opinion 12

25–29 Years

Approve............................56%
Disapprove 34
No opinion 10

30–49 Years

Approve............................56%
Disapprove 35
No opinion 9

50 Years and Over

Approve............................55%
Disapprove 33
No opinion 12

Do you approve or disapprove of the way Reagan is handling our foreign policy—that is, our relations with other nations?

Approve............................52%
Disapprove 26
No opinion 22

By Sex
Male

Approve............................57%
Disapprove 26
No opinion 17

Female

Approve............................48%
Disapprove 26
No opinion 26

By Race
White

Approve............................56%
Disapprove 22
No opinion 22

Nonwhite

Approve............................31%
Disapprove 48
No opinion 21

By Education
College

Approve............................56%
Disapprove 28
No opinion 16

High School

Approve............................54%
Disapprove 25
No opinion 21

Grade School

Approve............................38%
Disapprove 26
No opinion 36

By Region
East

Approve............................51%
Disapprove 24
No opinion 25

Midwest

Approve............................56%
Disapprove 23
No opinion 21

South

Approve............................50%
Disapprove 29
No opinion 21

West

Approve............................51%
Disapprove 29
No opinion 20

By Age
18–24 Years

Approve............................49%
Disapprove 34
No opinion 17

25–29 Years

Approve............................52%
Disapprove 29
No opinion 19

30–49 Years

Approve............................57%
Disapprove 24
No opinion 19

50 Years and Over

Approve............................50%
Disapprove 23
No opinion 27

Do you approve or disapprove of the way Reagan is dealing with economic conditions in this country?

Approve............................53%
Disapprove 35
No opinion 12

By Sex
Male

Approve............................58%
Disapprove 32
No opinion 10

Female

Approve............................48%
Disapprove 38
No opinion 14

By Race
White

Approve............................59%
Disapprove 29
No opinion 12

Nonwhite

Approve............................16%
Disapprove 72
No opinion 12

By Education
College

Approve............................63%
Disapprove 30
No opinion 7

High School

Approve............................51%
Disapprove 37
No opinion 12

Grade School

Approve............................34%
Disapprove 39
No opinion 27

By Region
East

Approve............................50%
Disapprove 35
No opinion 15

Midwest

Approve............................54%
Disapprove 36
No opinion 10

South

Approve............................52%
Disapprove 34
No opinion 14

West

Approve............................55%
Disapprove 36
No opinion 9

By Age
18–24 Years

Approve............................54%
Disapprove 36
No opinion 10

25–29 Years

Approve........................... 54%
Disapprove 37
No opinion 9

30–49 Years

Approve........................... 53%
Disapprove 38
No opinion 9

50 Years and Over

Approve........................... 50%
Disapprove 32
No opinion 18

Do you approve or disapprove of the way Reagan is dealing with inflation?

Approve........................... 53%
Disapprove 35
No opinion 12

By Sex
Male

Approve........................... 56%
Disapprove 34
No opinion 10

Female

Approve........................... 51%
Disapprove 35
No opinion 14

By Race
White

Approve........................... 59%
Disapprove 29
No opinion 12

Nonwhite

Approve........................... 17%
Disapprove 69
No opinion 14

By Education
College

Approve........................... 63%
Disapprove 28
No opinion 9

High School

Approve........................... 51%
Disapprove 36
No opinion 13

Grade School

Approve........................... 40%
Disapprove 42
No opinion 18

By Region
East

Approve........................... 48%
Disapprove 38
No opinion 14

Midwest

Approve........................... 57%
Disapprove 32
No opinion 11

South

Approve........................... 54%
Disapprove 33
No opinion 13

West

Approve........................... 55%
Disapprove 34
No opinion 11

By Age
18–24 Years

Approve........................... 50%
Disapprove 41
No opinion 9

25–29 Years

Approve...........................60%
Disapprove 29
No opinion 11

30–49 Years

Approve...........................54%
Disapprove 35
No opinion 11

50 Years and Over

Approve...........................53%
Disapprove 32
No opinion 15

Do you approve or disapprove of the way Reagan is dealing with unemployment?

Approve...........................39%
Disapprove 38
No opinion 23

By Sex
Male

Approve...........................42%
Disapprove 36
No opinion 22

Female

Approve...........................37%
Disapprove 39
No opinion 24

By Race
White

Approve...........................44%
Disapprove 32
No opinion 24

Nonwhite

Approve...........................14%
Disapprove 73
No opinion 13

By Education
College

Approve...........................45%
Disapprove 34
No opinion 21

High School

Approve...........................39%
Disapprove 38
No opinion 23

Grade School

Approve...........................30%
Disapprove 44
No opinion 26

By Region
East

Approve...........................38%
Disapprove 39
No opinion 23

Midwest

Approve...........................41%
Disapprove 35
No opinion 24

South

Approve...........................40%
Disapprove 37
No opinion 23

West

Approve...........................38%
Disapprove 42
No opinion 20

By Age
18–24 Years

Approve...........................35%
Disapprove 48
No opinion 17

25–29 Years

Approve.............................44%
Disapprove 36
No opinion 20

30–49 Years

Approve.............................42%
Disapprove 34
No opinion 24

50 Years and Over

Approve.............................38%
Disapprove 36
No opinion 26

Do you think the Reagan administration will or will not be able to reduce inflation?

Will 50%
Will not 35
No opinion 15

By Sex
Male

Will 52%
Will not 34
No opinion 14

Female

Will 48%
Will not 36
No opinion 16

By Race
White

Will 54%
Will not 31
No opinion 15

Nonwhite

Will 27%
Will not 56
No opinion 17

By Education
College

Will 61%
Will not 29
No opinion 10

High School

Will 48%
Will not 36
No opinion 16

Grade School

Will 36%
Will not 42
No opinion 22

By Region
East

Will 50%
Will not 35
No opinion 15

Midwest

Will 49%
Will not 35
No opinion 16

South

Will 49%
Will not 35
No opinion 16

West

Will 55%
Will not 34
No opinion 11

By Age
18–24 Years

Will 50%
Will not 38
No opinion 12

25–29 Years

Will 52%
Will not 33
No opinion 15

30–49 Years

Will 52%
Will not 35
No opinion 13

50 Years and Over

Will 48%
Will not 33
No opinion 19

Do you think the Reagan administration will or will not be able to reduce unemployment?

Will 40%
Will not 43
No opinion 17

By Sex
Male

Will 41%
Will not 43
No opinion 16

Female

Will 39%
Will not 42
No opinion 19

By Race
White

Will 43%
Will not 39
No opinion 18

Nonwhite

Will 21%
Will not 63
No opinion 16

By Education
College

Will 42%
Will not 41
No opinion 17

High School

Will 39%
Will not 43
No opinion 18

Grade School

Will 37%
Will not 46
No opinion 17

By Region
East

Will 38%
Will not 48
No opinion 14

Midwest

Will 38%
Will not 43
No opinion 19

South

Will 41%
Will not 40
No opinion 19

West

Will 44%
Will not 39
No opinion 17

By Age
18–24 Years

Will 40%
Will not 45
No opinion 15

25–29 Years

Will 38%
Will not 46
No opinion 16

30–49 Years

Will 40%
Will not 44
No opinion 16

50 Years and Over

Will 40%
Will not 40
No opinion 20

Do you think the Reagan administration will or will not be able to reduce the size of the federal government?

Will 56%
Will not 30
No opinion 14

By Sex
Male

Will 61%
Will not 29
No opinion 10

Female

Will 52%
Will not 31
No opinion 17

By Race
White

Will 60%
Will not 28
No opinion 12

Nonwhite

Will 33%
Will not 45
No opinion 22

By Education
College

Will 65%
Will not 26
No opinion 9

High School

Will 54%
Will not 31
No opinion 15

Grade School

Will 48%
Will not 33
No opinion 19

By Region
East

Will 60%
Will not 28
No opinion 12

Midwest

Will 57%
Will not 29
No opinion 14

South

Will 50%
Will not 33
No opinion 17

West

Will 59%
Will not 30
No opinion 11

By Age
18–24 Years

Will 45%
Will not 40
No opinion 15

25–29 Years

Will 58%
Will not 32
No opinion 10

30–49 Years

Will 61%
Will not 26
No opinion 13

50 Years and Over

Will 57%
Will not 29
No opinion 14

Do you think the Reagan administration will or will not be able to balance the budget?

Will 37%
Will not 48
No opinion 15

By Sex
Male

Will 38%
Will not 50
No opinion 12

Female

Will 37%
Will not 45
No opinion 18

By Race
White

Will 39%
Will not 46
No opinion 15

Nonwhite

Will 24%
Will not 56
No opinion 20

By Education
College

Will 35%
Will not 54
No opinion 11

High School

Will 39%
Will not 45
No opinion 16

Grade School

Will 32%
Will not 43
No opinion 25

By Region
East

Will 35%
Will not 46
No opinion 19

Midwest

Will 39%
Will not 47
No opinion 14

South

Will 37%
Will not 45
No opinion 18

West

Will 37%
Will not 55
No opinion 8

By Age
18–24 Years

Will 38%
Will not 48
No opinion 14

25–29 Years

Will 42%
Will not 45
No opinion 13

30–49 Years

Will 36%
Will not 50
No opinion 14

50 Years and Over

Will 36%
Will not 46
No opinion 18

Note: President Ronald Reagan's popularity trend line has remained remarkably stable over the last ten weeks, a period marked by major developments on the world and national scenes. In the latest survey, six in ten continue to express approval of his performance in office.

Little change is noted not only in the president's overall performance rating but also in the percentage of Americans who approve of his handling of specific problems. In the latest survey, 53% approve of his handling of economic conditions, while 35% disapprove and 12% are undecided. These are the same percentages accorded the president for his dealing with inflation and parallel those recorded in a late June survey. However, President Reagan scores less well on his dealing with the problem of unemployment, with 39% approving and 38% disapproving. Again, these are a virtual carbon copy of previous survey results.

President Reagan wins about equal approval for his overall handling of domestic and foreign policy. In the latest survey, 55% express approval of the way he is handling domestic problems, while 52% do so in the case of foreign policy.

While little change is found in terms of public response to the president's performance in office in general and his efforts in certain key areas, the public's earlier optimism regarding Reagan's key goals is now somewhat tempered. Considerably fewer today than in May believe Reagan will be able to lower inflation, reduce the size of government, decrease unemployment, or balance the budget.

SEPTEMBER 10
PERSONAL FINANCIAL SITUATION

Interviewing Date: 8/14–17/81
Survey #181-G

Now, let's talk about the Reagan administration's economic policies. What effect do you think that these policies will have on your own and your family's financial situation? Do you feel your financial situation will be much better, somewhat better, somewhat worse, or much worse as a result of the Reagan economic policies?

	August 14–17	May 8–11*
Much better	5%	7%
Somewhat better	43	41
Somewhat worse	28	28
Much worse	8	9
No opinion	16	15

*Included for comparative purposes

By Income
$25,000 and Over

Much better......................... 8%
Somewhat better..................... 59
Somewhat worse 20
Much worse......................... 3
No opinion 10

$20,000–$24,999

Much better......................... 5%
Somewhat better..................... 57
Somewhat worse 20
Much worse......................... 3
No opinion 15

$15,000–$19,999

Much better......................... 1%
Somewhat better..................... 45
Somewhat worse 32
Much worse......................... 8
No opinion 14

$10,000–$14,999

Much better. 5%
Somewhat better. 36
Somewhat worse 30
Much worse. 10
No opinion 19

$5,000–$9,999

Much better. 6%
Somewhat better. 27
Somewhat worse 28
Much worse. 14
No opinion 25

Under $5,000

Much better. 3%
Somewhat better. 24
Somewhat worse 43
Much worse. 18
No opinion 12

The following table shows the comparison when the categories are combined:

	Somewhat better, much better	Somewhat worse, much worse
$25,000 and over . . .	67%	23%
$20,000–$24,999. . .	62	23
$15,000–$19,999. . .	46	40
$10,000–$14,999. . .	41	40
$5,000–$9,999	33	42
Under $5,000	27	61

By Politics
Republicans

Much better. 10%
Somewhat better. 59
Somewhat worse 15
Much worse. 3
No opinion 13

Democrats

Much better. 2%
Somewhat better. 32

Somewhat worse 38
Much worse. 12
No opinion 16

Independents

Much better. 4%
Somewhat better. 43
Somewhat worse 27
Much worse. 8
No opinion 18

Note: The American people continue to lean toward an optimistic point of view regarding the impact of the Reagan administration's economic policies on their own personal or family financial situation. Almost half (48%) believe that their situation will get better as a result of these policies, while 36% say worse. While optimism outweighs pessimism by about a 5-to-4 ratio, survey results indicate a lack of extreme feelings about the impact of Reagan's policies on one's personal or family situation.

Despite the intense debate over the administration's economic policies in recent weeks and passage of the tax cut bill in late July, today's findings are virtually the same as those recorded in May. That survey showed 48% saying they will be better off as a result of the Reagan economic policies and 37% saying worse.

The higher the income level of the persons interviewed, the more likely they are to say they will be better off as a result of the Reagan administration's overall economic package. Nearly seven in ten in the $25,000 and over income bracket, for example, express this view. In contrast, only about one-third of those earning under $10,000 have a similar optimistic outlook.

Views regarding the impact of Reagan's economic program relate closely to one's response to the recent tax cut program. The overwhelming majority (approximately eight in ten) of those who think they will be better off as a result of Reaganomics favor the president's tax cut program, compared to only about three in ten who believe they will be worse off even though they express support for the tax cut.

SEPTEMBER 13
REAGAN'S TAX CUT PROGRAM

Interviewing Date: 8/14–17/81
Survey #181-G

Have you heard or read about the Reagan administration's tax cut program?

Yes.................................87%
No; don't know.......................13

Asked of those who replied in the affirmative: Do you favor or oppose Reagan's tax cut program?

Favor...............................59%
Oppose...............................30
No opinion 11

By Income
$25,000 and Over

Favor...............................74%
Oppose...............................20
No opinion 6

$20,000–$24,999

Favor...............................64%
Oppose...............................23
No opinion 13

$15,000–$19,999

Favor...............................59%
Oppose...............................30
No opinion 11

$10,000–$14,999

Favor...............................57%
Oppose...............................33
No opinion 10

$5,000–$9,999

Favor...............................49%
Oppose...............................35
No opinion 16

Under $5,000

Favor...............................36%
Oppose...............................45
No opinion 19

By Politics
Republicans

Favor...............................83%
Oppose...............................10
No opinion 7

Democrats

Favor...............................42%
Oppose...............................44
No opinion 14

Independents

Favor...............................57%
Oppose...............................32
No opinion 11

Also asked of those who had heard of the Reagan administration's tax cut program: To what extent do you think the taxes you pay will be reduced—a great deal, a fair amount, not very much, or none at all?

Great deal.......................... 3%
Fair amount 23
Not very much 53
None at all.........................16
Don't know 5

By Income
$25,000 and Over

Great deal.......................... 3%
Fair amount 29
Not very much 60
None at all......................... 7
Don't know 1

$20,000–$24,999

Great deal.......................... 2%
Fair amount 26
Not very much 60

None at all. 10
Don't know 2

$15,000–$19,999

Great deal. 3%
Fair amount 21
Not very much 57
None at all. 15
Don't know 4

$10,000–$14,999

Great deal. 4%
Fair amount 19
Not very much 56
None at all. 17
Don't know 4

$5,000–$9,999

Great deal. 2%
Fair amount 22
Not very much 41
None at all. 25
Don't know 10

Under $5,000

Great deal. 8%
Fair amount 16
Not very much 28
None at all. 34
Don't know 14

By Politics
Republicans

Great deal. 6%
Fair amount 31
Not very much 49
None at all. 10
Don't know 4

Democrats

Great deal. 1%
Fair amount 18
Not very much 53
None at all. 21
Don't know 7

Independents

Great deal. 3%
Fair amount 21
Not very much 59
None at all. 14
Don't know 3

Also asked of those who heard or read about the Reagan tax cut program: If you do have some extra money as a result of the cut in federal income taxes, are you more likely to spend it, or are you more likely to save or invest it?

Spend. 40%
Save 51
Both equally (volunteered) 4
Other; don't know 5

By Income
$25,000 and Over

Spend. 35%
Save 59
Both equally (volunteered) 4
Other; don't know 2

$20,000–$24,999

Spend. 40%
Save 53
Both equally (volunteered) 5
Other; don't know 2

$15,000–$19,999

Spend. 44%
Save 49
Both equally (volunteered) 6
Other; don't know 1

$10,000–$14,999

Spend. 42%
Save 50
Both equally (volunteered) 2
Other; don't know 6

$5,000–$9,999

Spend 41%
Save 46
Both equally (volunteered) 4
Other; don't know 9

Under $5,000

Spend 40%
Save 36
Both equally (volunteered) 4
Other; don't know 20

Note: The American people appear prepared to give President Ronald Reagan a chance to test his economic program, which includes the largest tax and budget cuts ever enacted.

Here are the highlights of the current survey, based on those who have heard or read about Reagan's program:

1. The public and all income groups, especially those with incomes of $25,000 or more, are overwhelmingly of the opinion that the Reagan tax cut program favors upper-income more than lower-income families. At the same time, however, support outweighs opposition in each income group except under $5,000.

2. Seven in ten Americans think that the taxes they pay will not be reduced very much or not at all.

3. Fifty-one percent say they plan to save or invest the extra money they hope to receive as a result of the cut in federal income taxes, while 40% are more likely to spend it. Most inclined to save are those in higher income brackets.

Reagan's economic program is based on the premise that Americans, both individuals and businesses, will have new incentives to work, save, and invest because of lower taxes and reduced government spending. Combined with slower monetary growth and regulatory reform, lower taxes and reduced spending are expected by the Reagan administration to produce lower inflation, faster economic growth, and lower interest rates in the years ahead. The new laws slash individual and business taxes by $750 billion through fiscal 1986 and reduce earlier budgeted spending on domestic programs by an estimated $130.5 billion during the next three years.

SEPTEMBER 14
ECONOMY SURPRISES BUSINESSMEN*

Special Survey

For the first time since he took office, President Ronald Reagan has serious political trouble, and it comes from an unexpected quarter—the business community. Wall Street is reported to have lost confidence in Reagan's economic policies. Last week the stock market reached a fifteen-month low. Since April alone the Dow Jones industrial average is off some 170 points. Market analysts attribute the fall to anxiety over continuing high interest rates related to concern that the Reagan administration will not be able to stem the tide of government spending.

Opinion polls conducted late last year of business executives suggest that the 1981 economy has failed to meet businesses' expectations in many respects. Last December a *Wall Street Journal*/Gallup Survey of 300 top executives from the nation's largest businesses helped explain the reaction that investors are now having to the 1981 economy. That survey and others like it showed that the business community looked upon the change of administrations with great enthusiasm. In particular, businesses' expectations about 1981 were far more optimistic than were those of the general public.

Right after the election a Gallup Poll found the public expecting no easing of inflation in 1981 and expressing some concern that unemployment might rise. Business leaders anticipated much better things. Here is what top executives told the *Wall Street Journal* and Gallup they expected of 1981 and what has occurred:

1. Late last year the average business leader was forecasting a prime interest rate of 12% by the end of the year and long-term corporate bond

*This Gallup analysis was written by Andrew Kohut, president, The Gallup Organization Inc.

rates of 11%. The prime is now at 20% and the highest quality corporate bonds are being offered at about 17%. It will take either a miracle or a total disaster for the prime to be near 12% by December, as anticipated by top executives.

2. A solid majority (65%) of businessmen expected profits to be higher in 1981, and 61% saw Reagan's election improving their company's outlook. In the second quarter of 1981 profits were 10% below the fourth quarter of 1980 and only 3% above the second quarter, which was a recessionary period. It seems quite unlikely that 1981 will be even a moderately better year for profits than was 1980.

3. Sixty-eight percent of those polled in the *Wall Street Journal*/Gallup Survey anticipated a stock market that would be at least moderately up in 1981. This is clearly not the case.

4. At the end of last year top corporate officers expected to see improvements in productivity, increased capital spending, and more hiring. The 1981 economy has been disappointing in each of these categories.

5. The optimistic expectations of the business community regarding inflation were far closer to the mark than those of the general public. Businessmen were anticipating a 9% to 10% inflation rate, which is close to the underlying rate, while the public foresaw a 13% rate.

The critical factor that has depressed the stock market and inhibited business and consumer spending is high interest rates. The *Wall Street Journal*/Gallup Survey pinpoints a misreading of Federal Reserve Board Chairman Paul Volcker's resolve as a critical factor in why many executives were expecting somewhat better times than have occurred.

In June 1980 a survey showed that while 88% of chief executive officers from major corporations approved of Volcker's stewardship of the Federal Reserve Board, only 42% believed that he would stay with a tight monetary policy long enough to deal with inflation. When asked in December whether they expected Volcker's monetary policies to remain the same, be more restrained, or less restrained under Reagan, a majority (75%) expected the same level of restraint or less. In fact, since Reagan

took office Volcker's policies have been clearly tougher, something anticipated by only 31% of the top executives.

Small business men who rely more on borrowing have to be the most surprised and most disillusioned. While big business was giving Volcker an 88% approval rating in June 1980, only 39% of the owners and managers of small businesses were approving. However, small businesses saw monetary policies changing with Reagan's election. Close to a majority (46%) believed that under Reagan the Federal Reserve Board would loosen its grip on the money supply; very few expected more stringency.

The extent to which business confidence in Reaganomics has been shaken is no doubt overstated by the recent stock plunge. Wall Street is the most jittery sector of the business community, and whether its doubts will spread to the general public remains a question. The latest Gallup Poll suggests that the public by a 5-to-4 margin continues to express moderate faith in the Reagan program.

It should be kept in mind, however, that 1981 actually has exceeded the economic expectations of the public, expectations that did not foresee lower inflation. As with inflation, the public probably has become habituated to some extent to high interest rates. The more critical issue for the Reagan administration with the public would be an upturn in the unemployment rate. Even a modest increase in the number of jobless by year's end, given high interest rates, could unsettle public support for the administration.

SEPTEMBER 17
LABOR UNIONS/STRIKES BY PUBLIC EMPLOYEES

Interviewing Date: 8/14–17/81
Survey #181-G

Do you approve or disapprove of labor unions?

Approve. 55%
Disapprove 35
No opinion 10

By Sex
Male

Approve.............................58%
Disapprove 35
No opinion 7

Female

Approve.............................52%
Disapprove 35
No opinion 13

By Race
White

Approve.............................53%
Disapprove 37
No opinion 10

Nonwhite

Approve.............................63%
Disapprove 25
No opinion 12

By Education
College

Approve.............................56%
Disapprove 37
No opinion 7

High School

Approve.............................56%
Disapprove 33
No opinion 11

Grade School

Approve.............................46%
Disapprove 37
No opinion 17

By Region
East

Approve.............................61%
Disapprove 29
No opinion 10

Midwest

Approve.............................54%
Disapprove 35
No opinion 11

South

Approve.............................49%
Disapprove 38
No opinion 13

West

Approve.............................54%
Disapprove 39
No opinion 7

By Age
18–24 Years

Approve.............................69%
Disapprove 23
No opinion 8

25–29 Years

Approve.............................56%
Disapprove 37
No opinion 7

30–49 Years

Approve.............................54%
Disapprove 37
No opinion 9

50 Years and Over

Approve.............................48%
Disapprove 38
No opinion 14

By Income
$15,000 and Over

Approve.............................55%
Disapprove 37
No opinion 8

Under $15,000

Approve.............................54%
Disapprove 32
No opinion 14

By Politics

Republicans

Approve...........................47%
Disapprove 42
No opinion 11

Democrats

Approve...........................59%
Disapprove 30
No opinion 11

Independents

Approve...........................55%
Disapprove 36
No opinion 9

Labor Union Families Only

Approve...........................73%
Disapprove 21
No opinion 6

Nonlabor Union Families Only

Approve...........................50%
Disapprove 38
No opinion 12

National Trend

	Approve	Dis-approve	No opinion
August 14–17,			
1981	55%	35%	10%
1978..............	59	31	10
1967..............	66	23	11
1959..............	68	19	13
1953..............	75	18	7
1947..............	64	25	11
1941..............	61	30	9
1936..............	72	20	8

Here are some questions about strikes by persons in various occupations: Should the following be permitted to strike, or not?

Policemen?

Should 27%
Should not........................69
No opinion 4

Labor Union Families Only

Should 35%
Should not........................60
No opinion 5

Nonlabor Union Families Only

Should 25%
Should not........................71
No opinion 4

National Trend

	Should	Should not	No opinion
August 14–17,			
1981	27%	69%	4%
1979	34	61	5
1978	33	61	6
1975	41	52	7

Firemen?

Should 27%
Should not........................70
No opinion 3

Labor Union Families Only

Should 35%
Should not........................60
No opinion 5

Nonlabor Union Families Only

Should 25%
Should not........................72
No opinion 3

National Trend

	Should	Should not	No opinion
August 14–17,			
1981	27%	70%	3%
1979	34	61	5
1978	32	62	6
1975	39	55	6

Sanitation workers?

Should 40%
Should not........................55
No opinion 5

Labor Union Families Only

Should 51%
Should not 46
No opinion 3

Nonlabor Union Families Only

Should 38%
Should not 57
No opinion 5

National Trend

	Should	Should not	No opinion
August 14–17,			
1981	40%	55%	5%
1978	40	53	7

Postal workers?

Should 33%
Should not 64
No opinion 3

Labor Union Families Only

Should 44%
Should not 52
No opinion 4

Nonlabor Union Families Only

Should 30%
Should not 67
No opinion 3

National Trend

	Should	Should not	No opinion
August 14–17,			
1981	33%	64%	3%
1978	37	58	5

Air traffic controllers?

Should 28%
Should not 68
No opinion 4

Labor Union Families Only

Should 40%
Should not 55
No opinion 5

Nonlabor Union Families Only

Should 25%
Should not 71
No opinion 4

Note: The September 19 "Solidarity Day" rally in Washington, DC, comes at a time when there is greater public disapproval of labor unions than at any time in the past forty-five years. Nevertheless, positive attitudes toward the labor movement outweigh negative by a 3-to-2 ratio, with 55% expressing approval in the latest Gallup Poll and 35% disapproving. Since 1965 the trend in favorable attitudes toward labor unions has been consistently down, while negative attitudes have grown. In 1936, when the Gallup Poll first measured public opinion of unions, 72% offered a positive assessment.

At least part of Americans' disaffection with the union movement may be traced to their general disapproval of strikes by public employees, the air traffic controllers' walkout being a recent and highly publicized example. Americans always have drawn a distinction between the right to strike of government employees whose work involves the safety of the public and those whose jobs are unrelated to safety. Thus, members of labor union and nonunion families alike regularly have voted against permitting police and firemen to strike, while opinion has been more evenly divided in the case of postal workers and sanitation workers. Air traffic control clearly is in the safety-related job category as far as the public is concerned.

By a 2-to-1 ratio the public supports President Reagan's handling of the air traffic controllers' strike, 59% to 30%. Even among members of labor union families, a 49% plurality approves of the president's actions.

This year organized labor marks its one hundredth anniversary, with much of the celebration centered on what union leadership perceives as the Reagan administration's anti-labor policies. Among the targets of union protests are expected to be the president's proposed cuts in Social Security payments, a weakening of the Davis-Bacon Act, and reduced enforcement of OSHA job safety rules.

Although President Reagan has denied that his administration is antiunion, maintaining that his economic program will increase employment, it is significant to note that fewer labor union members voted for Reagan than for Jimmy Carter in the November election and that Reagan is currently less popular among union members than he is in nonunion households. For example, the president is given a favorable rating by 47% of labor union families, compared with 63% approval in nonunion households. This 16-point difference is the greatest since Reagan's inauguration.

In addition, labor union members are less sanguine than nonunionists about the likelihood of the Reagan administration's reducing inflation, unemployment, and the size of the federal government as well as balancing the budget. Also, fewer union than nonunion members think that their financial situation will be improved as a result of Reagan's economic policies.

SEPTEMBER 20
HONESTY AND ETHICAL STANDARDS

Interviewing Date: 7/24–27/81
Survey #178-G

How would you rate the honesty and ethical standards of people in these different fields—very high, high, average, low, or very low?

Clergymen?

Very high; high	63%
Average	28
Low; very low	6
No opinion	3

Druggists; pharmacists?

Very high; high	59%
Average	33
Low; very low	5
No opinion	3

Dentists?

Very high; high	52%
Average	38
Low; very low	7
No opinion	3

Medical doctors?

Very high; high	50%
Average	38
Low; very low	10
No opinion	2

Engineers?

Very high; high	48%
Average	35
Low; very low	5
No opinion	12

College teachers?

Very high; high	45%
Average	36
Low; very low	8
No opinion	11

Policemen?

Very high; high	44%
Average	41
Low; very low	13
No opinion	2

Bankers?

Very high; high	39%
Average	47
Low; very low	10
No opinion	4

Television reporters; commentators?

Very high; high	36%
Average	45
Low; very low	15
No opinion	4

Newspaper reporters?

Very high; high 30%
Average 49
Low; very low 16
No opinion 5

Funeral directors?

Very high; high 30%
Average 41
Low; very low 19
No opinion 10

Lawyers?

Very high; high 25%
Average 41
Low; very low 27
No opinion 7

Stockbrokers?

Very high; high 21%
Average 46
Low; very low 7
No opinion 26

Senators?

Very high; high 20%
Average 50
Low; very low 25
No opinion 5

Business executives?

Very high; high 19%
Average 53
Low; very low 19
No opinion 9

Building contractors?

Very high; high 19%
Average 48
Low; very low 27
No opinion 6

Congressmen?

Very high; high 15%
Average 47
Low; very low 32
No opinion 6

Local political officeholders?

Very high; high 14%
Average 51
Low; very low 30
No opinion 5

Realtors?

Very high; high 14%
Average 48
Low; very low 30
No opinion 8

Labor union leaders?

Very high; high 14%
Average 29
Low; very low 48
No opinion 9

State political officeholders?

Very high; high 12%
Average 50
Low; very low 30
No opinion 8

Insurance salesmen?

Very high; high 11%
Average 49
Low; very low 36
No opinion 4

Advertising practitioners?

Very high; high 9%
Average 41
Low; very low 38
No opinion 12

Car salesmen?

Very high; high....................... 6%
Average............................33
Low; very low........................55
No opinion 6

Note: Among twenty-four professions and occupations tested, clergymen and pharmacists are rated highest by the public in terms of honesty and ethical standards. While certain professions or occupations do not fare too well in these studies, it is important to bear in mind that these findings reflect public perceptions only and are not necessarily a true indication of the ethical standards of a particular group. At the same time, however, the results suggest the need for a strong public relations effort on the part of certain professions or occupations.

The current findings give evidence of the poor public image of politicians in the United States. Although U.S. senators fare relatively well on this ethics scale, state and local officeholders are among the lowest rated of the occupations tested.

Collectively, the professions and occupations that received the lowest scores for honesty and ethics are those that involve selling—realtors, insurance salesmen, and advertising practitioners. This suggests that occupations that depend heavily on personal salesmanship to promote their products and services ironically have done a poor job of selling themselves.

SEPTEMBER 24
NEUTRON BOMB

Interviewing Date: 8/14–17/81
Survey #181-G

Have you heard or read about the decision of the Reagan administration to start production of neutron bombs?

Yes................................74%
No; don't know......................26

Asked of those who responded in the affirmative: To the best of your knowledge, *what makes the neutron bomb different from other types of nuclear weapons? Those giving a correct answer (60% of the total sample) were asked: Do you approve or disapprove of the Reagan administration's decision to start production of these bombs?**

Approve............................48%
Disapprove 44
No opinion 8

By Sex
Male

Approve............................54%
Disapprove 38
No opinion 8

Female

Approve............................39%
Disapprove 53
No opinion 8

By Race
White

Approve............................51%
Disapprove 40
No opinion 9

Nonwhite

Approve............................28%
Disapprove 67
No opinion 5

*This question was asked in 1978: Do you think the United States should or should not proceed to equip our armed forces and our allies with the neutron bomb? The results, based on the informed group, were: should (46%), should not (45%), and no opinion (9%).

By Education
College

Approve............................45%
Disapprove 48
No opinion 7

High School

Approve.............................54%
Disapprove 39
No opinion 7

Grade School

Approve.............................38%
Disapprove 45
No opinion 17

By Region
East

Approve.............................45%
Disapprove 45
No opinion 10

Midwest

Approve.............................52%
Disapprove 40
No opinion 8

South

Approve.............................52%
Disapprove 42
No opinion 6

West

Approve.............................44%
Disapprove 49
No opinion 7

By Age
18–24 Years

Approve.............................41%
Disapprove 53
No opinion 6

25–29 Years

Approve.............................54%
Disapprove 41
No opinion 5

30–49 Years

Approve.............................44%
Disapprove 47
No opinion 9

50 Years and Over

Approve.............................53%
Disapprove 37
No opinion 10

Also asked of the informed group: Do you think this decision will make the chances of nuclear war more likely or less likely?

More likely 36%
Less likely 44
No difference (volunteered) 15
No opinion 5

By Sex
Male

More likely 30%
Less likely 49
No difference (volunteered) 16
No opinion 5

Female

More likely 46%
Less likely 36
No difference (volunteered) 13
No opinion 5

By Race
White

More likely 34%
Less likely 47
No difference (volunteered) 14
No opinion 5

Nonwhite

More likely 53%
Less likely 24
No difference (volunteered) 18
No opinion 5

By Education

College

More likely 36%
Less likely 39
No difference (volunteered) 19
No opinion 6

High School

More likely 34%
Less likely 51
No difference (volunteered) 11
No opinion 4

Grade School

More likely 48%
Less likely 30
No difference (volunteered) 14
No opinion 8

By Region

East

More likely 35%
Less likely 40
No difference (volunteered) 18
No opinion 7

Midwest

More likely 32%
Less likely 46
No difference (volunteered) 17
No opinion 5

South

More likely 42%
Less likely 44
No difference (volunteered) 10
No opinion 4

West

More likely 38%
Less likely 46
No difference (volunteered) 12
No opinion 4

By Age

18–24 Years

More likely 54%
Less likely 28
No difference (volunteered) 15
No opinion 3

25–29 Years

More likely 34%
Less likely 46
No difference (volunteered) 18
No opinion 2

30–49 Years

More likely 38%
Less likely 44
No difference (volunteered) 14
No opinion 4

50 Years and Over

More likely 29%
Less likely 49
No difference (volunteered) 15
No opinion 7

Those Who Approve of Reagan's Neutron Bomb Decision

More likely 9%
Less likely 76
No difference (volunteered) 14
No opinion 1

Those Who Disapprove of Reagan's Neutron Bomb Decision

More likely 70%
Less likely 11
No difference (volunteered) 14
No opinion 5

Note: The informed segment of the U.S. public (60%) continues to be almost evenly divided over the controversial issue of producing neutron bombs—48% approve and 44% are opposed, compared to 46% and 45%, respectively, in a similar 1978 survey. Current findings also show that 44% of the informed group say that the decision to produce neutron bombs will make nuclear war less likely, with 36% holding the opposite view.

Although 60% of the public has a general idea of how a neutron bomb differs from other nuclear devices, their comments indicate that many are not familiar with the administration's reasons for proceeding with its production, or of the primarily defensive nature of the weapon.

Neutron warheads are designed to kill through radiation. The weapons have smaller blast and shock effects than older nuclear weapons. The military advantage of the neutron warhead lies in its ability, through intense radiation, to penetrate enemy armor, kill troops within tanks, but leave surrounding property relatively unscathed.

Defense Department Secretary Caspar Weinberger recently summed up the administration's case for the production of neutron bombs as follows:

. . . The weapon adds very substantially to the capability of the United States and its allies to deter an attack based upon a tremendous preponderance of armor and infantry that would be one of the characteristics of a Soviet attack on the central front [in Europe]. . . . We think [it] enormously increases our deterrent, our ability to demonstrate to the Soviets . . . that we have the capability to respond, and to inflict a cost which we hope they would regard as unacceptably high. . . .

SEPTEMBER 27
PRESIDENT REAGAN—
A GALLUP ANALYSIS

Special Survey

An unusual degree of polarization in President Ronald Reagan's standing with the American public has become evident. In forty-five years of Gallup measurements there never has been greater disagreement between men and women, or whites and blacks, on the performance of a presidential incumbent.

In seven Gallup surveys conducted during June, July, and August, Reagan's approval rating averaged 60% for the adult population as a whole. Yet during this period Reagan's handling of his presidential duties won a positive rating from 64% of men but only 56% of women, an 8-point difference. In another survey 63% of men and 49% of women approved of Reagan's performance in office—a difference of 14 points. Typically, only 2 or 3 percentage points have separated the sexes in presidential approval ratings.

There are other points of demographic divergence in President Reagan's approval profile, including age, income, and education, but none compares with the discrepancy by race. During the period studied, President Reagan had the confidence of 66% of whites but merely 14% of blacks. Conversely, 70% of blacks disapproved of Reagan's actions, while only 20% of whites offered a negative assessment.

White and black approval ratings have tended to be similar in the case of Democratic presidents. For Republicans Eisenhower, Ford, and Nixon, black approval has ranged from about two-fifths to two-thirds that of whites. Today the ratio is even smaller; for every five whites who approve of Reagan, only one black shares that view.

A rationale for these wide differences of opinion by population groups may be found in individual Gallup surveys conducted earlier this year. For example, at least part of Reagan's lower standing among women may be due to the belief of many that the president's actions may lead to war. An early April survey revealed that 46% of women fear President Reagan might get the United States into a shooting war, while only 37% of men hold this view.

Furthermore, in a late June survey 65% of men and 49% of women approved of the way Reagan was handling our national defense. The same survey showed 55% of men and 42% of women approving of the way the president was handling our relations with the Soviet Union. And female opinion on the president's decision to begin production of the neutron bomb is likewise opposite. Fifty-four percent of men approve this move, while 38% are opposed; the figures for women are 39% and 53%, respectively.

In the November 1980 election only one black voter out of ten supported Reagan, and the president's standing with blacks hardly can be said to have improved since then. On every issue studied by the Gallup Poll since the election, blacks have been consistently negative in their attitudes toward President Reagan. For instance, while 14% of whites approved of the president's performance on seven specific issues or problems (defense, relations with Russia, environmental issues, economic conditions, inflation, unemployment, and energy), less than 1% of blacks approved of all issues; 52% disapproved or withheld judgment.

In early August, when survey participants were asked to select from a list, blacks were named by 9% of whites as one of the groups unfairly treated by the Reagan administration, while 42% of blacks made the same designation.

The analysis reported here is based on personal interviews with 9,735 adults, eighteen years and older, and was conducted in more than 300 scientifically selected localities across the nation from June 5 to August 17. For results based on the full sample, it can be said with 95% confidence that the error attributable to sampling and other random effects could be 1½ percentage points in either direction. Findings for subgroups would be subject to a somewhat higher error; for example, those based on blacks would have an error margin of plus or minus 4 percentage points.

OCTOBER 1
CENTER PARTY/POLITICAL VIEWS

Various surveys conducted during the past eighteen months

Asked of registered voters: Suppose there were three major parties—the Republican party, the Democratic party, and a new Center party that would appeal to people whose political views are middle of the road, in between those of the Republicans and Democrats. If there were three such parties, which party would you favor—the Republican party, the Democratic party, or the Center party?

Republican 20%
Democratic 36
Center 31
No opinion 13

Interviewing Date: 6/19–22/81
Survey #175-G

People who are conservative in their political views are referred to as being right of center and people who are liberal in their political views are referred to as being left of center. Which one of these categories best describes your own political position? [Respondents were given a card listing eight political positions.]

Right of center 32%
Center 40
Left of center....................... 20
Don't know 8

By Sex
Male

Right of center 34%
Center 40
Left of center....................... 20
Don't know 6

Female

Right of center 30%
Center 40
Left of center....................... 20
Don't know 10

By Race
White

Right of center 33%
Center 41
Left of center....................... 19
Don't know 7

Nonwhite

Right of center 24%
Center 34
Left of center...........................24
Don't know 18

West

Right of center 33%
Center 39
Left of center...........................23
Don't know 5

By Education
College

Right of center 32%
Center 41
Left of center...........................24
Don't know 3

By Age
18–29 Years

Right of center 29%
Center 36
Left of center...........................27
Don't know 8

High School

Right of center 35%
Center 39
Left of center...........................17
Don't know 9

30–49 Years

Right of center 32%
Center 44
Left of center...........................17
Don't know 7

Grade School

Right of center 18%
Center 40
Left of center...........................21
Don't know 21

50 Years and Over

Right of center 34%
Center 39
Left of center...........................16
Don't know 11

By Region
East

Right of center 28%
Center 40
Left of center...........................24
Don't know 8

By Income
$15,000 and Over

Right of center 35%
Center 41
Left of center...........................18
Don't know 6

Midwest

Right of center 28%
Center 48
Left of center...........................18
Don't know 6

Under $15,000

Right of center 26%
Center 38
Left of center...........................21
Don't know 15

Note: The British political system is experiencing what has been described as the "most momentous change since World War I." This change could very well be the forerunner of political realignments here in the United States.

Many voters in Great Britain have concluded that Prime Minister Margaret Thatcher and the

South

Right of center 39%
Center 32
Left of center...........................15
Don't know 14

ruling Conservative party have gone too far to the right. At the same time many believe that the opposition Labour party has turned too far to the left. A new party that reflects middle-of-the-road views—a Center party made up of an alliance of Liberals and Social Democrats—shows surprising appeal to British voters. In fact, the British Gallup Poll has found that this new Center party would draw more votes than either the Conservative or the Labour party.

A mid-September British Gallup Poll finding on party strength shows the following standings if elections were being held now:

Strength of
British Political Parties

Center party (Liberal-SDP)............40%
Labour party........................32
Conservative party...................28

A significant number of Americans share the views of the British in supporting a Center party in the United States. They believe that the Republicans have taken a position too far to the right and the Democrats too far to the left. Of particular significance is the fact that two bell-wether groups in the total adult population—the college-educated voters and younger voters (eighteen to twenty-four years old)—favor a Center party over either of the two traditional parties.

These findings showing the appeal of a Center party are reflective of Gallup survey results spanning more than forty years, which show the American people to be more comfortable toward the center of the political spectrum than to the right or left.

OCTOBER 4
BIGGEST THREAT TO NATION

Interviewing Date: 9/18–21/81
Survey #182-G

In your opinion, which of the following will be the biggest threat to the country in the future—big business, big labor, or big government?

Big business 22%
Big labor 22
Big government.......................46
No opinion 10

By Education
College

Big business 26%
Big labor 24
Big government.......................44
No opinion 6

High School

Big business 21%
Big labor 21
Big government.......................51
No opinion 7

Grade School

Big business 21%
Big labor 21
Big government.......................33
No opinion 25

By Region
East

Big business 27%
Big labor 26
Big government.......................37
No opinion 10

Midwest

Big business 19%
Big labor 23
Big government.......................50
No opinion 8

South

Big business 18%
Big labor 17
Big government.......................52
No opinion 13

West

Big business	27%
Big labor	21
Big government	45
No opinion	7

By Age
18–24 Years

Big business	26%
Big labor	13
Big government	56
No opinion	5

25–29 Years

Big business	28%
Big labor	20
Big government	46
No opinion	6

30–49 Years

Big business	21%
Big labor	22
Big government	48
No opinion	9

50 Years and Over

Big business	20%
Big labor	26
Big government	40
No opinion	14

By Politics
Republicans

Big business	14%
Big labor	32
Big government	46
No opinion	8

Democrats

Big business	26%
Big labor	17
Big government	46
No opinion	11

Independents

Big business	23%
Big labor	20
Big government	51
No opinion	6

Labor Union Families Only

Big business	30%
Big labor	15
Big government	49
No opinion	6

Nonlabor Union Families Only

Big business	20%
Big labor	24
Big government	45
No opinion	11

National Trend

	Business	Labor	Government	No opinion
May 1979	28%	17%	43%	12%
January 1977	23	26	39	12
January 1967	14	21	49	16
October 1959	15	41	14	30

Note: President Ronald Reagan's renewed demands for a reduction in the size of the federal government strikes a responsive chord with the American people. In a recently completed Gallup Poll almost half of Americans (46%) single out big government as the greatest threat to the nation, while 22% name big business and a like percentage cite big labor. The proportion naming big government has been on a steady uptrend since 1977, when 39% gave this response.

In his televised speech on September 24, President Reagan asked for a reduction in the size of the federal government and called for cutting the 1982 budget by $13 billion and by $58 billion in the next three years. In addition, he called for the dismantling of the Departments of Energy and Education and the reduction of the federal payroll by 75,000 persons.

OCTOBER 8
PRESIDENT REAGAN

Interviewing Date: 10/2–5/81
Survey #183-G

*Do you approve or disapprove of the way
Reagan is handling his job as president?*

Approve............................56%
Disapprove 35
No opinion 9

By Sex
Male

Approve............................61%
Disapprove 32
No opinion 7

Female

Approve............................51%
Disapprove 37
No opinion 12

By Race
White

Approve............................62%
Disapprove 30
No opinion 8

Nonwhite

Approve............................12%
Disapprove 71
No opinion 17

By Education
College

Approve............................63%
Disapprove 31
No opinion 6

High School

Approve............................56%
Disapprove 33
No opinion 11

Grade School

Approve............................39%
Disapprove 48
No opinion 13

By Region
East

Approve............................56%
Disapprove 36
No opinion 8

Midwest

Approve............................57%
Disapprove 33
No opinion 10

South

Approve............................57%
Disapprove 32
No opinion 11

West

Approve............................51%
Disapprove 41
No opinion 8

By Age
18–29 Years

Approve............................56%
Disapprove 36
No opinion 8

30–49 Years

Approve............................58%
Disapprove 33
No opinion 9

50 Years and Over

Approve............................54%
Disapprove 36
No opinion 10

By Income

$15,000 and Over

Approve............................64%
Disapprove.........................29
No opinion......................... 7

Under $15,000

Approve............................44%
Disapprove.........................43
No opinion.........................13

By Politics

Republicans

Approve............................87%
Disapprove......................... 8
No opinion......................... 5

Democrats

Approve............................36%
Disapprove.........................56
No opinion......................... 8

Independents

Approve............................55%
Disapprove.........................31
No opinion.........................14

By Religion

Protestants

Approve............................56%
Disapprove.........................34
No opinion.........................10

Catholics

Approve............................58%
Disapprove.........................33
No opinion......................... 9

By Occupation

Professional and Business

Approve............................67%
Disapprove.........................28
No opinion......................... 5

Clerical and Sales

Approve............................45%
Disapprove.........................43
No opinion.........................12

Manual Workers

Approve............................52%
Disapprove.........................37
No opinion.........................11

Labor Union Families Only

Approve............................47%
Disapprove.........................40
No opinion.........................13

Nonlabor Union Families Only

Approve............................58%
Disapprove.........................33
No opinion......................... 9

National Trend

	Approve	Dis-approve	No opinion
Sept. 18–21	52%	37%	11%
Aug. 14–17	60	29	11
July 31–Aug. 2	60	28	12
July 24–27	56	30	14
July 17–20	60	29	11
June 26–29	58	30	12
June 19–22	59	29	12
June 5–8	59	28	13

Do you approve or disapprove of the way Reagan is handling economic conditions in this country?

Approve............................44%
Disapprove.........................47
No opinion......................... 9

By Sex

Male

Approve............................46%
Disapprove.........................46
No opinion......................... 8

Female

Approve...........................42%
Disapprove 48
No opinion 10

By Race
White

Approve...........................49%
Disapprove 42
No opinion 9

Nonwhite

Approve...........................10%
Disapprove 81
No opinion 9

By Education
College

Approve...........................52%
Disapprove 41
No opinion 7

High School

Approve...........................43%
Disapprove 48
No opinion 9

Grade School

Approve...........................31%
Disapprove 57
No opinion 12

By Region
East

Approve...........................41%
Disapprove 48
No opinion 11

Midwest

Approve...........................47%
Disapprove 46
No opinion 7

South

Approve...........................45%
Disapprove 46
No opinion 9

West

Approve...........................42%
Disapprove 52
No opinion 6

By Age
18–24 Years

Approve...........................37%
Disapprove 53
No opinion 10

25–29 Years

Approve...........................40%
Disapprove 52
No opinion 8

30–49 Years

Approve...........................48%
Disapprove 44
No opinion 8

50 Years and Over

Approve...........................44%
Disapprove 47
No opinion 9

By Income
$25,000 and Over

Approve...........................55%
Disapprove 38
No opinion 7

$20,000–$24,999

Approve...........................48%
Disapprove 44
No opinion 8

$15,000–$19,999

Approve............................47%
Disapprove 42
No opinion 11

$10,000–$14,999

Approve............................39%
Disapprove 51
No opinion 10

$5,000–$9,999

Approve............................36%
Disapprove 53
No opinion 11

Under $5,000

Approve............................19%
Disapprove 74
No opinion 7

By Occupation
Professional and Business

Approve............................54%
Disapprove 38
No opinion 8

Clerical and Sales

Approve............................40%
Disapprove 56
No opinion 9

Manual Workers

Approve............................39%
Disapprove 53
No opinion 8

Nonlabor Force

Approve............................45%
Disapprove 45
No opinion 10

By Community Size
One Million and Over

Approve............................31%
Disapprove 55
No opinion 14

500,000–999,999

Approve............................44%
Disapprove 54
No opinion 2

50,000–499,999

Approve............................43%
Disapprove 51
No opinion 6

2,500–49,999

Approve............................50%
Disapprove 42
No opinion 8

Under 2,500; Rural

Approve............................49%
Disapprove 40
No opinion 11

Labor Union Families Only

Approve............................39%
Disapprove 55
No opinion 6

Nonlabor Union Families Only

Approve............................45%
Disapprove 46
No opinion 9

National Trend

	Approve	Dis-approve	No opinion
Aug. 14–17	53%	35%	12%
June 26–29..........	51	40	9
May 8–11............	58	31	11
Apr. 3–6	60	29	11
Mar. 13–16	56	32	12

Do you approve or disapprove of the way Reagan is handling inflation?

Approve........................42%
Disapprove 48
No opinion 10

By Sex
Male

Approve........................46%
Disapprove 44
No opinion 10

Female

Approve........................38%
Disapprove 52
No opinion 10

By Race
White

Approve........................46%
Disapprove 44
No opinion 10

Nonwhite

Approve........................14%
Disapprove 78
No opinion 8

By Education
College

Approve........................51%
Disapprove 41
No opinion 8

High School

Approve........................41%
Disapprove 49
No opinion 10

Grade School

Approve........................27%
Disapprove 60
No opinion 13

By Region
East

Approve........................42%
Disapprove 47
No opinion 11

Midwest

Approve........................44%
Disapprove 47
No opinion 9

South

Approve........................41%
Disapprove 49
No opinion 10

West

Approve........................39%
Disapprove 51
No opinion 10

By Age
18–29 Years

Approve........................37%
Disapprove 51
No opinion 12

30–49 Years

Approve........................44%
Disapprove 47
No opinion 9

50 Years and Over

Approve........................43%
Disapprove 48
No opinion 9

By Income
$25,000 and Over

Approve........................54%
Disapprove 39
No opinion 7

$20,000–$24,999

Approve......................................48%
Disapprove................................42
No opinion................................10

$15,000–$19,999

Approve......................................43%
Disapprove................................46
No opinion................................11

$10,000–$14,999

Approve......................................40%
Disapprove................................50
No opinion................................10

$5,000–$9,999

Approve......................................31%
Disapprove................................58
No opinion................................11

Under $5,000

Approve......................................13%
Disapprove................................73
No opinion................................14

By Occupation
Professional and Business

Approve......................................55%
Disapprove................................37
No opinion.................................8

Clerical and Sales

Approve......................................38%
Disapprove................................59
No opinion.................................3

Manual Workers

Approve......................................37%
Disapprove................................52
No opinion................................11

Nonlabor Force

Approve......................................38%
Disapprove................................51
No opinion................................11

Labor Union Families Only

Approve......................................37%
Disapprove................................52
No opinion................................11

Nonlabor Union Families Only

Approve......................................43%
Disapprove................................47
No opinion................................10

National Trend

	Approve	Dis-approve	No opinion
Aug. 14–17	53%	35%	12%
June 26–29	53	35	12
May 8–11	56	30	14
Apr. 3–6	58	28	14
Mar. 13–16	56	30	14

Do you approve or disapprove of the way Reagan is handling unemployment?

Approve......................................33%
Disapprove................................53
No opinion................................14

By Sex
Male

Approve......................................36%
Disapprove................................51
No opinion................................13

Female

Approve......................................30%
Disapprove................................55
No opinion................................15

By Race
White

Approve.............................36%
Disapprove 49
No opinion 15

Nonwhite

Approve.............................11%
Disapprove 80
No opinion 9

By Education
College

Approve.............................36%
Disapprove 50
No opinion 14

High School

Approve.............................35%
Disapprove 51
No opinion 14

Grade School

Approve.............................20%
Disapprove 64
No opinion 16

By Region
East

Approve.............................32%
Disapprove 54
No opinion 14

Midwest

Approve.............................34%
Disapprove 53
No opinion 13

South

Approve.............................34%
Disapprove 52
No opinion 14

West

Approve.............................30%
Disapprove 52
No opinion 18

By Age
18–24 Years

Approve.............................29%
Disapprove 57
No opinion 14

25–29 Years

Approve.............................34%
Disapprove 53
No opinion 13

30–49 Years

Approve.............................34%
Disapprove 51
No opinion 15

50 Years and Over

Approve.............................33%
Disapprove 52
No opinion 15

By Income
$25,000 and Over

Approve.............................41%
Disapprove 42
No opinion 17

$20,000–$24,999

Approve.............................42%
Disapprove 46
No opinion 12

$15,000–$19,999

Approve.............................33%
Disapprove 51
No opinion 16

$10,000–$14,999

Approve............................31%
Disapprove 55
No opinion 14

$5,000–$9,999

Approve............................25%
Disapprove 63
No opinion 12

Under $5,000

Approve............................12%
Disapprove 74
No opinion 14

By Occupation

Professional and Business

Approve............................41%
Disapprove 44
No opinion 15

Clerical and Sales

Approve............................35%
Disapprove 59
No opinion 6

Manual Workers

Approve............................29%
Disapprove 58
No opinion 13

Nonlabor Force

Approve............................30%
Disapprove 53
No opinion 17

Labor Union Families Only

Approve............................27%
Disapprove 58
No opinion 15

Nonlabor Union Families Only

Approve............................34%
Disapprove 52
No opinion 14

National Trend

	Approve	Dis-approve	No opinion
Aug. 14–17	39%	38%	23%
June 26–29	39	40	21
May 8–11	42	34	24
Apr. 3–6	43	34	23
Mar. 13–16	40	37	23

Now let's talk about the Reagan administration's economic policies. What effect do you think that these policies will have on your own and your family's financial situation? Do you feel your financial situation will be much better, somewhat better, somewhat worse, or much worse as a result of the Reagan economic policies?

Much better......................... 4%
Somewhat better.....................38
Same (volunteered) 13
Somewhat worse 27
Much worse.........................12
No opinion 6

By Sex
Male

Much better......................... 4%
Somewhat better.....................43
Same (volunteered) 14
Somewhat worse 24
Much worse.........................11
No opinion 4

Female

Much better......................... 4%
Somewhat better.....................33
Same (volunteered) 12
Somewhat worse 30
Much worse.........................14
No opinion 7

By Race

White

Much better	4%
Somewhat better	42
Same (volunteered)	14
Somewhat worse	26
Much worse	9
No opinion	5

Nonwhite

Much better	2%
Somewhat better	12
Same (volunteered)	7
Somewhat worse	33
Much worse	36
No opinion	10

By Income

$25,000 and Over

Much better	4%
Somewhat better	53
Same (volunteered)	12
Somewhat worse	20
Much worse	8
No opinion	3

$20,000–$24,999

Much better	6%
Somewhat better	45
Same (volunteered)	13
Somewhat worse	25
Much worse	6
No opinion	5

$15,000–$19,999

Much better	2%
Somewhat better	39
Same (volunteered)	14
Somewhat worse	30
Much worse	10
No opinion	5

$10,000–$14,999

Much better	4%
Somewhat better	31

Same (volunteered)	13
Somewhat worse	30
Much worse	14
No opinion	8

$5,000–$9,999

Much better	5%
Somewhat better	28
Same (volunteered)	13
Somewhat worse	31
Much worse	16
No opinion	7

Under $5,000

Much better	1%
Somewhat better	15
Same (volunteered)	14
Somewhat worse	29
Much worse	32
No opinion	9

By Occupation

Professional and Business

Much better	5%
Somewhat better	48
Same (volunteered)	12
Somewhat worse	22
Much worse	10
No opinion	3

Clerical and Sales

Much better	8%
Somewhat better	29
Same (volunteered)	12
Somewhat worse	32
Much worse	17
No opinion	2

Manual Workers

Much better	2%
Somewhat better	41
Same (volunteered)	10
Somewhat worse	29
Much worse	13
No opinion	5

Nonlabor Force

Much better 2%
Somewhat better 25
Same (volunteered) 21
Somewhat worse 28
Much worse 15
No opinion 9

Labor Union Families Only

Much better 2%
Somewhat better 35
Same (volunteered) 12
Somewhat worse 34
Much worse 13
No opinion 4

Nonlabor Union Families Only

Much better 4%
Somewhat better 39
Same (volunteered) 13
Somewhat worse 25
Much worse 13
No opinion 6

National Trend
August 14–17

Much better 5%
Somewhat better 43
Somewhat worse 28
Much worse 8
Same; no opinion...................... 16

May 8–11

Much better 7%
Somewhat better 41
Somewhat worse 28
Much worse 9
Same; no opinion 15

We are interested in how people's financial situation may have changed. Would you say that you are financially better off now than you were a year ago or are you financially worse off now?

Better 28%
Same (volunteered) 28
Worse................................. 43
Don't know 1

By Sex
Male

Better 29%
Same (volunteered) 29
Worse................................. 41
Don't know 1

Female

Better 26%
Same (volunteered) 27
Worse................................. 45
Don't know 2

By Race
White

Better 29%
Same (volunteered) 29
Worse................................. 41
Don't know 1

Nonwhite

Better 15%
Same (volunteered) 23
Worse................................. 58
Don't know 4

By Income
$25,000 and Over

Better 41%
Same (volunteered) 25
Worse................................. 34
Don't know .... *

$20,000–$24,999

Better 32%
Same (volunteered) 32
Worse................................. 33
Don't know 3

$15,000–$19,999

Better 29%
Same (volunteered) 33
Worse 37
Don't know 1

$10,000–$14,999

Better 24%
Same (volunteered) 27
Worse 48
Don't know 1

$5,000–$9,999

Better 15%
Same (volunteered) 28
Worse 55
Don't know 2

Under $5,000

Better 11%
Same (volunteered) 19
Worse 68
Don't know 2

By Occupation
Professional and Business

Better 37%
Same (volunteered) 27
Worse 36
Don't know . . . . *

Clerical and Sales

Better 29%
Same (volunteered) 25
Worse 45
Don't know 1

Manual Workers

Better 28%
Same (volunteered) 25
Worse 46
Don't know 1

Nonlabor Force

Better 16%
Same (volunteered) 36
Worse 45
Don't know 3

Labor Union Families Only

Better 30%
Same (volunteered) 29
Worse 40
Don't know 1

Nonlabor Union Families Only

Better 27%
Same (volunteered) 28
Worse 44
Don't know 1

*Less than 1%

Now looking ahead—do you expect that at this time next year you will be financially better off than now or worse off than now?

Better 40%
Same (volunteered) 21
Worse 31
Don't know 8

By Sex
Male

Better 44%
Same (volunteered) 19
Worse 31
Don't know 6

Female

Better 36%
Same (volunteered) 23
Worse 31
Don't know 10

By Race
White

Better 43%
Same (volunteered) 21
Worse 28
Don't know 8

Nonwhite

Better............................21%
Same (volunteered).................20
Worse............................48
Don't know........................11

By Income

$25,000 and Over

Better............................53%
Same (volunteered).................16
Worse............................26
Don't know......................... 5

$20,000–$24,999

Better............................51%
Same (volunteered).................17
Worse............................24
Don't know......................... 8

$15,000–$19,999

Better............................46%
Same (volunteered).................24
Worse............................26
Don't know......................... 4

$10,000–$14,999

Better............................37%
Same (volunteered).................21
Worse............................33
Don't know......................... 9

$5,000–$9,999

Better............................21%
Same (volunteered).................28
Worse............................41
Don't know........................10

Under $5,000

Better............................23%
Same (volunteered).................20
Worse............................41
Don't know........................16

By Occupation

Professional and Business

Better............................53%
Same (volunteered).................18
Worse............................26
Don't know......................... 3

Clerical and Sales

Better............................44%
Same (volunteered).................19
Worse............................30
Don't know......................... 7

Manual Workers

Better............................43%
Same (volunteered).................17
Worse............................33
Don't know......................... 7

Nonlabor Force

Better............................19%
Same (volunteered).................33
Worse............................33
Don't know........................15

Labor Union Families Only

Better............................37%
Same (volunteered).................22
Worse............................34
Don't know......................... 7

Nonlabor Union Families Only

Better............................41%
Same (volunteered).................21
Worse............................30
Don't know......................... 8

Note: A recent nationwide survey shows growing pessimism among Americans over President Ronald Reagan's economic program:

1. The proportions of Americans who approve of President Reagan's handling of the nation's economy, specifically of inflation, have fallen below the 50% level for the first time. In addition, only one-third of the public now approves of the president's handling of unemployment, the low point of a steady downtrend since April.

2. The president's overall job rating, while showing a slight boost in the aftermath of his October 2 press conference, is below the average approval level he has maintained since taking office. In the current survey, 56% of all persons interviewed say they approve of the way Reagan is handling his job as chief executive.

3. The decline in approval of the president's handling of economic problems has been accompanied by lowered expectations about the administration's ability to reach three key economic goals by 1984: reducing inflation, balancing the federal budget, and reducing unemployment.

Opinion is 2 to 1 that the president's program will not balance the federal budget by 1984. Furthermore, those who think that the Reagan administration will reduce unemployment within three years are far outweighed by those who do not share this view.

4. Finally, in terms of the perceived impact of Reaganomics on Americans' own financial situation, a steady decrease has been recorded since May in the percentage who believe their financial situation will improve. At the same time, however, those saying better still outnumber those saying worse by the narrow margin of 42% to 39%.

When those interviewed were asked about their own financial situation without reference to the Reagan administration, similar responses emerged. For example, whereas opinion was closely divided in June on whether they are financially better or worse off than one year ago, today it is clearly on the negative side. Furthermore, those who predict their financial situation will get worse has grown during this period. At the same time, however, it should be noted that optimism regarding the future outweighs pessimism, although by a narrow margin.

OCTOBER 11
FEDERAL BUDGET CUTS

Interviewing Date: 10/2–5/81
Survey #183-G

Did you happen to see or read about President Reagan's television speech on September 24 in which he proposed federal budget cuts in addition to those approved earlier this year?

	Yes
National	59%

Asked of the entire sample: In general, are you in favor of budget cuts in addition to those approved earlier this year or are you opposed to more cuts?

	Total sample	Saw or read about Reagan's speech
Favor	42%	47%
Oppose	46	47
No opinion	12	6

Asked of those who approve of the president's additional cuts: To reduce the size of the 1982 budget deficiency, President Reagan has proposed cutting $13 billion in addition to the $35 billion in cuts approved earlier this year. About $11 billion of the new cuts would come from social programs and about $2 billion from defense programs. In general, would you say you approve or disapprove of the president's proposal?

Approve	74%
Disapprove	20
No opinion	6

Asked of the entire sample: The additional cuts for social programs come to about $11 billion. Do you feel that this amount is too high, too low, or about right?

Too high 43%
Too low 8
About right 35
No opinion 14

By Sex
Male

Too high 38%
Too low 11
About right 39
No opinion 12

Female

Too high 48%
Too low 5
About right 31
No opinion 16

By Race
White

Too high 39%
Too low 8
About right 39
No opinion 14

Nonwhite

Too high 71%
Too low 5
About right 12
No opinion 12

By Education
College

Too high 43%
Too low 10
About right 36
No opinion 11

High School

Too high 42%
Too low 8
About right 37
No opinion 13

Grade School

Too high 47%
Too low 3
About right 27
No opinion 23

By Politics
Republicans

Too high 22%
Too low 11
About right 54
No opinion 13

Democrats

Too high 60%
Too low 6
About right 22
No opinion 12

Independents

Too high 37%
Too low 8
About right 38
No opinion 17

Asked of the entire sample: The additional cuts for defense programs come to about $2 billion. Do you feel that this amount is too high, too low, or about right?

Too high 26%
Too low 20
About right 40
No opinion 14

By Sex
Male

Too high 26%
Too low 25
About right 40
No opinion 9

Female

Too high	26%
Too low	16
About right	40
No opinion	18

By Race

White

Too high	25%
Too low	20
About right	42
No opinion	13

Nonwhite

Too high	34%
Too low	19
About right	26
No opinion	21

By Education

College

Too high	17%
Too low	32
About right	43
No opinion	8

High School

Too high	30%
Too low	16
About right	41
No opinion	13

Grade School

Too high	31%
Too low	9
About right	30
No opinion	30

By Politics

Republicans

Too high	27%
Too low	14
About right	47
No opinion	12

Democrats

Too high	27%
Too low	23
About right	35
No opinion	15

Independents

Too high	23%
Too low	24
About right	42
No opinion	11

Note: Public opinion on President Ronald Reagan's proposal to cut an additional $13 billion from the 1982 federal budget is closely divided, with 42% favoring and 46% opposed. A plurality, however, believes that the $11 billion earmarked for reductions in social programs is too high, while most of the public thinks that the $2 billion cut in defense spending is about the right amount.

Fifty-nine percent of the total sample who saw or read about President Reagan's September 24 television address do not differ significantly from the nation as a whole. But opinion does vary markedly by population groups. Among blacks, eight in ten express opposition to the new cuts.

All persons favoring additional cuts were then asked whether they approved or disapproved of the specific budget cuts proposed by the president in his recent speech. Among this group, opinion is 3 to 1 in favor of Reagan's program.

Opinion is strongly polarized along political lines, with a 54% majority of Republicans believing that the new social cuts are about right and 22% saying too high, compared with 22% and 60%, respectively, of Democrats.

Greater unanimity between groups is found in public attitudes toward the proposed defense budget cuts. However, college-educated persons are more likely to perceive the defense cuts as too low and those with less formal education as too high.

The public long has favored a law that would require the government to balance the federal budget each year. A September 1981 Gallup Poll indicated that of those who were aware of a proposed constitutional amendment to require such a law support was 67% to 19% in favor. Yet, while a large majority of Americans approve a balanced budget, opinion is 2 to 1 that it will not be possible for the Reagan administration to do so by 1984.

OCTOBER 15
CONGRESSIONAL ELECTIONS

Interviewing Date: 9/18–21/81
Survey #182-G

Asked of registered voters: If the elections for Congress were being held today, which party would you like to see win in this congressional district—the Democratic party or the Republican party? [Those who said they were undecided or who preferred another party were asked: As of today, do you lean more to the Democratic party or to the Republican party?]

Democratic 53%
Republican 35
Other 3
Undecided 9

By Sex
Male

Democratic 50%
Republican 41
Other 1
Undecided 8

Female

Democratic 56%
Republican 31
Other 3
Undecided 10

By Race
White

Democratic 48%
Republican 40
Other 3
Undecided 9

Nonwhite

Democratic 83%
Republican 9
Other .... *
Undecided 8

By Education
College

Democratic 48%
Republican 44
Other 1
Undecided 7

High School

Democratic 54%
Republican 34
Other 3
Undecided 9

Grade School

Democratic 60%
Republican 26
Other 3
Undecided 11

By Region
East

Democratic 55%
Republican 35
Other 2
Undecided 8

Midwest

Democratic 50%
Republican 38
Other 2
Undecided 10

South

Democratic........................56%
Republican 33
Other 3
Undecided........................ 8

West

Democratic........................51%
Republican 38
Other 1
Undecided........................10

By Age
18–29 Years

Democratic........................54%
Republican 34
Other 3
Undecided........................ 9

30–49 Years

Democratic........................56%
Republican 31
Other 4
Undecided........................ 9

50 Years and Over

Democratic........................50%
Republican 41
Other 1
Undecided........................ 8

By Income
$15,000 and Over

Democratic........................47%
Republican 42
Other 3
Undecided........................ 8

Under $15,000

Democratic........................60%
Republican 28
Other 3
Undecided........................ 9

*Less than 1%

Note: After a strong surge by the Republicans earlier this year, the Democratic party again has taken a commanding lead in the national race for Congress. In a June 1981 survey the Republicans trailed the Democrats by 48% to 52%, the GOP's strongest showing in these measurements since the early years of the Eisenhower administration. Nevertheless, the Republican party still finds itself in the best position in over two decades. One must go back to 1957 to find a significantly stronger GOP position than at present.

The diminished standing of the Republican party in the national race for Congress undoubtedly reflects the public's growing uneasiness over President Ronald Reagan's economic program. The proportions of Americans who approve of the president's handling of the economy, specifically inflation, have fallen below the 50% level for the first time. In addition, only one-third now approves of his handling of unemployment, the low point of a steady downtrend since April.

The decline in approval of President Reagan's dealing with economic problems has been accompanied by lowered expectations about the administration's ability to reach three key economic goals by 1984: reducing inflation, balancing the federal budget, and reducing unemployment. In terms of the perceived impact of Reaganomics on Americans' own financial situation, a steady decrease has been recorded since May in the percentage who say that their financial state will improve as a result of Reagan's economic policies.

OCTOBER 18
FEDERAL VS. STATE GOVERNMENT

Interviewing Date: 9/18–21/81
Survey #182-G

Which theory of government do you favor— concentration of power in the federal government or concentration of power in the state government?

Federal government................... 28%
State government 56
No opinion 16

By Region
East

Federal government................... 33%
State government 51
No opinion 16

Midwest

Federal government................... 28%
State government 58
No opinion 14

South

Federal government................... 20%
State government 60
No opinion 20

West

Federal government................... 29%
State government 56
No opinion 15

Which do you think is more likely to administer social programs efficiently— the federal government in Washington or the government of this state?

Federal government................... 18%
This state............................ 67
Neither (volunteered) 8
No opinion 7

By Region
East

Federal government................... 19%
This state............................ 63
Neither (volunteered) 11
No opinion 7

Midwest

Federal government................... 17%
This state............................ 69
Neither (volunteered) 5
No opinion 9

South

Federal government................... 17%
This state............................ 65
Neither (volunteered) 8
No opinion 10

West

Federal government................... 20%
This state............................ 70
Neither (volunteered) 7
No opinion 3

Which do you think is more understanding of the real needs of the people of this community—the federal government in Washington or the government of this state?

Federal government................... 15%
This state............................ 67
Neither (volunteered) 9
No opinion 9

By Region
East

Federal government................... 17%
This state............................ 65
Neither (volunteered) 12
No opinion 6

Midwest

Federal government................... 13%
This state............................ 72
Neither (volunteered) 7
No opinion 8

South

Federal government................... 16%
This state............................ 62
Neither (volunteered) 9
No opinion 13

West

Federal government	15%
This state	72
Neither (volunteered)	7
No opinion	6

Which do you think is more likely to make decisions free of political corruption—the federal government in Washington or the government of this state?

Federal government	26%
This state	42
Neither (volunteered)	20
No opinion	12

By Region

East

Federal government	35%
This state	33
Neither (volunteered)	22
No opinion	10

Midwest

Federal government	22%
This state	47
Neither (volunteered)	16
No opinion	15

South

Federal government	20%
This state	45
Neither (volunteered)	20
No opinion	15

West

Federal government	23%
This state	44
Neither (volunteered)	24
No opinion	9

Of every tax dollar that goes to the federal government in Washington, DC, how many cents of each dollar would you say are wasted?

	Median average
National	42¢

And how many cents of each tax dollar that goes to the government of this state would you say are wasted?

	Median average
National	29¢

And how many cents of each tax dollar that goes to your local government would you say are wasted?

	Median average
National	23¢

Note: President Ronald Reagan's "New Federalism," in which the government in Washington would turn over much of its power to the states, strikes a responsive chord with the American public. The New Federalism would embrace cuts in federal spending and regulations and would substitute broad block grants to the states for health and education programs that previously have been run under close federal supervision.

Some taxpayers worry about the impact of the New Federalism on their state and local taxes. Others express concern about the ability of states and cities to serve adequately the needs of the disadvantaged through block grants, while still others are uneasy about the complexities of transferring responsibility from the federal to the state governments.

At the same time, however, the public as a whole is clearly receptive to the principles of the New Federalism, as evidenced by the following survey findings:

1. An almost complete reversal is noted in the public's views on federalism since a Gallup survey conducted in 1936 during the early days of Franklin Roosevelt's New Deal. In 1936, 56% of persons surveyed voted in favor of the concentration of power in the federal government, while 44% preferred that such power be vested in the state governments.

2. On three vital aspects of government, the public leans heavily in favor of the state as opposed to the federal government:

a) By a 67% to 15% vote, survey respondents believe that state governments are more understanding of the needs of the people than the federal government.

b) By a similar 67% to 18% margin, the public views their state government as more likely than the federal government to administer social programs efficiently. This opinion is shared even among those who favor the concentration of power in the federal government as opposed to the state.

c) Those interviewed also believe—42% to 26%—that the governments of states are more likely than the federal government to make decisions free of political corruption.

3. And Gallup polls consistently have shown that those surveyed believe that almost half (42¢) of every tax dollar that goes to Washington is wasted. In contrast, respondents estimate that 29¢ goes to state and 23¢ to local governments.

OCTOBER 22
MOST IMPORTANT PROBLEM

Interviewing Date: 10/2–5/81
Survey #183-G

What do you think is the most important problem facing this country today?

High cost of living; inflation 52%
Unemployment 17
Reagan budget cuts 6
Excessive government spending 4
Fear of war 4
Crime 4
Moral decline in society 4
Defense; national security 4
All others 15
No opinion 2
                                           112%*

*Total adds to more than 100% due to multiple responses.

Note: The high cost of living and unemployment are seen as the top problems facing the nation today, with 52% and 17% citing these issues, respectively. The percentage naming unemployment as the number one problem has been on an uptrend since January, when 8% said this was the most important problem.

Blacks are currently more than twice as likely as whites to name unemployment as the nation's most urgent problem, with 36% giving this response compared to 14% of whites. At the present time blacks are almost evenly divided between those who say the high cost of living is the top problem (40%) and those who name unemployment (36%). The September 1981 Labor Department figures show that joblessness among blacks is more than twice that of whites.

Named third most often as the nation's most pressing problem are the Reagan administration's budget cuts, cited by 6% of whites and 12% of nonwhites.

Analysis of the current findings also shows that persons in the $15,000 and above income bracket are about four times as likely to name the high cost of living as unemployment, while those earning under $15,000 are about twice as likely to do so.

Little difference is noted in the proportions of people from different regions of the nation naming the high cost of living, but unemployment is less often cited in the Sun Belt states in the South and West, as shown in the following:

By Region
East

High cost of living; inflation 52%
Unemployment 20

Midwest

High cost of living; inflation 53%
Unemployment 20

South

High cost of living; inflation 50%
Unemployment 12

West

High cost of living; inflation 54%
Unemployment 16

OCTOBER 25
ITEM VETO

Interviewing Date: 10/2–5/81
Survey #183-G

At the present time, when Congress passes a bill, the president cannot veto parts of that bill but must accept it in full or veto it. Do you think this should be changed so that the president can veto some items in a bill without vetoing the entire bill?

Should 64%
Should not 24
No opinion 12

By Education
College

Should 64%
Should not 30
No opinion 6

High School

Should 68%
Should not 21
No opinion 11

Grade School

Should 47%
Should not 27
No opinion 26

By Region
East

Should 63%
Should not 25
No opinion 12

Midwest

Should 67%
Should not 23
No opinion 10

South

Should 58%
Should not 27
No opinion 15

West

Should 71%
Should not 22
No opinion 7

By Age
18–29 Years

Should 64%
Should not 26
No opinion 10

30–49 Years

Should 68%
Should not 22
No opinion 10

50 Years and Over

Should 60%
Should not 25
No opinion 15

By Politics
Republicans

Should 72%
Should not 19
No opinion 9

Democrats

Should 57%
Should not 29
No opinion 14

Independents

Should 68%
Should not 23
No opinion 9

National Trend

	Should	Should not	No opinion
1981	64%	24%	12%
1978	70	19	11
1975	69	20	11
1953	63	24	13
1945	57	14	29

Note: A solid majority of Americans (64%) backs President Ronald Reagan in his request for the authority to veto individual items in appropriations bills passed by Congress. At present, bills must be approved or vetoed in their entirety. The president recently renewed interest in this issue when he called for a fundamental revision of the federal budget process, including the power to veto individual budget items.

More than half the states grant their governors the power of the item veto, but many scholars believe it would require a constitutional amendment to give presidents this authority. Those favoring the item veto think that such power would stop pork-barrel legislation, the inclusion of budget items that primarily serve the expedient political interests of congressmen without regard to the soundness of the measures on their own merits. Others believe that eliminating expensive riders frequently tacked onto proposed bills would save millions of dollars.

The main argument offered by those who favor the present system is that it gives the legislative branch more power by forcing a president to accept items, particularly in appropriations bills, that he might not otherwise accept.

OCTOBER 26
THE FORTRESS AMERICA SYNDROME*

One of the most profound changes in public opinion in the past few years has been America's revived concern for national defense. Public uneasiness over the nation's defense readiness

*This Gallup analysis was written by Andrew Kohut, president of the Gallup Organization Inc.

grew steadily throughout the mid-1970s as the country slowly shook off the effects of Vietnam. Uneasiness turned to fear with the apparent inability of the United States to handle the Iranian hostage situation and again in the aftermath of the Russian invasion of Afghanistan.

Polls conducted during that period showed a remarkable transformation of opinion. Measures of concern for military preparedness and the adequacy of defense spending, which has shown moderate upturns between 1975 and 1979, soared in late 1979 and early 1980. Since then American resolve to improve its defenses has been expressed in consistent support for the Reagan administration's defense policies. However, in the face of this determination a surprising countertrend in public opinion has developed. While the public seems increasingly willing to spend money for defense, it shows significantly less support for measures that involve U.S. military forces.

Recent polls indicate the following findings concerning Americans' opinions on defense spending:

1. In September a polling by major survey organizations showed declining support for the administration in general and its economic policies in particular. However, most Americans continued to express confidence in President Reagan's defense spending policies. In fact, Reagan's handling of the defense issue is currently his major strength.

2. The CBS/*New York Times* Poll showed 62% of the public saying that it could trust Reagan to make the right decisions on military defense. This figure is considerably higher than those who are in favor of his decisions on Social Security or the federal budget. The ABC/*Washington Post* Poll found 52% saying that the administration's increased defense spending was at about the right level, while 19% said not enough and 23% believed it had gone too far.

3. A *Newsweek* survey, conducted by the Gallup Organization earlier in the year, attested to the public's commitment to increased defense spending when it found two-thirds would opt for a smaller tax cut for the sake of more defense spending. A more recent CBS/*New York Times*

Poll reaffirmed that finding and indicated that 64% of its respondents would be willing to give up their recently passed tax cut rather than trim the defense budget in order to achieve a balanced federal budget. In that survey only preserving Social Security payments was given higher priority than defense spending.

These polls and others like them are testimony to the importance that the public attaches to bolstering its military forces and the extent to which the administration's spending policies are supported, but they seem inconsistent with other survey findings on defense.

In the past year, as the public favored mammoth increases in defense spending, support for a resumption of the draft fell sharply. In July 1980 the Gallup Poll registered 62% favoring a return of the draft, with 31% opposing. In its most recent survey, Gallup found the percentage who approved of a resumed draft had fallen to 48%, while opposition had risen to 45%.

Consistent with attitudes toward the draft are trends in opinion about the use of American forces in a number of potential trouble spots around the world. According to the *Newsweek* Poll, since February 1980 the percentage who would favor employing American forces if Western Europe were invaded by the Soviet Union has tumbled 20 percentage points—from 73% to 53% in July 1981.

Newsweek's July 1981 survey also shows a majority (57%) saying they would be opposed to the use of American forces if the U.S. Mideast oil supply were interrupted. This represents a 15 percentage point increase in opposition to the use of American forces in that situation when compared to an October 1980 survey.

The significance of these hypothetical opinion tests is not in how predictive they are of public views if these events were actually to occur but rather what they say about the overall direction of the public's mood with regard to military involvement in light of America's renewed commitment to defense.

Just recently, with the El Salvador situation, the public's reaction to potential military involvement was brought to the attention of the Reagan administration. The response was an overwhelming opposition to sending any weapons or troops to that country. Although as committed as Americans are to improving and expanding their own military capabilities, they show little interest for exporting arms to other nations. A recent ABC/*Washington Post* Poll showed continued opposition to the sale of airborne warning and control systems (AWACS) to Saudi Arabia despite the death of Egyptian President Anwar Sadat.

OCTOBER 29
PRESIDENT REAGAN

Interviewing Date: 10/2–5/81
Survey #183-G

Do you approve or disapprove of the way President Reagan is dealing with economic conditions in this country?

Approve............................44%
Disapprove 47
No opinion 9

By Sex
Male

Approve............................46%
Disapprove 46
No opinion 8

Female

Approve............................42%
Disapprove 48
No opinion 10

By Race
White

Approve............................49%
Disapprove 42
No opinion 9

Nonwhite

Approve............................10%
Disapprove 81
No opinion 9

By Education
College
Approve............................52%
Disapprove 41
No opinion 7

High School
Approve............................43%
Disapprove 48
No opinion 9

Grade School
Approve............................31%
Disapprove 57
No opinion 12

By Region
East
Approve............................41%
Disapprove 48
No opinion 11

Midwest
Approve............................47%
Disapprove 46
No opinion 7

South
Approve............................45%
Disapprove 46
No opinion 9

West
Approve............................42%
Disapprove 52
No opinion 6

By Age
18–29 Years
Approve............................39%
Disapprove 52
No opinion 9

30–49 Years
Approve............................48%
Disapprove 44
No opinion 8

50 Years and Over
Approve............................44%
Disapprove 47
No opinion 9

By Income
$15,000 and Over
Approve............................51%
Disapprove 41
No opinion 8

Under $15,000
Approve............................34%
Disapprove 56
No opinion 10

By Politics
Republicans
Approve............................70%
Disapprove 20
No opinion 10

Democrats
Approve............................25%
Disapprove 69
No opinion 6

Independents
Approve............................47%
Disapprove 43
No opinion 10

Labor Union Families Only
Approve............................39%
Disapprove 55
No opinion 6

Nonlabor Union Families Only

Approve..............................45%
Disapprove 46
No opinion 9

Do you approve or disapprove of the way President Reagan is dealing with inflation?

Approve..............................42%
Disapprove 48
No opinion 10

By Sex
Male

Approve..............................46%
Disapprove 44
No opinion 10

Female

Approve..............................38%
Disapprove 52
No opinion 10

By Race
White

Approve..............................46%
Disapprove 44
No opinion 10

Nonwhite

Approve..............................14%
Disapprove 78
No opinion 8

By Education
College

Approve..............................51%
Disapprove 41
No opinion 8

High School

Approve..............................41%
Disapprove 49
No opinion 10

Grade School

Approve..............................27%
Disapprove 60
No opinion 13

By Region
East

Approve..............................42%
Disapprove 47
No opinion 11

Midwest

Approve..............................44%
Disapprove 47
No opinion 9

South

Approve..............................41%
Disapprove 49
No opinion 10

West

Approve..............................39%
Disapprove 51
No opinion 10

By Age
18–29 Years

Approve..............................37%
Disapprove 51
No opinion 12

30–49 Years

Approve..............................44%
Disapprove 47
No opinion 9

50 Years and Over

Approve..............................43%
Disapprove 48
No opinion 9

By Income
$15,000 and Over
Approve............................50%
Disapprove 41
No opinion 9

Under $15,000
Approve............................31%
Disapprove 58
No opinion 11

By Politics
Republicans
Approve............................67%
Disapprove 24
No opinion 9

Democrats
Approve............................25%
Disapprove 67
No opinion 8

Independents
Approve............................43%
Disapprove 43
No opinion 14

Labor Union Families Only
Approve............................37%
Disapprove 52
No opinion 11

Nonlabor Union Families Only
Approve............................43%
Disapprove 47
No opinion 10

Do you approve or disapprove of the way President Reagan is dealing with unemployment?

Approve............................33%
Disapprove 53
No opinion 14

By Sex
Male
Approve............................36%
Disapprove 51
No opinion 13

Female
Approve............................30%
Disapprove 55
No opinion 15

By Race
White
Approve............................36%
Disapprove 49
No opinion 15

Nonwhite
Approve............................11%
Disapprove 80
No opinion 9

By Education
College
Approve............................36%
Disapprove 50
No opinion 14

High School
Approve............................35%
Disapprove 51
No opinion 14

Grade School
Approve............................20%
Disapprove 64
No opinion 16

By Region
East
Approve............................32%
Disapprove 54
No opinion 14

Midwest

Approve............................34%
Disapprove 53
No opinion 13

South

Approve............................34%
Disapprove 52
No opinion 14

West

Approve............................30%
Disapprove 52
No opinion 18

By Age
18–29 Years

Approve............................31%
Disapprove 55
No opinion 14

30–49 Years

Approve............................34%
Disapprove 51
No opinion 15

50 Years and Over

Approve............................33%
Disapprove 52
No opinion 15

By Income
$15,000 and Over

Approve............................39%
Disapprove 46
No opinion 15

Under $15,000

Approve............................25%
Disapprove 62
No opinion 13

By Politics
Republicans

Approve............................50%
Disapprove 31
No opinion 19

Democrats

Approve............................19%
Disapprove 70
No opinion 11

Independents

Approve............................39%
Disapprove 47
No opinion 14

Labor Union Families Only

Approve............................27%
Disapprove 58
No opinion 15

Nonlabor Union Families Only

Approve............................34%
Disapprove 52
No opinion 14

Do you approve or disapprove of the way President Reagan is handling our foreign policy—that is, our relations with other nations?

Approve............................56%
Disapprove 29
No opinion 15

By Sex
Male

Approve............................62%
Disapprove 27
No opinion 11

Female

Approve............................51%
Disapprove 31
No opinion 18

By Race

White

Approve...........................61%
Disapprove 26
No opinion 13

Nonwhite

Approve...........................27%
Disapprove 49
No opinion 24

By Education

College

Approve...........................63%
Disapprove 28
No opinion 9

High School

Approve...........................57%
Disapprove 28
No opinion 15

Grade School

Approve...........................38%
Disapprove 39
No opinion 23

By Income

$15,000 and Over

Approve...........................66%
Disapprove 23
No opinion 11

Under $15,000

Approve...........................43%
Disapprove 37
No opinion 20

By Politics

Republicans

Approve...........................76%
Disapprove 12
No opinion 12

Democrats

Approve...........................43%
Disapprove 42
No opinion 15

Independents

Approve...........................59%
Disapprove 28
No opinion 13

Do you approve or disapprove of the way President Reagan is handling our national defense?

Approve...........................61%
Disapprove 28
No opinion 11

By Sex

Male

Approve...........................68%
Disapprove 24
No opinion 8

Female

Approve...........................55%
Disapprove 31
No opinion 14

By Race

White

Approve...........................64%
Disapprove 26
No opinion 10

Nonwhite

Approve...........................41%
Disapprove 39
No opinion 20

By Education

College

Approve...........................63%
Disapprove 31
No opinion 6

High School

Approve............................64%
Disapprove.........................25
No opinion.........................11

Grade School

Approve............................48%
Disapprove.........................29
No opinion.........................23

By Income
$15,000 and Over

Approve............................68%
Disapprove.........................24
No opinion......................... 8

Under $15,000

Approve............................53%
Disapprove.........................31
No opinion.........................16

By Politics
Republicans

Approve............................78%
Disapprove.........................14
No opinion......................... 8

Democrats

Approve............................51%
Disapprove.........................35
No opinion.........................14

Independents

Approve............................62%
Disapprove.........................29
No opinion......................... 9

Do you approve or disapprove of the way President Reagan is handling relations with Russia?

Approve............................53%
Disapprove.........................25
No opinion.........................22

By Sex
Male

Approve............................62%
Disapprove.........................22
No opinion.........................16

Female

Approve............................44%
Disapprove.........................28
No opinion.........................28

By Race
White

Approve............................56%
Disapprove.........................23
No opinion.........................21

Nonwhite

Approve............................30%
Disapprove.........................38
No opinion.........................32

By Education
College

Approve............................58%
Disapprove.........................25
No opinion.........................17

High School

Approve............................55%
Disapprove.........................23
No opinion.........................22

Grade School

Approve............................32%
Disapprove.........................34
No opinion.........................34

By Income
$15,000 and Over

Approve............................62%
Disapprove.........................22
No opinion.........................16

Approve. 39%
Disapprove 30
No opinion 31

By Politics

Republicans

Approve. 68%
Disapprove 14
No opinion 18

Democrats

Approve. 42%
Disapprove 33
No opinion 25

Independents

Approve. 54%
Disapprove 25
No opinion 21

This card lists some things the president is sometimes criticized for. Some of these criticisms will reflect how you, yourself, feel and some will not. Would you read off all of the items, if any, which worry or bother you about Ronald Reagan, even if they worry you only a little bit?

Cut back in social programs. 48%
Sides with the rich 47
Sides with business; special interests 46
Unsympathetic to the elderly 46
Might get United States into a war 38
Might get United States into a recession . . . 28
Lost or reduced government payments . . . 27
Unsympathetic to minorities 26
Unsympathetic to women 16
Policies hurt our image abroad. 16
May lose job 15
Policies too conservative. 13

Note: The high regard in which the public held President Ronald Reagan's policies as recently as August shows serious signs of erosion. For the first time since he took office more Americans now disapprove than approve of the way Reagan is dealing with economic conditions in this country, specifically inflation and unemployment. However, despite the increase in pessimism about the president's domestic policies, his overall job approval rating is 56%.

With the 1982 congressional elections only a year away, mounting concern over Reagan's programs is reflected in the diminished standing of the Republican party in the national race for Congress. In the latest Gallup Poll the Democratic party holds a 55% to 45% lead over the GOP; in June the Republican party trailed the Democrats by only 4 percentage points—48% to 52%—the GOP's best showing in these measurements since the 1958 off-year elections.

The public is somewhat more positive in its appraisal of President Reagan's handling of the nation's foreign policy and defense and the way he is dealing with the Soviet Union. In each of these areas there has been an increase since earlier surveys in the proportion of the public's approval.

NOVEMBER 1
PARTY BEST FOR PEACE AND PROSPERITY

Interviewing Date: 10/2–5/81
Survey #183-G

Which political party do you think would be more likely to keep the United States out of World War III—the Republican party or the Democratic party?

Republican 29%
Democratic 34
No difference (volunteered) 22
No opinion 15

Which political party do you think will do a better job of keeping the country prosperous—the Republican party or the Democratic party?

Republican 40%
Democratic 31
No difference (volunteered) 15
No opinion 14

By comparison, the following shows the percentages of survey respondents ascribing which of the two major political parties they believe is better able to deal with the key issues of peace and prosperity. The no difference and no opinion figures have been omitted:

Party Better for Peace

	Republican	Democratic
June 1980..............	28%	32%
March 1978............	25	31
August 1976...........	29	32
March 1974............	24	33
September 1972	32	28

Party Better for Prosperity

	Republican	Democratic
June 1980..............	31%	37%
March 1978............	23	41
August 1976...........	23	47
March 1974............	19	49
September 1972	38	35

Note: For the first time since earlier this year the Republican party has retained the public image it acquired as the political party better able to keep the nation prosperous. And, although the GOP still trails the Democrats as the party more likely to keep the United States out of war, its deficit has been considerably reduced since April.

Currently, 40% of Americans believe that the Republicans will do a better job of keeping the country prosperous, while 31% name the Democrats. In an April survey the Democratic party, which virtually had owned the prosperity issue since these Gallup measurements began three decades ago, relinquished the lead for the first time to the Republican party.

Although the 13-percentage point lead enjoyed by the GOP has been reduced to 9 points, it is somewhat surprising that the Republicans continue to maintain an advantage over their Democratic rivals in the face of growing public pessimism that the Reagan administration's policies will solve the nation's economic problems. As reported, more Americans now disapprove than approve of the way President Reagan is dealing with economic conditions, especially inflation and unemployment.

Not only has the GOP been able to sustain most of its lead as the party of prosperity, but the Democrats' margin of superiority as the party of peace has dwindled from 13 to 5 percentage points. Currently, 34% of the public considers the Democrats to have the edge, while 29% name the Republicans. In the April survey the figures were 39% and 26%, respectively. Thus, the GOP now shows the potential for regaining the leadership position it has historically held as the party of peace, which in part may be attributed to President Reagan's positive ratings from the public for his handling of foreign policy and defense.

The following shows that equal proportions of Democrats and Republicans name the rival party as better for peace, and political independents are evenly divided. On the other hand, far more Republicans than Democrats think that their own party is better for prosperity, and independents side heavily with the GOP. Also, twice the proportion of Democrats as Republicans choose the rival party as more likely to keep the nation prosperous.

Party Better for Peace

Republicans

Republicans	63%
Democrats...........................	11
No difference (volunteered)	15
No opinion	11

Democrats

Republicans	11%
Democrats...........................	54
No difference (volunteered)	22
No opinion	13

Independents

Republicans	26%
Democrats...........................	26
No difference (volunteered)	30
No opinion	18

Party Better for Prosperity
Republicans

Republicans 77%
Democrats........................... 8
No difference (volunteered) 6
No opinion 9

Democrats

Republicans 16%
Democrats........................... 57
No difference (volunteered) 15
No opinion 12

Independents

Republicans 44%
Democrats........................... 17
No difference (volunteered) 21
No opinion 18

NOVEMBER 5
PRESIDENTIAL TERM OF OFFICE

Interviewing Date: 10/2–5/81
Survey #183-G

Have you heard or read about a proposal for changing the term of office of the president of the United States to one six-year term with no reelection?

	Yes
National	37%

Asked of the entire sample: Some people feel that limiting a president to one term of six years would best serve the national interest because he could devote all his energies to solving national problems rather than spending a lot of time trying to get reelected. Others prefer the present system because they feel it takes a president a long time learning how to do his job and that knowing that he will have to seek reelection will make him answerable to the wishes of the people. Which point of view comes closer to the way you, yourself, feel? Do you favor or oppose changing the term

of office of the president to one six-year term with no reelection?

	Entire sample	Informed group*
Favor	31%	47%
Oppose	61	49
No opinion	8	4

By Education
College

Favor	37%	54%
Oppose	58	42
No opinion	5	4

High School

Favor	30%	43%
Oppose	61	53
No opinion	9	4

Grade School

Favor	21%	37%
Oppose	67	56
No opinion	12	7

By Region
East

Favor	36%	55%
Oppose	56	40
No opinion	8	5

Midwest

Favor	30%	44%
Oppose	61	50
No opinion	9	6

South

Favor	24%	41%
Oppose	66	55
No opinion	10	4

West

Favor	35%	48%
Oppose	59	50
No opinion	6	2

By Age
18–24 Years

Favor 29%   45%
Oppose..................... 62   54
No opinion................. 9   1

25–29 Years

Favor 33%   55%
Oppose..................... 59   43
No opinion................. 8   2

30–49 Years

Favor 32%   47%
Oppose..................... 61   48
No opinion................. 7   5

50 Years and Over

Favor 30%   45%
Oppose..................... 61   50
No opinion................. 9   5

By Politics
Republicans

Favor 34%   45%
Oppose..................... 59   50
No opinion................. 7   5

Democrats

Favor 27%   45%
Oppose..................... 66   52
No opinion................. 7   3

Independents

Favor 35%   53%
Oppose..................... 55   42
No opinion................. 10   5

*The informed group is considered to include those who said they had heard or read of the proposal and could name an advantage or a disadvantage.

Note: By a 61% to 31% margin Americans reject a proposal for a single six-year term for U.S. presidents, as they have in surveys going back to the 1930s. However, opinion is evenly divided—47% favor and 49% oppose—among the informed public.

One advocate of a single six-year presidency, former Secretary of State Cyrus Vance, summed up the basic arguments as follows:

... One key proposal—which I support— would limit a President to one term of six years. The idea of a single, limited Presidential term is not new. It was proposed, debated and initially adopted by the Committee of the Whole at the Constitutional Convention in 1787. The issue was later revived by Andrew Jackson, and many Presidents since him have publicly subscribed to the belief that the national interest would be better served by Presidents who are not intent on being re-elected. The virtues of a single six-year term are that a President could devote his full attention to national needs, rather than spending much of his energy on trying to win re-election; the paralysis in decision-making that grips the executive branch during the long primary campaign could be eliminated, and a single-term President would be less inclined to use his office for the purpose of courting voters to win re-election.

A commonly held view among those opposed to changing the present system is that a single six-year term would be too long for a bad president and too short for a good one. In this century many proposals for six-year terms have been introduced in Congress, and once, in 1913, the Senate, not the House, passed such a resolution. Interestingly, the constitution of the Confederacy during the Civil War provided for a six-year term and Jefferson Davis took office on that basis.

NOVEMBER 8
PRESIDENTIAL TRIAL HEATS

Interviewing Date: 10/2–5/81
Survey #183-G

Asked of registered voters: Suppose the presidential election were being held today. If President Ronald Reagan were the Republican candidate and Senator Edward

Kennedy were the Democratic candidate, which would you like to see win? [Those who named another person or who were undecided were asked: As of today, do you lean more to Reagan, the Republican, or to Kennedy, the Democrat?]

Reagan............................56%
Kennedy 35
Other; undecided 9

By Sex
Male

Reagan............................59%
Kennedy 32
Other; undecided 9

Female

Reagan............................53%
Kennedy 37
Other; undecided 10

By Race
White

Reagan............................62%
Kennedy 28
Other; undecided 10

Nonwhite

Reagan............................ 8%
Kennedy 83
Other; undecided 9

By Education
College

Reagan............................62%
Kennedy 28
Other; undecided 10

High School

Reagan............................56%
Kennedy 34
Other; undecided 10

Grade School

Reagan............................39%
Kennedy 52
Other; undecided 9

By Region
East

Reagan............................50%
Kennedy 40
Other; undecided 10

Midwest

Reagan............................62%
Kennedy 30
Other; undecided 8

South

Reagan............................58%
Kennedy 33
Other; undecided 9

West

Reagan............................56%
Kennedy 34
Other; undecided 10

By Age
18–24 Years

Reagan............................48%
Kennedy 42
Other; undecided 10

25–29 Years

Reagan............................52%
Kennedy 44
Other; undecided 4

30–49 Years

Reagan............................59%
Kennedy 32
Other; undecided 9

50 Years and Over

Reagan.............................57%
Kennedy 32
Other; undecided 11

By Politics

Republicans

Reagan.............................92%
Kennedy 7
Other; undecided 1

Democrats

Reagan.............................31%
Kennedy 57
Other; undecided 12

Independents

Reagan.............................62%
Kennedy 24
Other; undecided 14

Asked of registered voters: Suppose the presidential election were being held today. If President Ronald Reagan were the Republican candidate and former Vice-President Walter Mondale were the Democratic candidate, which would you like to see win? [Those who named another person or who were undecided were asked: As of today, do you lean more to Reagan, the Republican, or to Mondale, the Democrat?]

Reagan.............................54%
Mondale............................37
Other; undecided 9

By Sex

Male

Reagan.............................57%
Mondale............................35
Other; undecided 8

Female

Reagan.............................52%
Mondale............................38
Other; undecided 10

By Race

White

Reagan.............................59%
Mondale............................33
Other; undecided 8

Nonwhite

Reagan.............................17%
Mondale............................67
Other; undecided 16

By Education

College

Reagan.............................58%
Mondale............................35
Other; undecided 7

High School

Reagan.............................58%
Mondale............................33
Other; undecided 9

Grade School

Reagan.............................33%
Mondale............................55
Other; undecided 12

By Region

East

Reagan.............................52%
Mondale............................34
Other; undecided 14

Midwest

Reagan.............................59%
Mondale............................36
Other; undecided 5

South

Reagan.............................53%
Mondale............................37
Other; undecided 10

West

Reagan	51%
Mondale	41
Other; undecided	8

By Age
18–24 Years

Reagan	58%
Mondale	30
Other; undecided	12

25–29 Years

Reagan	55%
Mondale	37
Other; undecided	8

30–49 Years

Reagan	57%
Mondale	33
Other; undecided	10

50 Years and Over

Reagan	50%
Mondale	41
Other; undecided	9

By Politics
Republicans

Reagan	94%
Mondale	3
Other; undecided	3

Democrats

Reagan	26%
Mondale	63
Other; undecided	11

Independents

Reagan	61%
Mondale	24
Other; undecided	15

Note: In early tests of President Ronald Reagan's potential election strength he wins greater voter support than two 1984 Democratic rivals—Senator Edward Kennedy and former Vice-President Walter Mondale. The president leads both these possible Democratic contenders in all regions and among every major population group, with the exception of nonwhites and persons with only a grade-school education.

The current figures on the Reagan-Kennedy race are similar to those recorded following the June 1980 primaries, when Reagan led Kennedy 58% to 32%. And the last trial heat between Reagan and Mondale, conducted in May 1980, showed Reagan leading 48% to 39%.

NOVEMBER 12
PROFESSIONS AND OCCUPATIONS*

Interviewing Date: 7/24–27/81
Survey #178-G

Now I'd like your impressions about different professions and occupations, based on your personal experience, on what you've heard or read, or anything at all. To indicate your impression please use this scale, which goes from a lowest rating of zero to the highest rating of ten. [Respondents were handed a card with a scale printed on it.] First would you rate the following professions for the amount each contributes to the general good of society? The more you feel it contributes to the good of society, the higher the number you would pick; the less you feel it contributes, the lower the number. How would you rate:

General Good of Society

	Percent giving 9 or 10 rating
Clergymen	46%
Medical doctors	41
Public-school teachers	29
Public-school principals	28

Judges 23
Funeral directors 20
Bankers 14
Lawyers 12
Business executives 10
Local political officeholders 8
Realtors 7
Advertising practitioners 4

Lawyers 31
Public-school principals 25
Business executives 23
Public-school teachers 19
Funeral directors 17
Local political officeholders 16
Advertising practitioners 8
Realtors 6

*This survey was sponsored by the Charles F. Kettering Foundation, the National Association of Elementary School Principals, and the National Association of Secondary School Principals.

Now, how would you rate the following for the amount of stress or pressure experienced by people working in each profession? The more stress or pressure you feel there is, the higher the number you would pick; the less you feel there is, the lower the number. How would you rate:

Stress or Pressure

	Percent giving 9 or 10 rating
Medical doctors	49%
Public-school teachers	43
Public-school principals	42
Judges	36
Business executives	30
Clergymen	26
Bankers	22
Lawyers	21
Local political officeholders	14
Funeral directors	13
Advertising practitioners	12
Realtors	10

And how would you rate the following for the amount of prestige or status people in each profession have in this community? The more prestige or status you feel they have, the higher the number you would pick; the less you feel they have, the lower the number. How would you rate:

Status or Prestige

	Percent giving 9 or 10 rating
Medical doctors	59%
Judges	48
Clergymen	42
Bankers	35

Note: The American public gives clergymen and medical doctors the highest ratings out of twelve professions for contributing to the general good of society, while local political officeholders, realtors, and advertising practitioners are rated lowest in this respect. The recent Gallup survey also found that doctors, lawyers, and the clergy are deemed to have more prestige and status within their community than other professionals. The leading occupation in terms of the perceived amount of stress and pressure their work entails is doctors, followed by public-school teachers and principals.

Generally, women are inclined to give higher ratings to the professions than men, as are persons who attended college and those from families with $15,000 or more yearly income.

NOVEMBER 15
CONGRESSIONAL ELECTIONS

Interviewing Date: 9/18–21; 10/2–5/81
Survey #182-G; #183-G

Asked of registered voters: If the elections for Congress were being held today, which party would you like to see win in this congressional district—the Republican party or the Democratic party? [Those who said they were undecided or who voted for a different party were asked: As of today, do you lean more to the Republican party or to the Democratic party?]

Republican 44%
Democratic 56

By Region
South

Republican 40%
Democratic 60

Non-South

Republican 45%
Democratic 55

When allowance is made for voter turnout based on the results of the 1970, 1974, and 1978 off-year congressional elections, the following is the projected vote for Congress:

Republican 47%
Democratic 53

By Region
South

Republican 40%
Democratic 60

Non-South

Republican 49%
Democratic 51

Note: Republican chances for winning a majority of seats in the House of Representatives in 1982 have shown little improvement in recent weeks. Nationally, the popular vote for House seats, based on the two latest Gallup surveys, shows the Democrats leading the Republicans 53% to 47%.

Regardless of the public's current sentiments, the congressional races may well hinge next fall on the success or failure of President Ronald Reagan's economic program and the unemployment rate. Only twice in the last fifty years—in 1946 and again in 1952—has the Republican party won more seats in the lower house than the Democrats. And Republican hopes for repeating these victories next year appear to be slight at the present time.

The continuing strong advantage that the Democratic party holds in the South is the chief obstacle facing the GOP in winning control of the House. With the reapportionment of House seats, based on the 1980 census, the South will gain 8 new seats, and the Midwest, the area that typically elects more Republican than Democratic congressmen, will lose 8. The West will pick up 9 seats, but in this region the two parties elect about the same number of representatives. And in the East, where Democrats normally have an advantage, they will lose 9 seats.

Although survey figures on the popular vote cannot be translated directly into seats, some indication of the relationship of the popular vote is seen in the results of the 1980 election. Of the 435 seats nationwide, 243 were won by Democrats and 192 by Republicans. In the South the division of the 121 seats was 78 for the Democrats and 43 for the Republicans. Outside the South the 314 seats were divided 165 and 149, respectively. As these results indicate, this situation makes it extremely difficult for the GOP to reduce the usual off-year election losses, let alone win control of the House.

Assuming that the Republicans win the same proportion of seats in the reapportioned South as they now hold, which would result in 46 GOP seats to 83 for the Democrats, the Republicans would have to pick up 172 seats outside the South in order to gain a 218-seat majority in the next Congress. This is a tough assignment because of the many areas of Democratic strength in the large cities of the North.

Congressional Apportionment

	Total 1982	Total 1980
National	435	435
East	108	117
Midwest.............	113	121
South	129	121
West	85	76
Non-South	306	314

NOVEMBER 19
PRESIDENT REAGAN

Interviewing Date: 10/30–11/2/81
Survey #184-G

Do you approve or disapprove of the way Reagan is handling his job as president?

Approve..............................53%
Disapprove 35
No opinion 12

Note: A remarkable parallel is found between the job performance rating given President Ronald Reagan ten months after taking office and the rating given President Jimmy Carter at the same point in his tenure in late October 1977. At that time 51% approved of the way Carter was handling his duties as chief executive, while 31% disapproved and 18% were undecided. In comparison, current survey results show that 53% approve of the way Reagan is handling his job as president, with 35% disapproving and 12% undecided. Reagan's approval figure is down 7 percentage points from the 60% rating he received in mid-March. Carter's mid-March rating was 75%, 24 points higher than his late October measurement.

Economic problems dominated the first ten months of each president's term, and the most recent audit of key concerns of the American people indicates that 52% cite the high cost of living and 17% name unemployment. During the same period in 1977 these figures were 35% and 25%, respectively. Furthermore, in May 1977, 57% of voters were skeptical about the Carter administration's stated goal of balancing the federal budget, compared to 62% who currently do not think that the Reagan administration will be able to do so by 1984.

Although the national ratings given each president ten months into their first terms are uncommonly similar, the pattern of approval differs dramatically among various demographic groups:

Reagan/Carter Ten-Month Approval Comparison

	Reagan	Carter
National	53%	51%

By Sex

Male	60%	52%
Female	47	51

By Race

White........................	61%	51%
Nonwhite	13	59

By Education

College	64%	53%
High school..................	52	52
Grade school	36	46

By Region

East	51%	55%
Midwest	60	40
South	49	55
West	55	50

By Age

18–29 years	53%	61%
30–49 years	56	50
50 years and over	51	45

By Income

$15,000 and over..............	65%	50%
Under $15,000.................	41	52
Labor union families	52%	53%
Nonlabor union families........	54	51

NOVEMBER 22
REAGANOMICS

Interviewing Date: 10/30–11/2/81
Survey #184-G

Now let us talk about the Reagan administration's economic policies. What effect do you think these policies will have on your own and your family's financial situation? Do you feel your financial situation will be much better, somewhat better, somewhat worse or much worse as a result of the Reagan economic policies?

Much better......................... 5%
Somewhat better.....................29
Somewhat worse 30
Much worse.........................15
Same (volunteered) 15
No opinion 6

By Sex
Male

Much better......................... 7%
Somewhat better.....................34
Somewhat worse 29
Much worse.........................11
Same (volunteered) 14
No opinion 5

Female

Much better......................... 4%
Somewhat better.....................25
Somewhat worse 30
Much worse.........................19
Same (volunteered) 16
No opinion 6

By Race
White

Much better......................... 6%
Somewhat better.....................34
Somewhat worse 28
Much worse.........................11
Same (volunteered) 16
No opinion 5

Nonwhite

Much better......................... 1%
Somewhat better..................... 6
Somewhat worse 37
Much worse.........................34
Same (volunteered) 13
No opinion 9

By Education
College

Much better......................... 7%
Somewhat better.....................38

Somewhat worse 29
Much worse.........................10
Same (volunteered) 13
No opinion 3

High School

Much better......................... 4%
Somewhat better.....................28
Somewhat worse 30
Much worse.........................16
Same (volunteered) 16
No opinion 6

Grade School

Much better......................... 4%
Somewhat better.....................16
Somewhat worse 30
Much worse.........................22
Same (volunteered) 17
No opinion 11

By Region
East

Much better......................... 5%
Somewhat better.....................30
Somewhat worse 29
Much worse.........................16
Same (volunteered) 16
No opinion 4

Midwest

Much better......................... 6%
Somewhat better.....................28
Somewhat worse 31
Much worse.........................13
Same (volunteered) 17
No opinion 5

South

Much better......................... 4%
Somewhat better.....................31
Somewhat worse 25
Much worse.........................17
Same (volunteered) 15
No opinion 8

West

Much better........................ 6%
Somewhat better.................... 26
Somewhat worse 38
Much worse........................ 13
Same (volunteered) 11
No opinion 6

By Age
18–29 Years

Much better........................ 4%
Somewhat better.................... 39
Somewhat worse 28
Much worse........................ 12
Same (volunteered) 13
No opinion 4

30–49 Years

Much better........................ 5%
Somewhat better.................... 29
Somewhat worse 32
Much worse........................ 14
Same (volunteered) 14
No opinion 6

50 Years and Over

Much better................. ...... 6%
Somewhat better.................... 22
Somewhat worse 29
Much worse........................ 18
Same (volunteered) 18
No opinion 7

By Income
$15,000 and Over

Much better........................ 7%
Somewhat better.................... 37
Somewhat worse 29
Much worse........................ 8
Same (volunteered) 15
No opinion 4

Under $15,000

Much better........................ 3%
Somewhat better.................... 21

Somewhat worse 31
Much worse........................ 22
Same (volunteered) 16
No opinion 7

By Occupation
Professional and Business

Much better........................ 8%
Somewhat better.................... 37
Somewhat worse 27
Much worse........................ 9
Same (volunteered) 14
No opinion 5

Clerical and Sales

Much better........................ 4%
Somewhat better.................... 33
Somewhat worse 34
Much worse........................ 8
Same (volunteered) 15
No opinion 6

Manual Workers

Much better........................ 5%
Somewhat better.................... 30
Somewhat worse 29
Much worse........................ 17
Same (volunteered) 15
No opinion 4

Nonlabor Force

Much better........................ 4%
Somewhat better.................... 19
Somewhat worse 27
Much worse........................ 22
Same (volunteered) 20
No opinion 8

Those Who Approve of Reagan*

Much better........................ 9%
Somewhat better.................... 47
Somewhat worse 19
Much worse........................ 2
Same (volunteered) 18
No opinion 5

Those Who Disapprove of Reagan*

Much better...................... 1%
Somewhat better.................... 7
Somewhat worse 45
Much worse........................ 35
Same (volunteered) 8
No opinion 4

*These findings tend to accent the strong link between President Reagan's popularity and the public's perceptions of the effectiveness of his economic policies.

How about the nation? What effect do you think the Reagan administration's economic policies will have on the nation's economic situation? Do you feel the nation's economic situation will be much better, somewhat better, somewhat worse or much worse as a result of the Reagan economic policies?

Much better...................... 9%
Somewhat better.................... 35
Somewhat worse 27
Much worse........................ 15
Same (volunteered) 7
No opinion 7

By Sex
Male

Much better......................13%
Somewhat better.................... 37
Somewhat worse 24
Much worse........................ 14
Same (volunteered) 7
No opinion 5

Female

Much better...................... 5%
Somewhat better.................... 35
Somewhat worse 29
Much worse........................ 16
Same (volunteered) 6
No opinion 9

By Race
White

Much better......................11%
Somewhat better.................... 40
Somewhat worse 25
Much worse........................ 12
Same (volunteered) 6
No opinion 6

Nonwhite

Much better...................... 1%
Somewhat better.................... 12
Somewhat worse 34
Much worse........................ 31
Same (volunteered) 9
No opinion 13

By Education
College

Much better......................13%
Somewhat better.................... 42
Somewhat worse 22
Much worse........................ 12
Same (volunteered) 5
No opinion 6

High School

Much better...................... 8%
Somewhat better.................... 36
Somewhat worse 29
Much worse........................ 15
Same (volunteered) 7
No opinion 5

Grade School

Much better...................... 5%
Somewhat better.................... 22
Somewhat worse 25
Much worse........................ 21
Same (volunteered) 9
No opinion 18

By Region
East

Much better.................................... 8%
Somewhat better.............................34
Somewhat worse 27
Much worse....................................16
Same (volunteered) 8
No opinion 7

Midwest

Much better...................................11%
Somewhat better.............................38
Somewhat worse 22
Much worse....................................16
Same (volunteered) 7
No opinion 6

South

Much better.................................... 8%
Somewhat better.............................34
Somewhat worse 27
Much worse....................................15
Same (volunteered) 7
No opinion 9

West

Much better...................................10%
Somewhat better.............................35
Somewhat worse 30
Much worse....................................13
Same (volunteered) 4
No opinion 8

By Age
18–29 Years

Much better...................................10%
Somewhat better.............................41
Somewhat worse 28
Much worse....................................11
Same (volunteered) 5
No opinion 5

30–49 Years

Much better.................................... 7%
Somewhat better.............................36

Somewhat worse 26
Much worse....................................17
Same (volunteered) 7
No opinion 7

50 Years and Over

Much better...................................10%
Somewhat better.............................31
Somewhat worse 26
Much worse....................................17
Same (volunteered) 7
No opinion 9

By Income
$15,000 and Over

Much better...................................11%
Somewhat better.............................42
Somewhat worse 24
Much worse....................................11
Same (volunteered) 6
No opinion 6

Under $15,000

Much better.................................... 6%
Somewhat better.............................28
Somewhat worse 30
Much worse....................................20
Same (volunteered) 7
No opinion 9

By Occupation
Professional and Business

Much better...................................12%
Somewhat better.............................41
Somewhat worse 25
Much worse....................................10
Same (volunteered) 7
No opinion 5

Clerical and Sales

Much better...................................10%
Somewhat better.............................36
Somewhat worse 24
Much worse.................................... 8
Same (volunteered) 10
No opinion 12

Manual Workers

Much better......................... 8%
Somewhat better..................... 34
Somewhat worse 28
Much worse.......................... 18
Same (volunteered) 6
No opinion 6

Nonlabor Force

Much better......................... 33%
Somewhat better..................... 8
Somewhat worse 24
Much worse.......................... 19
Same (volunteered) 5
No opinion 11

Those Who Approve of Reagan*

Much better......................... 16%
Somewhat better..................... 53
Somewhat worse 15
Much worse.......................... 3
Same (volunteered) 7
No opinion 6

Those Who Disapprove of Reagan*

Much better.......................... **%
Somewhat better..................... 13
Somewhat worse 43
Much worse.......................... 35
Same (volunteered) 3
No opinion 6

*These findings tend to accent the strong link between President Reagan's popularity and the public's perceptions of the effectiveness of his economic policies.

**Less than 1%

Note: More Americans now believe their family's financial condition will worsen rather than improve as a result of the Reagan administration's economic program. This is the first time since May that pessimistic attitudes have outweighed optimism about Reaganomics.

In the latest survey—completed before publication of the *Atlantic* magazine article detailing Budget Director David Stockman's misgivings about Reaganomics—34% of the public believes that their family's financial situation will be either much better (5%) or somewhat better (29%) because of President Ronald Reagan's economic policies, while 45% say somewhat worse (30%) or much worse (15%). The 21% balance is divided between those who think there will be no change (15%) or do not express an opinion (6%). In contrast, in a May survey conducted shortly after the announcement of the Reagan plan, 48% thought their finances would improve and 37% held the opposite view. Since then there has been a deterioration in positive appraisals of the program and a concomitant increase in negative attitudes.

The public is slightly more sanguine about the effect of Reaganomics on the country, with about equal proportions saying the nation's economic condition will get better (44%) or become worse (42%). However, in this assessment there also has been a decline in optimism about the administration's policies since the previous survey.

The fact that voters are more optimistic about the effect of Reaganomics on the nation than on their own financial situation suggests that the "bite-the-bullet" phenomenon—recognition that they may have to undergo personal hardship for the greater good of the country—is still operative.

NOVEMBER 26
PRESIDENTIAL TRIAL HEAT

Interviewing Date: 10/30–11/2/81
Survey #184-G

Asked of registered voters: Suppose Jimmy Carter were to decide to run again for president and the election were being held today. If Carter were the Democratic candidate and President Reagan were the Republican candidate, which would you like to see win? [Those who named another person or who were undecided were then asked: As of today, do you lean more to Carter, the Democrat, or to Reagan, the Republican?]

Carter............................35%
Reagan............................54
Other 5
Undecided......................... 6

By Sex
Male

Carter............................32%
Reagan............................59
Other 5
Undecided......................... 4

Female

Carter............................39%
Reagan............................50
Other 4
Undecided......................... 7

By Race
White

Carter............................27%
Reagan............................63
Other 5
Undecided......................... 5

Nonwhite

Carter............................76%
Reagan............................11
Other 6
Undecided......................... 7

By Education
College

Carter............................24%
Reagan............................66
Other 5
Undecided......................... 5

High School

Carter............................37%
Reagan............................53
Other 4
Undecided......................... 6

Grade School

Carter............................55%
Reagan............................33
Other 5
Undecided......................... 7

By Region
East

Carter............................35%
Reagan............................52
Other 6
Undecided......................... 7

Midwest

Carter............................34%
Reagan............................60
Other 2
Undecided......................... 4

South

Carter............................40%
Reagan............................52
Other 3
Undecided......................... 5

West

Carter............................32%
Reagan............................54
Other 7
Undecided......................... 7

By Age
18–29 Years

Carter............................36%
Reagan............................52
Other 7
Undecided......................... 5

30–49 Years

Carter............................32%
Reagan............................58
Other 4
Undecided......................... 6

50 Years and Over

Carter............................38%
Reagan...........................52
Other 4
Undecided........................ 6

By Politics
Republicans

Carter............................ 5%
Reagan...........................91
Other 2
Undecided........................ 2

Democrats

Carter............................59%
Reagan...........................28
Other 7
Undecided........................ 6

Independents

Carter............................23%
Reagan...........................64
Other 5
Undecided........................ 8

Note: With the off-year congressional elections less than a year away, debate already has begun over possible Democratic rivals for President Ronald Reagan. Judging by the views of the American electorate, Jimmy Carter is not the "forgotten man" when it comes to speculation about the 1984 presidential race. The latest Gallup results show that as high a proportion of registered voters select Carter in a test election against Reagan as choose either Senator Edward Kennedy or former Vice-President Walter Mondale, two candidates who have been widely discussed as possible Democratic nominees.

Although Carter has not given any indication that he might make another try for the White House, he wins 35% of the support of registered voters compared to Reagan who receives 54%. An earlier survey found Reagan ahead of Kennedy 56% to 35% and Mondale 54% to 37%.

NOVEMBER 29
BEST POLITICAL PARTY

Interviewing Date: 10/30–11/2/81
Survey #184-G

As you feel today, which political party— the Republican or the Democratic—do you think best serves the interests of the following groups:

Farmers?

Republican 23%
Democratic 44
Same; no opinion 33

Professional and business people?

Republican 55%
Democratic 22
Same; no opinion 23

Skilled workers?

Republican 21%
Democratic 51
Same; no opinion 28

Unskilled workers?

Republican 14%
Democratic 57
Same; no opinion 29

White-collar workers?

Republican 38%
Democratic 32
Same; no opinion 30

Upper-income people?

Republican 66%
Democratic 15
Same; no opinion 19

Corporate executives?

Republican 62%
Democratic 16
Same; no opinion 22

People like yourself?

Republican 29%
Democratic 45
Same; no opinion 26

Small business people?

Republican 27%
Democratic 47
Same; no opinion 26

Average citizen?

Republican 24%
Democratic 47
Same; no opinion 29

Young people?

Republican 18%
Democratic 43
Same; no opinion 39

Labor union members?

Republican 16%
Democratic 61
Same; no opinion 23

Women?

Republican 16%
Democratic 45
Same; no opinion 39

Retired people?

Republican 15%
Democratic 55
Same; no opinion 30

Unemployed people?

Republican 12%
Democratic 58
Same; no opinion 30

Blacks?

Republican 11%
Democratic 60
Same; no opinion 29

Note: Just as they did during the New Deal nearly a half century ago, voters today perceive the GOP to be the party of the rich and the Democrats to be the workingman's party. These enduring images help explain why the Republican party has controlled both the executive and legislative branches of government in only two out of the last fifty years.

In Gallup Polls conducted regularly over the past four decades, voters consistently have expressed the belief that the GOP best accommodates the interests of up-scale population groups. For example, in the current survey twice as many name the Republican than the Democratic party as better serving professional and business people.

The most recent findings also show Republicans to be heavily outnumbered by Democrats in political party affiliation, with 27% of the public describing themselves as Republicans, 45% as Democrats, and 28% as independents. The proportion of Republicans grew steadily between the first quarter of 1980, when 21% called themselves Republicans, to 28% in the second quarter of 1981.

NOVEMBER 30
CHILD ABUSE*

Interviewing Date: 10/30–11/2/81
Survey #184-G

Are you personally aware of any serious instances of physical abuse of children by their parents—that is, not just something you read about in the newspapers or saw on television but that happened to someone you know or someone who lives in your neighborhood?

Yes

National 15%

By Sex

Male................................ 13%
Female.............................. 16

By Race

White................................15%
Nonwhite.............................11

By Education

College...............................20%
High school...........................12
Grade school..........................12

By Region

East 14%
Midwest..............................15
South 14
West..................................14

By Income

$20,000 and over......................15%
$15,000 and over......................15
Under $15,000.........................13
Under $10,000.........................12

By Occupation

Professional and business..............18%
Clerical and sales.....................10
Manual workers 14
Nonlabor force 10

By Community Size

One million and over..................13%
500,000–999,999 16
50,000–499,999.......................13
2,500–49,999.........................23
Under 2,500; rural....................12

*This study was conducted for the National Coalition for Children's Justice.

Note: Some 24 million Americans, or 15% of the adult population, report at least one serious instance of physical abuse of children in their neighborhood. While it is generally assumed that child abuse is more common in less privileged neighborhoods, the study here suggests that this may not be the case. For example, 15% of persons in households with an annual income of $20,000 and over report knowledge of child abuse by someone they know or who lives in their neighborhood, compared to 12% whose income scale is under $10,000.

Analysis of the findings by various occupations provides still further evidence that child abuse cases might be more common in upper than lower-income neighborhoods. Among professional and business people 18% say that they know of at least one child abuse situation, while the proportion who report such cases is 14% among blue-collar households and 10% in the clerical and sales category.

DECEMBER 3
PRESIDENT REAGAN

Interviewing Date: 11/13–16/81
Survey #185-G

Do you approve or disapprove of the way Reagan is handling his job as president?

Approve...............................51%
Disapprove 39
No opinion 10

National Trend

	Approve	Dis-approve	No opinion
October 30– November 2	53%	35%	12%
October 2–5	56	35	9
September 18–21	52	37	11
August 14–17	60	29	11

Asked of those who replied that they either approve or disapprove: How strongly would you say you approve/disapprove—very strongly or not so strongly?

Approve...............................51%
  Very strongly......................27
  Not so strongly 24
Disapprove 39
  Not so strongly 16
  Very strongly......................23

Do you approve or disapprove of the way Reagan is handling economic conditions in this country?

Approve............................43%
Disapprove 48
No opinion 9

National Trend

	Approve	Dis- approve	No opinion
October 30–			
November 2	45%	43%	12%
October 2–5	44	47	9
August 14–17	53	35	12
June 26–29	51	40	9
May 8–11............	58	31	11
April 3–6	60	29	11
March 13–16........	56	32	12

Apart from whether you approve or dis-
approve of the way Reagan is handling his
job as president, what do you think of
Reagan as a person? Would you say you
approve or disapprove of him?

Approve............................74%
Disapprove 16
No opinion 10

Note: The high rating (74%) given President
Ronald Reagan as a person stands in sharp contrast to the 51% given him for his job performance. Approval of Reagan's performance in
office is based on a survey completed just before
his recent speech on U.S. nuclear arms policy.
In comparison, this rating stood at 60% in mid-
August.

A key factor in the decline in approval of the
president's overall performance in office has
been growing pessimism over his handling of
U.S. economic conditions. Approval has
dropped from 60% in April to 43% in the latest
survey.

DECEMBER 6
VOLUNTARISM

Interviewing Date: 9/18–21/81
Survey #182-G

Do you, yourself, happen to be involved in
any charity or social service activities such
as helping the poor, sick, or elderly?

	Yes
National	29%

By Sex

Male...............................	27%
Female.............................	30

By Education

College.............................	35%
High school........................	26
Grade school.......................	27

By Region

East	26%
Midwest...........................	30
South	33
West...............................	25

By Occupation

Professional and business..............	38%
Clerical and sales	28
Manual workers	24
Nonlabor force	27

By Views on Religion

Religion very important	36%
Religion fairly important...............	19
Religion not very important	19
Church members	34
Nonchurch members	18
Attend church regularly................	40
Do not attend church regularly	20

Note: With President Ronald Reagan calling for
a new "spirit of voluntarism" to pick up the slack
caused by his cuts in social programs, a recent
Gallup Poll reveals that three persons in ten
(29%) are presently engaged in volunteer activities such as helping the poor, sick, or elderly.
This level of involvement in charitable or social
service activities, which projects to more than
40 million adult Americans, is as high as it was
in a 1977 survey, when 27% of the public
engaged in volunteer work.

When the definition of a volunteer is broadened to include working in some way to help others without benefit of pay, as was done in a March 1981 survey conducted for the *Independent Sector* by the Gallup Organization Inc., it was found that 52% of American adults and 53% of teen-agers had served as volunteers during the year ending in March. Other highlights from the survey include:

1) The largest percentage of volunteers were found in the areas of religion (19%), health (12%), education (12%), and among those informal activities performed without organizational support (23%).

2) Persons from up-scale socioeconomic backgrounds were most likely to serve as volunteers. Other demographic groups more inclined to volunteer include women, those under the age of fifty-five, the employed, those with children still at home, suburban and rural residents, and people from larger households.

DECEMBER 10
DAVID STOCKMAN

Interviewing Date: 11/20–23/81
Survey #186-G

Did you happen to see, hear, or read about the situation in Washington involving David Stockman, the director of the Office of Management and Budget?

	Yes
National	66%

By Politics

Republicans	73%
Democrats	64
Independents	65

Asked of those who replied in the affirmative: From what you know about it, would you say you are more confident President Reagan's economic program will work, less confident, or haven't your feelings about it changed?

More confident	9%
Less confident	34
No change	53
No opinion	4

By Politics
Republicans

More confident	14%
Less confident	19
No change	64
No opinion	3

Democrats

More confident	6%
Less confident	47
No change	42
No opinion	5

Independents

More confident	10%
Less confident	29
No change	58
No opinion	3

Also asked of those who replied in the affirmative: Do you feel President Reagan should have accepted Stockman's offer to resign or not?

Should have	41%
Should not have	44
No opinion	15

By Politics
Republicans

Should have	30%
Should not have	55
No opinion	15

Democrats

Should have	51%
Should not have	35
No opinion	14

Independents

Should have 38%
Should not have 48
No opinion 14

Note: David Stockman, director of the Office of Management and Budget, came under fire recently when *Atlantic* magazine published a long article in which Stockman expressed his misgivings about whether President Ronald Reagan's economic program would work. With the Reagan administration currently weighing the political fallout of the Stockman affair, the latest nationwide Gallup Poll shows those who have followed the situation lean marginally—44% to 41%—toward the view that the budget director should remain in office.

Opinion divides sharply, however, on the basis of political party affiliation. Seventy-three percent of Republicans surveyed were understandably reluctant to say that their confidence in Reaganomics had been adversely affected by Stockman's remarks. Democrats aware of the Stockman situation (64% of the total) were only moderately ready to seize the obvious political advantage. Although a 47% plurality said their confidence had declined since Stockman's comments were made public, almost as many (42%) expressed that they had not changed their feelings about the Reagan plan.

Asked what effect the Stockman affair has had on their assessment of whether the Reagan economic program will work, a slim 53% majority of the public said that their opinion had remained unchanged. Of the balance, 34% were less confident and only 9% more confident.

DECEMBER 13
DISARMAMENT AND
ARMS CONTROL

Interviewing Date: 11/20–23/81
Survey #186-G

Would you approve or disapprove if President Reagan made a proposal to the Soviet Union that both countries reduce their present stock of nuclear weapons by 50%?

Approve............................... 76%
Disapprove 19
No opinion 5

By Education
College

Approve............................... 82%
Disapprove 16
No opinion 2

High School

Approve............................... 73%
Disapprove 22
No opinion 5

Grade School

Approve............................... 71%
Disapprove 16
No opinion 13

By Politics
Republicans

Approve............................... 72%
Disapprove 23
No opinion 5

Democrats

Approve............................... 77%
Disapprove 19
No opinion 4

Independents

Approve............................... 78%
Disapprove 16
No opinion 6

If an arms agreement between the United States and the Soviet Union is reached, would you favor or oppose setting up a worldwide organization which would make sure, by regular inspection, that neither the United States nor the Soviet Union violates this arms agreement?

Favor 83%
Oppose 10
No opinion 7

By Education
College

Favor 87%
Oppose 8
No opinion 5

High School

Favor 84%
Oppose 10
No opinion 6

Grade School

Favor 75%
Oppose 10
No opinion 15

By Politics
Republicans

Favor 83%
Oppose 11
No opinion 6

Democrats

Favor 86%
Oppose 8
No opinion 6

Independents

Favor 82%
Oppose 10
No opinion 8

Do you think the USSR is or is not doing all it can to keep peace in the world?

Is 7%
Is not 84
No opinion 9

Do you think the United States is or is not doing all it can to keep peace in the world?

Is 54%
Is not 39
No opinion 7

By Sex
Male

Is 56%
Is not 38
No opinion 6

Female

Is 53%
Is not 39
No opinion 8

By Race
White

Is 55%
Is not 38
No opinion 7

Nonwhite

Is 50%
Is not 41
No opinion 9

By Education
College

Is 45%
Is not 49
No opinion 6

High School

Is 57%
Is not 36
No opinion 7

Grade School

Is 63%
Is not 26
No opinion 11

By Region

East

Is.....................................56%
Is not 38
No opinion 6

Midwest

Is.....................................49%
Is not 44
No opinion 7

South

Is.....................................61%
Is not 30
No opinion 9

West

Is.....................................50%
Is not 44
No opinion 6

By Age

18–29 Years

Is.....................................46%
Is not 48
No opinion 6

30–49 Years

Is.....................................52%
Is not 41
No opinion 7

50 Years and Over

Is.....................................63%
Is not 29
No opinion 8

By Politics

Republicans

Is.....................................68%
Is not 24
No opinion 8

Democrats

Is.....................................49%
Is not 44
No opinion 7

Independents

Is.....................................50%
Is not 44
No opinion 6

Note: By an overwhelming 4-to-1 margin, the American people would back President Ronald Reagan if he were to propose to the Soviet Union that both nations reduce their present stock of nuclear weapons by one-half. Such a proposal was offered earlier this year by George Kennan, former ambassador to Moscow, as a way to break the spiral of a nuclear arms buildup.

In calling for this bold action by both nations, Ambassador Kennan proposed "an immediate across-the-board reduction by fifty percent of the nuclear arsenals now being maintained by the two superpowers—a reduction affecting in equal measure all forms of the weapons (strategic, medium-range, and tactical) as well as all means of their delivery—to be implemented at once and without further wrangling among the experts, and to be subject to such national means of verification as now lie at the disposal of the two powers." The Kennan plan receives solid support among all socioeconomic groups, in all regions of the nation, and by both Republicans and Democrats.

If an arms agreement between the Soviet Union and the United States were reached, the American public, by more than 9 to 1, would favor the establishment of a worldwide organization to ensure, by regular inspection, that neither the United States nor the Soviet Union violates this arms pact. The belief that such a plan is necessary stems from widespread public concern that the Soviet Union would not live up to an arms agreement. The Reagan administration has made it clear to the Soviet Union that any future arms control accords will have to include on-site inspection and other direct means of verification.

The public's views on the Kennan plan are seen against a background of opinion. While 54% believe the United States is doing all it can to maintain world peace, 39% hold the opposite view. In fact, slightly greater proportions among eighteen to twenty-nine year olds and those with a college education lean toward this latter view. Cynicism over the Soviet Union's peace intentions is also revealed in the latest survey, which shows that only 7% of Americans believe that the USSR is doing all it can to preserve peace in the world, while 84% think the opposite.

The survey was conducted the weekend following President Reagan's November 18 speech in which he proposed that the United States and the Soviet Union agree to a mutual reduction of conventional intermediate-range nuclear and strategic forces. The president said that the United States would drop its plan to deploy 572 new intermediate-range missiles in Western Europe if the Soviets dismantle 600 SS-4, SS-5, and SS-20 missiles already targeted in on NATO countries.

DECEMBER 17
INVESTIGATIVE REPORTING

Interviewing Date: 11/20–23/81
Survey #186-G

As you probably know, the news media—television, newspapers, and magazines—often do what is called "investigative reporting," or uncovering and reporting on corruption and fraud in business, government agencies, and other organizations. In general, do you approve or disapprove of investigative reporting by the news media?

Approve. 79%
Disapprove 18
No opinion 3

By Education
College

Approve. 83%
Disapprove 16
No opinion 1

High School

Approve. 79%
Disapprove 17
No opinion 4

Grade School

Approve. 68%
Disapprove 25
No opinion 7

By Age
18–29 Years

Approve. 86%
Disapprove 10
No opinion 4

30–49 Years

Approve. 80%
Disapprove 17
No opinion 3

50 Years and Over

Approve. 71%
Disapprove 25
No opinion 4

By Income
$15,000 and Over

Approve. 82%
Disapprove 16
No opinion 2

Under $15,000

Approve. 74%
Disapprove 21
No opinion 5

From what you have seen or read about it, would you like to see more of this type of reporting, or less?

Like to see more......................66%
Like to see less.......................19
Enough at present (volunteered).......11
No opinion..........................4

By Education
College

Like to see more......................67%
Like to see less.......................19
Enough at present (volunteered).......12
No opinion..........................2

High School

Like to see more......................69%
Like to see less.......................18
Enough at present (volunteered).......10
No opinion..........................3

Grade School

Like to see more......................57%
Like to see less.......................21
Enough at present (volunteered).......14
No opinion..........................8

By Age
18–29 Years

Like to see more......................76%
Like to see less.......................11
Enough at present (volunteered)........9
No opinion..........................4

30–49 Years

Like to see more......................68%
Like to see less.......................19
Enough at present (volunteered).......11
No opinion..........................2

50 Years and Over

Like to see more......................57%
Like to see less.......................26
Enough at present (volunteered).......12
No opinion..........................5

By Income
$15,000 and Over

Like to see more......................69%
Like to see less.......................18
Enough at present (volunteered).......11
No opinion..........................2

Under $15,000

Like to see more......................64%
Like to see less.......................20
Enough at present (volunteered).......11
No opinion..........................5

Now, I am going to read to you a list of techniques the media sometimes use when they are doing investigative reporting. Please tell me whether you approve or disapprove of each technique:

Using hidden cameras and microphones?

Approve..............................38%
Disapprove...........................58
No opinion..........................4

Having reporters not identify themselves as reporters?

Approve..............................32%
Disapprove...........................65
No opinion..........................3

Running stories that quote an unnamed source rather than giving the person's name?

Approve..............................42%
Disapprove...........................52
No opinion..........................6

Paying informers for their information or testimony?

Approve..............................36%
Disapprove...........................56
No opinion..........................8

Note: While investigative reporting—that which seeks out and exposes crime, waste, corruption, and other wrongdoing in business, government agencies, and elsewhere—plays an increasingly prominent role in the news media, a recent Gallup Poll showed that the public has some reservations on the techniques used in obtaining this information. Specifically, four out of five Americans (79%) approve while 18% disapprove. In addition, 66% indicate an interest in seeing more of this type of journalism, compared to 19% who would prefer less.

Of the techniques studied, having the news media misrepresent themselves in the course of gathering information for their reports by masquerading as prospective customers for a product or service draws the most objection from the public, with 65% opposed. Considered somewhat less objectionable—58% disapprove—are the use of hidden cameras and microphones and paying informers for information or testimony (56% disapprove). A slightly smaller majority (52%) disapproves of the common practice of citing an anonymous or nameless person as the source for a news item rather than identifying that individual by name. It is interesting to note that even among the large majorities who approve of investigative reporting in general and those who would like to see more of it, negative attitudes toward each of the four undercover techniques outweigh positive.

DECEMBER 20
MOST ADMIRED MAN

Interviewing Date: 11/20–23/81
Survey #186-G

What man that you have heard or read about, living today in any part of the world, do you admire the most? Who is your second choice?

The following are listed in order of frequency of mention with first and second choices combined:

Ronald Reagan
Pope John Paul II
Jimmy Carter
Billy Graham
Edward Kennedy

Menachem Begin
Bob Hope
Gerald Ford
Henry Kissinger
Jesse Jackson

Note: The name of the late president of Egypt, Anwar Sadat, is conspicuously missing from this list. Since the voting in these annual surveys is restricted to living men, it was not possible to accept nominations for Sadat, the victim of assassins' bullets in October. In each of the four previous years he had placed in the top five, trailing only Pope John Paul II and President Jimmy Carter in last year's survey.

Respondents in these survey studies, which have been conducted for more than three decades, are asked to give their choice without a list of names. This procedure, while opening the field to all possible choices, tends to favor those who are currently in the news. Receiving mention but not listed in the top ten were Muhammad Ali, Walter Cronkite, Walter Mondale, Richard Nixon, Burt Reynolds, and Andrew Young.

DECEMBER 22
RECESSION POLITICS*

Only a few months ago political analysts asked: Will the Republican party become the majority party? Will President Ronald Reagan's popularity result in Republican control of the House as well as the Senate in 1982? Now the proposed questions are: Will the Republican party sustain major losses in the '82 congressional elections? Can public support for the administration be revived? The critical difference between then and now is the continuing concern over inflation and rising unemployment.

Nothing dampens the mood of Americans as much as the prospect of increasing unemployment. And nothing is more powerful politically than fear among a substantial number of voters that they might lose their jobs. Concern for

*This Gallup analysis was written by Andrew Kohut, president of the Gallup Organization Inc.

inflation is more widespread, but unemployment has a much more profound effect on public opinion. Polling trends show that increasing inflation erodes support for an administration, as was the case with Jimmy Carter whose popularity declined as prices increased. In contrast, however, over the past twenty-five years there have been five periods when unemployment rose significantly and took its toll on public support for the administration in power.

The following shows the effects of unemployment on support for the incumbent administration:

Decline in Popularity

	High to low during period	Change in unemployment rate
Reagan/1981	59%- ?%	7%-8.4%
Carter/1980	56%-32%	6%-7.5%
Ford/1974	66%-37%	5%-9%
Nixon/1970	61%-52%	3.5%-6%
Eisenhower/1958	60%-48%	5%-7.5%

Each of these presidents experienced the political impact of high unemployment. Carter's handsome victories over Ted Kennedy in the early primaries of 1980 stood in sharp contrast to his defeats and narrow victories later in the campaign as the economy experienced a mild recession. Gerald Ford assumed the presidency just as the U.S. economy went into one of its most serious tailspins. Ford's pardon of Richard Nixon was perhaps the precipitating factor in his fall from public grace, but given the severity of the '74 recession, it is likely that the pardon only served to hasten an inevitable loss of support. And the Reagan administration has been particularly vulnerable on the employment issue. In March, when the president's overall popularity stood at 60%, only 40% of Americans approved of his handling of unemployment. Currently, as 51% approve of his overall job performance, barely a third (32%) approve and 49% disapprove.

Since its inception the current administration has inspired more public confidence with regard to inflation than unemployment. Unfortunately for the Reaganites the focus of the public's economic concerns has begun to shift. According to the NBC/AP Poll, between August and November concern for unemployment rose by 7 percentage points, while concern for inflation declined by 10 points. Currently, 34% believe the problem of unemployment should be given the highest priority, while 32% believe inflation is the most important economic issue.

A shift in concern from inflation to unemployment is also bad news for the Republican party. By a 48% to 27% margin the GOP is seen as better able to deal with inflation than the Democratic party, although according to the latest *Washington Post*/ABC Poll the Democrats are given the edge on reducing unemployment. The difference in the perceived abilities of the two parties on these economic issues could be crucial in the 1982 congressional elections.

Trends in opinion polls indicate that the greatest losses of support for the administration have occurred among those groups who are most susceptible to unemployment—white-collar workers, unskilled manual workers, and those earning less than $15,000. The critical issue for the GOP in 1982 will be how much further change occurs among these groups. Should unemployment continue to rise, or even not significantly decline, those voting blocs will bear the brunt of further recession.

DECEMBER 24
MOST ADMIRED WOMAN

Interviewing Date: 11/20–23/81
Survey #186-G

What woman that you have heard or read about, living today in any part of the world, do you admire the most? Who is your second choice?

The following are listed in order of frequency of mention with first and second choices combined:

Nancy Reagan
Margaret Thatcher

Sandra O'Connor
Mother Teresa of Calcutta
Betty Ford
Jacqueline Onassis
Rosalynn Carter
Barbara Walters
Queen Elizabeth II
Jane Fonda

Note: Many of this year's most admired women were represented on the 1980 roster. Of the top ten only two—Sandra O'Connor and Queen Elizabeth—did not appear in last year's ranking. Absent from the 1981 list are 1980 leaders Barbara Jordan, former Texas congresswoman; Indian Prime Minister Indira Gandhi; and Ella Grasso, former governor of Connecticut who died of cancer during the year. And receiving frequent mention but not included were Jordan, Gandhi, actress Farrah Fawcett, civil rights activist Coretta King, and film star Elizabeth Taylor.

Survey respondents in these studies, which the Gallup Poll has conducted for more than three decades, are asked to give their choices without the aid of a prearranged list of names. This procedure, while opening the field to all possible choices, tends to favor those who are currently or recently have been in the news.

The wives of incumbent U.S. presidents have been frequently, but not always, at the top of the national rankings. A notable exception was from 1948 to 1961, when Eleanor Roosevelt won the top position thirteen out of fourteen years. Mrs. Roosevelt served as First Lady from the start of President Franklin D. Roosevelt's first term in 1933 until his death in 1945. Thus, First Ladies Bess Truman, Mamie Eisenhower, and Jacqueline Kennedy were overshadowed during all or part of their tenure by the dominant personality of Eleanor Roosevelt, who died in 1962.

The top five choices of men in the survey were Margaret Thatcher, Sandra O'Connor, Nancy Reagan, Mother Teresa, and Betty Ford. Women chose Nancy Reagan, Mother Teresa, Margaret Thatcher, Betty Ford, and Jacqueline Onassis.

DECEMBER 27
ECONOMIC OUTLOOK FOR 1982

Interviewing Date: 11/20–23/81 (USA)
Special Survey

Asked in twenty-seven nations: As far as you are concerned, do you think that 1982 will be better or worse than 1981?

Industrialized Nations Only*

Better than 1981 ....25%
Worse than 1981 37
Remain the same (volunteered) 31
Don't know 7

Developing Nations Only**

Better than 1981 ....41%
Worse than 1981 29
Remain the same (volunteered) 19
Don't know 11

Asked in twenty-seven nations: Will it be a year of economic prosperity, economic difficulty, or remain the same?

Industrialized Nations Only*

Economic prosperity.................. 7%
Economic difficulty 55
Remain the same (volunteered) 32
Don't know 6

Developing Nations Only**

Economic prosperity..................22%
Economic difficulty 44
Remain the same (volunteered) 24
Don't know 10

Asked in twenty-seven nations: Looking ahead to 1982, do you think the number of unemployed (in this country) will increase, decrease, or remain the same?

Industrialized Nations Only*

Will increase	62%
Will decrease	11
Remain the same	22
Don't know (volunteered)	5

Developing Nations Only**

Will increase	53%
Will decrease	20
Remain the same (volunteered)	17
Don't know	10

*Industrialized nations: Australia, Austria, Belgium, Canada, Denmark, Finland, France, Germany, Great Britain, Ireland, Italy, Japan, Luxembourg, the Netherlands, Norway, Spain, Sweden, Switzerland, and the United States.

**Developing nations: Argentina, Brazil, Chile, Colombia, Ecuador, India, Korea, and Uruguay.

Note: On the average only 11%—the smallest proportion to hold this view since the 1974 recession—of the residents in twenty-seven nations around the world expect 1982 to be a year of economic prosperity, while almost five times that (52%) foresee economic troubles. A brighter outlook is found in the less-developed countries, but nevertheless pessimism outweighs optimism by a 2-to-1 ratio. In sharp contrast, an average of 55% of the citizens of the industrialized nations anticipate economic difficulty, while 7% foresee prosperity, an 8-to-1 deficit. These are among the key findings of a major international survey conducted at year-end by Gallup International Research Institutes and that has been carried out annually for more than twenty years.

The international outlook for employment is equally grim. In the average nation surveyed, more than four times as many people predict increased joblessness (60%) as think the employment picture will improve (14%). Residents of the underdeveloped countries are distinctly more optimistic about employment than those of the industrial nations. Among the latter only the Japanese have a really sanguine attitude, with merely 2% forecasting an increase in unemployment in 1982, while 38% foresee less.

When personal expectations are examined without regard to specific economic issues, the outlook is considerably brighter. In total, 30% of the participants in the global study think 1982 will be better than 1981, while 35% think it will be worse. In the industrialized nations pessimism outweighs optimism by a 3-to-2 ratio, but in the Third World optimism prevails by about the same margin.

American men, whites, the college educated, persons from upper-income families, and Republicans are more optimistic in their personal expectations for 1982. In the United States a better year is foreseen by 41%, while 44% believe it will be worse than 1981. In last year's survey optimists outnumbered pessimists 49% to 26%.

DECEMBER 31
OUTLOOK FOR PEACE IN 1982

Interviewing Date: 11/20–23/81 (USA)
Special Survey

Asked in twenty-six nations: Looking ahead to 1982, do you think it will be a peaceful year more or less free of international disputes, a troubled year with much international discord, or remain the same?

	Peaceful year	Troubled year	Remain the same; don't know
Europe			
Finland	16%	48%	36%
Ireland	13	46	41
Austria	12	49	39
Italy	11	48	42
Spain	11	47	42
Germany	10	54	36
Denmark	10	50	40
France	9	50	41
Switzerland	8	65	27
Luxembourg	7	61	32
Sweden	7	38	55
Great Britain	6	50	44
Belgium	4	61	35
Netherlands	4	57	39

North America

United States	12%	45%	43%
Canada	7	53	41

South America

Brazil	31%	46%	23%
Ecuador	31	29	40
Argentina	26	34	40
Chile	19	42	39
Uruguay	12	60	27
Colombia	11	56	33

Asia

India	15%	48%	37%
Korea	11	53	36
Australia	10	47	43
Japan	2	53	45

Asked in twenty-four nations: With the help of this card [respondents were handed a card listing positions from zero, or "no danger of war," to 100, or "world war certain."] Please tell me what you think the chances are of a world war breaking out in the next ten years. The more likely you think the chances are, the higher the number you would pick; the less likely, the lower the number. Please read off the number.

	More than 50%	50-50	Less than 50%*
Europe			
Spain	35%	15%	36%
Germany	28	13	49
Luxembourg	27	17	57
Belgium	27	13	44
Ireland	26	15	54
France	24	19	51
Denmark	23	15	54
Great Britain	20	16	59
Netherlands	19	21	55
Switzerland	19	19	55
Italy	18	14	67
Sweden	16	16	64
Austria	16	13	62
North America			
United States	31%	22%	41%
Canada	33	16	44
South America			
Colombia	47%	13%	37%
Uruguay	32	14	48
Brazil	30	13	55
Argentina	19	12	62
Ecuador	17	9	69
Chile	12	23	66
Asia			
Australia	32%	20%	39%
India	19	8	54
Korea	16	19	60

*The no opinion category has been omitted.

Note: The weight of public opinion in virtually all of the twenty-six nations of the world is that 1982 will be a troubled year with much international discord. These findings are based on an international survey conducted at year-end by Gallup International Research Institutes. These studies have been carried out annually for more than two decades.

Index

A

Abortion
  antiabortion, special-interest group, 178
  legal under some circumstances or illegal, 116-17
  life at conception or birth, 114-15
  national trend, 117
  and public opinion mired in middle ground (analysis by A. Kohut), 170-71
  and Reagan, 87
  special-interest group, 178
  Supreme Court decision, 112-14, 171
Advertising practitioners
  contribution to society rating, 255
  honesty rating, 210
  status rating, 255
  stress rating, 255
Affirmative action
  through preferential treatment or ability, 106-07
Air traffic controllers
  strikes by, 208
Alcohol/alcoholic beverages
  as cause of trouble in family, 30-31
    national trend, 31
  law forbidding sale of, 29-30
    national trend, 30
  as reason for more crime, 74
  use of, 29
    national trend, 29
Anti-Semitism
  any unpleasant experiences with Jews, 81
  power in United States of Jews, 81
  rating of Jews, 80-81
Argentina
  chances of world war, 278
  economic outlook, 276-77
  outlook for peace, 278
Arms control *see* Nuclear disarmament
Arms sales ban
  and United Nations resolution, 157-58

Assaults
  incidence of, 71-72
  reported to police, 73
Attitudes in society
  as reason for more crime, 74
Australia
  chances of world war, 278
  economic outlook, 276-77
  most important problem in, 10
  outlook for peace, 278
Austria
  chances of world war, 278
  economic outlook, 276-77
  most important problem in, 10
  outlook for peace, 277
Average citizen
  political party best serving, 265

B

Bankers
  contribution to society rating, 255
  honesty rating, 209
  status rating, 255
  stress rating, 255
Baseball
  favorite sport to watch, 32-33
Basketball
  favorite sport to watch, 32-33
Begin, Menachem
  as most admired man, 274
Belgium
  chances of world war, 278
  economic outlook, 276-77
  outlook for peace, 277
Big business
  Reagan sides with, 87, 248
  as threat to nation, 217-18
    national trend, 218
Big government
  as threat to nation, 217-18
    national trend, 218
Big labor
  as threat to nation, 217-18
    national trend, 218
Birth control
  special-interest group, 178
Birth defects
  and cigarette smoking, 188-89
Blacks
  political party best serving, 265
  quality of life, 20
  situation for, 105
    national trend, 105
  somber mood of (analysis by A. Kohut), 105-06
  special-interest group, 178
  status of, 20-21

Blacks (*continued*)
    treatment in community, 20
    unfairly treated by Reagan and Carter, 179-81
Bomb shelters *see* Civil defense
Bowling
    favorite sport to watch, 32-33
Brazil
    chances of world war, 278
    economic outlook, 276-77
    most important problem in; 10
    outlook for peace, 278
Budget (federal)
    balanced by Reagan, 199-200
    and Reagan's campaign promises, 127-28
Budget cuts (federal)
    approval of, 231
    as most important problem, 238
    proposed by Reagan, 231
Building contractors
    honesty rating, 210
Business executives
    contribution to society rating, 255
    honesty rating, 210
    status rating, 255
    stress rating, 255
    see also Corporation executives
Business investment
    and cut in income tax rates, 160
Businessmen
    surprised by economy (analysis by A. Kohut), 204-05
Busing *see* School busing

C

Canada
    chances of world war, 278
    economic outlook, 276-77
    outlook for peace, 278
Cancer
    lung, caused by cigarette smoking, 187-88
    throat, caused by cigarette smoking, 188
Car salesmen
    honesty rating, 211
Carter, Jimmy
    approval rating, 4-6, 34
    approval rating vs. predecessors, 7
    approval rating vs. Reagan, 60, 111, 257
    decline in popularity vs. unemployment rate, 275
    as most admired man, 274
    rating in history, 6
    in trial heats vs. Reagan, 262-64
    unfair treatment of groups compared to Reagan, 179-81
Carter, Rosalynn
    as most admired woman, 276

Catholics
    unfairly treated by Reagan and Carter, 179-81
Center party
    as major party, 215
Center party (Great Britain)
    strength, 217
CETA programs
    cut in government spending, 126
Child abuse
    personally aware of, 265-66
Children
    ideal number for family, 1-2
Chile
    chances of world war, 278
    economic outlook, 276-77
    most important problem in, 10
    outlook for peace, 278
Cigarette smoking
    each day, 185-86
    given up at least one day, 186
    harmful to health, 187
    length of time without, 186
    like to give up, 186
    national trends, 185, 186
    one cause of birth defects, 188-89
    one cause of cancer of the throat, 188
    one cause of heart disease, 188
    one cause of lung cancer, 187-88
    in past week, 185
Cigarettes
    ban on advertising of, 189
    ban on sale of, 189
    federal and state taxes increased on, 189
Civil defense
    and bomb shelter required, 168-69
    or national defense and military spending, 165-66
    and nearest public bomb shelter, 169
    and Russia's spending on, 166-68
Clergymen
    contribution to society rating, 254
    honesty rating, 209
    status rating, 255
    stress rating, 255
Climate
    as reason to move away from this city, 83
College students
    financial aid to, cut in government spending, 126
College teachers
    honesty rating, 209
Colombia
    chances of world war, 278
    economic outlook, 276-77
    outlook for peace, 278
Community needs
    understood by federal or state government, 236-37
Congress
    approval rating, 148-49
    and item veto by president, 239

Eisenhower, Dwight
 approval rating vs. Carter, 7
 approval rating vs. Reagan, 111
 decline in popularity vs. unemployment rate, 265
Elderly people
 aid to, cut in government spending, 126
 Reagan unsympathetic to, 248
 voluntarism as help to, 267
 work with, as nonmilitary national service, 143
Elizabeth II, Queen
 as most admired woman, 276
El Salvador
 heard of situation, 63
 helped by United States, 65-66
 helped by United States with which type of aid, 66
 side backed by United States, 63
 situation handled by Reagan, 67-68, 91-92, 118
 U.S. involvement could turn into a Vietnam, 63-65
 and U.S. position, 68-69
Employment
 and cut in income tax rates, 160
Energy situation
 dealt with by Reagan, 78, 94, 118, 156-57
 as most important problem, 9-11, 53
Engineers
 honesty rating, 209
Environmental issues
 dealt with by Reagan, 157
 special-interest group, 178
Equal Rights Amendment (ERA)
 approval rating, 171-74
 national trend, 174
 and Reagan, 87
Ethical standards *see* Honesty and ethical standards
Expectations for 1981
 better or worse than 1980, 7-8
 inflation rate, 2-3, 75
 unemployment rate, 3, 75
 see also Economic prosperity; Personal financial
  situation
Expectations for 1982
 better or worse than 1981, 228-29, 276-78
 unemployment rate, 276
 see also Economic prosperity; Personal financial
  situation

F

Family size
 ideal, 1
 national trend, 2
Farmers
 political party best serving, 264
 unfairly treated by Reagan and Carter, 179-81
Finances *see* Personal financial situation
Finland
 economic outlook, 276-77

most important problem in, 10
 outlook for peace, 277
Firemen
 strikes by, 207
Fonda, Jane
 as most admired woman, 276
Food stamps
 cut in government spending, 126
Football
 favorite sport to watch, 32-33
Ford, Betty
 as most admired woman, 276
Ford, Gerald
 approval rating, 34
 approval rating vs. Carter, 7
 decline in popularity vs. unemployment rate, 275
 as most admired man, 274
 rating in history, 6
Foreign affairs
 as most important problem, 53
Foreign policy
 handled by Reagan, 192-93, 245-46
Fortress America syndrome
 analysis by A. Kohut, 240-41
France
 chances of world war, 278
 economic outlook, 276-77
 most important problem in, 10
 outlook for peace, 277
Free enterprise
 special-interest group, 178
Fuel subsidies
 cut in government spending, 126
Funeral directors
 contribution to society rating, 255
 honesty rating, 210
 status rating, 255
 stress rating, 255

G

Gallup analyses
 of President Reagan, 278-79
 see also Kohut, Andrew
Golf
 favorite sport to watch, 32-33
Government (federal)
 administers social programs efficiently, 236
 cents wasted of tax dollar to, 35, 237
 concentration of power in, 235-36
 dissatisfaction with, as most important problem, 53
 free of political corruption, 237
 understands needs of community, 236-37
Government (local)
 cents wasted of tax dollar to, 35-36, 237
Government (state)
 administers social programs efficiently, 236

cents wasted of tax dollar to, 35, 237
concentration of power in, 235-36
free of political corruption, 237
understands needs of community, 236-37
Government size
and Reagan's campaign promises, 127-28
reduced by Reagan, 198-99
see also Big government
Government spending
as most important problem, 238
Graham, Billy
as most admired man, 274
Great Britain
chances of world war, 278
economic outlook, 276-77
most important problem in, 10
outlook for peace, 277
Gun control
antigun control, special-interest group, 178
law forbidding possession of handguns, 13-14, 85-86, 150-51
law making illegal import of gun parts, 151-52
law requiring license to carry gun, 83-85
laws covering sale of handguns, 12-13, 85
mandatory jail sentence for disobeying laws requiring license to carry gun, 85
national trends, 85, 86
special-interest group, 178
waiting period before gun can be purchased, 152

H

Handicapped persons
lowering the minimum wage for, 39-41
Happiness *see* Personal happiness
Heart disease
and cigarette smoking, 188
Homosexuals' rights
special-interest group, 178
Honesty and ethical standards
ratings by professions, 209-11
Hope, Bob
as most admired man, 274
Hospital work
as nonmilitary national service, 143
Housebreaking
incidence of, 71-72
reported to police, 73
Housing
as reason to move away from this city, 83

I

Independents
affiliation as, 53, 128-29, 153

national trend, 129
India
chances of world war, 278
economic outlook, 276-77
most important problem in, 10
outlook for peace, 278
Inflation
and cut in income tax rates, 160
dealt with/handled by Reagan, 75-76, 92-93, 118, 156, 194-95, 223-24, 243-44
national trend, 224
as most important problem, 9-11, 53, 238-39
and Reagan's campaign promises, 127-28
reduced by Reagan, 196-97
Inflation rate
by end of 1981, 2-3, 75
Insurance salesmen
honesty rating, 210
Integration *see* School busing
International relations
as most important problem, 9-11, 53
Investigative reporting
approval of techniques of, 273
like to see more of, 273
by news media, approval of, 272
Ireland
chances of world war, 278
economic outlook, 276-77
outlook for peace, 277
Italy
chances of world war, 278
economic outlook, 276-77
outlook for peace, 277

J

Jackson, Jesse
as most admired man, 274
Japan
economic outlook, 276-77
most important problem in, 10
outlook for peace, 278
Jews
and anti-Semitism, 80-82
unfairly treated by Reagan and Carter, 179-81
John Paul II, Pope
as most admired man, 274
Johnson, Lyndon
approval rating, 34
approval rating vs. Carter, 7
Judges
contribution to society rating, 255
leniency of, as reason for more crime, 74
status rating, 255
stress rating, 255

K

Kennedy, Edward
  as most admired man, 274
  in presidential trial heats vs. Reagan, 251-53
Kennedy, John
  approval rating vs. Carter, 7
  approval rating vs. Reagan, 111
Kissinger, Henry
  as most admired man, 274
Kohut, Andrew
  analysis, abortion mired in middle ground, 170-71
  analysis, economy surprises businessmen, 204-05
  analysis, Fortress America syndrome, 240-41
  analysis, opinion polling and the presidency, 33-35
  analysis, Reagan/Thatcher mirror, 140-42
  analysis, Reagan's fragile mandate, 79-80
  analysis, recession politics, 274-75
  analysis, somber mood of black America, 105-06
Korea
  chances of world war, 278
  economic outlook, 276-77
  outlook for peace, 278
Korean War
  as most important problem, 11

L

Labor union leaders
  honesty rating, 210
Labor union members
  political party best serving, 265
  unfairly treated by Reagan and Carter, 179-81
Labor unions
  approval rating, 205-07
    national trend, 207
  see also Big labor
Labor unrest
  as most important problem, 11
Labour party (Great Britain)
  strength, 217
  support for Thatcher, 141
Lawyers
  contribution to society rating, 255
  honesty rating, 210
  status rating, 255
  stress rating, 255
Liberal party (Great Britain)
  support for Thatcher, 141
Liberals
  affiliation as, 53, 215-16
  and Reagan's political position, 184
  and your political position, 184
Luxembourg
  chances of world war, 278
  economic outlook, 276-77
  outlook for peace, 277

M

Magazines
  investigative reporting for, 272-73
Media
  investigative reporting by, 272-73
Medical doctors
  contribution to society rating, 254
  honesty rating, 209
  status rating, 255
  stress rating, 255
Medicare/Medicaid
  cut in government spending, 126
Mental institutions
  and handgun owners, 152
Mexico
  most important problem in, 10
Military draft
  return to, 181-82
  Supreme Court ruling on women, 182-83
Military spending
  amount spent for national defense, 97
  cents wasted of dollar to federal government, 96-97
  or civil defense, 165-66
  national trend, 97-98
Minimum wage
  for handicapped persons, 39-41
  for teen-agers, 37-39
Minorities
  Reagan not sympathetic to, 87, 248
Mondale, Walter
  in presidential trial heats vs. Reagan, 253-54
Moral decline
  as most important problem, 53, 238
  as reason for more crime, 74
Most admired man
  choice for, 274
Most admired woman
  choice for, 275-76
Muggings
  incidence of, 71-72
  reported to police, 73

N

National defense
  or civil defense, 165-66
  handled by Reagan, 118, 156, 246-47
National security
  as most important problem, 238
National service
  military or nonmilitary for young men, 145-46
  military or nonmilitary for young women, 146
  required for young men, 143-44
  required for young women, 144-45
Netherlands
  chances of world war, 278

economic outlook, 276-77
most important problem in, 10
outlook for peace, 277
Neutron bomb
approval of decision to start production, 211-12
and chances of nuclear war, 212-13
decision to start production, 211
Newspaper reporters
honesty rating, 210
Newspapers
investigative reporting for, 272-73
Nixon, Richard
approval rating, 34
approval rating vs Carter, 7
approval rating vs. Reagan, 111
decline in popularity vs. unemployment rate, 275
Noise
as reason to move away from this city, 83
Norway
economic outlook, 276-77
most important problem in, 11
Nuclear disarmament
and agreement between United States and Soviet Union, 134
and agreement between United States and Soviet Union not to build more nuclear weapons, 134-35
and agreement between United States and Soviet Union to destroy all nuclear weapons, 135-36
and organization to ensure arms agreement, 269-70
and proposal that Soviet Union and United States reduce stock of weapons, 269
and United Nations referendum, 133
and vote in referendum, 133-34
Nuclear power
antinuclear power, special-interest group, 178
special-interest group, 178
Nuclear war
likely to get into, 164-65
national trend for chances of surviving, 165
and production of neutron bomb, 212-13
and your chances of living through it, 163-64

O

O'Connor, Sandra Day
as most admired woman, 276
qualified for Supreme Court, 175
Onassis, Jacqueline
as most admired woman, 276
Overcrowding
as reason for more crime, 74
as reason to move away from this city, 83

P

Parental guidance and discipline
lack of, as reason for more crime, 74
Peace (keeping out of war)
as most important problem, 11
outlook for 1982, in twenty-six nations, 277-78
see also Democratic party; Republican party
People like yourself
political party best serving, 265
unfairly treated by Reagan and Carter, 179-81
Permissiveness
as reason for more crime, 74
Personal financial situation
better next year than now, 161-62, 229-30
better now than a year ago, 161, 228-29
effect of Reagan's economic policies on, 200-01, 226-28
national trend, 228
Personal happiness
rated, 61-63
and religion, 61-63
Personal satisfaction see Satisfaction
Peru
most important problem in, 11
Pharmacists
honesty rating, 209
Philippines
most important problem in, 11
Police protection
inadequacy of, as reason for more crime, 74
Policemen
honesty rating, 209
strikes by, 207
Political affiliation, 53, 128-29, 153, 215-16
and most important problem, 53
national trend, 129
Political ideology
of Reagan, 184
your own, 184
Political officeholders (local)
contribution to society rating, 255
honesty rating, 210
status rating, 255
stress rating, 255
Political officeholders (state)
honesty rating, 210
Pollution
as reason to move away from this city, 83
Poor people
voluntarism as help to, 267
see also Urban poor people
Population increase
as reason for more crime, 74
Portugal
most important problem in, 11
Postal workers
strikes by, 208

Poverty
    as reason for more crime, 74
Presidential term of office
    change to one six-year term, 41-42, 250-51
        national trend, 42
Presidential trial heats
    Carter vs. Reagan, 262-64
    Reagan vs. Kennedy, 251-53
    Reagan vs. Mondale, 253-54
Price controls *see* Wage and price controls
Problems
    most important, 9, 53, 238-39
        national trend, 11-12
Professional and business people
    political party best serving, 264
Prosperity *see* Democratic party; Economic prosperity;
        Republican party
Public employees
    strikes by, 205-08
Public-school principals
    contribution to society rating, 254
    status rating, 255
    stress rating, 255
Public-school teachers
    contribution to society rating, 254
    status rating, 255
    stress rating, 255

R

Race relations
    as most important problem, 11
Reagan, Ronald
    and abortion, 87
    approval rating, 33-35, 57-59, 88-90, 110-11, 118,
        130, 147-48, 155-56, 190-91, 219-20, 257, 266
        national trend, 220, 266
        relative importance of, 95
    approval rating by degree, 130-32, 158-59, 266
    approval rating as person, 159-60, 267
    approval rating vs. Carter, 60, 257
    approval rating vs. predecessors, 111
    approval rating with reasons, 132
    balancing the budget, 199-200
    and big business, 87, 248
    and campaign promise to balance budget, 127-28
    and campaign promise to increase respect for United
        States abroad, 127-28
    and campaign promise to reduce inflation, 127
    and campaign promise to reduce size of government,
        127-28
    and campaign promise to reduce unemployment, 127
    compared to Margaret Thatcher (analysis by A.
        Kohut), 140-42
    criticism of, 87, 248
        national trend, 87
    decline in popularity vs. unemployment rate, 275

    and defense spending, 87
    and domestic problems, 191-92
    and economic conditions, 118, 156, 193-94, 220-22,
        241-43, 266-67, *see also* Reagan's economic
        plan
        national trend, 222, 267
    and the elderly, 248
    and El Salvador situation, 67-68, 91-92, 118
    and energy situation, 78, 94, 118, 156-57
    and environmental issues, 157
    and Equal Rights Amendment, 87
    and foreign policy, 192-93, 245-46
    and fragile mandate (analysis by A. Kohut), 79-80
    Gallup analysis of, 214-15
    getting United States into recession, 248
    getting United States into war, 248
    and inflation, 75-76, 92-93, 118, 156, 194-95, 223-
        24, 243-44
        national trend, 224
    and item veto, 239
    and minorities, 87, 248
    as most admired man, 274
    and national defense, 118, 156, 246-47
    opinion polling and the presidency (analysis by A.
        Kohut), 33-35
    political position to right or left, 184
    and production of neutron bombs, 211-12
    proposal of federal budget cuts, 231
    proposal to Soviet Union to reduce stocks of nuclear
        weapons, 269
    rating of kind of president, 36
    reducing inflation, 196-97
    reducing size of government, 198-99
    reducing unemployment, 197-98
    and relations with Russia, 87, 90-91, 118, 156, 247-
        48
    and the rich, 248
    and social programs, 87, 248
    and special-interest groups, 87, 248
    and Stockman's offer to resign, 268-69
    tax-cut program, 202-04
    in trial heats vs. Carter, 262-64
    in trial heats vs. Kennedy, 251-53
    in trial heats vs. Mondale, 253-54
    and unemployment, 76-78, 93-94, 118, 157, 195-
        196, 224-26, 244-45
        national trend, 226
    unfair treatment of groups compared to Carter, 179-
        81
    and United States image abroad, 248
    and women, 248
Reagan, Nancy
    as most admired woman, 275
Reaganomics *see* Reagan's economic plan
Reagan's economic plan/policies
    and amount of cuts in federal tax rates, 126
    confidence in, after Stockman, 268
    and cuts in government spending, 123-26

and cuts in government spending disapproved, 126
cuts in government spending and you/your family, 122-23
effect on nation's economic situation, 260-62
effect on your financial situation, 200-01, 226-28, 257-60
national trend, 228
and list of cuts in government spending disapproved, 126
your financial situation as result of, 119-22
Realtors
contribution to society rating, 255
honesty rating, 210
status rating, 255
stress rating, 255
Recession
as most important problem, 53
Reagan might get United States into, 248
Recession politics
analysis by A. Kohut, 274-75
Religion
as answer for today's problems, 60-61
national trend, 61
church or synagogue attendance, 15
national trend, 15-16
church or synagogue membership, 16
national trend, 16-17
and personal happiness, 61-63
religious television programs and involvement in local church, 17-19
religious television programs watched, 17
Rent subsidies
cut in government spending, 126
Republican party
affiliation in, 53, 128-29, 153, 215
national trend, 129
best for interests of certain groups, 264-65
and keeping country prosperous, 95, 248, 250
national trend, 96, 249
and keeping United States out of war, 95, 248, 249
national trend, 96, 249
and most important problem, 53
preference for, in Congressional elections, 154, 234-35, 255-56
Retired people
political party best serving, 265
Rich people
Reagan sides with, 248
Roosevelt, Franklin
approval rating vs. Carter, 7

S

Sanitation workers
strikes by, 207-08
Satisfaction
dissatisfaction with life, as reason for more crime, 74

national trend on views toward personal life, 139
national trend on views toward United States, 138
with personal life, 138-39
with United States, 137-38
School busing
for better racial balance, 21-23, 28
busing of Negro and white children, 27-28
children sent to school where others are black, 23–25
court order followed by violence, 27
courts order to integrate, 27
Deep South integration of schools gradually, 26-27
election day vote on, 29
government integration of schools gradually, 26
integration of schools gradually, 26
integration of schools too fast, 27
Little Rock ruling, 26
plans to integrate schools in community, 27
prohibited through Constitutional amendment, 29
Supreme Court decision, 26
national trend, 26
ways to achieve integration of schools, 28
School lunches
cut in government spending, 126
Schools
as reason to move away from this city, 83
Senators
honesty rating, 210
Senior citizens
unfairly treated by Reagan and Carter, 179-81
Sick people
voluntarism as help to, 267
Skilled workers
political party best serving, 264
Small business people
political party best serving, 265
unfairly treated by Reagan and Carter, 179-81
Social programs
administered by federal or state government, 236
approval of budget cuts in, 231-32
cut by Reagan, 87, 248
cut in government spending, 126
Social Security
cut in government spending, 126
Social services
voluntarism and, 267
South Africa
most important problem in, 11
Soviet Union (Russia, USSR)
agreement with United States not to build more nuclear weapons, 134-35
agreement with United States on nuclear disarmament, 134
agreement with United States to destroy all nuclear weapons, 135-36
doing all it can to keep peace, 270
likely to abide by agreement with United States not to build more nuclear weapons, 135

Soviet Union (*continued*)
  likely to abide by agreement with United States to destroy all nuclear weapons, 136
  and organization to ensure arms agreement with United States, 269-70
  and Reagan proposal to reduce stock of nuclear weapons, 269
  relations with, handled by Reagan, 87, 90-91, 118, 156, 247-48
  spending for civil defense, 166-68
Spain
  chances of world war, 278
  economic outlook, 276-77
  outlook for peace, 277
Special-interest groups
  contribution to/membership in, 177-78
  like to be member of, 178
  Reagan sides with, 87, 248
Speed limit
  exceed 55-mile-per-hour, 51-52
  keep present 55-mile-per-hour, 49-50
  obey 55-mile-per-hour, 50-51
  obeyed by most drivers, 52
Sports
  favorite to watch, 32-33
Status
  ratings by professions and occupations, 255
Stockbrokers
  honesty rating, 210
Stockman, David
  heard about, 268
  offer to resign, 268-69
Stress
  ratings by professions and occupations, 255
Strikes
  national trends, 207, 208
  by public employees, 205-08
Supreme Court
  decision on abortion, 112-14, 115, 171
  and Mrs. O'Connor, 175
  ruling that women cannot be drafted, 182-83
  woman serving on, 175
Sweden
  chances of world war, 278
  economic outlook, 276-77
  most important problem in, 11
  outlook for peace, 277
Switzerland
  chances of world war, 278
  economic outlook, 276-77
  most important problem in, 11
  outlook for peace, 277

T

Tax reduction
  special-interest group, 178

Taxes
  cents wasted of dollar to federal government, 35, 237
  cents wasted of dollar to local government, 35-36, 237
  cents wasted of dollar to state government, 35, 237
  effect of income tax rates cut on business investment and employment, 160
  effect of income tax rates cut on inflation, 160
  extent of Reagan's tax cut program, 202-03
  federal and state, increased on cigarettes, 189
  Reagan's tax-cut program, 202
  as reason to move away from this city, 83
  spend/save as result of Reagan's tax cut program, 203-04
  see also Military spending; Reagan's economic plan
Teen-agers
  lowering the minimum wage for, 37-39
Television
  investigative reporting for, 272-73
  see also Religion
Television commentators
  honesty rating, 209
Television reporters
  honesty rating, 209
Tennis
  favorite sport to watch, 32-33
Teresa of Calcutta, Mother
  as most admired woman, 276
Thatcher, Margaret
  compared to Ronald Reagan (analysis by A. Kohut), 140-42
  as most admired woman, 275
  trend of party support for, 141
Theft of car
  incidence of, 71-72
  reported to police, 73
Theft of money or property
  incidence of, 71-72
  reported to police, 73
Traffic congestion
  as reason to move away from this city, 83
Truman, Harry
  approval rating vs. Carter, 7

U

Underdeveloped countries
  and aid increased by United States, 176
  problems their own or shared by developed countries, 175-76
Unemployed people
  outlook in industrialized and developing nations, 276-77
  political party best serving, 265
  unfairly treated by Reagan and Carter, 179-81
Unemployment
  dealt with/handled by Reagan, 76-78, 93-94, 118,

157, 195-96, 224-26, 244-45
  national trend, 226
as most important problem, 9-12, 53, 238-39
and Reagan's campaign promises, 127-28
as reason for more crime, 74
as reason to move away from this city, 83
reduced by Reagan, 197-98
Unemployment rate
  by end of 1981, 3, 75
  and incumbent president's decline in popularity, 275
United Nations
  and arms sales ban, 157-58
  and nuclear disarmament, 133
United States
  agreements on nuclear disarmament, *see* Soviet Union
  chances of world war, 278
  doing all it can to keep peace, 270-71
  economic outlook, 276-77
  image abroad, 248
  outlook for peace, 278
  Reagan might get into recession, 248
  Reagan might get into war, 87, 248
  and Reagan's campaign promise to increase respect for abroad, 127-28
  satisfaction with way things are going in, 137-38
    national trend, 138
  see also Government (federal)
Unskilled workers
  political party best serving, 264
Upper-income people
  political party best serving, 264
Urban poor people
  list of reasons for relocation of, 99-100
  relocation of, 98-99
Urban problems
  move away from this city, 82
  national trend, 83
  reasons to move away from this city, 83
Uruguay
  chances of world war, 278
  economic outlook, 276-77
  outlook for peace, 278
Utility subsidies
  cut in government spending, 126

V

Vandalism of property
  incidence of, 71-72
  reported to police, 73
Venezuela
  most important problem in, 11
Veterans' benefits
  cut in government spending, 126

Vietnam
  as most important problem, 11
Vietnam veterans
  special-interest group, 178
Violence
  as most important problem, 9-11
Voluntarism
  yourself involved in, 267
Voting
  on national issue if petitioned for, 108-09
  on national issues as well as candidates, 108

W

Wage and price controls
  brought back by government, 142-43
Walters, Barbara
  as most admired woman, 276
War
  antiwar, special-interest group, 178
  chances for world war, in twenty-four nations, 278
  as most important problem, 11, 53, 238
  party likely to keep United States out of, 95, 248, 249
    national trend, 96, 249
  Reagan might get United States into, 87, 248
  see also Nuclear war
Watergate
  as most important problem, 11
Welfare
  cut in government spending, 126
  people on, unfairly treated by Reagan and Carter, 179-81
West Germany
  chances of world war, 278
  economic outlook, 276-77
  most important problem in, 11
  outlook for peace, 277
White-collar workers
  political party best serving, 264
Wildlife protection
  special-interest group, 178
Women
  and military draft, 182-83
  political party best serving, 265
  Reagan unsympathetic to, 248
  unfairly treated by Reagan and Carter, 179-81
  see also Most admired woman
Women's rights
  special-interest group, 178

Y

Young people
  political party best serving, 265